2015 STATUTORY AND CASE SUPPLEMENT TO

WHITE COLLAR CRIME

LAW AND PRACTICE

Fourth Edition

■ ■ ■

by

Jerold H. Israel

Alene and Allan F. Smith Professor of Law Emeritus,
University of Michigan Law School
Ed Rood Eminent Scholar Emeritus,
University of Florida, Levin College of Law

Ellen S. Podgor

Gary R. Trombley Family White-Collar Crime Research Professor
Professor of Law
Stetson University College of Law

Paul D. Borman

Judge, United States District Court for the
Eastern District of Michigan

Peter J. Henning

Professor of Law
Wayne State University Law School

AMERICAN CASEBOOK SERIES®

WEST
ACADEMIC
PUBLISHING

American Casebook Series is a trademark registered in the U.S. Patent and Trademark Office.

© West, a Thomson business, 2003-2006
© 2009 Thomson Reuters
© 2015 LEG, Inc. d/b/a West Academic
      444 Cedar Street, Suite 700
      St. Paul, MN 55101
      1-877-888-1330

West, West Academic Publishing, and West Academic are trademarks of West Publishing Corporation, used under license.

Printed in the United States of America

ISBN: 978-1-63459-755-5

TABLE OF CONTENTS

STATUTORY AND DOCUMENTARY MATERIALS

Title 26

Title 28

Title 31

Principles of Federal Prosecution

Principles of Federal Prosecution of Business Organizations

Organized Crime and Racketeering

2015 STATUTORY AND DOCUMENTARY SUPPLEMENT TO

WHITE COLLAR CRIME

LAW AND PRACTICE

Fourth Edition

Title 18, United States Code–
Crimes and Criminal Procedure

BANKRUPTCY

Sec. 152. Concealment of assets; false oaths and claims; bribery

A person who–

(1) knowingly and fraudulently conceals from a custodian, trustee, marshal, or other officer of the court charged with the control or custody of property, or, in connection with a case under title 11, from creditors or the United States Trustee, any property belonging to the estate of a debtor;

(2) knowingly and fraudulently makes a false oath or account in or in relation to any case under title 11;

(3) knowingly and fraudulently makes a false declaration, certificate, verification, or statement under penalty of perjury as permitted under section 1746 of title 28, in or in relation to any case under title 11;

(4) knowingly and fraudulently presents any false claim for proof against the estate of a debtor, or uses any such claim in any case under title 11, in a personal capacity or as or through an agent, proxy, or attorney;

(5) knowingly and fraudulently receives any material amount of property from a debtor after the filing of a case under title 11, with intent to defeat the provisions of title 11;

(6) knowingly and fraudulently gives, offers, receives, or attempts to obtain any money or property, remuneration, compensation, reward, advantage, or promise thereof for acting or forbearing to act in any case under title 11;

(7) in a personal capacity or as an agent or officer of any person or corporation, in contemplation of a case under title 11 by or against the person or any other person or corporation, or with intent to defeat the provisions of title 11, knowingly and fraudulently transfers or conceals any of his property or the property of such other person or corporation;

(8) after the filing of a case under title 11 or in contemplation thereof, knowingly and fraudulently conceals, destroys, mutilates, falsifies, or makes a false entry in any recorded information (including books, documents, records, and papers) relating to the property or financial affairs of a debtor; or

(9) after the filing of a case under title 11, knowingly and fraudulently withholds from a custodian, trustee, marshal, or other officer of the court or a United States Trustee entitled to its possession, any recorded information

(including books, documents, records, and papers) relating to the property or financial affairs of a debtor,

shall be fined under this title, imprisoned not more than 5 years, or both.

Sec. 157. - Bankruptcy fraud

A person who, having devised or intending to devise a scheme or artifice to defraud and for the purpose of executing or concealing such a scheme or artifice or attempting to do so--

(1) files a petition under title 11, including a fraudulent involuntary bankruptcy petition under section 303 of such title;

(2) files a document in a proceeding under title 11; or

(3) makes a false or fraudulent representation, claim, or promise concerning or in relation to a proceeding under title 11, at any time before or after the filing of the petition, or in relation to a proceeding falsely asserted to be pending under such title,

shall be fined under this title, imprisoned not more than 5 years, or both.

BRIBES & GRATUITIES (FEDERAL OFFICIALS)

Sec. 201. - Bribery of public officials and witnesses

(a) For the purpose of this section -

(1) the term "public official" means Member of Congress, Delegate, or Resident Commissioner, either before or after such official has qualified, or an officer or employee or person acting for or on behalf of the United States, or any department, agency or branch of Government thereof, including the District of Columbia, in any official function, under or by authority of any such department, agency, or branch of Government, or a juror;

(2) the term "person who has been selected to be a public official" means any person who has been nominated or appointed to be a public official, or has been officially informed that such person will be so nominated or appointed; and

(3) the term "official act" means any decision or action on any question, matter, cause, suit, proceeding or controversy, which may at any time be pending, or which may by law be brought before any public official, in such official's official capacity, or in such official's place of trust or profit.

(b) Whoever -

(1) directly or indirectly, corruptly gives, offers or promises anything of value to any public official or person who has been selected to be a public official, or offers or promises any public official or any person who has been selected to be a public official to give anything of value to any other person or entity, with intent -

(A) to influence any official act; or

(B) to influence such public official or person who has been selected to be a public official to commit or aid in committing, or collude in, or allow, any fraud, or make opportunity for the commission of any fraud, on the United States; or

(C) to induce such public official or such person who has been selected to be a public official to do or omit to do any act in violation of the lawful duty of such official or person;

(2) being a public official or person selected to be a public official, directly or indirectly, corruptly demands, seeks, receives, accepts, or agrees to receive or accept anything of value personally or for any other person or entity, in return for:

(A) being influenced in the performance of any official act;

(B) being influenced to commit or aid in committing, or to collude in, or allow, any fraud, or make opportunity for the commission of any fraud, on the United States; or

(C) being induced to do or omit to do any act in violation of the official duty of such official or person;

(3) directly or indirectly, corruptly gives, offers, or promises anything of value to any person, or offers or promises such person to give anything of value to any other person or entity, with intent to influence the testimony under oath or affirmation of such first-mentioned person as a witness upon a trial, hearing, or other proceeding, before any court, any committee of either House or both Houses of Congress, or any agency, commission, or officer authorized by the laws of the United States to hear evidence or take testimony, or with intent to influence such person to absent himself therefrom;

(4) directly or indirectly, corruptly demands, seeks, receives, accepts, or agrees to receive or accept anything of value personally or for any other person or entity in return for being influenced in testimony under oath or affirmation as a witness upon any such trial, hearing, or other proceeding, or in return for absenting himself therefrom; shall be fined under this title or not more than three times the monetary

equivalent of the thing of value, whichever is greater, or imprisoned for not more than fifteen years, or both, and may be disqualified from holding any office of honor, trust, or profit under the United States.

(c) Whoever -

(1) otherwise than as provided by law for the proper discharge of official duty -

(A) directly or indirectly gives, offers, or promises anything of value to any public official, former public official, or person selected to be a public official, for or because of any official act performed or to be performed by such public official, former public official, or person selected to be a public official; or

(B) being a public official, former public official, or person selected to be a public official, otherwise than as provided by law for the proper discharge of official duty, directly or indirectly demands, seeks, receives, accepts, or agrees to receive or accept anything of value personally for or because of any official act performed or to be performed by such official or person;

(2) directly or indirectly, gives, offers, or promises anything of value to any person, for or because of the testimony under oath or affirmation given or to be given by such person as a witness upon a trial, hearing, or other proceeding, before any court, any committee of either House or both Houses of Congress, or any agency, commission, or officer authorized by the laws of the United States to hear evidence or take testimony, or for or because of such person's absence therefrom;

(3) directly or indirectly, demands, seeks, receives, accepts, or agrees to receive or accept anything of value personally for or because of the testimony under oath or affirmation given or to be given by such person as a witness upon any such trial, hearing, or other proceeding, or for or because of such person's absence therefrom; shall be fined under this title or imprisoned for not more than two years, or both.

(d) Paragraphs (3) and (4) of subsection (b) and paragraphs (2) and (3) of subsection (c) shall not be construed to prohibit the payment or receipt of witness fees provided by law, or the payment, by the party upon whose behalf a witness is called and receipt by a witness, of the reasonable cost of travel and subsistence incurred and the reasonable value of time lost in attendance at any such trial, hearing, or proceeding, or in the case of expert witnesses, a reasonable fee for time spent in the preparation of such opinion, and in appearing and testifying.

(e) The offenses and penalties prescribed in this section are separate from and in addition to those prescribed in sections 1503, 1504, and 1505 of this title.

CONSPIRACY

Sec. 371. - Conspiracy to commit offense or to defraud United States

If two or more persons conspire either to commit any offense against the United States, or to defraud the United States, or any agency thereof in any manner or for any purpose, and one or more of such persons do any act to effect the object of the conspiracy, each shall be fined under this title or imprisoned not more than five years, or both.

If, however, the offense, the commission of which is the object of the conspiracy, is a misdemeanor only, the punishment for such conspiracy shall not exceed the maximum punishment provided for such misdemeanor

BRIBERY (FEDERAL PROGRAMS)

Sec. 666. - Theft or bribery concerning programs receiving Federal funds

(a) Whoever, if the circumstance described in subsection (b) of this section exists -

(1) being an agent of an organization, or of a State, local, or Indian tribal government, or any agency thereof -

(A) embezzles, steals, obtains by fraud, or otherwise without authority knowingly converts to the use of any person other than the rightful owner or intentionally misapplies, property that -

(i) is valued at $5,000 or more, and

(ii) is owned by, or is under the care, custody, or control of such organization, government, or agency; or

(B) corruptly solicits or demands for the benefit of any person, or accepts or agrees to accept, anything of value from any person, intending to be influenced or rewarded in connection with any business, transaction, or series of transactions of such organization, government, or agency involving any thing of value of $5,000 or more; or

(2) corruptly gives, offers, or agrees to give anything of value to any person, with intent to influence or reward an agent of an organization or of a State, local or Indian tribal government, or any agency thereof, in connection with any business, transaction, or series of transactions of such organization, government, or agency involving anything of value of $5,000 or more;

shall be fined under this title, imprisoned not more than 10 years, or both.

(b) The circumstance referred to in subsection (a) of this section is that the organization, government, or agency receives, in any one year period, benefits in excess of $10,000 under a Federal program involving a grant, contract, subsidy, loan, guarantee, insurance, or other form of Federal assistance.

(c) This section does not apply to bona fide salary, wages, fees, or other compensation paid, or expenses paid or reimbursed, in the usual course of business.

(d) As used in this section -

(1) the term "agent" means a person authorized to act on behalf of another person or a government and, in the case of an organization or government, includes a servant or employee, and a partner, director, officer, manager, and representative;

(2) the term "government agency" means a subdivision of the executive, legislative, judicial, or other branch of government, including a department, independent establishment, commission, administration, authority, board, and bureau, and a corporation or other legal entity established, and subject to control, by a government or governments for the execution of a governmental or intergovernmental program;

(3) the term "local" means of or pertaining to a political subdivision within a State;

(4) the term "State" includes a State of the United States, the District of Columbia, and any commonwealth, territory, or possession of the United States; and

(5) the term "in any one-year period" means a continuous period that commences no earlier than twelve months before the commission of the offense or that ends no later than twelve months after the commission of the offense. Such period may include time both before and after the commission of the offense.

FALSE STATEMENTS

Sec. 1001. - Statements or entries generally

(a) Except as otherwise provided in this section, whoever, in any matter within the jurisdiction of the executive, legislative, or judicial branch of the Government of the United States, knowingly and willfully--

(1) falsifies, conceals, or covers up by any trick, scheme, or device a material fact;

(2) makes any materially false, fictitious, or fraudulent statement or representation; or

(3) makes or uses any false writing or document knowing the same to contain any materially false, fictitious, or fraudulent statement or entry;

shall be fined under this title, imprisoned not more than 5 years or, if the offense involves international or domestic terrorism (as defined in section 2331), imprisoned not more than 8 years, or both. If the matter relates to an offense under chapter 109A, 109B, 110, or 117, or section 1591, then the term of imprisonment imposed under this section shall be not more than 8 years.

(b) Subsection (a) does not apply to a party to a judicial proceeding, or that party's counsel, for statements, representations, writings or documents submitted by such party or counsel to a judge or magistrate in that proceeding.

(c) With respect to any matter within the jurisdiction of the legislative branch, subsection (a) shall apply only to--

(1) administrative matters, including a claim for payment, a matter related to the procurement of property or services, personnel or employment practices, or support services, or a document required by law, rule, or regulation to be submitted to the Congress or any office or officer within the legislative branch; or

(2) any investigation or review, conducted pursuant to the authority of any committee, subcommittee, commission or office of the Congress, consistent with applicable rules of the House or Senate.

Sec. 1014. - Loan and credit applications generally; renewals and discounts; crop insurance

Whoever knowingly makes any false statement or report, or willfully overvalues any land, property or security, for the purpose of influencing in any way the action of the Federal Housing Administration, the Farm Credit

Administration, Federal Crop Insurance Corporation or a company the Corporation reinsures, the Secretary of Agriculture acting through the Farmers Home Administration or successor agency, the Rural Development Administration or successor agency, any Farm Credit Bank, production credit association, agricultural credit association, bank for cooperatives, or any division, officer, or employee thereof, or of any regional agricultural credit corporation established pursuant to law, or a Federal land bank, a Federal land bank association, a Federal Reserve bank, a small business investment company, as defined in section 103 of the Small Business Investment Act of 1958 (15 U.S.C. 662), or the Small Business Administration in connection with any provision of that Act, a Federal credit union, an insured State-chartered credit union, any institution the accounts of which are insured by the Federal Deposit Insurance Corporation, any Federal home loan bank, the Federal Housing Finance Agency, the Federal Deposit Insurance Corporation, the Farm Credit System Insurance Corporation, or the National Credit Union Administration Board, a branch or agency of a foreign bank (as such terms are defined in paragraphs (1) and (3) of section 1(b) of the International Banking Act of 1978), an organization operating under section 25 or section 25(a) of the Federal Reserve Act, or a mortgage lending business, or any person or entity that makes in whole or in part a federally related mortgage loan as defined in section 3 of the Real Estate Settlement Procedures Act of 1974, upon any application, advance, discount, purchase, purchase agreement, repurchase agreement, commitment, loan, or insurance agreement or application for insurance or a guarantee, or any change or extension of any of the same, by renewal, deferment of action or otherwise, or the acceptance, release, or substitution of security therefor, shall be fined not more than $1,000,000 or imprisoned not more than 30 years, or both. The term "State-chartered credit union" includes a credit union chartered under the laws of a State of the United States, the District of Columbia, or any commonwealth, territory, or possession of the United States.

Sec. 1015. - Naturalization, citizenship or alien registry

(a) Whoever knowingly makes any false statement under oath, in any case, proceeding, or matter relating to, or under, or by virtue of any law of the United States relating to naturalization, citizenship, or registry of aliens; or

(b) Whoever knowingly, with intent to avoid any duty or liability imposed or required by law, denies that he has been naturalized or admitted to be a citizen, after having been so naturalized or admitted; or

(c) Whoever uses or attempts to use any certificate of arrival, declaration of intention, certificate of naturalization, certificate of citizenship or other documentary evidence of naturalization or of citizenship, or any duplicate or copy thereof, knowing the same to have been procured by fraud or false evidence or without required appearance or hearing of the applicant in court or otherwise unlawfully obtained; or

(d) Whoever knowingly makes any false certificate, acknowledgment or statement concerning the appearance before him or the taking of an oath or affirmation or the signature, attestation or execution by any person with respect to any application, declaration, petition, affidavit, deposition, certificate of naturalization, certificate of citizenship or other paper or writing required or authorized by the laws relating to immigration, naturalization, citizenship, or registry of aliens; or

(e) Whoever knowingly makes any false statement or claim that he is, or at any time has been, a citizen or national of the United States, with the intent to obtain on behalf of himself, or any other person, any Federal or State benefit or service, or to engage unlawfully in employment in the United States; or

(f) Whoever knowingly makes any false statement or claim that he is a citizen of the United States in order to register to vote or to vote in any Federal, State, or local election (including an initiative, recall, or referendum) -

Shall be fined under this title or imprisoned not more than five years, or both. Subsection (f) does not apply to an alien if each natural parent of the alien (or, in the case of an adopted alien, each adoptive parent of the alien) is or was a citizen (whether by birth or naturalization), the alien permanently resided in the United States prior to attaining the age of 16, and the alien reasonably believed at the time of making the false statement or claim that he or she was a citizen of the United States.

COMPUTER FRAUD AND ABUSE

Sec. 1030. - Fraud and related activity in connection with computers

(a) Whoever--

(1) having knowingly accessed a computer without authorization or exceeding authorized access, and by means of such conduct having obtained information that has been determined by the United States Government pursuant to an Executive order or statute to require protection against unauthorized disclosure for reasons of national defense or foreign relations, or any restricted data, as defined in paragraph y. of section 11 of the Atomic Energy Act of 1954, with reason to believe that such information so obtained could be used to the injury of the United States, or to the advantage of any foreign nation willfully communicates, delivers, transmits, or causes to be communicated, delivered, or transmitted, or attempts to communicate, deliver, transmit or cause to be communicated, delivered, or transmitted the same to any person not entitled to receive it, or willfully retains the same and fails to deliver it to the officer or employee of the United States entitled to receive it;

(2) intentionally accesses a computer without authorization or exceeds authorized access, and thereby obtains--

(A) information contained in a financial record of a financial institution, or of a card issuer as defined in section 1602(n) of title 15, or contained in a file of a consumer reporting agency on a consumer, as such terms are defined in the Fair Credit Reporting Act (15 U.S.C. 1681 et seq.);

(B) information from any department or agency of the United States; or

(C) information from any protected computer;

(3) intentionally, without authorization to access any nonpublic computer of a department or agency of the United States, accesses such a computer of that department or agency that is exclusively for the use of the Government of the United States or, in the case of a computer not exclusively for such use, is used by or for the Government of the United States and such conduct affects that use by or for the Government of the United States;

(4) knowingly and with intent to defraud, accesses a protected computer without authorization, or exceeds authorized access, and by means of such conduct furthers the intended fraud and obtains anything of value, unless the object of the fraud and the thing obtained consists only of the use of the computer and the value of such use is not more than $5,000 in any 1-year period;

(5) (A) knowingly causes the transmission of a program, information, code, or command, and as a result of such conduct, intentionally causes damage without authorization, to a protected computer;

(B) intentionally accesses a protected computer without authorization, and as a result of such conduct, recklessly causes damage; or

(C) intentionally accesses a protected computer without authorization, and as a result of such conduct, causes damage and loss.

(6) knowingly and with intent to defraud traffics (as defined in section 1029) in any password or similar information through which a computer may be accessed without authorization, if--

(A) such trafficking affects interstate or foreign commerce; or

(B) such computer is used by or for the Government of the United States;

(7) with intent to extort from any person any money or other thing of value, transmits in interstate or foreign commerce any communication containing any--

(A) threat to cause damage to a protected computer;

(B) threat to obtain information from a protected computer without authorization or in excess of authorization or to impair the confidentiality of information obtained from a protected computer without authorization or by exceeding authorized access; or (C) demand or request for money or other thing of value in relation to damage to a protected computer, where such damage was caused to facilitate the extortion;

shall be punished as provided in subsection (c) of this section.

(b) Whoever conspires to commit or attempts to commit an offense under subsection (a) of this section shall be punished as provided in subsection (c) of this section. (c) The punishment for an offense under subsection (a) or (b) of this section is--

(1) (A) a fine under this title or imprisonment for not more than ten years, or both, in the case of an offense under subsection (a)(1) of this section which does not occur after a conviction for another offense under this section, or an attempt to commit an offense punishable under this subparagraph; and

(B) a fine under this title or imprisonment for not more than twenty years, or both, in the case of an offense under subsection (a)(1) of this section which occurs after a conviction for another offense under this section, or an attempt to commit an offense punishable under this subparagraph;

(2) (A) except as provided in subparagraph (B), a fine under this title or imprisonment for not more than one year, or both, in the case of an offense under subsection (a)(2), (a)(3), or (a)(6) of this section which does not occur after a conviction for another offense under this section, or an attempt to commit an offense punishable under this subparagraph;

(B) a fine under this title or imprisonment for not more than 5 years, or both, in the case of an offense under subsection (a)(2), or an attempt to commit an offense punishable under this subparagraph, if--

(i) the offense was committed for purposes of commercial advantage or private financial gain;

(ii) the offense was committed in furtherance of any criminal or tortious act in violation of the Constitution or laws of the United States or of any State;

or

(iii) the value of the information obtained exceeds $5,000; and

(C) a fine under this title or imprisonment for not more than ten years, or both, in the case of an offense under subsection (a)(2), (a)(3) or (a)(6) of this section which occurs after a conviction for another offense under this section, or an attempt to commit an offense punishable under this subparagraph;

(3) (A) a fine under this title or imprisonment for not more than five years, or both, in the case of an offense under subsection (a)(4) or (a)(7) of this section which does not occur after a conviction for another offense under this section, or an attempt to commit an offense punishable under this subparagraph; and

(B) a fine under this title or imprisonment for not more than ten years, or both, in the case of an offense under subsection (a)(4), or (a)(7) of this section which occurs after a conviction for another offense under this section, or an attempt to commit an offense punishable under this subparagraph;

(4) (A) except as provided in subparagraphs (E) and (F), a fine under this title, imprisonment for not more than 5 years, or both, in the case of--

(i) an offense under subsection (a)(5)(B), which does not occur after a conviction for another offense under this section, if the offense caused (or, in the case of an attempted offense, would, if completed, have caused)--

(I) loss to 1 or more persons during any 1-year period (and, for purposes of an investigation, prosecution, or other proceeding brought by the United States only, loss resulting from a related course of conduct affecting 1 or more other protected computers) aggregating at least $5,000 in value;

(II) the modification or impairment, or potential modification or impairment, of the medical examination, diagnosis, treatment, or care of 1 or more individuals;

(III) physical injury to any person;

(IV) a threat to public health or safety;

(V) damage affecting a computer used by or for an entity of the United States Government in furtherance of the administration of justice, national defense, or national security; or

(VI) damage affecting 10 or more protected computers during any 1-year period; or

(ii) an attempt to commit an offense punishable under this subparagraph;

(B) except as provided in subparagraphs (E) and (F), a fine under this title, imprisonment for not more than 10 years, or both, in the case of--

(i) an offense under subsection (a)(5)(A), which does not occur after a conviction for another offense under this section, if the offense caused (or, in the case of an attempted offense, would, if completed, have caused) a harm provided in subclauses (I) through (VI) of subparagraph (A)(i); or

(ii) an attempt to commit an offense punishable under this subparagraph;

(C) except as provided in subparagraphs (E) and (F), a fine under this title, imprisonment for not more than 20 years, or both, in the case of--

(i) an offense or an attempt to commit an offense under subparagraphs (A) or (B) of subsection (a)(5) that occurs after a conviction for another offense under this section; or

(ii) an attempt to commit an offense punishable under this subparagraph;

(D) a fine under this title, imprisonment for not more than 10 years, or both, in the case of--

(i) an offense or an attempt to commit an offense under subsection (a) (5)(C) that occurs after a conviction for another offense under this section; or

(ii) an attempt to commit an offense punishable under this subparagraph;

(E) if the offender attempts to cause or knowingly or recklessly causes serious bodily injury from conduct in violation of subsection (a)(5)(A), a fine under this title, imprisonment for not more than 20 years, or both;

(F) if the offender attempts to cause or knowingly or recklessly causes death from conduct in violation of subsection (a)(5)(A), a fine under this title, imprisonment for any term of years or for life, or both; or

(G) a fine under this title, imprisonment for not more than 1 year, or both, for--

(i) any other offense under subsection (a)(5); or

(ii) an attempt to commit an offense punishable under this subparagraph.

[(5) Repealed. Pub.L. 110-326, Title II, § 204(a)(2)(D), Sept. 26, 2008, 122 Stat. 3562]

(d)(1) The United States Secret Service shall, in addition to any other agency having such authority, have the authority to investigate offenses under this section.

(2) The Federal Bureau of Investigation shall have primary authority to investigate offenses under subsection (a)(1) for any cases involving espionage, foreign counterintelligence, information protected against unauthorized disclosure for reasons of national defense or foreign relations, or Restricted Data (as that term is defined in section 11y of the Atomic Energy Act of 1954 (42 U.S.C. 2014(y)), except for offenses affecting the duties of the United States Secret Service pursuant to section 3056(a) of this title.

(3) Such authority shall be exercised in accordance with an agreement which shall be entered into by the Secretary of the Treasury and the Attorney General.

(e) As used in this section--

(1) the term "computer" means an electronic, magnetic, optical, electrochemical, or other high speed data processing device performing logical, arithmetic, or storage functions, and includes any data storage facility or communications facility directly related to or operating in conjunction with such device, but such term does not include an automated typewriter or typesetter, a portable hand held calculator, or other similar device;

(2) the term "protected computer" means a computer--

(A) exclusively for the use of a financial institution or the United States Government, or, in the case of a computer not exclusively for such use, used by or for a financial institution or the United States Government and the conduct constituting the offense affects that use by or for the financial institution or the Government; or
(B) which is used in or affecting interstate or foreign commerce or communication, including a computer located outside the United

States that is used in a manner that affects interstate or foreign commerce or communication of the United States;

(3) the term "State" includes the District of Columbia, the Commonwealth of Puerto Rico, and any other commonwealth, possession or territory of the United States;

(4) the term "financial institution" means--

(A) an institution, with deposits insured by the Federal Deposit Insurance Corporation;

(B) the Federal Reserve or a member of the Federal Reserve including any Federal Reserve Bank;

(C) a credit union with accounts insured by the National Credit Union Administration;

(D) a member of the Federal home loan bank system and any home loan bank;

(E) any institution of the Farm Credit System under the Farm Credit Act of 1971;

(F) a broker-dealer registered with the Securities and Exchange Commission pursuant to section 15 of the Securities Exchange Act of 1934;

(G) the Securities Investor Protection Corporation;

(H) a branch or agency of a foreign bank (as such terms are defined in paragraphs (1) and (3) of section 1(b) of the International Banking Act of 1978); and

(I) an organization operating under section 25 or section 25(a) of the Federal Reserve Act;

(5) the term "financial record" means information derived from any record held by a financial institution pertaining to a customer's relationship with the financial institution;

(6) the term "exceeds authorized access" means to access a computer with authorization and to use such access to obtain or alter information in the computer that the accesser is not entitled so to obtain or alter;

(7) the term "department of the United States" means the legislative or judicial branch of the Government or one of the executive departments enumerated in section 101 of title 5;

(8) the term "damage" means any impairment to the integrity or availability of data, a program, a system, or information;

(9) the term "government entity" includes the Government of the United States, any State or political subdivision of the United States, any foreign country, and any state, province, municipality, or other political subdivision of a foreign country;

(10) the term "conviction" shall include a conviction under the law of any State for a crime punishable by imprisonment for more than 1 year, an element of which is unauthorized access, or exceeding authorized access, to a computer;

(11) the term "loss" means any reasonable cost to any victim, including the cost of responding to an offense, conducting a damage assessment, and restoring the data, program, system, or information to its condition prior to the offense, and any revenue lost, cost incurred, or other consequential damages incurred because of interruption of service; and

(12) the term "person" means any individual, firm, corporation, educational institution, financial institution, governmental entity, or legal or other entity.
(f) This section does not prohibit any lawfully authorized investigative, protective, or intelligence activity of a law enforcement agency of the United States, a State, or a political subdivision of a State, or of an intelligence agency of the United States.

(g) Any person who suffers damage or loss by reason of a violation of this section may maintain a civil action against the violator to obtain compensatory damages and injunctive relief or other equitable relief. A civil action for a violation of this section may be brought only if the conduct involves 1 of the factors set forth in subclauses (I), (II), (III), (IV), or (V) of subsection (c)(4)(A)(i). Damages for a violation involving only conduct described in subsection (c)(4)(A)(i)(I) are limited to economic damages. No action may be brought under this subsection unless such action is begun within 2 years of the date of the act complained of or the date of the discovery of the damage. No action may be brought under this subsection for the negligent design or manufacture of computer hardware, computer software, or firmware.

(h) The Attorney General and the Secretary of the Treasury shall report to the Congress annually, during the first 3 years following the date of the enactment of this subsection, concerning investigations and prosecutions under subsection (a)(5).

(i)(1) The court, in imposing sentence on any person convicted of a violation of this section, or convicted of conspiracy to violate this section, shall order, in addition to any other sentence imposed and irrespective of any provision of State law, that such person forfeit to the United States--

(A) such person's interest in any personal property that was used or intended to be used to commit or to facilitate the commission of such violation; and

(B) any property, real or personal, constituting or derived from, any proceeds that such person obtained, directly or indirectly, as a result of such violation.

(2) The criminal forfeiture of property under this subsection, any seizure and disposition thereof, and any judicial proceeding in relation thereto, shall be governed by the provisions of section 413 of the Comprehensive Drug Abuse Prevention and Control Act of 1970 (21 U.S.C. 853), except subsection (d) of that section.

(j) For purposes of subsection (i), the following shall be subject to forfeiture to the United States and no property right shall exist in them:

(1) Any personal property used or intended to be used to commit or to facilitate the commission of any violation of this section, or a conspiracy to violate this section.

(2) Any property, real or personal, which constitutes or is derived from proceeds traceable to any violation of this section, or a conspiracy to violate this section.

FRAUD AGAINST THE UNITED STATES

Sec. 1031. - Major fraud against the United States

(a) Whoever knowingly executes, or attempts to execute, any scheme or artifice with the intent--

(1) to defraud the United States; or

(2) to obtain money or property by means of false or fraudulent pretenses, representations, or promises,

in any grant, contract, subcontract, subsidy, loan, guarantee, insurance, or other form of Federal assistance, including through the Troubled Asset Relief Program, an economic stimulus, recovery or rescue plan provided by the Government, or the Government's purchase of any troubled asset as defined in the Emergency Economic Stabilization Act of 2008, or in any procurement of property or services as a prime contractor with the United States or as a subcontractor or supplier on a contract in which there is a prime contract with the United States, if the value of such grant, contract, subcontract, subsidy, loan, guarantee, insurance, or other form of Federal assistance, or any constituent part thereof, is $1,000,000 or more shall, subject to the applicability of subsection (c) of this section, be fined not more than $1,000,000, or imprisoned not more than 10 years, or both.

(b) The fine imposed for an offense under this section may exceed the maximum otherwise provided by law, if such fine does not exceed $5,000,000 and--

> (1) the gross loss to the Government or the gross gain to a defendant is $500,000 or greater; or

> (2) the offense involves a conscious or reckless risk of serious personal injury.

(c) The maximum fine imposed upon a defendant for a prosecution including a prosecution with multiple counts under this section shall not exceed $10,000,000.

(d) Nothing in this section shall preclude a court from imposing any other sentences available under this title, including without limitation a fine up to twice the amount of the gross loss or gross gain involved in the offense pursuant to 18 U.S.C. section 3571(d).

(e) In determining the amount of the fine, the court shall consider the factors set forth in 18 U.S.C. sections 3553 and 3572, and the factors set forth in the guidelines and policy statements of the United States Sentencing Commission, including--

> (1) the need to reflect the seriousness of the offense, including the harm or loss to the victim and the gain to the defendant;

> (2) whether the defendant previously has been fined for a similar offense; and

> (3) any other pertinent equitable considerations.

(f) A prosecution of an offense under this section may be commenced any time not later than 7 years after the offense is committed, plus any additional time otherwise allowed by law.

(g) (1) In special circumstances and in his or her sole discretion, the Attorney General is authorized to make payments from funds appropriated to the Department of Justice to persons who furnish information relating to a possible prosecution under this section. The amount of such payment shall not exceed $250,000. Upon application by the Attorney General, the court may order that the Department shall be reimbursed for a payment from a criminal fine imposed under this section.

> (2) An individual is not eligible for such a payment if--

(A) that individual is an officer or employee of a Government agency who furnishes information or renders service in the performance of official duties;

(B) that individual failed to furnish the information to the individual's employer prior to furnishing it to law enforcement authorities, unless the court determines the individual has justifiable reasons for that failure;

(C) the furnished information is based upon public disclosure of allegations or transactions in a criminal, civil, or administrative hearing, in a congressional, administrative, or GAO report, hearing, audit or investigation, or from the news media unless the person is the original source of the information. For the purposes of this subsection, "original source" means an individual who has direct and independent knowledge of the information on which the allegations are based and has voluntarily provided the information to the Government; or

(D) that individual participated in the violation of this section with respect to which such payment would be made.

(3) The failure of the Attorney General to authorize a payment shall not be subject to judicial review.

(h) Any individual who--

(1) is discharged, demoted, suspended, threatened, harassed, or in any other manner discriminated against in the terms and conditions of employment by an employer because of lawful acts done by the employee on behalf of the employee or others in furtherance of a prosecution under this section (including investigation for, initiation of, testimony for, or assistance in such prosecution), and

(2) was not a participant in the unlawful activity that is the subject of said prosecution, may, in a civil action, obtain all relief necessary to make such individual whole. Such relief shall include reinstatement with the same seniority status such individual would have had but for the discrimination, 2 times the amount of back pay, interest on the back pay, and compensation for any special damages sustained as a result of the discrimination, including litigation costs and reasonable attorney's fees.

FRAUDS

Sec. 1341. - Frauds and swindles

Whoever, having devised or intending to devise any scheme or artifice to defraud, or for obtaining money or property by means of false or fraudulent pretenses, representations, or promises, or to sell, dispose of, loan, exchange, alter, give away, distribute, supply, or furnish or procure for unlawful use any counterfeit or spurious coin, obligation, security, or other article, or anything represented to be or intimated or held out to be such counterfeit or spurious article, for the purpose of executing such scheme or artifice or attempting so to do, places in any post office or authorized depository for mail matter, any matter or thing whatever to be sent or delivered by the Postal Service, or deposits or causes to be deposited any matter or thing whatever to be sent or delivered by any private or commercial interstate carrier, or takes or receives therefrom, any such matter or thing, or knowingly causes to be delivered by mail or such carrier according to the direction thereon, or at the place at which it is directed to be delivered by the person to whom it is addressed, any such matter or thing, shall be fined under this title or imprisoned not more than 20 years, or both. If the violation occurs in relation to, or involving any benefit authorized, transported, transmitted, transferred, disbursed, or paid in connection with, a presidentially declared major disaster or emergency (as those terms are defined in section 102 of the Robert T. Stafford Disaster Relief and Emergency Assistance Act (42 U.S.C. 5122)), or affects a financial institution, such person shall be fined not more than $1,000,000 or imprisoned not more than 30 years, or both.

Sec. 1343. - Fraud by wire, radio, or television

Whoever, having devised or intending to devise any scheme or artifice to defraud, or for obtaining money or property by means of false or fraudulent pretenses, representations, or promises, transmits or causes to be transmitted by means of wire, radio, or television communication in interstate or foreign commerce, any writings, signs, signals, pictures, or sounds for the purpose of executing such scheme or artifice, shall be fined under this title or imprisoned not more than 20 years, or both. If the violation occurs in relation to, or involving any benefit authorized, transported, transmitted, transferred, disbursed, or paid in connection with, a presidentially declared major disaster or emergency (as those terms are defined in section 102 of the Robert T. Stafford Disaster Relief and Emergency Assistance Act (42 U.S.C. 5122)), or affects a financial institution, such person shall be fined not more than $1,000,000 or imprisoned not more than 30 years, or both.

Sec. 1344. - Bank fraud

Whoever knowingly executes, or attempts to execute, a scheme or artifice -

(1) to defraud a financial institution; or

(2) to obtain any of the moneys, funds, credits, assets, securities, or other property owned by, or under the custody or control of, a financial institution, by means of false or fraudulent pretenses, representations, or promises;

shall be fined not more than $1,000,000 or imprisoned not more than 30 years, or both

Sec. 1346. - Definition of "scheme or artifice to defraud"

For the purposes of this chapter, the term "scheme or artifice to defraud" includes a scheme or artifice to deprive another of the intangible right of honest services

Sec. 1347. - Health care fraud

(a) Whoever knowingly and willfully executes, or attempts to execute, a scheme or artifice -
(1) to defraud any health care benefit program; or

(2) to obtain, by means of false or fraudulent pretenses, representations, or promises, any of the money or property owned by, or under the custody or control of, any health care benefit program,

in connection with the delivery of or payment for health care benefits, items, or services, shall be fined under this title or imprisoned not more than 10 years, or both. If the violation results in serious bodily injury (as defined in section 1365 of this title), such person shall be fined under this title or imprisoned not more than 20 years, or both; and if the violation results in death, such person shall be fined under this title, or imprisoned for any term of years or for life, or both.

(b) With respect to violations of this section, a person need not have actual knowledge of this section or specific intent to commit a violation of this section.

§ 1348. Securities and commodities fraud

Whoever knowingly executes, or attempts to execute, a scheme or artifice--

(1) to defraud any person in connection with any commodity for future delivery, or any option on a commodity for future delivery, or any security of an issuer with a class of securities registered under section

12 of the Securities Exchange Act of 1934 (15 U.S.C. 78l) or that is required to file reports under section 15(d) of the Securities Exchange Act of 1934 (15 U.S.C. 78o(d)); or

(2) to obtain, by means of false or fraudulent pretenses, representations, or promises, any money or property in connection with the purchase or sale of any commodity for future delivery, or any option on a commodity for future delivery, or any security of an issuer with a class of securities registered under section 12 of the Securities Exchange Act of 1934 (15 U.S.C. 78l) or that is required to file reports under section 15(d) of the Securities Exchange Act of 1934 (15 U.S.C. 78o(d));

shall be fined under this title, or imprisoned not more than 25 years, or both.

OBSTRUCTION OF JUSTICE

Sec. 1503. - Influencing or injuring officer or juror generally

(a) Whoever corruptly, or by threats or force, or by any threatening letter or communication, endeavors to influence, intimidate, or impede any grand or petit juror, or officer in or of any court of the United States, or officer who may be serving at any examination or other proceeding before any United States magistrate judge or other committing magistrate, in the discharge of his duty, or injures any such grand or petit juror in his person or property on account of any verdict or indictment assented to by him, or on account of his being or having been such juror, or injures any such officer, magistrate judge, or other committing magistrate in his person or property on account of the performance of his official duties, or corruptly or by threats or force, or by any threatening letter or communication, influences, obstructs, or impedes, or endeavors to influence, obstruct, or impede, the due administration of justice, shall be punished as provided in subsection (b). If the offense under this section occurs in connection with a trial of a criminal case, and the act in violation of this section involves the threat of physical force or physical force, the maximum term of imprisonment which may be imposed for the offense shall be the higher of that otherwise provided by law or the maximum term that could have been imposed for any offense charged in such case.

(b) The punishment for an offense under this section is -

(1) in the case of a killing, the punishment provided in sections 1111 and 1112;

(2) in the case of an attempted killing, or a case in which the offense was committed against a petit juror and in which a class A or B felony was charged, imprisonment for not more than 20 years, a fine under this title, or both; and

(3) in any other case, imprisonment for not more than 10 years, a fine under this title, or both.

§ 1505. Obstruction of proceedings before departments, agencies, and committees

Whoever, with intent to avoid, evade, prevent, or obstruct compliance, in whole or in part, with any civil investigative demand duly and properly made under the Antitrust Civil Process Act, willfully withholds, misrepresents, removes from any place, conceals, covers up, destroys, mutilates, alters, or by other means falsifies any documentary material, answers to written interrogatories, or oral testimony, which is the subject of such demand; or attempts to do so or solicits another to do so; or

Whoever corruptly, or by threats or force, or by any threatening letter or communication influences, obstructs, or impedes or endeavors to influence, obstruct, or impede the due and proper administration of the law under which any pending proceeding is being had before any department or agency of the United States, or the due and proper exercise of the power of inquiry under which any inquiry or investigation is being had by either House, or any committee of either House or any joint committee of the Congress--

Shall be fined under this title, imprisoned not more than 5 years or, if the offense involves international or domestic terrorism (as defined in section 2331), imprisoned not more than 8 years, or both.

§ 1510. Obstruction of criminal investigations

(a) Whoever willfully endeavors by means of bribery to obstruct, delay, or prevent the communication of information relating to a violation of any criminal statute of the United States by any person to a criminal investigator shall be fined under this title, or imprisoned not more than five years, or both.

(b) (1) Whoever, being an officer of a financial institution, with the intent to obstruct a judicial proceeding, directly or indirectly notifies any other person about the existence or contents of a subpoena for records of that financial institution, or information that has been furnished in response to that subpoena, shall be fined under this title or imprisoned not more than 5 years, or both.

(2) Whoever, being an officer of a financial institution, directly or indirectly notifies--

(A) a customer of that financial institution whose records are sought by a subpoena for records; or

(B) any other person named in that subpoena;

about the existence or contents of that subpoena or information that has been furnished in response to that subpoena, shall be fined under this title or imprisoned not more than one year, or both.

(3) As used in this subsection--

(A) the term "an officer of a financial institution" means an officer, director, partner, employee, agent, or attorney of or for a financial institution; and

(B) the term "subpoena for records" means a Federal grand jury subpoena or a Department of Justice subpoena (issued under section 3486 of title 18), for customer records that has been served relating to a violation of, or a conspiracy to violate--

(i) section 215, 656, 657, 1005, 1006, 1007, 1014, 1344, 1956, 1957, or chapter 53 of title 31; or

(ii) section 1341 or 1343 affecting a financial institution.

(c) As used in this section, the term "criminal investigator" means any individual duly authorized by a department, agency, or armed force of the United States to conduct or engage in investigations of or prosecutions for violations of the criminal laws of the United States.

(d) (1) Whoever--

(A) acting as, or being, an officer, director, agent or employee of a person engaged in the business of insurance whose activities affect interstate commerce, or

(B) is engaged in the business of insurance whose activities affect interstate commerce or is involved (other than as an insured or beneficiary under a policy of insurance) in a transaction relating to the conduct of affairs of such a business,

with intent to obstruct a judicial proceeding, directly or indirectly notifies any other person about the existence or contents of a subpoena for records of that person engaged in such business or information that has been furnished to a Federal grand jury in response to that subpoena, shall be fined as provided by this title or imprisoned not more than 5 years, or both.

(2) As used in paragraph (1), the term "subpoena for records" means a Federal grand jury subpoena for records that has been served

relating to a violation of, or a conspiracy to violate, section 1033 of this title.

(e) Whoever, having been notified of the applicable disclosure prohibitions or confidentiality requirements of section 2709(c)(1) of this title, section 626(d)(1) or 627(c)(1) of the Fair Credit Reporting Act (15 U. S.C. 1681u(d)(1) or 1681v(c)(1)), section 1114(a)(3)(A) or 1114(a)(5)(D)(i) of the Right to Financial Privacy Act (12 U.S.C. 3414(a)(3)(A) or 3414(a)(5)(D)(i)), or section 802(b)(1) of the National Security Act of 1947 (50 U.S.C. 436(b)(1)), knowingly and with the intent to obstruct an investigation or judicial proceeding violates such prohibitions or requirements applicable by law to such person shall be imprisoned for not more than five years, fined under this title, or both.

§ 1512. Tampering with a witness, victim, or an informant

(a)(1) Whoever kills or attempts to kill another person, with intent to--

> (A) prevent the attendance or testimony of any person in an official proceeding;

> (B) prevent the production of a record, document, or other object, in an official proceeding; or

> (C) prevent the communication by any person to a law enforcement officer or judge of the United States of information relating to the commission or possible commission of a Federal offense or a violation of conditions of probation, parole, or release pending judicial proceedings;

shall be punished as provided in paragraph (3).

(2) Whoever uses physical force or the threat of physical force against any person, or attempts to do so, with intent to--

> (A) influence, delay, or prevent the testimony of any person in an official proceeding;

> (B) cause or induce any person to--

>> (i) withhold testimony, or withhold a record, document, or other object, from an official proceeding;

>> (ii) alter, destroy, mutilate, or conceal an object with intent to impair the integrity or availability of the object for use in an official proceeding;

>> (iii) evade legal process summoning that person to appear as a witness, or to produce a record,

document, or other object, in an official proceeding; or

    (iv) be absent from an official proceeding to which that person has been summoned by legal process; or

(C) hinder, delay, or prevent the communication to a law enforcement officer or judge of the United States of information relating to the commission or possible commission of a Federal offense or a violation of conditions of probation, supervised release, parole, or release pending judicial proceedings;

shall be punished as provided in paragraph (3).

(3) The punishment for an offense under this subsection is--

    (A) in the case of a killing, the punishment provided in sections 1111 and 1112;

    (B) in the case of--

        (i) an attempt to murder; or

        (ii) the use or attempted use of physical force against any person;

imprisonment for not more than 30 years; and

    (C) in the case of the threat of use of physical force against any person, imprisonment for not more than 20 years.

(b) Whoever knowingly uses intimidation, threatens, or corruptly persuades another person, or attempts to do so, or engages in misleading conduct toward another person, with intent to--

    (1) influence, delay, or prevent the testimony of any person in an official proceeding;

    (2) cause or induce any person to--

        (A) withhold testimony, or withhold a record, document, or other object, from an official proceeding;

        (B) alter, destroy, mutilate, or conceal an object with intent to impair the object's integrity or availability for use in an official proceeding;

(C) evade legal process summoning that person to appear as a witness, or to produce a record, document, or other object, in an official proceeding; or

(D) be absent from an official proceeding to which such person has been summoned by legal process; or

(3) hinder, delay, or prevent the communication to a law enforcement officer or judge of the United States of information relating to the commission or possible commission of a Federal offense or a violation of conditions of probation supervised release, parole, or release pending judicial proceedings;

shall be fined under this title or imprisoned not more than 20 years, or both.

(c) Whoever corruptly--

(1) alters, destroys, mutilates, or conceals a record, document, or other object, or attempts to do so, with the intent to impair the object's integrity or availability for use in an official proceeding; or

(2) otherwise obstructs, influences, or impedes any official proceeding, or attempts to do so,

shall be fined under this title or imprisoned not more than 20 years, or both.

(d) Whoever intentionally harasses another person and thereby hinders, delays, prevents, or dissuades any person from--

(1) attending or testifying in an official proceeding;

(2) reporting to a law enforcement officer or judge of the United States the commission or possible commission of a Federal offense or a violation of conditions of probation, supervised release, parole, or release pending judicial proceedings;

(3) arresting or seeking the arrest of another person in connection with a Federal offense; or

(4) causing a criminal prosecution, or a parole or probation revocation proceeding, to be sought or instituted, or assisting in such prosecution or proceeding;

or attempts to do so, shall be fined under this title or imprisoned not more than 3 years, or both.

(e) In a prosecution for an offense under this section, it is an affirmative defense, as to which the defendant has the burden of proof by a preponderance of the evidence, that the conduct consisted solely of lawful conduct and that the defendant's sole intention was to encourage, induce, or cause the other person to testify truthfully.

(f) For the purposes of this section--

(1) an official proceeding need not be pending or about to be instituted at the time of the offense; and

(2) the testimony, or the record, document, or other object need not be admissible in evidence or free of a claim of privilege.

(g) In a prosecution for an offense under this section, no state of mind need be proved with respect to the circumstance--

(1) that the official proceeding before a judge, court, magistrate judge, grand jury, or government agency is before a judge or court of the United States, a United States magistrate judge, a bankruptcy judge, a Federal grand jury, or a Federal Government agency; or

(2) that the judge is a judge of the United States or that the law enforcement officer is an officer or employee of the Federal Government or a person authorized to act for or on behalf of the Federal Government or serving the Federal Government as an adviser or consultant.

(h) There is extraterritorial Federal jurisdiction over an offense under this section.

(i) A prosecution under this section or section 1503 may be brought in the district in which the official proceeding (whether or not pending or about to be instituted) was intended to be affected or in the district in which the conduct constituting the alleged offense occurred.

(j) If the offense under this section occurs in connection with a trial of a criminal case, the maximum term of imprisonment which may be imposed for the offense shall be the higher of that otherwise provided by law or the maximum term that could have been imposed for any offense charged in such case.

(k) Whoever conspires to commit any offense under this section shall be subject to the same penalties as those prescribed for the offense the commission of which was the object of the conspiracy.

§ 1515. Definitions for certain provisions; general provision

(a) As used in sections 1512 and 1513 of this title and in this section--

(1) the term "official proceeding" means--

(A) a proceeding before a judge or court of the United States, a United States magistrate judge, a bankruptcy judge, a judge of the United States Tax Court, a special trial judge of the Tax Court, a judge of the United States Court of Federal Claims, or a Federal grand jury;

(B) a proceeding before the Congress;

(C) a proceeding before a Federal Government agency which is authorized by law; or

(D) a proceeding involving the business of insurance whose activities affect interstate commerce before any insurance regulatory official or agency or any agent or examiner appointed by such official or agency to examine the affairs of any person engaged in the business of insurance whose activities affect interstate commerce;

(2) the term "physical force" means physical action against another, and includes confinement;

(3) the term "misleading conduct" means--

(A) knowingly making a false statement;

(B) intentionally omitting information from a statement and thereby causing a portion of such statement to be misleading, or intentionally concealing a material fact, and thereby creating a false impression by such statement;

(C) with intent to mislead, knowingly submitting or inviting reliance on a writing or recording that is false, forged, altered, or otherwise lacking in authenticity;

(D) with intent to mislead, knowingly submitting or inviting reliance on a sample, specimen, map, photograph, boundary mark, or other object that is misleading in a material respect; or

(E) knowingly using a trick, scheme, or device with intent to mislead;

(4) the term "law enforcement officer" means an officer or employee of the Federal Government, or a person authorized to act for or on behalf of the Federal Government or serving the Federal Government as an adviser or consultant--

(A) authorized under law to engage in or supervise the prevention, detection, investigation, or prosecution of an offense; or

(B) serving as a probation or pretrial services officer under this title;

(5) the term "bodily injury" means--

(A) a cut, abrasion, bruise, burn, or disfigurement;

(B) physical pain;

(C) illness;

(D) impairment of the function of a bodily member, organ, or mental faculty; or

(E) any other injury to the body, no matter how temporary; and

(6) the term "corruptly persuades" does not include conduct which would be misleading conduct but for a lack of a state of mind.

(b) As used in section 1505, the term "corruptly" means acting with an improper purpose, personally or by influencing another, including making a false or misleading statement, or withholding, concealing, altering, or destroying a document or other information.

(c) This chapter does not prohibit or punish the providing of lawful, bona fide, legal representation services in connection with or anticipation of an official proceeding.

§ 1518. Obstruction of criminal investigations of health care offenses

(a) Whoever willfully prevents, obstructs, misleads, delays or attempts to prevent, obstruct, mislead, or delay the communication of information or records relating to a violation of a Federal health care offense to a criminal investigator shall be fined under this title or imprisoned not more than 5 years, or both.

(b) As used in this section the term "criminal investigator" means any individual duly authorized by a department, agency, or armed force of the United States to conduct or engage in investigations for prosecutions for violations of health care offenses.

§ 1519. Destruction, alteration, or falsification of records in Federal investigations and bankruptcy

Whoever knowingly alters, destroys, mutilates, conceals, covers up, falsifies, or makes a false entry in any record, document, or tangible object with the intent to impede, obstruct, or influence the investigation or proper administration of any matter within the jurisdiction of any department or agency of the United States or any case filed under title 11, or in relation to or contemplation of any such matter or case, shall be fined under this title, imprisoned not more than 20 years, or both.

§ 1520. Destruction of corporate audit records

(a)(1) Any accountant who conducts an audit of an issuer of securities to which section 10A(a) of the Securities Exchange Act of 1934 (15 U.S.C. 78j-1(a)) applies, shall maintain all audit or review workpapers for a period of 5 years from the end of the fiscal period in which the audit or review was concluded.

(2) The Securities and Exchange Commission shall promulgate, within 180 days, after adequate notice and an opportunity for comment, such rules and regulations, as are reasonably necessary, relating to the retention of relevant records such as workpapers, documents that form the basis of an audit or review, memoranda, correspondence, communications, other documents, and records (including electronic records) which are created, sent, or received in connection with an audit or review and contain conclusions, opinions, analyses, or financial data relating to such an audit or review, which is conducted by any accountant who conducts an audit of an issuer of securities to which section 10A(a) of the Securities Exchange Act of 1934 (15 U.S.C. 78j-1(a)) applies. The Commission may, from time to time, amend or supplement the rules and regulations that it is required to promulgate under this section, after adequate notice and an opportunity for comment, in order to ensure that such rules and regulations adequately comport with the purposes of this section.

(b) Whoever knowingly and willfully violates subsection (a)(1), or any rule or regulation promulgated by the Securities and Exchange Commission under subsection (a)(2), shall be fined under this title, imprisoned not more than 10 years, or both.

(c) Nothing in this section shall be deemed to diminish or relieve any person of any other duty or obligation imposed by Federal or State law or regulation to maintain, or refrain from destroying, any document.

PERJURY

Sec. 1621. - Perjury generally

Whoever -

(1) having taken an oath before a competent tribunal, officer, or person, in any case in which a law of the United States authorizes an oath to be administered, that he will testify, declare, depose, or certify truly, or that any written testimony, declaration, deposition, or certificate by him subscribed, is true, willfully and contrary to such oath states or subscribes any material matter which he does not believe to be true; or

(2) in any declaration, certificate, verification, or statement under penalty of perjury as permitted under section 1746 of title 28, United States Code, willfully subscribes as true any material matter which he does not believe to be true;

is guilty of perjury and shall, except as otherwise expressly provided by law, be fined under this title or imprisoned not more than five years, or both. This section is applicable whether the statement or subscription is made within or without the United States

Sec. 1623. - False declarations before grand jury or court

(a) Whoever under oath (or in any declaration, certificate, verification, or statement under penalty of perjury as permitted under section 1746 of title 28, United States Code) in any proceeding before or ancillary to any court or grand jury of the United States knowingly makes any false material declaration or makes or uses any other information, including any book, paper, document, record, recording, or other material, knowing the same to contain any false material declaration, shall be fined under this title or imprisoned not more than five years, or both.

(b) This section is applicable whether the conduct occurred within or without the United States.

(c) An indictment or information for violation of this section alleging that, in any proceedings before or ancillary to any court or grand jury of the United States, the defendant under oath has knowingly made two or more declarations, which are inconsistent to the degree that one of them is necessarily false, need not specify which declaration is false if -

(1) each declaration was material to the point in question, and

(2) each declaration was made within the period of the statute of limitations for the offense charged under this section.

In any prosecution under this section, the falsity of a declaration set forth in the indictment or information shall be established sufficient for conviction by proof that the defendant while under oath made irreconcilably contradictory declarations material to the point in question in any proceeding before or ancillary to any court or grand jury. It shall be a defense to an indictment or information made pursuant to the first sentence of this subsection that the defendant at the time he made each declaration believed the declaration was true.

(d) Where, in the same continuous court or grand jury proceeding in which a declaration is made, the person making the declaration admits such declaration to be false, such admission shall bar prosecution under this section if, at the time the admission is made, the declaration has not substantially affected the proceeding, or it has not become manifest that such falsity has been or will be exposed.

(e) Proof beyond a reasonable doubt under this section is sufficient for conviction. It shall not be necessary that such proof be made by any particular number of witnesses or by documentary or other type of evidence.

ECONOMIC ESPIONAGE

Sec. 1831. - Economic espionage

(a) In General. Whoever, intending or knowing that the offense will benefit any foreign government, foreign instrumentality, or foreign agent, knowingly -

(1) steals, or without authorization appropriates, takes, carries away, or conceals, or by fraud, artifice, or deception obtains a trade secret;

(2) without authorization copies, duplicates, sketches, draws, photographs, downloads, uploads, alters, destroys, photocopies, replicates, transmits, delivers, sends, mails, communicates, or conveys a trade secret;

(3) receives, buys, or possesses a trade secret, knowing the same to have been stolen or appropriated, obtained, or converted without authorization;

(4) attempts to commit any offense described in any of paragraphs (1) through (3); or

(5) conspires with one or more other persons to commit any offense described in any of paragraphs (1) through (3), and one or more of such persons do any act to effect the object of the conspiracy,

shall, except as provided in subsection (b), be fined not more than $5,000,000 or imprisoned not more than 15 years, or both.

(b) Organizations. Any organization that commits any offense described in subsection (a) shall be fined not more than the greater of $10,000,000 or 3 times the value of the stolen trade secret to the organization, including expenses for research and design and other costs of reproducing the trade secret that the organization has thereby avoided.

Sec. 1832. - Theft of trade secrets

(a) Whoever, with intent to convert a trade secret, that is related to a product or service used in or intended for use in interstate or foreign commerce, to the economic benefit of anyone other than the owner thereof, and intending or knowing that the offense will, injure any owner of that trade secret, knowingly -

(1) steals, or without authorization appropriates, takes, carries away, or conceals, or by fraud, artifice, or deception obtains such information;

(2) without authorization copies, duplicates, sketches, draws, photographs, downloads, uploads, alters, destroys, photocopies, replicates, transmits, delivers, sends, mails, communicates, or conveys such information;

(3) receives, buys, or possesses such information, knowing the same to have been stolen or appropriated, obtained, or converted without authorization;

(4) attempts to commit any offense described in paragraphs (1) through (3); or

(5) conspires with one or more other persons to commit any offense described in paragraphs (1) through (3), and one or more of such persons do any act to effect the object of the conspiracy,

shall, except as provided in subsection (b), be fined under this title or imprisoned not more than 10 years, or both.

(b) Any organization that commits any offense described in subsection (a) shall be fined not more than $5,000,000

Sec. 1839. - Definitions

As used in this chapter -

(1) the term "foreign instrumentality" means any agency, bureau, ministry, component, institution, association, or any legal, commercial, or business organization, corporation, firm, or entity that is substantially owned,

controlled, sponsored, commanded, managed, or dominated by a foreign government;

(2) the term "foreign agent" means any officer, employee, proxy, servant, delegate, or representative of a foreign government;

(3) the term "trade secret" means all forms and types of financial, business, scientific, technical, economic, or engineering information, including patterns, plans, compilations, program devices, formulas, designs, prototypes, methods, techniques, processes, procedures, programs, or codes, whether tangible or intangible, and whether or how stored, compiled, or memorialized physically, electronically, graphically, photographically, or in writing if -

(A) the owner thereof has taken reasonable measures to keep such information secret; and

(B) the information derives independent economic value, actual or potential, from not being generally known to, and not being readily ascertainable through proper means by, the public; and

(4) the term "owner", with respect to a trade secret, means the person or entity in whom or in which rightful legal or equitable title to, or license in, the trade secret is reposed.

HOBBS ACT

Sec. 1951. - Interference with commerce by threats or violence

(a) Whoever in any way or degree obstructs, delays, or affects commerce or the movement of any article or commodity in commerce, by robbery or extortion or attempts or conspires so to do, or commits or threatens physical violence to any person or property in furtherance of a plan or purpose to do anything in violation of this section shall be fined under this title or imprisoned not more than twenty years, or both.

(b) As used in this section -

(1) The term "robbery" means the unlawful taking or obtaining of personal property from the person or in the presence of another, against his will, by means of actual or threatened force, or violence, or fear of injury, immediate or future, to his person or property, or property in his custody or possession, or the person or property of a relative or member of his family or of anyone in his company at the time of the taking or obtaining.

(2) The term "extortion" means the obtaining of property from another, with his consent, induced by wrongful use of actual or threatened force, violence, or fear, or under color of official right.

(3) The term "commerce" means commerce within the District of Columbia, or any Territory or Possession of the United States; all commerce between any point in a State, Territory, Possession, or the District of Columbia and any point outside thereof; all commerce between points within the same State through any place outside such State; and all other commerce over which the United States has jurisdiction.

(c) This section shall not be construed to repeal, modify or affect section 17 of Title 15, sections 52, 101-115, 151-166 of Title 29 or sections 151-188 of Title 45.

MONEY LAUNDERING

§ 1956. Laundering of monetary instruments

(a)(1) Whoever, knowing that the property involved in a financial transaction represents the proceeds of some form of unlawful activity, conducts or attempts to conduct such a financial transaction which in fact involves the proceeds of specified unlawful activity--

    (A)(i) with the intent to promote the carrying on of specified unlawful activity; or

        (ii) with intent to engage in conduct constituting a violation of section 7201 or 7206 of the Internal Revenue Code of 1986; or

    (B) knowing that the transaction is designed in whole or in part--

        (i) to conceal or disguise the nature, the location, the source, the ownership, or the control of the proceeds of specified unlawful activity; or

        (ii) to avoid a transaction reporting requirement under State or Federal law,

shall be sentenced to a fine of not more than $500,000 or twice the value of the property involved in the transaction, whichever is greater, or imprisonment for not more than twenty years, or both.

(2) Whoever transports, transmits, or transfers, or attempts to transport, transmit, or transfer a monetary instrument or funds from a place in the United States to or through a place outside the United States or to a place in the United States from or through a place outside the United States--

(A) with the intent to promote the carrying on of specified unlawful activity; or

(B) knowing that the monetary instrument or funds involved in the transportation, transmission, or transfer represent the proceeds of some form of unlawful activity and knowing that such transportation, transmission, or transfer is designed in whole or in part--

(i) to conceal or disguise the nature, the location, the source, the ownership, or the control of the proceeds of specified unlawful activity; or

(ii) to avoid a transaction reporting requirement under State or Federal law,

shall be sentenced to a fine of not more than $500,000 or twice the value of the monetary instrument or funds involved in the transportation, transmission, or transfer whichever is greater, or imprisonment for not more than twenty years, or both. For the purpose of the offense described in subparagraph (B), the defendant's knowledge may be established by proof that a law enforcement officer represented the matter specified in subparagraph (B) as true, and the defendant's subsequent statements or actions indicate that the defendant believed such representations to be true.

(3) Whoever, with the intent--

(A) to promote the carrying on of specified unlawful activity;

(B) to conceal or disguise the nature, location, source, ownership, or control of property believed to be the proceeds of specified unlawful activity; or

(C) to avoid a transaction reporting requirement under State or Federal law,

conducts or attempts to conduct a financial transaction involving property represented to be the proceeds of specified unlawful activity, or property used to conduct or facilitate specified unlawful activity, shall be fined under this title or imprisoned for not more than 20 years, or both. For purposes of this paragraph and paragraph (2), the term "represented" means any representation made by a law enforcement officer or by another person at the direction of, or with the approval of, a Federal official authorized to investigate or prosecute violations of this section.

(b) Penalties.--

(1) In general.--Whoever conducts or attempts to conduct a transaction described in subsection (a)(1) or (a)(3), or section 1957, or a transportation, transmission, or transfer described in subsection (a)(2), is liable to the United States for a civil penalty of not more than the greater of--

(A) the value of the property, funds, or monetary instruments involved in the transaction; or

(B) $10,000.

(2) Jurisdiction over foreign persons.--For purposes of adjudicating an action filed or enforcing a penalty ordered under this section, the district courts shall have jurisdiction over any foreign person, including any financial institution authorized under the laws of a foreign country, against whom the action is brought, if service of process upon the foreign person is made under the Federal Rules of Civil Procedure or the laws of the country in which the foreign person is found, and--

(A) the foreign person commits an offense under subsection (a) involving a financial transaction that occurs in whole or in part in the United States;

(B) the foreign person converts, to his or her own use, property in which the United States has an ownership interest by virtue of the entry of an order of forfeiture by a court of the United States; or

(C) the foreign person is a financial institution that maintains a bank account at a financial institution in the United States. * * *

(c) As used in this section--

(1) the term "knowing that the property involved in a financial transaction represents the proceeds of some form of unlawful activity" means that the person knew the property involved in the transaction represented proceeds from some form, though not necessarily which form, of activity that constitutes a felony under State, Federal, or foreign law, regardless of whether or not such activity is specified in paragraph (7);

(2) the term "conducts" includes initiating, concluding, or participating in initiating, or concluding a transaction;

(3) the term "transaction" includes a purchase, sale, loan, pledge, gift, transfer, delivery, or other disposition, and with respect to a financial

institution includes a deposit, withdrawal, transfer between accounts, exchange of currency, loan, extension of credit, purchase or sale of any stock, bond, certificate of deposit, or other monetary instrument, use of a safe deposit box, or any other payment, transfer, or delivery by, through, or to a financial institution, by whatever means effected;

(4) the term "financial transaction" means (A) a transaction which in any way or degree affects interstate or foreign commerce (i) involving the movement of funds by wire or other means or (ii) involving one or more monetary instruments, or (iii) involving the transfer of title to any real property, vehicle, vessel, or aircraft, or (B) a transaction involving the use of a financial institution which is engaged in, or the activities of which affect, interstate or foreign commerce in any way or degree;

(5) the term "monetary instruments" means

(i) coin or currency of the United States or of any other country, travelers' checks, personal checks, bank checks, and money orders, or

(ii) investment securities or negotiable instruments, in bearer form or otherwise in such form that title thereto passes upon delivery;

(6) the term "financial institution" includes--

(A) any financial institution, as defined in section 5312(a)(2) of title 31, United States Code, or the regulations promulgated thereunder; and

(B) any foreign bank, as defined in section 1 of the International Banking Act of 1978 (12 U.S.C. 3101);

(7) the term "specified unlawful activity" means--

(A) any act or activity constituting an offense listed in section 1961(1) of this title except an act which is indictable under subchapter II of chapter 53 of title 31;

(B) with respect to a financial transaction occurring in whole or in part in the United States, an offense against a foreign nation involving--

(i) the manufacture, importation, sale, or distribution of a controlled substance (as such term is defined for the purposes of the Controlled Substances Act);

(ii) murder, kidnapping, robbery, extortion, destruction of property by means of explosive or fire, or a crime of violence (as defined in section 16);

(iii) fraud, or any scheme or attempt to defraud, by or against a foreign bank (as defined in paragraph 7 of section 1(b) of the International Banking Act of 1978);

(iv) bribery of a public official, or the misappropriation, theft, or embezzlement of public funds by or for the benefit of a public official;

(v) smuggling or export control violations involving--

(I) an item controlled on the United States Munitions List established under section 38 of the Arms Export Control Act (22 U.S.C. 2778); or

(II) an item controlled under regulations under the Export Administration Regulations (15 C.F.R. Parts 730-774); or

(vi) an offense with respect to which the United States would be obligated by a multilateral treaty, either to extradite the alleged offender or to submit the case for prosecution, if the offender were found within the territory of the United States;

(C) any act or acts constituting a continuing criminal enterprise, as that term is defined in section 408 of the Controlled Substances Act (21 U.S.C. 848);

(D) an offense under section 32 (relating to the destruction of aircraft), section 37 (relating to violence at international airports), section 115 (relating to influencing, impeding, or retaliating against a Federal official by threatening or injuring a family member), section 152 (relating to concealment of assets; false oaths and claims; bribery), section 175c (relating to the variola virus), section 215 (relating to commissions or gifts for procuring loans), section 351 (relating to congressional or Cabinet officer assassination), any of sections 500 through 503 (relating to certain counterfeiting offenses), section 513 (relating to securities of States and private entities), section 541 (relating to goods falsely classified), section 542 (relating to entry of goods by means of false statements), section 545 (relating to smuggling goods into the United States), section 549 (relating to removing goods from Customs custody), section 554 (relating to smuggling goods from the United States), section 555 (relating to border tunnels), section 641 (relating to public money, property, or records), section 656 (relating to theft, embezzlement, or misapplication by bank officer or employee), section 657 (relating to lending, credit, and insurance institutions), section 658 (relating to property mortgaged or pledged to farm credit agencies), section 666 (relating to theft or bribery concerning programs receiving Federal funds), section 793, 794, or 798 (relating to espionage), section 831 (relating to prohibited transactions involving nuclear materials), section 844(f) or (i) (relating to destruction by explosives or fire of Government property or property affecting interstate or foreign commerce), section 875 (relating to interstate communications), section 922(1) (relating to the unlawful importation of firearms), section 924(n) (relating to firearms trafficking), section 956 (relating to conspiracy to kill, kidnap, maim, or injure certain property in a foreign country), section 1005 (relating to fraudulent bank entries), 1006 (relating to fraudulent Federal credit institution entries), 1007 (relating to fraudulent Federal Deposit Insurance transactions), 1014 (relating to fraudulent loan or credit applications), section 1030 (relating to computer fraud and abuse), 1032 (relating to concealment of assets from conservator, receiver, or liquidating agent of financial institution), section 1111 (relating to murder), section 1114 (relating to murder of United States law enforcement officials), section 1116 (relating to murder of foreign officials, official guests, or internationally protected persons), section 1201 (relating to kidnaping), section 1203 (relating to hostage taking), section 1361 (relating to willful injury of Government property), section 1363 (relating to destruction of property within the special maritime and territorial jurisdiction), section 1708 (theft from the mail), section 1751 (relating to Presidential assassination), section 2113 or 2114 (relating to bank and postal robbery and theft), section 2252A (relating to child pornography) where the child pornography contains a visual depiction of an actual minor engaging in sexually explicit conduct, section 2260 (production of certain child pornography for importation into the United States), section 2280 (relating to violence against maritime navigation), section 2281 (relating to violence against maritime fixed platforms), section 2319 (relating to copyright infringement), section 2320 (relating to trafficking in counterfeit goods and services), section 2332 (relating to terrorist acts abroad against United States nationals), section 2332a (relating to use of weapons of mass destruction), section 2332b (relating to international terrorist acts transcending national boundaries), section 2332g (relating to missile systems designed to destroy aircraft), section 2332h (relating to radiological dispersal devices), section 2339A or 2339B (relating to providing material support to terrorists), section 2339C (relating to financing of terrorism), or section 2339D (relating to receiving military-type training from a foreign terrorist organization) of this title, section 46502 of title 49, United States Code, a felony violation of the Chemical Diversion and Trafficking Act of 1988 (relating to precursor and essential chemicals), section 590 of the Tariff Act of 1930 (19 U.S.C. 1590) (relating to aviation smuggling), section 422 of the Controlled Substances Act (relating to transportation of drug paraphernalia), section 38(c) (relating to criminal violations) of the Arms Export Control Act, section 11 (relating to violations) of the Export Administration Act of 1979, section 206 (relating to penalties) of the International Emergency Economic Powers Act, section 16 (relating to offenses and punishment) of the Trading with the Enemy Act, any felony violation of section 15 of the Food and Nutrition Act of 2008 [7 U.S.C.A. § 2024] (relating to supplemental nutrition assistance program benefits fraud) involving a quantity of benefits having a value of not less than $5,000, any violation of section 543(a)(1) of the Housing Act of 1949 [42 U.S.C.A. § 1490s(a)(1)] (relating to equity skimming), any felony violation of the Foreign Agents Registration Act of 1938, any felony violation of the Foreign Corrupt Practices Act, or section 92 of the Atomic Energy Act of 1954 (42 U.S.C. 2122) (relating to prohibitions governing atomic weapons);

(E) a felony violation of the Federal Water Pollution Control Act (33 U.S.C. 1251 et seq.), the Ocean Dumping Act (33 U.S.C. 1401 et seq.), the Act to Prevent Pollution from Ships (33 U.S.C. 1901 et seq.), the Safe Drinking Water Act (42 U.S.C. 300f et seq.), or the Resources Conservation and Recovery Act (42 U.S.C. 6901 et seq.); or

(F) any act or activity constituting an offense involving a Federal health care offense;

(8) the term "State" includes a State of the United States, the District of Columbia, and any commonwealth, territory, or possession of the United States; and

(9) the term "proceeds" means any property derived from or obtained or retained, directly or indirectly, through some form of unlawful activity, including the gross receipts of such activity.

(d) Nothing in this section shall supersede any provision of Federal, State, or other law imposing criminal penalties or affording civil remedies in addition to those provided for in this section.

(e) Violations of this section may be investigated by such components of the Department of Justice as the Attorney General may direct, and by such components of the Department of the Treasury as the Secretary of the Treasury may direct, as appropriate, and, with respect to offenses over which the Department of Homeland Security has jurisdiction, by such components of the Department of Homeland Security as the Secretary of Homeland Security may direct, and, with respect to offenses over which the United States Postal Service has jurisdiction, by the Postal Service. Such authority of the Secretary of the Treasury, the Secretary of Homeland Security, and the Postal Service shall be exercised in accordance with an agreement which shall be entered into by the Secretary of the Treasury, the Secretary of Homeland Security, the Postal Service, and the Attorney General. Violations of this section involving offenses described in paragraph (c)(7)(E) may be investigated by such components of the Department of Justice as the Attorney General may direct, and the National Enforcement Investigations Center of the Environmental Protection Agency.

(f) There is extraterritorial jurisdiction over the conduct prohibited by this section if--

(1) the conduct is by a United States citizen or, in the case of a non-United States citizen, the conduct occurs in part in the United States; and

(2) the transaction or series of related transactions involves funds or monetary instruments of a value exceeding $10,000.

(g) Notice of conviction of financial institutions.--If any financial institution or any officer, director, or employee of any financial institution has been found guilty of an offense under this section, section 1957 or 1960 of this title, or section 5322 or 5324 of title 31, the Attorney General shall provide written notice of such fact to the appropriate regulatory agency for the financial institution.

(h) Any person who conspires to commit any offense defined in this section or section 1957 shall be subject to the same penalties as those prescribed for the offense the commission of which was the object of the conspiracy.

(i) Venue.--

(1) Except as provided in paragraph (2), a prosecution for an offense under this section or section 1957 may be brought in--

(A) any district in which the financial or monetary transaction is conducted; or

(B) any district where a prosecution for the underlying specified unlawful activity could be brought, if the defendant participated in the transfer of the proceeds of the specified unlawful activity from that district to the district where the financial or monetary transaction is conducted.

(2) A prosecution for an attempt or conspiracy offense under this section or section 1957 may be brought in the district where venue would lie for the completed offense under paragraph (1), or in any other district where an act in furtherance of the attempt or conspiracy took place.

(3) For purposes of this section, a transfer of funds from 1 place to another, by wire or any other means, shall constitute a single, continuing transaction. Any person who conducts (as that term is defined in subsection (c)(2)) any portion of the transaction may be charged in any district in which the transaction takes place.

§ 1957. Engaging in monetary transactions in property derived from specified unlawful activity

(a) Whoever, in any of the circumstances set forth in subsection (d), knowingly engages or attempts to engage in a monetary transaction in criminally derived property of a value greater than $10,000 and is derived from specified unlawful activity, shall be punished as provided in subsection (b).

(b)(1) Except as provided in paragraph (2), the punishment for an offense under this section is a fine under title 18, United States Code, or imprisonment for not more than ten years or both. If the offense involves a pre-retail medical product (as defined in section 670) the punishment for the offense shall be the same as the punishment for an offense under section 670 unless the punishment under this subsection is greater.

(2) The court may impose an alternate fine to that imposable under paragraph (1) of not more than twice the amount of the criminally derived property involved in the transaction.

(c) In a prosecution for an offense under this section, the Government is not required to prove the defendant knew that the offense from which the criminally derived property was derived was specified unlawful activity.

(d) The circumstances referred to in subsection (a) are--

(1) that the offense under this section takes place in the United States or in the special maritime and territorial jurisdiction of the United States; or

(2) that the offense under this section takes place outside the United States and such special jurisdiction, but the defendant is a United States person (as defined in section 3077 of this title, but excluding the class described in paragraph (2)(D) of such section).

(e) Violations of this section may be investigated by such components of the Department of Justice as the Attorney General may direct, and by such components of the Department of the Treasury as the Secretary of the Treasury may direct, as appropriate, and, with respect to offenses over which the Department of Homeland Security has jurisdiction, by such components of the Department of Homeland Security as the Secretary of Homeland Security may direct, and, with respect to offenses over which the United States Postal Service has jurisdiction, by the Postal Service. Such authority of the Secretary of the Treasury, the Secretary of Homeland Security, and the Postal Service shall be exercised in accordance with an agreement which shall be entered into by the Secretary of the Treasury, the Secretary of Homeland Security, the Postal Service, and the Attorney General.

(f) As used in this section--

(1) the term "monetary transaction" means the deposit, withdrawal, transfer, or exchange, in or affecting interstate or foreign commerce, of funds or a monetary instrument (as defined in section 1956(c)(5) of this title) by, through, or to a financial institution (as defined in section 1956 of this title), including any transaction that would be a financial transaction under section 1956(c)(4)(B) of this title, but such term does not include any transaction necessary to preserve a person's right to representation as guaranteed by the sixth amendment to the Constitution;

(2) the term "criminally derived property" means any property constituting, or derived from, proceeds obtained from a criminal offense; and

(3) the terms "specified unlawful activity" and "proceeds" shall have the meaning given those terms in section 1956 of this title.

RICO

Sec. 1961. - Definitions

As used in this chapter -

(1) "racketeering activity" means

(A) any act or threat involving murder, kidnapping, gambling, arson, robbery, bribery, extortion, dealing in obscene matter, or dealing in a controlled substance or listed chemical (as defined in section 102 of the

Controlled Substances Act), which is chargeable under State law and punishable by imprisonment for more than one year;

(B) any act which is indictable under any of the following provisions of title 18, United States Code: Section 201 (relating to bribery), section 224 (relating to sports bribery), sections 471, 472, and 473 (relating to counterfeiting), section 659 (relating to theft from interstate shipment) if the act indictable under section 659 is felonious, section 664 (relating to embezzlement from pension and welfare funds), sections 891-894 (relating to extortionate credit transactions), section 1028 (relating to fraud and related activity in connection with identification documents), section 1029 (relating to fraud and related activity in connection with access devices), section 1084 (relating to the transmission of gambling information), section 1341 (relating to mail fraud), section 1343 (relating to wire fraud), section 1344 (relating to financial institution fraud), section 1351 (relating to fraud in foreign labor contracting), section 1425 (relating to the procurement of citizenship or nationalization unlawfully), section 1426 (relating to the reproduction of naturalization or citizenship papers), section 1427 (relating to the sale of naturalization or citizenship papers), sections 1461-1465 (relating to obscene matter), section 1503 (relating to obstruction of justice), section 1510 (relating to obstruction of criminal investigations), section 1511 (relating to the obstruction of State or local law enforcement), section 1512 (relating to tampering with a witness, victim, or an informant), section 1513 (relating to retaliating against a witness, victim, or an informant), section 1542 (relating to false statement in application and use of passport), section 1543 (relating to forgery or false use of passport), section 1544 (relating to misuse of passport), section 1546 (relating to fraud and misuse of visas, permits, and other documents), sections 1581-1592 (relating to peonage, slavery, and trafficking in persons), section 1951 (relating to interference with commerce, robbery, or extortion), section 1952 (relating to racketeering), section 1953 (relating to interstate transportation of wagering paraphernalia), section 1954 (relating to unlawful welfare fund payments), section 1955 (relating to the prohibition of illegal gambling businesses), section 1956 (relating to the laundering of monetary instruments), section 1957 (relating to engaging in monetary transactions in property derived from specified unlawful activity), section 1958 (relating to use of interstate commerce facilities in the commission of murder-for-hire), section 1960 (relating to illegal money transmitters), sections 2251, 2251A, 2252, and 2260 (relating to sexual exploitation of children), sections 2312 and 2313 (relating to interstate transportation of stolen motor vehicles), sections 2314 and 2315 (relating to interstate transportation of stolen property), section 2318 (relating to trafficking in counterfeit labels for phonorecords, computer programs or computer program documentation or packaging and copies of motion pictures or other audiovisual works), section 2319 (relating to criminal infringement of a copyright), section 2319A (relating to unauthorized fixation of and trafficking in sound recordings and music videos of live musical performances), section 2320 (relating to trafficking in goods or services bearing counterfeit marks), section 2321 (relating to trafficking in certain motor vehicles or motor vehicle parts), sections 2341-2346 (relating to trafficking in contraband cigarettes), sections 2421-24 (relating to white slave traffic), sections 175-178 (relating to biological weapons), sections 229-229F (relating to chemical weapons), section 831 (relating to nuclear materials),

(C) any act which is indictable under title 29, United States Code, section 186 (dealing with restrictions on payments and loans to labor organizations) or section 501(c) (relating to embezzlement from union funds),

(D) any offense involving fraud connected with a case under title 11 (except a case under section 157 of this title), fraud in the sale of securities, or the felonious manufacture, importation, receiving, concealment, buying, selling, or otherwise dealing in a controlled substance or listed chemical (as defined in section 102 of the Controlled Substances Act), punishable under any law of the United States,

(E) any act which is indictable under the Currency and Foreign Transactions Reporting Act,

(F) any act which is indictable under the Immigration and Nationality Act, section 274 (relating to bringing in and harboring certain aliens), section 277 (relating to aiding or assisting certain aliens to enter the United States), or section 278 (relating to importation of alien for immoral purpose) if the act indictable under such section of such Act was committed for the purpose of financial gain, or

(G) any act that is indictable under any provision listed in section 2332b(g)(5)(B);

(2) "State" means any State of the United States, the District of Columbia, the Commonwealth of Puerto Rico, any territory or possession of the United States, any political subdivision, or any department, agency, or instrumentality thereof;

(3) "person" includes any individual or entity capable of holding a legal or beneficial interest in property;

(4) "enterprise" includes any individual, partnership, corporation, association, or other legal entity, and any union or group of individuals associated in fact although not a legal entity;

(5) "pattern of racketeering activity" requires at least two acts of racketeering activity, one of which occurred after the effective date of this chapter and the last of which occurred within ten years (excluding any period of imprisonment) after the commission of a prior act of racketeering activity;

(6) "unlawful debt" means a debt

(A) incurred or contracted in gambling activity which was in violation of the law of the United States, a State or political subdivision thereof, or which is unenforceable under State or Federal law in whole or in part as to principal or interest because of the laws relating to usury, and

(B) which was incurred in connection with the business of gambling in violation of the law of the United States, a State or political subdivision thereof, or the business of lending money or a thing of value at a rate usurious under State or Federal law, where the usurious rate is at least twice the enforceable rate;

(7) "racketeering investigator" means any attorney or investigator so designated by the Attorney General and charged with the duty of enforcing or carrying into effect this chapter;

(8) "racketeering investigation" means any inquiry conducted by any racketeering investigator for the purpose of ascertaining whether any person has been involved in any violation of this chapter or of any final order, judgment, or decree of any court of the United States, duly entered in any case or proceeding arising under this chapter;

(9) "documentary material" includes any book, paper, document, record, recording, or other material; and

(10) "Attorney General" includes the Attorney General of the United States, the Deputy Attorney General of the United States, the Associate Attorney General of the United States, any Assistant Attorney General of the United States, or any employee of the Department of Justice or any employee of any department or agency of the United States so designated by the Attorney General to carry out the powers conferred on the Attorney General by this chapter. Any department or agency so designated may use in investigations authorized by this chapter either the investigative provisions of this chapter or the investigative power of such department or agency otherwise conferred by law

Sec. 1962. - Prohibited activities

(a) It shall be unlawful for any person who has received any income derived, directly or indirectly, from a pattern of racketeering activity or through collection of an unlawful debt in which such person has participated as a principal within the meaning of section 2, title 18, United States Code, to use or invest, directly or indirectly, any part of such income, or the proceeds of such income, in acquisition of any interest in, or the establishment or operation of, any enterprise which is engaged in, or the activities of which affect, interstate or foreign commerce. A purchase of securities on the open market for purposes of investment, and without the intention of controlling or participating in the control of the issuer, or of assisting another to do so, shall not be unlawful under this subsection if the securities of the issuer held by the purchaser, the members of his immediate family, and his or their accomplices in any pattern or racketeering activity or the collection of an unlawful debt after such purchase do not amount in the aggregate to one percent of the outstanding securities of any one class, and do not confer, either in law or in fact, the power to elect one or more directors of the issuer.

(b) It shall be unlawful for any person through a pattern of racketeering activity or through collection of an unlawful debt to acquire or maintain, directly or indirectly, any interest in or control of any enterprise which is engaged in, or the activities of which affect, interstate or foreign commerce.

(c) It shall be unlawful for any person employed by or associated with any enterprise engaged in, or the activities of which affect, interstate or foreign commerce, to conduct or participate, directly or indirectly, in the conduct of such enterprise's affairs through a pattern of racketeering activity or collection of unlawful debt.

(d) It shall be unlawful for any person to conspire to violate any of the provisions of subsection (a), (b), or (c) of this section

Sec. 1963. - Criminal penalties

(a) Whoever violates any provision of section 1962 of this chapter shall be fined under this title or imprisoned not more than 20 years (or for life if the violation is based on a racketeering activity for which the maximum penalty includes life imprisonment), or both, and shall forfeit to the United States, irrespective of any provision of State law -

(1) any interest the person has acquired or maintained in violation of section 1962;

(2) any -

(A) interest in;

(B) security of;

(C) claim against; or

(D) property or contractual right of any kind affording a source of influence over;

any enterprise which the person has established, operated, controlled, conducted, or participated in the conduct of, in violation of section 1962; and

(3) any property constituting, or derived from, any proceeds which the person obtained, directly or indirectly, from racketeering activity or unlawful debt collection in violation of section 1962.

The court, in imposing sentence on such person shall order, in addition to any other sentence imposed pursuant to this section, that the person forfeit to the United States all property described in this subsection. In lieu of a fine otherwise authorized by this section, a defendant who derives profits or other proceeds from an offense may be fined not more than twice the gross profits or other proceeds.

(b) Property subject to criminal forfeiture under this section includes -

(1) real property, including things growing on, affixed to, and found in land; and

(2) tangible and intangible personal property, including rights, privileges, interests, claims, and securities.

(c) All right, title, and interest in property described in subsection (a) vests in the United States upon the commission of the act giving rise to forfeiture under this section. Any such property that is subsequently transferred to a person other than the defendant may be the subject of a special verdict of forfeiture and thereafter shall be ordered forfeited to the United States, unless the transferee establishes in a hearing pursuant to subsection (l) that he is a bona fide purchaser for value of such property who at the time of purchase was reasonably without cause to believe that the property was subject to forfeiture under this section.

(d) (1) Upon application of the United States, the court may enter a restraining order or injunction, require the execution of a satisfactory performance bond, or take any other action to preserve the availability of property described in subsection (a) for forfeiture under this section -

(A) upon the filing of an indictment or information charging a violation of section 1962 of this chapter and alleging that the property with respect to which the order is sought would, in the event of conviction, be subject to forfeiture under this section; or

(B) prior to the filing of such an indictment or information, if, after notice to persons appearing to have an interest in the property and opportunity for a hearing, the court determines that -

(i) there is a substantial probability that the United States will prevail on the issue of forfeiture and that failure to enter the order will result in the property being destroyed, removed from the jurisdiction of the court, or otherwise made unavailable for forfeiture; and

(ii) the need to preserve the availability of the property through the entry of the requested order outweighs the hardship on any party against whom the order is to be entered:

Provided, however, That an order entered pursuant to subparagraph (B) shall be effective for not more than ninety days, unless extended by the court for good cause shown or unless an indictment or information described in subparagraph (A) has been filed.

(2) A temporary restraining order under this subsection may be entered upon application of the United States without notice or opportunity for a hearing when an information or indictment has not yet been filed with respect to the property, if the United States demonstrates that there is probable cause to believe that the property with respect to which the order is sought would, in the event of conviction, be subject to forfeiture under this section and that provision of notice will jeopardize the availability of the property for forfeiture. Such a temporary order shall expire not more than ten days after the date on which it is entered, unless extended for good cause shown or unless the party against whom it is entered consents to an extension for a longer period. A hearing requested concerning an order entered under this paragraph shall be held at the earliest possible time, and prior to the expiration of the temporary order.

(3) The court may receive and consider, at a hearing held pursuant to this subsection, evidence and information that would be inadmissible under the Federal Rules of Evidence.

(e) Upon conviction of a person under this section, the court shall enter a judgment of forfeiture of the property to the United States and shall also authorize the Attorney General to seize all property ordered forfeited upon such terms and conditions as the court shall deem proper. Following the entry of an order declaring the property forfeited, the court may, upon application of the United States, enter such appropriate restraining orders or injunctions, require the execution of satisfactory performance bonds, appoint receivers, conservators, appraisers, accountants, or trustees, or take any other action to protect the interest of the United States in the property ordered forfeited. Any income accruing to, or derived from, an enterprise or an interest in an enterprise which has been ordered forfeited under this section may be used to offset ordinary and necessary expenses to the enterprise which are required by law, or which are necessary to protect the interests of the United States or third parties.

(f) Following the seizure of property ordered forfeited under this section, the Attorney General shall direct the disposition of the property by sale or any other commercially feasible means, making due provision for the rights of any innocent persons. Any property right or interest not exercisable by, or transferable for value to, the United States shall expire and shall not revert to the defendant, nor shall the defendant or any person acting in concert with or on behalf of the defendant be eligible to purchase forfeited property at any sale held by the United States. Upon application of a person, other than the defendant or a person acting in concert with or on behalf of the defendant, the court may restrain or stay the sale or disposition of the property pending the conclusion of any appeal of the criminal case giving rise to the forfeiture, if the applicant demonstrates that proceeding with the sale or disposition of the property will result in irreparable injury, harm or loss to him. Notwithstanding 31 U.S.C. 3302(b), the proceeds of any sale or other disposition of property forfeited under this section and any moneys forfeited shall be used to pay all proper expenses for the forfeiture and the sale, including expenses of seizure, maintenance and custody of the property pending its disposition, advertising and court costs. The Attorney General shall deposit in the Treasury any amounts of such proceeds or moneys remaining after the payment of such expenses.

(g) With respect to property ordered forfeited under this section, the Attorney General is authorized to -

   (1) grant petitions for mitigation or remission of forfeiture, restore forfeited property to victims of a violation of this chapter, or take any other action to protect the rights of innocent persons which is in the interest of justice and which is not inconsistent with the provisions of this chapter;

   (2) compromise claims arising under this section;

   (3) award compensation to persons providing information resulting in a forfeiture under this section;

   (4) direct the disposition by the United States of all property ordered forfeited under this section by public sale or any other commercially feasible means, making due provision for the rights of innocent persons; and

   (5) take appropriate measures necessary to safeguard and maintain property ordered forfeited under this section pending its disposition.

(h) The Attorney General may promulgate regulations with respect to -

(1) making reasonable efforts to provide notice to persons who may have an interest in property ordered forfeited under this section;

(2) granting petitions for remission or mitigation of forfeiture;

(3) the restitution of property to victims of an offense petitioning for remission or mitigation of forfeiture under this chapter;

(4) the disposition by the United States of forfeited property by public sale or other commercially feasible means;

(5) the maintenance and safekeeping of any property forfeited under this section pending its disposition; and

(6) the compromise of claims arising under this chapter.
Pending the promulgation of such regulations, all provisions of law relating to the disposition of property, or the proceeds from the sale thereof, or the remission or mitigation of forfeitures for violation of the customs laws, and the compromise of claims and the award of compensation to informers in respect of such forfeitures shall apply to forfeitures incurred, or alleged to have been incurred, under the provisions of this section, insofar as applicable and not inconsistent with the provisions hereof. Such duties as are imposed upon the Customs Service or any person with respect to the disposition of property under the customs law shall be performed under this chapter by the Attorney General.

(i) Except as provided in subsection (l), no party claiming an interest in property subject to forfeiture under this section may -

(1) intervene in a trial or appeal of a criminal case involving the forfeiture of such property under this section; or

(2) commence an action at law or equity against the United States concerning the validity of his alleged interest in the property subsequent to the filing of an indictment or information alleging that the property is subject to forfeiture under this section.

(j) The district courts of the United States shall have jurisdiction to enter orders as provided in this section without regard to the location of any property which may be subject to forfeiture under this section or which has been ordered forfeited under this section.

(k) In order to facilitate the identification or location of property declared forfeited and to facilitate the disposition of petitions for remission or mitigation of forfeiture, after the entry of an order declaring property forfeited to the United States the court may, upon application of the United

States, order that the testimony of any witness relating to the property forfeited be taken by deposition and that any designated book, paper, document, record, recording, or other material not privileged be produced at the same time and place, in the same manner as provided for the taking of depositions under Rule 15 of the Federal Rules of Criminal Procedure.

(l) (1) Following the entry of an order of forfeiture under this section, the United States shall publish notice of the order and of its intent to dispose of the property in such manner as the Attorney General may direct. The Government may also, to the extent practicable, provide direct written notice to any person known to have alleged an interest in the property that is the subject of the order of forfeiture as a substitute for published notice as to those persons so notified.

(2) Any person, other than the defendant, asserting a legal interest in property which has been ordered forfeited to the United States pursuant to this section may, within thirty days of the final publication of notice or his receipt of notice under paragraph (1), whichever is earlier, petition the court for a hearing to adjudicate the validity of his alleged interest in the property. The hearing shall be held before the court alone, without a jury.

(3) The petition shall be signed by the petitioner under penalty of perjury and shall set forth the nature and extent of the petitioner's right, title, or interest in the property, the time and circumstances of the petitioner's acquisition of the right, title, or interest in the property, any additional facts supporting the petitioner's claim, and the relief sought.

(4) The hearing on the petition shall, to the extent practicable and consistent with the interests of justice, be held within thirty days of the filing of the petition. The court may consolidate the hearing on the petition with a hearing on any other petition filed by a person other than the defendant under this subsection.

(5) At the hearing, the petitioner may testify and present evidence and witnesses on his own behalf, and cross-examine witnesses who appear at the hearing. The United States may present evidence and witnesses in rebuttal and in defense of its claim to the property and cross-examine witnesses who appear at the hearing. In addition to testimony and evidence presented at the hearing, the court shall consider the relevant portions of the record of the criminal case which resulted in the order of forfeiture.

(6) If, after the hearing, the court determines that the petitioner has established by a preponderance of the evidence that -

    (A) the petitioner has a legal right, title, or interest in the property, and such right, title, or interest renders the order of forfeiture invalid in whole or in part because the right, title, or interest was vested in the petitioner rather than the defendant or was superior to any right, title, or interest of the defendant at the time of the commission of the acts which gave rise to the forfeiture of the property under this section; or

(B) the petitioner is a bona fide purchaser for value of the right, title, or interest in the property and was at the time of purchase reasonably without cause to believe that the property was subject to forfeiture under this section;

the court shall amend the order of forfeiture in accordance with its determination.

(7) Following the court's disposition of all petitions filed under this subsection, or if no such petitions are filed following the expiration of the period provided in paragraph (2) for the filing of such petitions, the United States shall have clear title to property that is the subject of the order of forfeiture and may warrant good title to any subsequent purchaser or transferee.

(m) If any of the property described in subsection (a), as a result of any act or omission of the defendant -

(1) cannot be located upon the exercise of due diligence;

(2) has been transferred or sold to, or deposited with, a third party;

(3) has been placed beyond the jurisdiction of the court;

(4) has been substantially diminished in value; or

(5) has been commingled with other property which cannot be divided without difficulty;
the court shall order the forfeiture of any other property of the defendant up to the value of any property described in paragraphs (1) through (5)

Sec. 1964. - Civil remedies

(a) The district courts of the United States shall have jurisdiction to prevent and restrain violations of section 1962 of this chapter by issuing appropriate orders, including, but not limited to: ordering any person to divest himself of any interest, direct or indirect, in any enterprise; imposing reasonable restrictions on the future activities or investments of any person, including, but not limited to, prohibiting any person from engaging in the same type of endeavor as the enterprise engaged in, the activities of which affect interstate or foreign commerce; or ordering dissolution or reorganization of any enterprise, making due provision for the rights of innocent persons.

(b) The Attorney General may institute proceedings under this section. Pending final determination thereof, the court may at any time enter such restraining orders or prohibitions, or take such other actions, including the acceptance of satisfactory performance bonds, as it shall deem proper.

(c) Any person injured in his business or property by reason of a violation of section 1962 of this chapter may sue therefor in any appropriate United States district court and shall recover threefold the damages he sustains and the cost of the suit, including a reasonable attorney's fee, except that no person may rely upon any conduct that would have been actionable as fraud in the purchase or sale of securities to establish a violation of section 1962. The exception contained in the preceding sentence does not apply to an action against any person that is criminally convicted in connection with the fraud, in which case the statute of limitations shall start to run on the date on which the conviction becomes final.

(d) A final judgment or decree rendered in favor of the United States in any criminal proceeding brought by the United States under this chapter shall estop the defendant from denying the essential allegations of the criminal offense in any subsequent civil proceeding brought by the United States

INTERSTATE TRANSPORTATION OF STOLEN PROPERTY

Sec. 2314. - Transportation of stolen goods, securities, moneys, fraudulent State tax stamps, or articles used in counterfeiting

Whoever transports, transmits, or transfers in interstate or foreign commerce any goods, wares, merchandise, securities or money, of the value of $5,000 or more, knowing the same to have been stolen, converted or taken by fraud; or

Whoever, having devised or intending to devise any scheme or artifice to defraud, or for obtaining money or property by means of false or fraudulent pretenses, representations, or promises, transports or causes to be transported, or induces any person or persons to travel in, or to be transported in interstate or foreign commerce in the execution or concealment of a scheme or artifice to defraud that person or those persons of money or property having a value of $5,000 or more; or

Whoever, with unlawful or fraudulent intent, transports in interstate or foreign commerce any falsely made, forged, altered, or counterfeited securities or tax stamps, knowing the same to have been falsely made, forged, altered, or counterfeited; or

Whoever, with unlawful or fraudulent intent, transports in interstate or foreign commerce any traveler's check bearing a forged countersignature; or

Whoever, with unlawful or fraudulent intent, transports in interstate or foreign commerce, any tool, implement, or thing used or fitted to be used in falsely making, forging, altering, or counterfeiting any security or tax stamps, or any part thereof -

Shall be fined under this title or imprisoned not more than ten years, or both.

This section shall not apply to any falsely made, forged, altered, counterfeited or spurious representation of an obligation or other security of the United States, or of an obligation, bond, certificate, security, treasury note, bill, promise to pay or bank note issued by any foreign government. This section also shall not apply to any falsely made, forged, altered, counterfeited, or spurious representation of any bank note or bill issued by a bank or corporation of any foreign country which is intended by the laws or usage of such country to circulate as money.

Sentencing Reform Act

§ 3553. Imposition of a sentence

(a) Factors to be considered in imposing a sentence.--The court shall impose a sentence sufficient, but not greater than necessary, to comply with the purposes set forth in paragraph (2) of this subsection. The court, in determining the particular sentence to be imposed, shall consider--

(1) the nature and circumstances of the offense and the history and characteristics of the defendant;

(2) the need for the sentence imposed--

(A) to reflect the seriousness of the offense, to promote respect for the law, and to provide just punishment for the offense;

(B) to afford adequate deterrence to criminal conduct;

(C) to protect the public from further crimes of the defendant; and

(D) to provide the defendant with needed educational or vocational training, medical care, or other correctional treatment in the most effective manner;

(3) the kinds of sentences available;

(4) the kinds of sentence and the sentencing range established for--

(A) the applicable category of offense committed by the applicable category of defendant as set forth in the guidelines--

(i) issued by the Sentencing Commission pursuant to section 994(a)(1) of title 28, United States Code, subject to any amendments made to such guidelines by act of Congress (regardless of whether such amendments have yet to be incorporated by the Sentencing Commission into amendments issued under section 994(p) of title 28); and

(ii) that, except as provided in section 3742(g), are in effect on the date the defendant is sentenced; or

(B) in the case of a violation of probation or supervised release, the applicable guidelines or policy statements issued by the Sentencing Commission pursuant to section 994(a)(3) of title 28, United States Code, taking into account any amendments made to such guidelines or policy statements by act of Congress (regardless of whether such amendments have yet to be incorporated by the Sentencing Commission into amendments issued under section 994(p) of title 28);

(5) any pertinent policy statement--

(A) issued by the Sentencing Commission pursuant to section 994(a)(2) of title 28, United States Code, subject to any amendments made to such policy statement by act of Congress (regardless of whether such amendments have yet to be incorporated by the Sentencing Commission into amendments issued under section 994(p) of title 28); and

(B) that, except as provided in section 3742(g), is in effect on the date the defendant is sentenced.

(6) the need to avoid unwarranted sentence disparities among defendants with similar records who have been found guilty of similar conduct; and

(7) the need to provide restitution to any victims of the offense.

* * *

Witness Immunity

Sec. 6001. - Definitions

As used in this chapter -

(1) "agency of the United States" means any executive department as defined in section 101 of title 5, United States Code, a military department as defined in section 102 of title 5, United States Code, the Nuclear Regulatory Commission, the Board of Governors of the Federal Reserve System, the China Trade Act registrar appointed under 53 Stat. 1432 (15 U.S.C. sec. 143), the Commodity Futures Trading Commission, the Federal Communications Commission, the Federal Deposit Insurance Corporation, the Federal Maritime Commission, the Federal Power Commission, the Federal Trade Commission, the Surface Transportation Board, the National Labor Relations Board, the National Transportation Safety Board, the Railroad Retirement Board, an arbitration board established under 48 Stat. 1193 (45 U.S.C. sec. 157), the Securities and Exchange Commission, or a board established under 49 Stat. 31 (15 U.S.C. sec. 715d);

(2) "other information" includes any book, paper, document, record, recording, or other material;

(3) "proceeding before an agency of the United States" means any proceeding before such an agency with respect to which it is authorized to issue subpenas and to take testimony or receive other information from witnesses under oath; and

(4) "court of the United States" means any of the following courts: the Supreme Court of the United States, a United States court of appeals, a United States district court established under chapter 5, title 28, United States Code, a United States bankruptcy court established under chapter 6, title 28, United States Code, the District of Columbia Court of Appeals, the Superior Court of the District of Columbia, the District Court of Guam, the District Court of the Virgin Islands, the United States Court of Federal Claims, the Tax Court of the United States, the Court of International Trade, and the Court of Appeals for the Armed Forces.

Sec. 6002. - Immunity generally

Whenever a witness refuses, on the basis of his privilege against self-incrimination, to testify or provide other information in a proceeding before or ancillary to -

(1) a court or grand jury of the United States,

(2) an agency of the United States, or

(3) either House of Congress, a joint committee of the two Houses, or a committee or a subcommittee of either House,

and the person presiding over the proceeding communicates to the witness an order issued under this title, the witness may not refuse to comply with the order on the basis of his privilege against self-incrimination; but no testimony or other information compelled under the order (or any information directly or indirectly derived from such testimony or other information) may be used against the witness in any criminal case, except a prosecution for perjury, giving a false statement, or otherwise failing to comply with the order.

Sec. 6003. - Court and grand jury proceedings

(a) In the case of any individual who has been or may be called to testify or provide other information at any proceeding before or ancillary to a court of the United States or a grand jury of the United States, the United States district court for the judicial district in which the proceeding is or may be held shall issue, in accordance with subsection (b) of this section, upon the request of the United States attorney for such district, an order requiring such individual to give testimony or provide other information which he refuses to give or provide on the basis of his privilege against self-incrimination, such order to become effective as provided in section 6002 of this title.

(b) A United States attorney may, with the approval of the Attorney General, the Deputy Attorney General, the Associate Attorney General, or any designated Assistant Attorney General or Deputy Assistant Attorney General, request an order under subsection (a) of this section when in his judgment -

    (1) the testimony or other information from such individual may be necessary to the public interest; and

    (2) such individual has refused or is likely to refuse to testify or provide other information on the basis of his privilege against self-incrimination.

Sec. 6004. - Certain administrative proceedings

(a) In the case of any individual who has been or who may be called to testify or provide other information at any proceeding before an agency of the United States, the agency may, with the approval of the Attorney General, issue, in accordance with subsection (b) of this section, an order requiring the individual to give testimony or provide other information which he refuses to give or provide on the basis of his privilege against self-incrimination, such order to become effective as provided in section 6002 of this title.

(b) An agency of the United States may issue an order under subsection (a) of this section only if in its judgment -

(1) the testimony or other information from such individual may be necessary to the public interest; and

(2) such individual has refused or is likely to refuse to testify or provide other information on the basis of his privilege against self-incrimination.

Title 26, United States Code–
Internal Revenue Code

Sec. 7201. - Attempt to evade or defeat tax

Any person who willfully attempts in any manner to evade or defeat any tax imposed by this title or the payment thereof shall, in addition to other penalties provided by law, be guilty of a felony and, upon conviction thereof, shall be fined not more than $100,000 ($500,000 in the case of a corporation), or imprisoned not more than 5 years, or both, together with the costs of prosecution

Sec. 7203. - Willful failure to file return, supply information, or pay tax

Any person required under this title to pay any estimated tax or tax, or required by this title or by regulations made under authority thereof to make a return, keep any records, or supply any information, who willfully fails to pay such estimated tax or tax, make such return, keep such records, or supply such information, at the time or times required by law or regulations, shall, in addition to other penalties provided by law, be guilty of a misdemeanor and, upon conviction thereof, shall be fined not more than $25,000 ($100,000 in the case of a corporation), or imprisoned not more than 1 year, or both, together with the costs of prosecution. In the case of any person with respect to whom there is a failure to pay any estimated tax, this section shall not apply to such person with respect to such failure if there is no addition to tax under section 6654 or 6655 with respect to such failure. In the case of a willful violation of any provision of section 6050I, the first sentence of this section shall be applied by substituting "felony" for "misdemeanor" and "5 years" for "1 year".

Sec. 7206. - Fraud and false statements

Any person who -

(1) Declaration under penalties of perjury

Willfully makes and subscribes any return, statement, or other document, which contains or is verified by a written declaration that it is made under the penalties of perjury, and which he does not believe to be true and correct as to every material matter; or

(2) Aid or assistance

Willfully aids or assists in, or procures, counsels, or advises the preparation or presentation under, or in connection with any matter arising under, the internal revenue laws, of a return, affidavit, claim, or other document, which is fraudulent or is false as to any material matter, whether or not such falsity or fraud is with the knowledge or consent of the person authorized or required to present such return, affidavit, claim, or document; or

(3) Fraudulent bonds, permits, and entries

Simulates or falsely or fraudulently executes or signs any bond, permit, entry, or other document required by the provisions of the internal revenue laws, or by any regulation made in pursuance thereof, or procures the same to be falsely or fraudulently executed, or advises, aids in, or connives at such execution thereof; or

(4) Removal or concealment with intent to defraud

Removes, deposits, or conceals, or is concerned in removing, depositing, or concealing, any goods or commodities for or in respect whereof any tax is or shall be imposed, or any property upon which levy is authorized by section 6331, with intent to evade or defeat the assessment or collection of any tax imposed by this title; or

(5) Compromises and closing agreements

In connection with any compromise under section 7122, or offer of such compromise, or in connection with any closing agreement under section 7121, or offer to enter into any such agreement, willfully -

   (A) Concealment of property

   Conceals from any officer or employee of the United States any property belonging to the estate of a taxpayer or other person liable in respect of the tax, or

   (B) Withholding, falsifying, and destroying records

   Receives, withholds, destroys, mutilates, or falsifies any book, document, or record, or makes any false statement, relating to the estate or financial condition of the taxpayer or other person liable in respect of the tax; shall be guilty of a felony and, upon conviction thereof, shall be fined not more than $100,000 ($500,000 in the case of a corporation), or imprisoned not more than 3 years, or both, together with the costs of prosecution.

Sec. 7213. - Unauthorized disclosure of information

(a) Returns and return information

(1) Federal employees and other persons

It shall be unlawful for any officer or employee of the United States or any person described in section 6103(n) (or an officer or employee of any such person), or any former officer or employee, willfully to disclose to any person, except as authorized in this title, any return or return information (as defined in section 6103(b)). Any violation of this paragraph shall be a felony punishable upon conviction by a fine in any amount not exceeding $5,000, or imprisonment of not more than 5 years, or both, together with the costs of prosecution, and if such offense is committed by any officer or employee of the United States, he shall, in addition to any other punishment, be dismissed from office or discharged from employment upon conviction for such offense.

(2) State and other employees

It shall be unlawful for any person (not described in paragraph (1)) willfully to disclose to any person, except as authorized in this title, any return or return information (as defined in section 6103(b)) acquired by him or another person under subsection (d), (i)(3)(B)(I), or (7)(A)(I), (k)(10), (l)(6), (7), (8), (9), (10), (12), (15), (16), (19), (20), or (21) or (m)(2), (4), (5), (6), or (7) of section 6103 or under section 6104(c). Any violation of this paragraph shall be a felony punishable by a fine in any amount not exceeding $5,000, or imprisonment of not more than 5 years, or both, together with the costs of prosecution.

(3) Other persons

It shall be unlawful for any person to whom any return or return information (as defined in section 6103(b)) is disclosed in a manner unauthorized by this title thereafter willfully to print or publish in any manner not provided by law any such return or return information. Any violation of this paragraph shall be a felony punishable by a fine in any amount not exceeding $5,000, or imprisonment of not more than 5 years, or both, together with the costs of prosecution.

(4) Solicitation

It shall be unlawful for any person willfully to offer any item of material value in exchange for any return or return information (as defined in section 6103(b)) and to receive as a result of such solicitation any such return or return information. Any violation of this paragraph shall be a felony punishable by a fine in any amount not exceeding $5,000, or imprisonment of not more than 5 years, or both, together with the costs of prosecution.

(5) Shareholders

It shall be unlawful for any person to whom a return or return information (as defined in section 6103(b)) is disclosed pursuant to the provisions of section 6103(e)(1)(D)(iii) willfully to disclose such return or return information in any manner not provided by law. Any violation of this paragraph shall be a felony punishable by a fine in any amount not to exceed $5,000, or imprisonment of not more than 5 years, or both, together with the costs of prosecution.

(b) Disclosure of operations of manufacturer or producer

Any officer or employee of the United States who divulges or makes known in any manner whatever not provided by law to any person the operations, style of work, or apparatus of any manufacturer or producer visited by him in the discharge of his official duties shall be guilty of a misdemeanor and, upon conviction thereof, shall be fined not more than $1,000, or imprisoned not more than 1 year, or both, together with the costs of prosecution; and the offender shall be dismissed from office or discharged from employment.

(c) Disclosures by certain delegates of Secretary

All provisions of law relating to the disclosure of information, and all provisions of law relating to penalties for unauthorized disclosure of information, which are applicable in respect of any function under this title when performed by an officer or employee of the Treasury Department are likewise applicable in respect of such function when performed by any person who is a "delegate" within the meaning of section 7701(a)(12)(B).

(d) Disclosure of software

Any person who willfully divulges or makes known software (as defined in section 7612(d)(1)) to any person in violation of section 7612 shall be guilty of a felony and, upon conviction thereof, shall be fined not more than $5,000, or imprisoned not more than 5 years, or both, together with the costs of prosecution. * * *

Sec. 7213A. - Unauthorized inspection of returns or return information

(a) Prohibitions

(1) Federal employees and other persons

It shall be unlawful for -

(A) any officer or employee of the United States, or

(B) any person described in section 6103(n) or an officer or employee of any such person, willfully to inspect, except as authorized in this title, any return or return information.

(2) State and other employees

It shall be unlawful for any person (not described in paragraph (1)) willfully to inspect, except as authorized in this title, any return or return information acquired by such person or another person under a provision of section 6103 or under section 6104(c) referred to in section 7213(a)(2).

(b) Penalty

(1) In general

Any violation of subsection (a) shall be punishable upon conviction by a fine in any amount not exceeding $1,000, or imprisonment of not more than 1 year, or both, together with the costs of prosecution.

(2) Federal officers or employees

An officer or employee of the United States who is convicted of any violation of subsection (a) shall, in addition to any other punishment, be dismissed from office or discharged from employment.

(c) Definitions

For purposes of this section, the terms "inspect", "return", and "return information" have the respective meanings given such terms by section 6103(b).

Title 28, United States Code–
Judiciary and Judicial Procedure

McDade Act

§ 530B. Ethical standards for attorneys for the Government

(a) An attorney for the Government shall be subject to State laws and rules, and local Federal court rules, governing attorneys in each State where such attorney engages in that attorney's duties, to the same extent and in the same manner as other attorneys in that State.

(b) The Attorney General shall make and amend rules of the Department of Justice to assure compliance with this section.

(c) As used in this section, the term "attorney for the Government" includes any attorney described in section 77.2(a) of part 77 of title 28 of the Code of Federal Regulations and also includes any independent counsel, or employee of such a counsel, appointed under chapter 40.

Title 31, United States Code– Money and Finance

Sec. 5312. - Definitions and application

(a) In this subchapter -

(1) "financial agency" means a person acting for a person (except for a country, a monetary or financial authority acting as a monetary or financial authority, or an international financial institution of which the United States Government is a member) as a financial institution, bailee, depository trustee, or agent, or acting in a similar way related to money, credit, securities, gold, or a transaction in money, credit, securities, or gold.

(2) "financial institution" means -

　(A) an insured bank (as defined in section 3(h) of the Federal Deposit Insurance Act (12 U.S.C. 1813(h)));

　(B) a commercial bank or trust company;

　(C) a private banker;

　(D) an agency or branch of a foreign bank in the United States;

　(E) an insured institution (as defined in section 401(a) [1] See References in Text note below.

　(F) a thrift institution;

　(G) a broker or dealer registered with the Securities and Exchange Commission under the Securities Exchange Act of 1934 (15 U.S.C. 78a et seq.);

　(H) a broker or dealer in securities or commodities;

　(I) an investment banker or investment company;

　(J) a currency exchange;

(K) an issuer, redeemer, or cashier of travelers' checks, checks, money orders, or similar instruments;

(L) an operator of a credit card system;

(M) an insurance company;

(N) a dealer in precious metals, stones, or jewels;

(O) a pawnbroker;

(P) a loan or finance company;

(Q) a travel agency;

(R) a licensed sender of money;

(S) a telegraph company;

(T) a business engaged in vehicle sales, including automobile, airplane, and boat sales;

(U) persons involved in real estate closings and settlements;

(V) the United States Postal Service;

(W) an agency of the United States Government or of a State or local government carrying out a duty or power of a business described in this paragraph;

(X) a casino, gambling casino, or gaming establishment with an annual gaming revenue of more than $1,000,000 which -

(i) is licensed as a casino, gambling casino, or gaming establishment under the laws of any State or any political subdivision of any State; or

(ii) is an Indian gaming operation conducted under or pursuant to the Indian Gaming Regulatory Act other than an operation which is limited to class I gaming (as defined in section 4(6) of such Act);

(Y) any business or agency which engages in any activity which the Secretary of the Treasury determines, by regulation, to be an activity which is similar to, related to, or a substitute for any activity in which any business described in this paragraph is authorized to engage; or

(Z) any other business designated by the Secretary whose cash transactions have a high degree of usefulness in criminal, tax, or regulatory matters.

(3) "monetary instruments" means -

(A) United States coins and currency;

(B) as the Secretary may prescribe by regulation, coins and currency of a foreign country, travelers' checks, bearer negotiable instruments, bearer investment securities, bearer securities, stock on which title is passed on delivery, and similar material; and

(C) as the Secretary of the Treasury shall provide by regulation for purposes of section 5316, checks, drafts, notes, money orders, and other similar instruments which are drawn on or by a foreign financial institution and are not in bearer form.

(4) "person", in addition to its meaning under section 1 of title 1, includes a trustee, a representative of an estate and, when the Secretary prescribes, a governmental entity.

(5) "United States" means the States of the United States, the District of Columbia, and, when the Secretary prescribes by regulation, the Commonwealth of Puerto Rico, the Virgin Islands, Guam, the Northern Mariana Islands, American Samoa, the Trust Territory of the Pacific Islands, a territory or possession of the United States, or a military or diplomatic establishment.

(b) In this subchapter -

(1) "domestic financial agency" and "domestic financial institution" apply to an action in the United States of a financial agency or institution.

(2) "foreign financial agency" and "foreign financial institution" apply to an action outside the United States of a financial agency or institution

Sec. 5313. - Reports on domestic coins and currency transactions

(a) When a domestic financial institution is involved in a transaction for the payment, receipt, or transfer of United States coins or currency (or other monetary instruments the Secretary of the Treasury prescribes), in an amount, denomination, or amount and denomination, or under circumstances the Secretary prescribes by regulation, the institution and any other participant in the transaction the Secretary may prescribe shall file a report on the transaction at the time and in the way the Secretary prescribes. A participant acting for another person shall make the report as the agent or bailee of the person and identify the person for whom the transaction is being made.

(b) The Secretary may designate a domestic financial institution as an agent of the United States Government to receive a report under this section. However, the Secretary may designate a domestic financial institution that is not insured, chartered, examined, or registered as a domestic financial institution only if the institution consents. The Secretary may suspend or revoke a designation for a violation of this subchapter or a regulation under this subchapter (except a violation of section 5315 of this title or a regulation prescribed under section 5315), section 411 [1] of the National Housing Act (12 U.S.C. 1730d), or section 21 of the Federal Deposit Insurance Act (12 U.S.C. 1829b).

(c) (1) A person (except a domestic financial institution designated under subsection (b) of this section) required to file a report under this section shall file the report -

　　(A) with the institution involved in the transaction if the institution was designated;

　　(B) in the way the Secretary prescribes when the institution was not designated; or

　　(C) with the Secretary.

(2) The Secretary shall prescribe -

　　(A) the filing procedure for a domestic financial institution designated under subsection (b) of this section; and

　　(B) the way the institution shall submit reports filed with it.

(d) Mandatory Exemptions From Reporting Requirements.

(1) In general. The Secretary of the Treasury shall exempt, pursuant to section 5318(a)(6), a depository institution from the reporting requirements of subsection (a) with respect to transactions between the depository institution and the following categories of entities:

　　(A) Another depository institution.

　　(B) A department or agency of the United States, any State, or any political subdivision of any State.

　　(C) Any entity established under the laws of the United States, any State, or any political subdivision of any State, or under an interstate compact between 2 or more States, which exercises governmental authority on behalf of the United States or any such State or political subdivision.

(D) Any business or category of business the reports on which have little or no value for law enforcement purposes.

(2) Notice of exemption. The Secretary of the Treasury shall publish in the Federal Register at such times as the Secretary determines to be appropriate (but not less frequently than once each year) a list of all the entities whose transactions with a depository institution are exempt under this subsection from the reporting requirements of subsection (a).

(e) Discretionary Exemptions From Reporting Requirements.

(1) In general. The Secretary of the Treasury may exempt, pursuant to section 5318(a)(6), a depository institution from the reporting requirements of subsection (a) with respect to transactions between the depository institution and a qualified business customer of the institution on the basis of information submitted to the Secretary by the institution in accordance with procedures which the Secretary shall establish.

(2) Qualified business customer defined. For purposes of this subsection, the term "qualified business customer" means a business which -

(A) maintains a transaction account (as defined in section 19(b)(1)(C) of the Federal Reserve Act) at the depository institution;

(B) frequently engages in transactions with the depository institution which are subject to the reporting requirements of subsection (a); and

(C) meets criteria which the Secretary determines are sufficient to ensure that the purposes of this subchapter are carried out without requiring a report with respect to such transactions.

(3) Criteria for exemption. The Secretary of the Treasury shall establish, by regulation, the criteria for granting and maintaining an exemption under paragraph (1).

(4) Guidelines.

(A) In general. The Secretary of the Treasury shall establish guidelines for depository institutions to follow in selecting customers for an exemption under this subsection.

(B) Contents. The guidelines may include a description of the types of businesses or an itemization of specific businesses for which no exemption will be granted under this subsection to any depository institution. * * *

(g) Depository Institution Defined. For purposes of this section, the term "depository institution" -

(1) has the meaning given to such term in section 19(b)(1)(A) of the Federal Reserve Act; and

(2) includes -

(A) any branch, agency, or commercial lending company (as such terms are defined in section 1(b) of the International Banking Act of 1978);

(B) any corporation chartered under section 25A of the Federal Reserve Act; and

(C) any corporation having an agreement or undertaking with the Board of Governors of the Federal Reserve System under section 25 of the Federal Reserve Act.

Sec. 5324. - Structuring transactions to evade reporting requirement prohibited

(a) Domestic Coin and Currency Transactions. No person shall for the purpose of evading the reporting requirements of section 5313(a) or 5325 or any regulation prescribed under any such section -

(1) cause or attempt to cause a domestic financial institution to fail to file a report required under section 5313(a) or 5325 or any regulation prescribed under any such section;

(2) cause or attempt to cause a domestic financial institution to file a report required under section 5313(a) or 5325 or any regulation prescribed under any such section that contains a material omission or misstatement of fact; or

(3) structure or assist in structuring, or attempt to structure or assist in structuring, any transaction with one or more domestic financial institutions.

(b) International Monetary Instrument Transactions. No person shall, for the purpose of evading the reporting requirements of section 5316 -

(1) fail to file a report required by section 5316, or cause or attempt to cause a person to fail to file such a report;

(2) file or cause or attempt to cause a person to file a report required under section 5316 that contains a material omission or misstatement of fact; or

(3) structure or assist in structuring, or attempt to structure or assist in structuring, any importation or exportation of monetary instruments.

(c) Criminal Penalty.

(1) In general. Whoever violates this section shall be fined in accordance with title 18, United States Code, imprisoned for not more than 5 years, or both.

(2) Enhanced penalty for aggravated cases. Whoever violates this section while violating another law of the United States or as part of a pattern of any illegal activity involving more than $100,000 in a 12-month period shall be fined twice the amount provided in subsection (b)(3) or (c)(3) (as the case may be) of section 3571 of title 18, United States Code, imprisoned for not more than 10 years, or both.

Title 15, United States Code–
Commerce and Trade

SECURITIES EXCHANGES

Sec. 78dd-1. Prohibited foreign trade practices by issuers

(a) Prohibition

It shall be unlawful for any issuer which has a class of securities registered pursuant to section 78l of this title or which is required to file reports under section 78o(d) of this title, or for any officer, director, employee, or agent of such issuer or any stockholder thereof acting on behalf of such issuer, to make use of the mails or any means or instrumentality of interstate commerce corruptly in furtherance of an offer, payment, promise to pay, or authorization of the payment of any money, or offer, gift, promise to give, or authorization of the giving of anything of value to--

(1) any foreign official for purposes of--

(A)(i) influencing any act or decision of such foreign official in his official capacity, (ii) inducing such foreign official to do or omit to do any act in violation of the lawful duty of such official, or (iii) securing any improper advantage; or

(B) inducing such foreign official to use his influence with a foreign government or instrumentality thereof to affect or influence any act or decision of such government or instrumentality,

in order to assist such issuer in obtaining or retaining business for or with, or directing business to, any person;

(2) any foreign political party or official thereof or any candidate for foreign political office for purposes of--

(A)(i) influencing any act or decision of such party, official, or candidate in its or his official capacity, (ii) inducing such party, official, or candidate to do or omit to do an act in violation of the lawful duty of such party, official, or candidate, or (iii) securing any improper advantage; or

(B) inducing such party, official, or candidate to use its or his influence with a foreign government or instrumentality thereof to affect or influence any act or decision of such government or instrumentality.

in order to assist such issuer in obtaining or retaining business for or with, or directing business to, any person; or

(3) any person, while knowing that all or a portion of such money or thing of value will be offered, given, or promised, directly or indirectly, to any foreign official, to any foreign political party or official thereof, or to any candidate for foreign political office, for purposes of--

(A)(i) influencing any act or decision of such foreign official, political party, party official, or candidate in his or its official capacity, (ii) inducing such foreign official, political party, party official, or candidate to do or omit to do any act in violation of the lawful duty of such foreign official, political party, party official, or candidate, or (iii) securing any improper advantage; or

(B) inducing such foreign official, political party, party official, or candidate to use his or its influence with a foreign government or instrumentality thereof to affect or influence any act or decision of such government or instrumentality,

in order to assist such issuer in obtaining or retaining business for or with, or directing business to, any person.

(b) Exception for routine governmental action

Subsections (a) and (g) of this section shall not apply to any facilitating or expediting payment to a foreign official, political party, or party official the purpose of which is to expedite or to secure the performance of a routine governmental action by a foreign official, political party, or party official.

(c) Affirmative defenses

It shall be an affirmative defense to actions under subsection (a) or (g) of this section that--

(1) the payment, gift, offer, or promise of anything of value that was made, was lawful under the written laws and regulations of the foreign official's, political party's, party official's, or candidate's country; or

(2) the payment, gift, offer, or promise of anything of value that was made, was a reasonable and bona fide expenditure, such as travel and lodging expenses, incurred by or on behalf of a foreign official, party, party official, or candidate and was directly related to--

(A) the promotion, demonstration, or explanation of products or services; or

(B) the execution or performance of a contract with a foreign government or agency thereof.

(d) Guidelines by Attorney General

Not later than one year after August 23, 1988, the Attorney General, after consultation with the Commission, the Secretary of Commerce, the United States Trade Representative, the Secretary of State, and the Secretary of the Treasury, and after obtaining the views of all interested persons through public notice and comment procedures, shall determine to what extent compliance with this section would be enhanced and the business community would be assisted by further clarification of the preceding provisions of this section and may, based on such determination and to the extent necessary and appropriate, issue--

(1) guidelines describing specific types of conduct, associated with common types of export sales arrangements and business contracts, which for purposes of the Department of Justice's present enforcement policy, the Attorney General determines would be in conformance with the preceding provisions of this section; and

(2) general precautionary procedures which issuers may use on a voluntary basis to conform their conduct to the Department of Justice's present enforcement policy regarding the preceding provisions of this section.

The Attorney General shall issue the guidelines and procedures referred to in the preceding sentence in accordance with the provisions of subchapter II of chapter 5 of Title 5 and those guidelines and procedures shall be subject to the provisions of chapter 7 of that title.

(e) Opinions of Attorney General

(1) The Attorney General, after consultation with appropriate departments and agencies of the United States and after obtaining the views of all interested persons through public notice and comment procedures, shall establish a procedure to provide responses to specific inquiries by issuers concerning conformance of their conduct with the Department of Justice's present enforcement policy regarding the preceding provisions of this section. The Attorney General shall, within 30 days after receiving such a request, issue an opinion in response to that request. The opinion shall state whether or not certain specified prospective conduct would, for purposes of the Department of Justice's present enforcement policy, violate the preceding provisions of this section. Additional requests for opinions may be filed with the Attorney General regarding other specified prospective conduct that is beyond the scope of conduct specified in previous requests. In any action brought under the applicable provisions of this section, there shall be a rebuttable presumption that conduct, which is specified in a request by an issuer and for which the Attorney General has issued an opinion that such conduct is in conformity with the Department of Justice's present enforcement policy, is in compliance with the preceding provisions of this section. Such a presumption may be rebutted by a preponderance of the evidence. In considering the presumption for purposes of this paragraph, a court shall weight all relevant factors, including but not limited to whether the information submitted to the Attorney General was accurate and complete and whether it was within the scope of the conduct specified in any request received by the Attorney General. The Attorney General shall establish the procedure required by this paragraph in accordance with the provisions of subchapter II of chapter 5 of Title 5 and that procedure shall be subject to the provisions of chapter 7 of that title.

(2) Any document or other material which is provided to, received by, or prepared in the Department of Justice or any other department or agency of the United States in connection with a request by an issuer under the procedure established under paragraph (1), shall be exempt from disclosure under section 552 of Title 5 and shall not, except with the consent of the issuer, be made publicly available, regardless of whether the Attorney General responds to such a request or the issuer withdraws such request before receiving a response.

(3) Any issuer who has made a request to the Attorney General under paragraph (1) may withdraw such request prior to the time the Attorney General issues an opinion in response to such request. Any request so withdrawn shall have no force or effect.

(4) The Attorney General shall, to the maximum extent practicable, provide timely guidance concerning the Department of Justice's present enforcement policy with respect to the preceding provisions of this section to potential exporters and small businesses that are unable to obtain specialized counsel on issues pertaining to such provisions. Such guidance shall be limited to

responses to requests under paragraph (1) concerning conformity of specified prospective conduct with the Department of Justice's present enforcement policy regarding the preceding provisions of this section and general explanations of compliance responsibilities and of potential liabilities under the preceding provisions of this section.

(f) Definitions

For purposes of this section:

(1)(A) The term "foreign official" means any officer or employee of a foreign government or any department, agency, or instrumentality thereof, or of a public international organization, or any person acting in an official capacity for or on behalf of any such government or department, agency, or instrumentality, or for or on behalf of any such public international organization.

(B) For purposes of subparagraph (A), the term "public international organization" means--

(i) an organization that is designated by Executive order pursuant to section 1 of the International Organizations Immunities Act (22 U.S.C. 288); or

(ii) any other international organization that is designated by the President by Executive order for the purposes of this section, effective as of the date of publication of such order in the Federal Register.

(2)(A) A person's state of mind is "knowing" with respect to conduct, a circumstance, or a result if--

(i) such person is aware that such person is engaging in such conduct, that such circumstance exists, or that such result is substantially certain to occur; or

(ii) such person has a firm belief that such circumstance exists or that such result is substantially certain to occur.

(B) When knowledge of the existence of a particular circumstance is required for an offense, such knowledge is established if a person is aware of a high probability of the existence of such circumstance, unless the person actually believes that such circumstance does not exist.

(3)(A) The term "routine governmental action" means only an action which is ordinarily and commonly performed by a foreign official in--

(i) obtaining permits, licenses, or other official documents to qualify a person to do business in a foreign country;

(ii) processing governmental papers, such as visas and work orders;

(iii) providing police protection, mail pick-up and delivery, or scheduling inspections associated with contract performance or inspections related to transit of goods across country;

(iv) providing phone service, power and water supply, loading and unloading cargo, or protecting perishable products or commodities from deterioration; or

(v) actions of a similar nature.

(B) The term "routine governmental action" does not include any decision by a foreign official whether, or on what terms, to award new business to or to continue business with a particular party, or any action taken by a foreign official involved in the decision-making process to encourage a decision to award new business to or continue business with a particular party.

(g) Alternative jurisdiction

(1) It shall also be unlawful for any issuer organized under the laws of the United States, or a State, territory, possession, or commonwealth of the United States or a political subdivision thereof and which has a class of securities registered pursuant to section 78l of this title or which is required to file reports under section 78o(d) of this title, or for any United States person that is an officer, director, employee, or agent of such issuer or a stockholder thereof acting on behalf of such issuer, to corruptly do any act outside the United States in furtherance of an offer, payment, promise to pay, or authorization of the payment of any money, or offer, gift, promise to give, or authorization of the giving of anything of value to any of the persons or entities set forth in paragraphs (1), (2), and (3) of subsection (a) of this section for the purposes set forth therein, irrespective of whether such issuer or such officer, director, employee, agent, or stockholder makes use of the mails or any means or instrumentality of interstate commerce in furtherance of such offer, gift, payment, promise, or authorization.

(2) As used in this subsection, the term "United States person" means a national of the United States (as defined in section 101 of the Immigration and Nationality Act (8 U.S.C. 1101)) or any corporation, partnership, association, joint-stock company, business trust, unincorporated organization, or sole proprietorship organized under the laws of the United States or any State, territory, possession, or commonwealth of the United States, or any political subdivision thereof.

Sec. 78dd-2. Prohibited foreign trade practices by domestic concerns

(a) Prohibition

It shall be unlawful for any domestic concern, other than an issuer which is subject to section 78dd-1 of this title, or for any officer, director, employee, or agent of such domestic concern or any stockholder thereof acting on behalf of such domestic concern, to make use of the mails or any means or instrumentality of interstate commerce corruptly in furtherance of an offer, payment, promise to pay, or authorization of the payment of any money, or offer, gift, promise to give, or authorization of the giving of anything of value to--

(1) any foreign official for purposes of--

(A)(i) influencing any act or decision of such foreign official in his official capacity, (ii) inducing such foreign official to do or omit to do any act in violation of the lawful duty of such official, or (iii) securing any improper advantage; or

(B) inducing such foreign official to use his influence with a foreign government or instrumentality thereof to affect or influence any act or decision of such government or instrumentality,

in order to assist such domestic concern in obtaining or retaining business for or with, or directing business to, any person;

(2) any foreign political party or official thereof or any candidate for foreign political office for purposes of--

(A)(i) influencing any act or decision of such party, official, or candidate in its or his official capacity, (ii) inducing such party, official, or candidate to do or omit to do an act in violation of the lawful duty of such party, official, or candidate, or (iii) securing any improper advantage; or

(B) inducing such party, official, or candidate to use its or his influence with a foreign government or instrumentality thereof to affect or influence any act or decision of such government or instrumentality,

in order to assist such domestic concern in obtaining or retaining business for or with, or directing business to, any person; or

(3) any person, while knowing that all or a portion of such money or thing of value will be offered, given, or promised, directly or indirectly, to any foreign official, to any foreign political party or official thereof, or to any candidate for foreign political office, for purposes of--

(A)(i) influencing any act or decision of such foreign official, political party, party official, or candidate in his or its official capacity, (ii) inducing such foreign official, political party, party official, or candidate to do or omit to do any act in violation of the lawful duty of such foreign official, political party, party official, or candidate, or (iii) securing any improper advantage; or

(B) inducing such foreign official, political party, party official, or candidate to use his or its influence with a foreign government or instrumentality thereof to affect or influence any act or decision of such government or instrumentality,

in order to assist such domestic concern in obtaining or retaining business for or with, or directing business to, any person.

(b) Exception for routine governmental action

Subsections (a) and (i) of this section shall not apply to any facilitating or expediting payment to a foreign official, political party, or party official the purpose of which is to expedite or to secure the performance of a routine governmental action by a foreign official, political party, or party official.

(c) Affirmative defenses

It shall be an affirmative defense to actions under subsection (a) or (i) of this section that--

(1) the payment, gift, offer, or promise of anything of value that was made, was lawful under the written laws and regulations of the foreign official's, political party's, party official's, or candidate's country; or

(2) the payment, gift, offer, or promise of anything of value that was made, was a reasonable and bona fide expenditure, such as travel and lodging expenses, incurred by or on behalf of a foreign official, party, party official, or candidate and was directly related to--

(A) the promotion, demonstration, or explanation of products or services; or

(B) the execution or performance of a contract with a foreign government or agency thereof.

(d) Injunctive relief

(1) When it appears to the Attorney General that any domestic concern to which this section applies, or officer, director, employee, agent, or stockholder thereof, is engaged, or about to engage, in any act or practice constituting a violation of subsection (a) or (i) of this section, the Attorney General may, in his discretion, bring a civil action in an appropriate district court of the United States to enjoin such act or practice, and upon a proper showing, a permanent injunction or a temporary restraining order shall be granted without bond.

(2) For the purpose of any civil investigation which, in the opinion of the Attorney General, is necessary and proper to enforce this section, the Attorney General or his designee are empowered to administer oaths and

affirmations, subpoena witnesses, take evidence, and require the production of any books, papers, or other documents which the Attorney General deems relevant or material to such investigation. The attendance of witnesses and the production of documentary evidence may be required from any place in the United States, or any territory, possession, or commonwealth of the United States, at any designated place of hearing.

(3) In case of contumacy by, or refusal to obey a subpoena issued to, any person, the Attorney General may invoke the aid of any court of the United States within the jurisdiction of which such investigation or proceeding is carried on, or where such person resides or carries on business, in requiring the attendance and testimony of witnesses and the production of books, papers, or other documents. Any such court may issue an order requiring such person to appear before the Attorney General or his designee, there to produce records, if so ordered, or to give testimony touching the matter under investigation. Any failure to obey such order of the court may be punished by such court as a contempt thereof.

All process in any such case may be served in the judicial district in which such person resides or may be found. The Attorney General may make such rules relating to civil investigations as may be necessary or appropriate to implement the provisions of this subsection.

(e) Guidelines by Attorney General

Not later than 6 months after August 23, 1988, the Attorney General, after consultation with the Securities and Exchange Commission, the Secretary of Commerce, the United States Trade Representative, the Secretary of State, and the Secretary of the Treasury, and after obtaining the views of all interested persons through public notice and comment procedures, shall determine to what extent compliance with this section would be enhanced and the business community would be assisted by further clarification of the preceding provisions of this section and may, based on such determination and to the extent necessary and appropriate, issue--

(1) guidelines describing specific types of conduct, associated with common types of export sales arrangements and business contracts, which for purposes of the Department of Justice's present enforcement policy, the Attorney General determines would be in conformance with the preceding provisions of this section; and

(2) general precautionary procedures which domestic concerns may use on a voluntary basis to conform their conduct to the Department of Justice's present enforcement policy regarding the preceding provisions of this section.

The Attorney General shall issue the guidelines and procedures referred to in the preceding sentence in accordance with the provisions of subchapter II of chapter 5 of Title 5 and those guidelines and procedures shall be subject to the provisions of chapter 7 of that title.

(f) Opinions of Attorney General

(1) The Attorney General, after consultation with appropriate departments and agencies of the United States and after obtaining the views of all interested persons through public notice and comment procedures, shall establish a procedure to provide responses to specific inquiries by domestic concerns concerning conformance of their conduct with the Department of Justice's present enforcement policy regarding the preceding provisions of this section. The Attorney General shall, within 30 days after receiving such a request, issue an opinion in response to that request. The opinion shall state whether or not certain specified prospective conduct would, for purposes of the Department of Justice's present enforcement policy, violate the preceding provisions of this section. Additional requests for opinions may be filed with the Attorney General regarding other specified prospective conduct that is beyond the scope of conduct specified in previous requests. In any action brought under the applicable provisions of this section, there shall be a rebuttable presumption that conduct, which is specified in a request by a domestic concern and for which the Attorney General has issued an opinion that such conduct is in conformity with the Department of Justice's present enforcement policy, is in compliance with the preceding provisions of this section. Such a presumption may be rebutted by a preponderance of the evidence. In considering the presumption for purposes of this paragraph, a court shall weigh all relevant factors, including but not limited to whether the information submitted to the Attorney General was accurate and complete and whether it was within the scope of the conduct specified in any request received by the Attorney General. The Attorney General shall establish the procedure required by this paragraph in accordance with the provisions of subchapter II of chapter 5 of Title 5 and that procedure shall be subject to the provisions of chapter 7 of that title.

(2) Any document or other material which is provided to, received by, or prepared in the Department of Justice or any other department or agency of the United States in connection with a request by a domestic concern under the procedure established under paragraph (1), shall be exempt from disclosure under section 552 of Title 5 and shall not, except with the consent of the domestic concern, by made publicly available, regardless of whether the Attorney General response to such a request or the domestic concern withdraws such request before receiving a response.

(3) Any domestic concern who has made a request to the Attorney General under paragraph (1) may withdraw such request prior to the time the Attorney General issues an opinion in response to such request. Any request so withdrawn shall have no force or effect.

(4) The Attorney General shall, to the maximum extent practicable, provide timely guidance concerning the Department of Justice's present enforcement

policy with respect to the preceding provisions of this section to potential exporters and small businesses that are unable to obtain specialized counsel on issues pertaining to such provisions. Such guidance shall be limited to responses to requests under paragraph (1) concerning conformity of specified prospective conduct with the Department of Justice's present enforcement policy regarding the preceding provisions of this section and general explanations of compliance responsibilities and of potential liabilities under the preceding provisions of this section.

(g) Penalties

(1)(A) Any domestic concern that is not a natural person and that violates subsection (a) or (i) of this section shall be fined not more than $2,000,000.

(B) Any domestic concern that is not a natural person and that violates subsection (a) or (i) of this section shall be subject to a civil penalty of not more than $10,000 imposed in an action brought by the Attorney General.

(2)(A) Any natural person that is an officer, director, employee, or agent of a domestic concern, or stockholder acting on behalf of such domestic concern, who willfully violates subsection (a) or (i) of this section shall be fined not more than $100,000 or imprisoned not more than 5 years, or both.

(B) Any natural person that is an officer, director, employee, or agent of a domestic concern, or stockholder acting on behalf of such domestic concern, who violates subsection (a) or (i) of this section shall be subject to a civil penalty of not more than $10,000 imposed in an action brought by the Attorney General.

(3) Whenever a fine is imposed under paragraph (2) upon any officer, director, employee, agent, or stockholder of a domestic concern, such fine may not be paid, directly or indirectly, by such domestic concern.

(h) Definitions

For purposes of this section:

  (1) The term "domestic concern" means--

    (A) any individual who is a citizen, national, or resident of the United States; and

    (B) any corporation, partnership, association, joint-stock company, business trust, unincorporated organization, or sole proprietorship which has its principal place of business in the United States, or which is organized under the laws of a State of the United States or a territory, possession, or commonwealth of the United States.

(2)(A) The term "foreign official" means any officer or employee of a foreign government or any department, agency, or instrumentality thereof, or of a public international organization, or any person acting in an official capacity for or on behalf of any such government or department, agency, or instrumentality, or for or on behalf of any such public international organization.

(B) For purposes of subparagraph (A), the term "public international organization" means--

(i) an organization that is designated by Executive order pursuant to section 1 of the International Organizations Immunities Act (22 U.S.C. 288); or

(ii) any other international organization that is designated by the President by Executive order for the purposes of this section, effective as of the date of publication of such order in the Federal Register.

(3)(A) A person's state of mind is "knowing" with respect to conduct, a circumstance, or a result if--

(i) such person is aware that such person is engaging in such conduct, that such circumstance exists, or that such result is substantially certain to occur; or

(ii) such person has a firm belief that such circumstance exists or that such result is substantially certain to occur.

(B) When knowledge of the existence of a particular circumstance is required for an offense, such knowledge is established if a person is aware of a high probability of the existence of such circumstance, unless the person actually believes that such circumstance does not exist.

(4)(A) The term "routine governmental action" means only an action which is ordinarily and commonly performed by a foreign official in--

(i) obtaining permits, licenses, or other official documents to qualify a person to do business in a foreign country;

(ii) processing governmental papers, such as visas and work orders;

(iii) providing police protection, mail pick-up and delivery, or scheduling inspections associated with contract performance or inspections related to transit of goods across country;

(iv) providing phone service, power and water supply, loading and unloading cargo, or protecting perishable products or commodities from deterioration; or

(v) actions of a similar nature.

(B) The term "routine governmental action" does not include any decision by a foreign official whether, or on what terms, to award new business to or to continue business with a particular party, or any action taken by a foreign official involved in the decision-making process to encourage a decision to award new business to or continue business with a particular party.

(5) The term "interstate commerce" means trade, commerce, transportation, or communication among the several States, or between any foreign country and any State or between any State and any place or ship outside thereof, and such term includes the intrastate use of--

(A) a telephone or other interstate means of communication, or

(B) any other interstate instrumentality.

(i) Alternative jurisdiction

(1) It shall also be unlawful for any United States person to corruptly do any act outside the United States in furtherance of an offer, payment, promise to pay, or authorization of the payment of any money, or offer, gift, promise to give, or authorization of the giving of anything of value to any of the persons or entities set forth in paragraphs (1), (2), and (3) of subsection (a), for the purposes set forth therein, irrespective of whether such United States person makes use of the mails or any means or instrumentality of interstate commerce in furtherance of such offer, gift, payment, promise, or authorization.

(2) As used in this subsection, the term "United States person" means a national of the United States (as defined in section 101 of the Immigration and Nationality Act (8 U.S.C. 1101)) or any corporation, partnership, association, joint-stock company, business trust, unincorporated organization, or sole proprietorship organized under the laws of the United States or any State, territory, possession, or commonwealth of the United States, or any political subdivision thereof.";

78j. Manipulative and deceptive devices

It shall be unlawful for any person, directly or indirectly, by the use of any means or instrumentality of interstate commerce or of the mails, or of any facility of any national securities exchange--

(a) (1) To effect a short sale, or to use or employ any stop-loss order in connection with the purchase or sale, of any security registered on a national securities exchange, in contravention of such rules and regulations as the Commission may prescribe as necessary or appropriate in the public interest or for the protection of investors.

(2) Paragraph (1) of this subsection shall not apply to security futures products.

(b) To use or employ, in connection with the purchase or sale of any security registered on a national securities exchange or any security not so registered, or any securities-based swap agreement, any manipulative or deceptive device or contrivance in contravention of such rules and regulations as the Commission may prescribe as necessary or appropriate in the public interest or for the protection of investors.

(c) (1) To effect, accept, or facilitate a transaction involving the loan or borrowing of securities in contravention of such rules and regulations as the Commission may prescribe as necessary or appropriate in the public interest or for the protection of investors.

(2) Nothing in paragraph (1) may be construed to limit the authority of the appropriate Federal banking agency (as defined in section 1813(q) of Title 12), the National Credit Union Administration, or any other Federal department or agency having a responsibility under Federal law to prescribe rules or regulations restricting transactions involving the loan or borrowing of securities in order to protect the safety and soundness of a financial institution or to protect the financial system from systemic risk.

Rules promulgated under subsection (b) of this section that prohibit fraud, manipulation, or insider trading (but not rules imposing or specifying reporting or recordkeeping requirements, procedures, or standards as prophylactic measures against fraud, manipulation, or insider trading), and judicial precedents decided under subsection (b) of this section and rules promulgated thereunder that prohibit fraud, manipulation, or insider trading, shall apply to security-based swap agreements to the same extent as they apply to securities. Judicial precedents decided under section 77q(a) of this title and sections 78i, 78o, 78p, 78t, and 78u-1 of this title, and judicial precedents decided under applicable rules promulgated under such sections, shall apply to security-based swap agreements to the same extent as they apply to securities.

Federal Rules of Criminal Procedure

Rule 6. The Grand Jury

(a) Summoning a Grand Jury.

(1) In General. When the public interest so requires, the court must order that one or more grand juries be summoned. A grand jury must have 16 to 23 members, and the court must order that enough legally qualified persons be summoned to meet this requirement.

(2) Alternate Jurors. When a grand jury is selected, the court may also select alternate jurors. Alternate jurors must have the same qualifications and be selected in the same manner as any other juror. Alternate jurors replace jurors in the same sequence in which the alternates were selected. An alternate juror who replaces a juror is subject to the same challenges, takes the same oath, and has the same authority as the other jurors.

(b) Objection to the Grand Jury or to a Grand Juror.

(1) Challenges. Either the government or a defendant may challenge the grand jury on the ground that it was not lawfully drawn, summoned, or selected, and may challenge an individual juror on the ground that the juror is not legally qualified.

(2) Motion to Dismiss an Indictment. A party may move to dismiss the indictment based on an objection to the grand jury or on an individual juror's lack of legal qualification, unless the court has previously ruled on the same objection under Rule 6(b)(1). The motion to dismiss is governed by 28 U.S.C. § 1867(e). The court must not dismiss the indictment on the ground that a grand juror was not legally qualified if the record shows that at least 12 qualified jurors concurred in the indictment.

(c) Foreperson and Deputy Foreperson. The court will appoint one juror as the foreperson and another as the deputy foreperson. In the foreperson's absence, the deputy foreperson will act as the foreperson. The foreperson may administer oaths and affirmations and will sign all indictments. The foreperson—or another juror designated by the foreperson—will record the number of jurors concurring in every indictment and will file the record with the clerk, but the record may not be made public unless the court so orders.

(d) Who May Be Present.

(1) While the Grand Jury Is in Session. The following persons may be present while the grand jury is in session: attorneys for the government, the witness being questioned, interpreters when needed, and a court reporter or an operator of a recording device.

(2) During Deliberations and Voting. No person other than the jurors, and any interpreter needed to assist a hearing-impaired or speech-impaired juror, may be present while the grand jury is deliberating or voting.

(e) Recording and Disclosing the Proceedings.

(1) Recording the Proceedings. Except while the grand jury is deliberating or voting, all proceedings must be recorded by a court reporter or by a suitable recording device. But the validity of a prosecution is not affected by the unintentional failure to make a recording. Unless the court orders otherwise, an attorney for the government will retain control of the recording, the reporter's notes, and any transcript prepared from those notes.

(2) Secrecy.

(A) No obligation of secrecy may be imposed on any person except in accordance with Rule 6(e)(2)(B).

(B) Unless these rules provide otherwise, the following persons must not disclose a matter occurring before the grand jury:

(i) a grand juror;

(ii) an interpreter;

(iii) a court reporter;

(iv) an operator of a recording device;

(v) a person who transcribes recorded testimony;

(vi) an attorney for the government; or

(vii) a person to whom disclosure is made under Rule 6(e)(3)(A)(ii) or (iii).

(3) Exceptions.

(A) Disclosure of a grand-jury matter--other than the grand jury's deliberations or any grand juror's vote--may be made to:

(i) an attorney for the government for use in performing that attorney's duty;

(ii) any government personnel--including those of a state, state subdivision, Indian tribe, or foreign government--that an attorney for the government considers necessary to assist in performing that attorney's duty to enforce federal criminal law; or

(iii) a person authorized by 18 U.S.C. § 3322.

(B) A person to whom information is disclosed under Rule 6(e)(3)(A)(ii) may use that information only to assist an attorney for the government in performing that attorney's duty to enforce federal criminal law. An attorney for the government must promptly provide the court that impaneled the grand jury with the names of all persons to whom a disclosure has been made, and must certify that the attorney has advised those persons of their obligation of secrecy under this rule.

(C) An attorney for the government may disclose any grand-jury matter to another federal grand jury.

(D) An attorney for the government may disclose any grand-jury matter involving foreign intelligence, counterintelligence (as defined in 50 U.S.C. § 3003), or foreign intelligence information (as defined in Rule 6(e)(3)(D)(iii)) to any federal law enforcement, intelligence, protective, immigration, national defense, or national security official to assist the official receiving the information in the performance of that official's duties. An attorney for the government may also disclose any grand-jury matter involving, within the United States or elsewhere, a threat of attack or other grave hostile acts of a foreign power or its agent, a threat of domestic or international sabotage or terrorism, or clandestine intelligence gathering activities by an intelligence service or network of a foreign power or by its agent, to any appropriate federal, state, state subdivision, Indian tribal, or foreign government official, for the purpose of preventing or responding to such threat or activities.

(i) Any official who receives information under Rule 6(e)(3)(D) may use the information only as necessary in the conduct of that person's official duties subject to any limitations on the unauthorized disclosure of such information. Any state, state subdivision, Indian tribal, or foreign government official who receives information under Rule 6(e)(3)(D) may use the information only in a manner consistent with any guidelines issued by the Attorney General and the Director of National Intelligence.

(ii) Within a reasonable time after disclosure is made under Rule 6(e)(3)(D), an attorney for the government must file, under seal, a notice with the court in the district where the grand jury convened stating that such information was disclosed and the departments, agencies, or entities to which the disclosure was made.

(iii) As used in Rule 6(e)(3)(D), the term "foreign intelligence information" means:

(a) information, whether or not it concerns a United States person, that relates to the ability of the United States to protect against--

• actual or potential attack or other grave hostile acts of a foreign power or its agent;

• sabotage or international terrorism by a foreign power or its agent; or

• clandestine intelligence activities by an intelligence service or network of a foreign power or by its agent; or

(b) information, whether or not it concerns a United States person, with respect to a foreign power or foreign territory that relates to--

• the national defense or the security of the United States; or

• the conduct of the foreign affairs of the United States.

(E) The court may authorize disclosure – at a time, in a manner, and subject to any other conditions that it directs – of a grand-jury matter:

(i) preliminarily to or in connection with a judicial proceeding;

(ii) at the request of a defendant who shows that a ground may exist to dismiss the indictment because of a matter that occurred before the grand jury;

(iii) at the request of the government, when sought by a foreign court or prosecutor for use in an official criminal investigation;

(iv) at the request of the government if it shows that the matter may disclose a violation of State, Indian tribal, or foreign criminal law, as long as the disclosure is to an appropriate state, state-subdivision, Indian tribal, or foreign government official for the purpose of enforcing that law; or

(v) at the request of the government if it shows that the matter may disclose a violation of military criminal law under the Uniform Code of Military Justice, as long as the disclosure is to an appropriate military official for the purpose of enforcing that law.

(F) A petition to disclose a grand-jury matter under Rule 6(e)(3)(E)(i) must be filed in the district where the grand jury convened. Unless the hearing is ex parte—as it may be when the government is the petitioner—the petitioner must serve the petition on, and the court must afford a reasonable opportunity to appear and be heard to:

(i) an attorney for the government;

(ii) the parties to the judicial proceeding; and

(iii) any other person whom the court may designate.

(G) If the petition to disclose arises out of a judicial proceeding in another district, the petitioned court must transfer the petition to the other court unless the petitioned court can reasonably determine whether disclosure is proper. If the petitioned court decides to transfer, it must send to the transferee court the material sought to be disclosed, if feasible, and a written evaluation of the need for continued grand-jury secrecy. The transferee court must afford those persons identified in Rule 6(e)(3)(F) a reasonable opportunity to appear and be heard.

(4) **Sealed Indictment.** The magistrate judge to whom an indictment is returned may direct that the indictment be kept secret until the defendant is in custody or has been released pending trial. The clerk must then seal the indictment, and no person may disclose the indictment's existence except as necessary to issue or execute a warrant or summons.

(5) Closed Hearing. Subject to any right to an open hearing in a contempt proceeding, the court must close any hearing to the extent necessary to prevent disclosure of a matter occurring before a grand jury.

(6) Sealed Records. Records, orders, and subpoenas relating to grand-jury proceedings must be kept under seal to the extent and as long as necessary to prevent the unauthorized disclosure of a matter occurring before a grand jury.

(7) Contempt. A knowing violation of Rule 6, or any of any guidelines jointly issued by the Attorney General and the Director of National Intelligence under Rule 6, may be punished as a contempt of court.

(f) Indictment and Return. A grand jury may indict only if at least 12 jurors concur. The grand jury—or its foreperson or deputy foreperson—must return the indictment to a magistrate judge in open court. To avoid unnecessary cost or delay, the magistrate judge may take the return by video teleconference from the court where the grand jury sits. If a complaint or information is pending against the defendant and 12 jurors do not concur in the indictment, the foreperson must promptly and in writing report the lack of concurrence to the magistrate judge.

(g) Discharging the Grand Jury. A grand jury must serve until the court discharges it, but it may serve more than 18 months only if the court, having determined that an extension is in the public interest, extends the grand jury's service. An extension may be granted for no more than 6 months, except as otherwise provided by statute.

(h) Excusing a Juror. At any time, for good cause, the court may excuse a juror either temporarily or permanently, and if permanently, the court may impanel an alternate juror in place of the excused juror.

(i) "Indian Tribe" Defined. "Indian tribe" means an Indian tribe recognized by the Secretary of the Interior on a list published in the Federal Register under 25 U.S.C. § 479a–1.

Rule 11. Pleas

(a) Entering a Plea.

(1) In General. A defendant may plead not guilty, guilty, or (with the court's consent) nolo contendere.

(2) Conditional Plea. With the consent of the court and the government, a defendant may enter a conditional plea of guilty or nolo contendere, reserving in writing the right to have an appellate court

review an adverse determination of a specified pretrial motion. A defendant who prevails on appeal may then withdraw the plea.

(3) Nolo Contendere Plea. Before accepting a plea of nolo contendere, the court must consider the parties' views and the public interest in the effective administration of justice.

(4) Failure to Enter a Plea. If a defendant refuses to enter a plea or if a defendant organization fails to appear, the court must enter a plea of not guilty.

(b) Considering and Accepting a Guilty or Nolo Contendere Plea.

(1) Advising and Questioning the Defendant. Before the court accepts a plea of guilty or nolo contendere, the defendant may be placed under oath, and the court must address the defendant personally in open court. During this address, the court must inform the defendant of, and determine that the defendant understands, the following:

(A) the government's right, in a prosecution for perjury or false statement, to use against the defendant any statement that the defendant gives under oath;

(B) the right to plead not guilty, or having already so pleaded, to persist in that plea;

(C) the right to a jury trial;

(D) the right to be represented by counsel—and if necessary have the court appoint counsel—at trial and at every other stage of the proceeding;

(E) the right at trial to confront and cross-examine adverse witnesses, to be protected from compelled self-incrimination, to testify and present evidence, and to compel the attendance of witnesses;

(F) the defendant's waiver of these trial rights if the court accepts a plea of guilty or nolo contendere;

(G) the nature of each charge to which the defendant is pleading;

(H) any maximum possible penalty, including imprisonment, fine, and term of supervised release;

(I) any mandatory minimum penalty;

(J) any applicable forfeiture;

(K) the court's authority to order restitution;

(L) the court's obligation to impose a special assessment;

(M) in determining a sentence, the court's obligation to calculate the applicable sentencing-guideline range and to consider that range, possible departures under the Sentencing Guidelines, and other sentencing factors under 18 U.S.C. § 3553(a); and

(N) the terms of any plea-agreement provision waiving the right to appeal or to collaterally attack the sentence.

(O) that, if convicted, a defendant who is not a United States citizen may be removed from the United States, denied citizenship, and denied admission to the United States in the future.

(2) Ensuring That a Plea Is Voluntary. Before accepting a plea of guilty or nolo contendere, the court must address the defendant personally in open court and determine that the plea is voluntary and did not result from force, threats, or promises (other than promises in a plea agreement).

(3) Determining the Factual Basis for a Plea. Before entering judgment on a guilty plea, the court must determine that there is a factual basis for the plea.

(c) Plea Agreement Procedure.

(1) In General. An attorney for the government and the defendant's attorney, or the defendant when proceeding pro se, may discuss and reach a plea agreement. The court must not participate in these discussions. If the defendant pleads guilty or nolo contendere to either a charged offense or a lesser or related offense, the plea agreement may specify that an attorney for the government will:

(A) not bring, or will move to dismiss, other charges;

(B) recommend, or agree not to oppose the defendant's request, that a particular sentence or sentencing range is appropriate or that a particular provision of the Sentencing Guidelines, or policy statement, or sentencing factor does or does not apply (such a recommendation or request does not bind the court); or

(C) agree that a specific sentence or sentencing range is the appropriate disposition of the case, or that a particular provision of the Sentencing Guidelines, or policy statement, or sentencing factor does or does not apply (such a recommendation or request binds the court once the court accepts the plea agreement).

(2) Disclosing a Plea Agreement. The parties must disclose the plea agreement in open court when the plea is offered, unless the court for good cause allows the parties to disclose the plea agreement in camera.

(3) Judicial Consideration of a Plea Agreement.

(A) To the extent the plea agreement is of the type specified in Rule 11(c)(1)(A) or (C), the court may accept the agreement, reject it, or defer a decision until the court has reviewed the presentence report.

(B) To the extent the plea agreement is of the type specified in Rule 11(c)(1)(B), the court must advise the defendant that the defendant has no right to withdraw the plea if the court does not follow the recommendation or request.

(4) Accepting a Plea Agreement. If the court accepts the plea agreement, it must inform the defendant that to the extent the plea agreement is of the type specified in Rule 11(c)(1)(A) or (C), the agreed disposition will be included in the judgment.

(5) Rejecting a Plea Agreement. If the court rejects a plea agreement containing provisions of the type specified in Rule 11(c)(1)(A) or (C), the court must do the following on the record and in open court (or, for good cause, in camera):

(A) inform the parties that the court rejects the plea agreement;

(B) advise the defendant personally that the court is not required to follow the plea agreement and give the defendant an opportunity to withdraw the plea; and

(C) advise the defendant personally that if the plea is not withdrawn, the court may dispose of the case less favorably toward the defendant than the plea agreement contemplated.

(d) Withdrawing a Guilty or Nolo Contendere Plea. A defendant may withdraw a plea of guilty or nolo contendere:

(1) before the court accepts the plea, for any reason or no reason; or

(2) after the court accepts the plea, but before it imposes sentence if:

(A) the court rejects a plea agreement under Rule 11(c)(5); or

(B) the defendant can show a fair and just reason for requesting the withdrawal.

(e) **Finality of a Guilty or Nolo Contendere Plea.** After the court imposes sentence, the defendant may not withdraw a plea of guilty or nolo contendere, and the plea may be set aside only on direct appeal or collateral attack.

(f) **Admissibility or Inadmissibility of a Plea, Plea Discussions, and Related Statements.** The admissibility or inadmissibility of a plea, a plea discussion, and any related statement is governed by Federal Rule of Evidence 410. * * *

(h) **Harmless Error.** A variance from the requirements of this rule is harmless error if it does not affect substantial rights.

Rule 17. Subpoena

* * *

(c) **Producing Documents and Objects.**

(1) **In General.** A subpoena may order the witness to produce any books, papers, documents, data, or other objects the subpoena designates. The court may direct the witness to produce the designated items in court before trial or before they are to be offered in evidence. When the items arrive, the court may permit the parties and their attorneys to inspect all or part of them.

(2) **Quashing or Modifying the Subpoena.** On motion made promptly, the court may quash or modify the subpoena if compliance would be unreasonable or oppressive.

(3) **Subpoena for Personal or Confidential Information About a Victim.** After a complaint, indictment, or information is filed, a subpoena requiring the production of personal or confidential information about a victim may be served on a third party only by court order. Before entering the order and unless there are exceptional circumstances, the court must require giving notice to the victim so that the victim can move to quash or modify the subpoena or otherwise object. * * *

(g) **Contempt.** The court (other than a magistrate judge) may hold in contempt a witness who, without adequate excuse, disobeys a subpoena issued by a federal court in that district. A magistrate judge may hold in contempt a witness who, without adequate excuse, disobeys a subpoena issued by that magistrate judge as provided in 28 U.S.C. § 636(e).

Rule 41. Search and Seizure

(a) Scope and Definitions.

    (1) Scope. This rule does not modify any statute regulating search or seizure, or the issuance and execution of a search warrant in special circumstances.

    (2) Definitions. The following definitions apply under this rule:

        (A) "Property" includes documents, books, papers, any other tangible objects, and information.

        (B) "Daytime" means the hours between 6:00 a.m. and 10:00 p.m. according to local time.

        (C) "Federal law enforcement officer" means a government agent (other than an attorney for the government) who is engaged in enforcing the criminal laws and is within any category of officers authorized by the Attorney General to request a search warrant.

        (D) "Domestic terrorism" and "international terrorism" have the meanings set out in 18 U.S.C. § 2331.

        (E) "Tracking device" has the meaning set out in 18 U.S.C. § 3117(b).

(b) Authority to Issue a Warrant. At the request of a federal law enforcement officer or an attorney for the government:

    (1) a magistrate judge with authority in the district—or if none is reasonably available, a judge of a state court of record in the district—has authority to issue a warrant to search for and seize a person or property located within the district;

    (2) a magistrate judge with authority in the district has authority to issue a warrant for a person or property outside the district if the person or property is located within the district when the warrant is issued but might move or be moved outside the district before the warrant is executed; and

    (3) a magistrate judge—in an investigation of domestic terrorism or international terrorism—with authority in any district in which activities related to the terrorism may have occurred, has authority

to issue a warrant for a person or property within or outside that district.

(4) a magistrate judge with authority in the district has authority to issue a warrant to install within the district a tracking device; the warrant may authorize use of the device to track the movement of a person or property located within the district, outside the district, or both; and

(5) a magistrate judge having authority in any district where activities related to the crime may have occurred, or in the District of Columbia, may issue a warrant for property that is located outside the jurisdiction of any state or district, but within any of the following:

    (A) a United States territory, possession, or commonwealth;

    (B) the premises—no matter who owns them—of a United States diplomatic or consular mission in a foreign state, including any appurtenant building, part of a building, or land used for the mission's purposes; or

    (C) a residence and any appurtenant land owned or leased by the United States and used by United States personnel assigned to a United States diplomatic or consular mission in a foreign state.

(c) Persons or Property Subject to Search or Seizure. A warrant may be issued for any of the following:

    (1) evidence of a crime;

    (2) contraband, fruits of crime, or other items illegally possessed;

    (3) property designed for use, intended for use, or used in committing a crime; or

    (4) a person to be arrested or a person who is unlawfully restrained.

(d) Obtaining a Warrant.

    (1) In General. After receiving an affidavit or other information, a magistrate judge—or if authorized by Rule 41(b), a judge of a state court of record—must issue the warrant if there is probable cause to search for and seize a person or property or to install and use a tracking device.

    (2) Requesting a Warrant in the Presence of a Judge.

(A) Warrant on an Affidavit.   When a federal law enforcement officer or an attorney for the government presents an affidavit in support of a warrant, the judge may require the affiant to appear personally and may examine under oath the affiant and any witness the affiant produces.

(B) Warrant on Sworn Testimony. The judge may wholly or partially dispense with a written affidavit and base a warrant on sworn testimony if doing so is reasonable under the circumstances.

(C) Recording Testimony. Testimony taken in support of a warrant must be recorded by a court reporter or by a suitable recording device, and the judge must file the transcript or recording with the clerk, along with any affidavit.

(3) Requesting a Warrant by Telephonic or Other Reliable Electronic Means. In accordance with Rule 4.1, a magistrate judge may issue a warrant based on information communicated by telephone or other reliable electronic means.

(e) Issuing the Warrant.

(1) In General. The magistrate judge or a judge of a state court of record must issue the warrant to an officer authorized to execute it.

(2) Contents of the Warrant.

(A) Warrant to Search for and Seize a Person or Property. Except for a tracking-device warrant, the warrant must identify the person or property to be searched, identify any person or property to be seized, and designate the magistrate judge to whom it must be returned. The warrant must command the officer to:

(i) execute the warrant within a specified time no longer than 14 days;

(ii) execute the warrant during the daytime, unless the judge for good cause expressly authorizes execution at another time; and

(iii) return the warrant to the magistrate judge designated in the warrant.

(B) Warrant Seeking Electronically Stored Information. A warrant Tule 41(e)(2)(A) may authorize the seizure of electronic storage media or the seizure or copying of electronically stored information. Unless otherwise specified, the warrant authorizes a later review of the media or information consistnet with the warrant. The time of executing the warrant in Rule 41(e)(2)(A) and (f)(1)(A) refers to the seizure or on-site copying of the media or information, and not to any later off-site copying or review.

(C) Warrant for a Tracking Device. A tracking-device warrant must identify the person or property to be tracked, designate the magistrate judge to whom it must be returned, and specify a reasonable length of time that the device may be used. The time must not exceed 45 days from the date the warrant was issued. The court may, for good cause, grant one or more extensions for a reasonable period not to exceed 45 days each. The warrant must command the officer to:

(i) complete any installation authorized by the warrant within a specified time no longer than 10 calendar days;

(ii) perform any installation authorized by the warrant during the daytime, unless the judge for good cause expressly authorizes installation at another time; and

(iii) return the warrant to the judge designated in the warrant.

(f) Executing and Returning the Warrant.

(1) Warrant to Search for and Seize a Person or Property.

(A) Noting the Time. The officer executing the warrant must enter on it the exact date and time it was executed.

(B) Inventory. An officer present during the execution of the warrant must prepare and verify an inventory of any property seized. The officer must do so in the presence of another officer and the person from whom, or from whose premises, the property was taken. If either one is not present, the officer must prepare and verify the inventory in the presence of at least one other credible person. In a case involving the seizure of electronic storage media or the seizure of copying of electronically stored information, the inventory may be limited to describing the physical storage media that were seized or copied. The officer may retain a copy of the electronically stored information that was seized or copied.

(C) Receipt. The officer executing the warrant must give a copy of the warrant and a receipt for the property taken to the person from whom, or from whose premises, the property was taken or leave a copy of the warrant and receipt at the place where the officer took the property.

(D) Return. The officer executing the warrant must promptly return it–together with a copy of the inventory–to the magistrate judge designated on the warrant. The officer may do so by reliable electronic means. The judge must, on request, give a copy of the inventory to the person from whom, or from whose premises, the property was taken and to the applicant for the warrant.

(2) Warrant for a Tracking Device.

(A) Noting the Time. The officer executing a tracking-device warrant must enter on it the exact date and time the device was installed and the period during which it was used.

(B) Return. Within 10 calendar days after the use of the tracking device has ended, the officer executing the warrant must return it to the judge designated in the warrant. The officer may do so by reliable electronic means.

(C) Service. Within 10 calendar days after the use of the tracking device has ended, the officer executing a tracking-device warrant must serve a copy of the warrant on the person who was tracked or whose property was tracked. Service may be accomplished by delivering a copy to the person who, or whose property, was tracked; or by leaving a copy at the person's residence or usual place of abode with an individual of suitable age and discretion who resides at that location and by mailing a copy to the person's last known address. Upon request of the government, the judge may delay notice as provided in Rule 41(f)(3).

(3) Delayed Notice. Upon the government's request, a magistrate judge–or if authorized by Rule 41(b), a judge of a state court of record–may delay any notice required by this rule if the delay is authorized by statute.

(g) Motion to Return Property. A person aggrieved by an unlawful search and seizure of property or by the deprivation of property may move for the property's return. The motion must be filed in the district where the property was seized. The court must receive evidence on any factual issue necessary to decide the motion. If it grants the motion, the court must return the property to the movant, but may impose reasonable conditions to protect access to the property and its use in later proceedings.

(h) Motion to Suppress. A defendant may move to suppress evidence in the court where the trial will occur, as Rule 12 provides.

(i) Forwarding Papers to the Clerk. The magistrate judge to whom the warrant is returned must attach to the warrant a copy of the return, or the inventory, and of all other related papers and must deliver them to the clerk in the district where the property was seized.

Federal Rules of Civil Procedure

Rule 26.   General Provisions Governing Discovery; Duty of Disclosure

* * * (b) Discovery Scope and Limits. Unless otherwise limited by order of the court in accordance with these rules, the scope of discovery is as follows: * * *

(3) Trial Preparation: Materials.

(A) Documents and Tangible Things. Ordinarily, a party may not discover documents and tangible things that are prepared in anticipation of litigation or for trial by or for another party or its representative (including the other party's attorney, consultant, surety, indemnitor, insurer, or agent). But, subject to Rule 26(b)(4), those materials may be discovered if:

(i) they are otherwise discoverable under Rule 26(b)(1); and

(ii) the party shows that it has substantial need for the materials to prepare its case and cannot, without undue hardship, obtain their substantial equivalent by other means.

(B) Protection Against Disclosure. If the court orders discovery of those materials, it must protect against disclosure of the mental impressions, conclusions, opinions, or legal theories of a party's attorney or other representative concerning the litigation.

(C) Previous Statement. Any party or other person may, on request and without the required showing, obtain the person's own previous statement about the action or its subject matter. If the request is refused, the person may move for a court order, and Rule 37(a)(5) applies to the award of expenses. A previous statement is either:

(i) a written statement that the person has signed or otherwise adopted or approved; or

(ii) a contemporaneous stenographic, mechanical, electrical, or other recording—or a transcription of it—that recites substantially verbatim the person's oral statement.

* * *

(c) Protective Orders.

(1) In General. A party or any person from whom discovery is sought may move for a protective order in the court where the action is pending—or as an alternative on matters relating to a deposition, in the court for the district where the deposition will be taken. The motion must include a certification that the movant has in good faith conferred or attempted to confer with other affected parties in an effort to resolve the dispute without court action. The court may, for good cause, issue an order to protect a party or person from annoyance, embarrassment, oppression, or undue burden or expense, including one or more of the following:

(A) forbidding the disclosure or discovery;

(B) specifying terms, including time and place, for the disclosure or discovery;

(C) prescribing a discovery method other than the one selected by the party seeking discovery;

(D) forbidding inquiry into certain matters, or limiting the scope of disclosure or discovery to certain matters;

(E) designating the persons who may be present while the discovery is conducted;

(F) requiring that a deposition be sealed and opened only on court order;

(G) requiring that a trade secret or other confidential research, development, or commercial information not be revealed or be revealed only in a specified way; and

(H) requiring that the parties simultaneously file specified documents or information in sealed envelopes, to be opened as the court directs.

(2) Ordering Discovery. If a motion for a protective order is wholly or partly denied, the court may, on just terms, order that any party or person provide or permit discovery.

(3) Awarding Expenses. Rule 37(a)(5) applies to the award of expenses.

Federal Rules of Evidence

Rule 502. Attorney-Client Privilege and Work Product; Limitations on Waiver

The following provisions apply, in the circumstances set out, to disclosure of a communication or information covered by the attorney-client privilege or work-product protection.

(a) Disclosure Made in a Federal Proceeding or to a Federal Office or Agency; Scope of a Waiver

When the disclosure is made in a federal proceeding or to a federal office or agency and waives the attorney-client privilege or work-product protection, the waiver extends to an undisclosed communication or information in a federal or state proceeding only if:

1. the waiver is intentional;

2. the disclosed and undisclosed communications or information concern the same subject matter; and

3. they ought in fairness to be considered together.

(b) Inadvertent disclosure.

When made in a federal proceeding or to a federal office or agency, the disclosure does not operate as a waiver in a federal or state proceeding if:

1. the disclosure is inadvertent;

2. the holder of the privilege or protection took reasonable steps to prevent disclosure; and

3. the holder promptly took reasonable steps to rectify the error, including (if applicable) following Federal Rule of Civil Procedure 26(b)(5)(B).

(c) Disclosure Made in a State Proceeding

When the disclosure is made in a state proceeding and is not the subject of a state-court order concerning waiver, the disclosure does not operate as a waiver in a federal proceeding if the disclosure:

1. would not be a waiver under this rule if it had been made in a federal proceeding; or

2. is not a waiver under the law of the state where the disclosure occurred.

(d) Controlling effect of court orders.

A federal court may order that the privilege or protection is not waived by disclosure connected with the litigation pending before the court--in which event the disclosure is also not a waiver in any other federal or state proceeding.

(e) Controlling Effect of a Party Agreement

An agreement on the effect of disclosure in a federal proceeding is binding only on the parties to the agreement, unless it is incorporated into a court order.

(f) Controlling Effect of This Rule

Notwithstanding Rules 101 and 1101, this rule applies to state proceedings and to federal court-annexed and federal court-mandated arbitration proceedings, in the circumstances set out in the rule. And notwithstanding Rule 501, this rule applies even if State law provides the rule of decision.

(g) Definitions

In this rule:

1. "attorney-client privilege" means the protection that applicable law provides for confidential attorney-client communications; and

2. "work-product protection" means the protection that applicable law provides for tangible material (or its intangible equivalent) prepared in anticipation of litigation or for trial."

Advisory Committee Notes

This new rule has two major purposes:

1) It resolves some longstanding disputes in the courts about the effect of certain disclosures of communications or information protected by the attorney-client privilege or as work product — specifically those disputes involving inadvertent disclosure and subject matter waiver.

2) It responds to the widespread complaint that litigation costs necessary to protect against waiver of attorney-client privilege or work product have become prohibitive due to the concern that any disclosure (however innocent or minimal) will operate as a subject matter waiver of all protected communications or information. This concern is especially troubling in cases involving electronic discovery. See, e.g., *Hopson v. City of Baltimore*, 232 F.R.D. 228, 244 (D.Md. 2005) (electronic discovery may encompass "millions of documents" and to insist upon "record-by-record pre-production privilege review, on pain of subject matter waiver, would impose upon parties costs of production that bear no proportionality to what is at stake in the litigation").

The rule seeks to provide a predictable, uniform set of standards under which parties can determine the consequences of a disclosure of a communication or information covered by the attorney-client privilege or work-product protection. Parties to litigation need to know, for example, that if they exchange privileged information pursuant to a confidentiality order, the court's order will be enforceable. Moreover, if a federal court's confidentiality order is not enforceable in a state court then the burdensome costs of privilege review and retention are unlikely to be reduced.

The rule makes no attempt to alter federal or state law on whether a communication or information is protected under the attorney-client privilege or work-product immunity as an initial matter. Moreover, while establishing some exceptions to waiver, the rule does not purport to supplant applicable waiver doctrine generally.

The rule governs only certain waivers by disclosure. Other common-law waiver doctrines may result in a finding of waiver even where there is no disclosure of privileged information or work product. See, e.g., *Nguyen v. Excel Corp.*, 197 F.3d 200 (5th Cir. 1999) (reliance on an advice of counsel defense waives the privilege with respect to attorney-client communications pertinent to that defense); *Ryers v. Burleson*, 100 F.R.D. 436 (D.D.C. 1983) (allegation of lawyer malpractice constituted a waiver of confidential communications under the circumstances). The rule is not intended to displace or modify federal common law concerning waiver of privilege or work product where no disclosure has been made.

Subdivision (a). The rule provides that a voluntary disclosure in a federal proceeding or to a federal office or agency, if a waiver, generally results in a waiver only of the communication or information disclosed; a subject matter waiver (of either privilege or work product) is reserved for those unusual situations in which fairness requires a further disclosure of related, protected information, in order to prevent a selective and misleading presentation of evidence to the disadvantage of the adversary. See, e.g., *In re United Mine Workers of America Employee Benefit Plans Litig.*, 159 F.R.D. 307, 312 (D.D.C. 1994) (waiver of work product limited to materials actually disclosed, because the party did not deliberately disclose documents in an attempt to gain a tactical advantage). Thus, subject matter waiver is limited to situations in which a party intentionally puts protected information into the litigation in a selective, misleading and unfair manner. It follows that an inadvertent disclosure of protected information can never result in a subject matter waiver. See Rule 502(b). The rule rejects the result in *In re Sealed Case*, 877 F.2d 976 (D.C.Cir. 1989), which held that inadvertent disclosure of documents during discovery automatically constituted a subject matter waiver.

The language concerning subject matter waiver – "ought in fairness" – is taken from Rule 106, because the animating principle is the same. Under both Rules, a party that makes a selective, misleading presentation that is unfair to the adversary opens itself to a more complete and accurate presentation.

To assure protection and predictability, the rule provides that if a disclosure is made at the federal level, the federal rule on subject matter waiver governs subsequent state court determinations on the scope of the waiver by that disclosure.

Subdivision (b). Courts are in conflict over whether an inadvertent disclosure of a communication or information protected as privileged or work product constitutes a waiver. A few courts find that a disclosure must be intentional to be a waiver. Most courts find a waiver only if the disclosing party acted carelessly in disclosing the communication or information and failed to request its return in a timely manner. And a few courts hold that any inadvertent disclosure of a communication or information protected under the attorney-client privilege or as work product constitutes a waiver without regard to the protections taken to avoid such a disclosure. See generally *Hopson v. City of Baltimore*, 232 F.R.D. 228 (D.Md. 2005), for a discussion of this case law.

The rule opts for the middle ground: inadvertent disclosure of protected communications or information in connection with a federal proceeding or to a federal office or agency does not constitute a waiver if the holder took reasonable steps to prevent disclosure and also promptly took reasonable steps to rectify the error. This position is in accord with the majority view on whether inadvertent disclosure is a waiver.

Cases such as *Lois Sportswear, U.S.A., Inc. v. Levi Strauss & Co.*, 104 F.R.D. 103, 105 (S.D.N.Y. 1985) and *Hartford Fire Ins. Co. v. Garvey*, 109 F.R.D. 323, 332 (N.D.Cal. 1985), set out a multi-factor test for determining whether inadvertent disclosure is a waiver. The stated factors (none of which is dispositive) are the reasonableness of precautions taken, the time taken to rectify the error, the scope of discovery, the extent of disclosure and the overriding issue of fairness. The rule does not explicitly codify that test, because it is really a set of non-determinative guidelines that vary from case to case. The rule is flexible enough to accommodate any of those listed factors. Other considerations bearing on the reasonableness of a producing party's efforts include the number of documents to be reviewed and the time constraints for production. Depending on the circumstances, a party that uses advanced analytical software applications and linguistic tools in screening for privilege and work product may be found to have taken "reasonable steps" to prevent inadvertent disclosure. The implementation of an efficient system of records management before litigation may also be relevant.

The rule does not require the producing party to engage in a post-production review to determine whether any protected communication or information has been produced by mistake. But the rule does require the producing party to follow up on any obvious indications that a protected communication or information has been produced inadvertently.

The rule applies to inadvertent disclosures made to a federal office or agency, including but not limited to an office or agency that is acting in the course of its regulatory, investigative or enforcement authority. The consequences of waiver, and the concomitant costs of pre-production privilege review, can be as great with respect to disclosures to offices and agencies as they are in litigation.

Subdivision (c). Difficult questions can arise when 1) a disclosure of a communication or information protected by the attorney-client privilege or as work product is made in a state proceeding, 2) the communication or information is offered in a subsequent federal proceeding on the ground that the disclosure waived the privilege or protection, and 3) the state and federal laws are in conflict on the question of waiver. The Committee determined that the proper solution for the federal court is to apply the law that is most protective of privilege and work product. If the state law is more protective (such as where the state law is that an inadvertent disclosure can never be a waiver), the holder of the privilege or protection may well have relied on that law when making the disclosure in the state proceeding. Moreover, applying a more restrictive federal law of waiver could impair the state objective of preserving the privilege or work-product protection for disclosures made in state proceedings. On the other hand, if the federal law is more protective, applying the state law of waiver to determine admissibility in federal court is likely to undermine the federal objective of limiting the costs of production.

The rule does not address the enforceability of a state court confidentiality order in a federal proceeding, as that question is covered both by statutory law and principles of federalism and comity. See 28 U.S.C. § 1738 (providing that state judicial proceedings "shall have the same full faith and credit in every court within the United States . . . as they have by law or usage in the courts of such State . . . from which they are taken"). See also *Tucker v. Ohtsu Tire & Rubber Co.*, 191 F.R.D. 495, 499 (D.Md. 2000) (noting that a federal court considering the enforceability of a state confidentiality order is "constrained by principles of comity, courtesy, and . . . federalism"). Thus, a state court order finding no waiver in connection with a disclosure made in a state court proceeding is enforceable under existing law in subsequent federal proceedings.

Subdivision (d). Confidentiality orders are becoming increasingly important in limiting the costs of privilege review and retention, especially in cases involving electronic discovery. But the utility of a confidentiality order in reducing discovery costs is substantially diminished if it provides no protection outside the particular litigation in which the order is entered. Parties are unlikely to be able to reduce the costs of pre-production review for privilege and work product if the consequence of disclosure is that the communications or information could be used by non-parties to the litigation.

There is some dispute on whether a confidentiality order entered in one case is enforceable in other proceedings. See generally *Hopson v. City of Baltimore*, 232 F.R.D. 228 (D.Md. 2005), for a discussion of this case law. The rule provides that when a confidentiality order governing the consequences of disclosure in that case is entered in a federal proceeding, its terms are enforceable against non-parties in any federal or state proceeding. For example, the court order may provide for return of documents without waiver irrespective of the care taken by the disclosing party; the rule contemplates enforcement of "claw-back" and "quick peek" arrangements as a way to avoid the excessive costs of pre-production review for privilege and work product. See *Zubulake v. UBS Warburg LLC*, 216 F.R.D. 280, 290 (S.D.N.Y. 2003) (noting that parties may enter into "so-called 'claw-back' agreements that allow the parties to forego privilege review altogether in favor of an agreement to return inadvertently produced privilege documents"). The rule provides a party with a predictable protection from a court order – predictability that is needed to allow the party to plan in advance to limit the prohibitive costs of privilege and work product review and retention.

Under the rule, a confidentiality order is enforceable whether or not it memorializes an agreement among the parties to the litigation. Party agreement should not be a condition of enforceability of a federal court's order.

Under subdivision (d), a federal court may order that disclosure of privileged or protected information "in connection with" a federal proceeding does not result in waiver. But subdivision (d) does not allow the federal court to enter an order determining the waiver effects of a separate disclosure of the same information in other proceedings, state or federal. If a disclosure has been made in a state proceeding (and is not the subject of a state-court order on waiver), then subdivision (d) is inapplicable. Subdivision (c) would govern the federal court's determination whether the state-court disclosure waived the privilege or protection in the federal proceeding.

Subdivision (e). Subdivision (e) codifies the well-established proposition that parties can enter an agreement to limit the effect of waiver by disclosure between or among them. Of course such an agreement can bind only the parties to the agreement. The rule makes clear that if parties want protection against non-parties from a finding of waiver by disclosure, the agreement must be made part of a court order.

Subdivision (f). The protections against waiver provided by Rule 502 must be applicable when protected communications or information disclosed in federal proceedings are subsequently offered in state proceedings. Otherwise the holders of protected communications and information, and their lawyers, could not rely on the protections provided by the Rule, and the goal of limiting costs in discovery would be substantially undermined. Rule 502(f) is intended to resolve any potential tension between the provisions of Rule 502 that apply to state proceedings and the possible limitations on the applicability of the Federal Rules of Evidence otherwise provided by Rules 101 and 1101.

The rule is intended to apply in all federal court proceedings, including court-annexed and court-ordered arbitrations, without regard to any possible limitations of Rules 101 and 1101. This provision is not intended to raise an inference about the applicability of any other rule of evidence in arbitration proceedings more generally.

The costs of discovery can be equally high for state and federal causes of action, and the rule seeks to limit those costs in all federal proceedings, regardless of whether the claim arises under state or federal law. Accordingly, the rule applies to state law causes of action brought in federal court.

Subdivision (g). The rule's coverage is limited to attorney-client privilege and work product. The operation of waiver by disclosure, as applied to other evidentiary privileges, remains a question of federal common law. Nor does the rule purport to apply to the Fifth Amendment privilege against compelled self-incrimination.

The definition of work product "materials" is intended to include both tangible and intangible information. See *In re Cendant Corp. Sec. Litig.*, 343

F.3d 658, 662 (3d Cir. 2003) ("work product protection extends to both tangible and intangible work product").

Standards of Professional Conduct for Attorneys Appearing and Practicing Before the Commission in the Representation of an Issuer
17 C.F.R. Part 205.

§ 205.1 Purpose and scope.

This part sets forth minimum standards of professional conduct for attorneys appearing and practicing before the Commission in the representation of an issuer. These standards supplement applicable standards of any jurisdiction where an attorney is admitted or practices and are not intended to limit the ability of any jurisdiction to impose additional obligations on an attorney not inconsistent with the application of this part. Where the standards of a state or other United States jurisdiction where an attorney is admitted or practices conflict with this part, this part shall govern.

§ 205.2 Definitions.

For purposes of this part, the following definitions apply:

(a) Appearing and practicing before the Commission:

    (1) Means:

        (i) Transacting any business with the Commission, including communications in any form;

        (ii) Representing an issuer in a Commission administrative proceeding or in connection with any Commission investigation, inquiry, information request, or subpoena;

        (iii) Providing advice in respect of the United States securities laws or the Commission's rules or regulations thereunder regarding any document that the attorney has notice will be filed with or submitted to, or incorporated into any document that will be filed with or submitted to, the Commission, including the provision of such advice in the context of preparing, or participating in the preparation of, any such document; or

        (iv) Advising an issuer as to whether information or a statement, opinion, or other writing is required under the United States securities laws or the Commission's rules or regulations thereunder to be filed with or submitted to, or incorporated into any document that will be filed with or submitted to, the Commission; but

111

(2) Does not include an attorney who:

(i) Conducts the activities in paragraphs (a)(1)(i) through (a)(1)(iv) of this section other than in the context of providing legal services to an issuer with whom the attorney has an attorney-client relationship; or

(ii) Is a non-appearing foreign attorney.

(b) Appropriate response means a response to an attorney regarding reported evidence of a material violation as a result of which the attorney reasonably believes:

(1) That no material violation, as defined in paragraph (i) of this section, has occurred, is ongoing, or is about to occur;

(2) That the issuer has, as necessary, adopted appropriate remedial measures, including appropriate steps or sanctions to stop any material violations that are ongoing, to prevent any material violation that has yet to occur, and to remedy or otherwise appropriately address any material violation that has already occurred and to minimize the likelihood of its recurrence; or

(3) That the issuer, with the consent of the issuer's board of directors, a committee thereof to whom a report could be made pursuant to § 205.3(b)(3), or a qualified legal compliance committee, has retained or directed an attorney to review the reported evidence of a material violation and either:

(i) Has substantially implemented any remedial recommendations made by such attorney after a reasonable investigation and evaluation of the reported evidence; or

(ii) Has been advised that such attorney may, consistent with his or her professional obligations, assert a colorable defense on behalf of the issuer (or the issuer's officer, director, employee, or agent, as the case may be) in any investigation or judicial or administrative proceeding relating to the reported evidence of a material violation.

(c) Attorney means any person who is admitted, licensed, or otherwise qualified to practice law in any jurisdiction, domestic or foreign, or who holds himself or herself out as admitted, licensed, or otherwise qualified to practice law.

(d) Breach of fiduciary duty refers to any breach of fiduciary or similar duty to the issuer recognized under an applicable Federal or State statute or at common law, including but not limited to misfeasance, nonfeasance, abdication of duty, abuse of trust, and approval of unlawful transactions.

(e) Evidence of a material violation means credible evidence, based upon which it would be unreasonable, under the circumstances, for a prudent and competent attorney not to conclude that it is reasonably likely that a material violation has occurred, is ongoing, or is about to occur.

(f) Foreign government issuer means a foreign issuer as defined in 17 CFR 230.405 eligible to register securities on Schedule B of the Securities Act of 1933 (15 U.S.C. 77a et seq., Schedule B).

(g) In the representation of an issuer means providing legal services as an attorney for an issuer, regardless of whether the attorney is employed or retained by the issuer.

(h) Issuer means an issuer (as defined in section 3 of the Securities Exchange Act of 1934 (15 U.S.C. 78c)), the securities of which are registered under section 12 of that Act (15 U.S.C. 78l), or that is required to file reports under section 15(d) of that Act (15 U.S.C. 78o(d)), or that files or has filed a registration statement that has not yet become effective under the Securities Act of 1933 (15 U.S.C. 77a et seq.), and that it has not withdrawn, but does not include a foreign government issuer. For purposes of paragraphs (a) and (g) of this section, the term "issuer" includes any person controlled by an issuer, where an attorney provides legal services to such person on behalf of, or at the behest, or for the benefit of the issuer, regardless of whether the attorney is employed or retained by the issuer.

(i) Material violation means a material violation of an applicable United States federal or state securities law, a material breach of fiduciary duty arising under United States federal or state law, or a similar material violation of any United States federal or state law.

(j) Non-appearing foreign attorney means an attorney:

   (1) Who is admitted to practice law in a jurisdiction outside the United States;

   (2) Who does not hold himself or herself out as practicing, and does not give legal advice regarding, United States federal or state securities or other laws (except as provided in paragraph (j)(3)(ii) of this section); and

   (3) Who:

      (i) Conducts activities that would constitute appearing and practicing before the Commission only incidentally to, and in the ordinary course of, the practice of law in a jurisdiction outside the United States; or

      (ii) Is appearing and practicing before the Commission only in consultation with counsel, other than a non-appearing foreign attorney, admitted or licensed to practice in a state or other United States jurisdiction.

(k) Qualified legal compliance committee means a committee of an issuer (which also may be an audit or other committee of the issuer) that:

(1) Consists of at least one member of the issuer's audit committee (or, if the issuer has no audit committee, one member from an equivalent committee of independent directors) and two or more members of the issuer's board of directors who are not employed, directly or indirectly, by the issuer and who are not, in the case of a registered investment company, "interested persons" as defined in section 2(a)(19) of the Investment Company Act of 1940 (15 U.S.C. 80a-2(a)(19));

(2) Has adopted written procedures for the confidential receipt, retention, and consideration of any report of evidence of a material violation under § 205.3;

(3) Has been duly established by the issuer's board of directors, with the authority and responsibility:

(i) To inform the issuer's chief legal officer and chief executive officer (or the equivalents thereof) of any report of evidence of a material violation (except in the circumstances described in § 205.3(b)(4));

(ii) To determine whether an investigation is necessary regarding any report of evidence of a material violation by the issuer, its officers, directors, employees or agents and, if it determines an investigation is necessary or appropriate, to:

(A) Notify the audit committee or the full board of directors;

(B) Initiate an investigation, which may be conducted either by the chief legal officer (or the equivalent thereof) or by outside attorneys; and

(C) Retain such additional expert personnel as the committee deems necessary; and

(iii) At the conclusion of any such investigation, to:

(A) Recommend, by majority vote, that the issuer implement an appropriate response to evidence of a material violation; and

(B) Inform the chief legal officer and the chief executive officer (or the equivalents thereof) and the board of directors of the results of any such investigation under this section and the appropriate remedial measures to be adopted; and

(4) Has the authority and responsibility, acting by majority vote, to take all other appropriate action, including the authority to notify the Commission in the event that the issuer fails in any material respect to implement an appropriate response that the qualified legal compliance committee has recommended the issuer to take.

(l) Reasonable or reasonably denotes, with respect to the actions of an attorney, conduct that would not be unreasonable for a prudent and competent attorney.

(m) Reasonably believes means that an attorney believes the matter in question and that the circumstances are such that the belief is not unreasonable.

(n) Report means to make known to directly, either in person, by telephone, by e-mail, electronically, or in writing.

§ 205.3 Issuer as client.

(a) Representing an issuer. An attorney appearing and practicing before the Commission in the representation of an issuer owes his or her professional and ethical duties to the issuer as an organization. That the attorney may work with and advise the issuer's officers, directors, or employees in the course of representing the issuer does not make such individuals the attorney's clients.

(b) Duty to report evidence of a material violation.

(1) If an attorney, appearing and practicing before the Commission in the representation of an issuer, becomes aware of evidence of a material violation by the issuer or by any officer, director, employee, or agent of the issuer, the attorney shall report such evidence to the issuer's chief legal officer (or the equivalent thereof) or to both the issuer's chief legal officer and its chief executive officer (or the equivalents thereof) forthwith. By communicating such information to the issuer's officers or directors, an attorney does not reveal client confidences or secrets or privileged or otherwise protected information related to the attorney's representation of an issuer.

(2) The chief legal officer (or the equivalent thereof) shall cause such inquiry into the evidence of a material violation as he or she reasonably believes is appropriate to determine whether the material violation described in the report has occurred, is ongoing,

or is about to occur. If the chief legal officer (or the equivalent thereof) determines no material violation has occurred, is ongoing, or is about to occur, he or she shall notify the reporting attorney and advise the reporting attorney of the basis for such determination. Unless the chief legal officer (or the equivalent thereof) reasonably believes that no material violation has occurred, is ongoing, or is about to occur, he or she shall take all reasonable steps to cause the issuer to adopt an appropriate response, and shall advise the reporting attorney thereof. In lieu of causing an inquiry under this paragraph (b), a chief legal officer (or the equivalent thereof) may refer a report of evidence of a material violation to a qualified legal compliance committee under paragraph (c)(2) of this section if the issuer has duly established a qualified legal compliance committee prior to the report of evidence of a material violation.

(3) Unless an attorney who has made a report under paragraph (b)(1) of this section reasonably believes that the chief legal officer or the chief executive officer of the issuer (or the equivalent thereof) has provided an appropriate response within a reasonable time, the attorney shall report the evidence of a material violation to:

(i) The audit committee of the issuer's board of directors;

(ii) Another committee of the issuer's board of directors consisting solely of directors who are not employed, directly or indirectly, by the issuer and are not, in the case of a registered investment company, "interested persons" as defined in section 2(a)(19) of the Investment Company Act of 1940 (15 U.S.C. 80a-2(a)(19)) (if the issuer's board of directors has no audit committee); or

(iii) The issuer's board of directors (if the issuer's board of directors has no committee consisting solely of directors who are not employed, directly or indirectly, by the issuer and are not, in the case of a registered investment company, "interested persons" as defined in section 2(a)(19) of the Investment Company Act of 1940 (15 U.S.C. 80a-2(a)(19))).

(4) If an attorney reasonably believes that it would be futile to report evidence of a material violation to the issuer's chief legal officer and chief executive officer (or the equivalents thereof) under paragraph (b)(1) of this section, the attorney may report such evidence as provided under paragraph (b)(3) of this section.

(5) An attorney retained or directed by an issuer to investigate evidence of a material violation reported under paragraph (b)(1), (b)(3), or (b)(4) of this section shall be deemed to be appearing and practicing before the Commission. Directing or retaining an attorney to investigate reported evidence of a material violation does not

relieve an officer or director of the issuer to whom such evidence has been reported under paragraph (b)(1), (b)(3), or (b)(4) of this section from a duty to respond to the reporting attorney.

(6) An attorney shall not have any obligation to report evidence of a material violation under this paragraph (b) if:

(i) The attorney was retained or directed by the issuer's chief legal officer (or the equivalent thereof) to investigate such evidence of a material violation and:

(A) The attorney reports the results of such investigation to the chief legal officer (or the equivalent thereof); and

(B) Except where the attorney and the chief legal officer (or the equivalent thereof) each reasonably believes that no material violation has occurred, is ongoing, or is about to occur, the chief legal officer (or the equivalent thereof) reports the results of the investigation to the issuer's board of directors, a committee thereof to whom a report could be made pursuant to paragraph (b)(3) of this section, or a qualified legal compliance committee; or

(ii) The attorney was retained or directed by the chief legal officer (or the equivalent thereof) to assert, consistent with his or her professional obligations, a colorable defense on behalf of the issuer (or the issuer's officer, director, employee, or agent, as the case may be) in any investigation or judicial or administrative proceeding relating to such evidence of a material violation, and the chief legal officer (or the equivalent thereof) provides reasonable and timely reports on the progress and outcome of such proceeding to the issuer's board of directors, a committee thereof to whom a report could be made pursuant to paragraph (b)(3) of this section, or a qualified legal compliance committee.

(7) An attorney shall not have any obligation to report evidence of a material violation under this paragraph (b) if such attorney was retained or directed by a qualified legal compliance committee:

(i) To investigate such evidence of a material violation; or

(ii) To assert, consistent with his or her professional obligations, a colorable defense on behalf of the issuer (or the issuer's officer, director, employee, or agent, as the case may be) in any investigation or judicial or administrative proceeding relating to such evidence of a material violation.

(8) An attorney who receives what he or she reasonably believes is an appropriate and timely response to a report he or she has made pursuant to paragraph (b)(1), (b)(3), or (b)(4) of this section need do nothing more under this section with respect to his or her report.

(9) An attorney who does not reasonably believe that the issuer has made an appropriate response within a reasonable time to the report or reports made pursuant to paragraph (b)(1), (b)(3), or (b)(4) of this section shall explain his or her reasons therefor to the chief legal officer (or the equivalent thereof), the chief executive officer (or the equivalent thereof), and directors to whom the attorney reported the evidence of a material violation pursuant to paragraph (b)(1), (b)(3), or (b)(4) of this section.

(10) An attorney formerly employed or retained by an issuer who has reported evidence of a material violation under this part and reasonably believes that he or she has been discharged for so doing may notify the issuer's board of directors or any committee thereof that he or she believes that he or she has been discharged for reporting evidence of a material violation under this section.

(c) Alternative reporting procedures for attorneys retained or employed by an issuer that has established a qualified legal compliance committee.

(1) If an attorney, appearing and practicing before the Commission in the representation of an issuer, becomes aware of evidence of a material violation by the issuer or by any officer, director, employee, or agent of the issuer, the attorney may, as an alternative to the reporting requirements of paragraph (b) of this section, report such evidence to a qualified legal compliance committee, if the issuer has previously formed such a committee. An attorney who reports evidence of a material violation to such a qualified legal compliance committee has satisfied his or her obligation to report such evidence and is not required to assess the issuer's response to the reported evidence of a material violation.

(2) A chief legal officer (or the equivalent thereof) may refer a report of evidence of a material violation to a previously established qualified legal compliance committee in lieu of causing an inquiry to be conducted under paragraph (b)(2) of this section. The chief legal officer (or the equivalent thereof) shall inform the reporting attorney that the report has been referred to a qualified legal compliance committee. Thereafter, pursuant to the requirements under § 205.2(k), the qualified legal compliance committee shall be responsible for responding to the evidence of a material violation reported to it under this paragraph (c).

(d) Issuer confidences.

(1) Any report under this section (or the contemporaneous record thereof) or any response thereto (or the contemporaneous record thereof) may be used by an attorney in connection with any investigation, proceeding, or litigation in which the attorney's compliance with this part is in issue.

(2) An attorney appearing and practicing before the Commission in the representation of an issuer may reveal to the Commission, without the issuer's consent, confidential information related to the representation to the extent the attorney reasonably believes necessary:

(i) To prevent the issuer from committing a material violation that is likely to cause substantial injury to the financial interest or property of the issuer or investors;

(ii) To prevent the issuer, in a Commission investigation or administrative proceeding from committing perjury, proscribed in 18 U.S.C. 1621; suborning perjury, proscribed in 18 U.S.C. 1622; or committing any act proscribed in 18 U.S.C. 1001 that is likely to perpetrate a fraud upon the Commission; or

(iii) To rectify the consequences of a material violation by the issuer that caused, or may cause, substantial injury to the financial interest or property of the issuer or investors in the furtherance of which the attorney's services were used.

§ 205.4 Responsibilities of supervisory attorneys.

(a) An attorney supervising or directing another attorney who is appearing and practicing before the Commission in the representation of an issuer is a supervisory attorney. An issuer's chief legal officer (or the equivalent thereof) is a supervisory attorney under this section.

(b) A supervisory attorney shall make reasonable efforts to ensure that a subordinate attorney, as defined in § 205.5(a), that he or she supervises or directs conforms to this part. To the extent a subordinate attorney appears and practices before the Commission in the representation of an issuer, that subordinate attorney's supervisory attorneys also appear and practice before the Commission.

(c) A supervisory attorney is responsible for complying with the reporting requirements in § 205.3 when a subordinate attorney has reported to the supervisory attorney evidence of a material violation.

(d) A supervisory attorney who has received a report of evidence of a material violation from a subordinate attorney under § 205.3 may report such evidence to the issuer's qualified legal compliance committee if the issuer has duly formed such a committee.

§ 205.5 Responsibilities of a subordinate attorney.

(a) An attorney who appears and practices before the Commission in the representation of an issuer on a matter under the supervision or direction of another attorney (other than under the direct supervision or direction of the issuer's chief legal officer (or the equivalent thereof)) is a subordinate attorney.

(b) A subordinate attorney shall comply with this part notwithstanding that the subordinate attorney acted at the direction of or under the supervision of another person.

(c) A subordinate attorney complies with § 205.3 if the subordinate attorney reports to his or her supervising attorney under § 205.3(b) evidence of a material violation of which the subordinate attorney has become aware in appearing and practicing before the Commission.

(d) A subordinate attorney may take the steps permitted or required by § 205.3(b) or (c) if the subordinate attorney reasonably believes that a supervisory attorney to whom he or she has reported evidence of a material violation under § 205.3(b) has failed to comply with § 205.3.

§ 205.6 Sanctions and discipline.

(a) A violation of this part by any attorney appearing and practicing before the Commission in the representation of an issuer shall subject such attorney to the civil penalties and remedies for a violation of the federal securities laws available to the Commission in an action brought by the Commission thereunder.

(b) An attorney appearing and practicing before the Commission who violates any provision of this part is subject to the disciplinary authority of the Commission, regardless of whether the attorney may also be subject to discipline for the same conduct in a jurisdiction where the attorney is admitted or practices. An administrative disciplinary proceeding initiated by the Commission for violation of this part may result in an attorney being censured, or being temporarily or permanently denied the privilege of appearing or practicing before the Commission.

(c) An attorney who complies in good faith with the provisions of this part shall not be subject to discipline or otherwise liable under inconsistent standards imposed by any state or other United States jurisdiction where the attorney is admitted or practices.

(d) An attorney practicing outside the United States shall not be required to comply with the requirements of this part to the extent that such compliance is prohibited by applicable foreign law.

Office of Professional Responsibility
Department of Justice
28 C.F.R., Part 0

§ 0.39 Organization.

The Office of Professional Responsibility (DOJ-OPR) shall be headed by a Counsel, who shall be appointed by the Attorney General and subject to the general supervision and direction of the Attorney General or, whenever appropriate, the Deputy Attorney General.

§ 0.39a Functions.

(a) The Counsel shall:

(1) Receive, review, investigate and refer for appropriate action allegations of misconduct involving Department attorneys that relate to the exercise of their authority to investigate, litigate or provide legal advice, as well as allegations of misconduct by law enforcement personnel when such allegations are related to allegations of attorney misconduct within the jurisdiction of DOJ-OPR;

(2) Receive, review, investigate and refer for appropriate action:

(i) Any allegation of reprisal against an employee or applicant who discloses information pursuant to paragraph (a)(1) of this section; and

(ii) Allegations of reprisal taken against any Federal Bureau of Investigation employee for disclosing information pursuant to 28 CFR 27.1;

(3) Report to the responsible Department official the results of inquiries and investigations arising under paragraphs (a)(1) and (2) of this section, and, when appropriate, make recommendations for disciplinary and other corrective action;

(4) Refer any allegation not arising under paragraphs (a)(1) or (2) of this section to the Inspector General or another appropriate Department official;

(5) Notify any person who has made allegations pursuant to paragraphs (a)(1) or (2) of this section and any person who was the

subject of such allegations of the completion and, as appropriate, the results of, any inquiry or investigation undertaken, where such notification is permitted by law and consistent with the law enforcement interests of the Department;

(6) Engage in liaison with the bar disciplinary authorities of the states, territories, and the District of Columbia with respect to professional misconduct matters;

(7) Submit an annual report to the Attorney General summarizing the work of the Office;

(8) Submit recommendations to the Attorney General and the Deputy Attorney General on the need for changes in policies and procedures that become evident during the course of the Counsel's inquiries and investigations;

(9) Review proposals from Department employees to refer to appropriate licensing authorities apparent professional misconduct by attorneys outside the Department, and make such referrals where warranted, except that referrals made pursuant to 8 CFR 1003.106(d) do not require the Counsel's review; and

(10) Perform any other responsibilities assigned by the Attorney General or the Deputy Attorney General.

(b) For the purpose of paragraph (a)(2)(i) of this section, any disclosure by an employee or applicant to a supervisor, Professional Responsibility Officer, the Office of Professional Responsibility, the Office of the Inspector General, the Executive Office for United States Attorneys, or other appropriate individual or component shall constitute disclosure to the Attorney General or the Counsel.

§ 0.39b Confidentiality of Information.

The Counsel shall not disclose the identity of any person submitting an allegation of misconduct or reprisal pursuant to 28 CFR 0.39a(a)(1) or (2) unless the person consents to the disclosure of his identity or the disclosure is necessary to carry out the authority of the Office of Professional Responsibility, including conducting an investigation or referring the allegation to another component.

STATEMENTS OF POLICY
28 C.F.R., Part 50

§ 50.10 Policy regarding obtaining information from, or records of, members of the news media; and regarding questioning, arresting, or charging members of the news media.

(a) Statement of principles.

(1) Because freedom of the press can be no broader than the freedom of members of the news media to investigate and report the news, the Department's policy is intended to provide protection to members of the news media from certain law enforcement tools, whether criminal or civil, that might unreasonably impair newsgathering activities. The policy is not intended to extend special protections to members of the news media who are subjects or targets of criminal investigations for conduct not based on, or within the scope of, newsgathering activities.

(2) In determining whether to seek information from, or records of, members of the news media, the approach in every instance must be to strike the proper balance among several vital interests: Protecting national security, ensuring public safety, promoting effective law enforcement and the fair administration of justice, and safeguarding the essential role of the free press in fostering government accountability and an open society.

(3) The Department views the use of certain law enforcement tools, including subpoenas, court orders issued pursuant to 18 U.S.C. 2703(d) or 3123, and search warrants to seek information from, or records of, non-consenting members of the news media as extraordinary measures, not standard investigatory practices. In particular, subpoenas or court orders issued pursuant to 18 U.S.C. 2703(d) or 3123 may be used, after authorization by the Attorney General, or by another senior official in accordance with the exceptions set forth in paragraph (c)(3) of this section, only to obtain information from, or records of, members of the news media when the information sought is essential to a successful investigation, prosecution, or litigation; after all reasonable alternative attempts have been made to obtain the information from alternative sources; and after negotiations with the affected member of the news media have been pursued and appropriate notice to the affected member of the news media has been provided, unless the Attorney General determines that, for compelling reasons, such negotiations or notice would pose a clear and substantial threat to the integrity of the investigation, risk grave harm to national security, or present an imminent risk of death or serious bodily harm.

(4) When the Attorney General has authorized the use of a subpoena, court order issued pursuant to 18 U.S.C. 2703(d) or 3123, or warrant

to obtain from a third party communications records or business records of a member of the news media, the affected member of the news media shall be given reasonable and timely notice of the Attorney General's determination before the use of the subpoena, court order, or warrant, unless the Attorney General determines that, for compelling reasons, such notice would pose a clear and substantial threat to the integrity of the investigation, risk grave harm to national security, or present an imminent risk of death or serious bodily harm.

(b) Scope.—

(1) Covered individuals and entities.

(i) The policy governs the use of certain law enforcement tools to obtain information from, or records of, members of the news media.

(ii) The protections of the policy do not extend to any individual or entity where there are reasonable grounds to believe that the individual or entity is—

(A) A foreign power or agent of a foreign power, as those terms are defined in section 101 of the Foreign Intelligence Surveillance Act of 1978 (50 U.S.C. 1801);

(B) A member or affiliate of a foreign terrorist organization designated under section 219(a) of the Immigration and Nationality Act (8 U.S.C. 1189(a));

(C) Designated as a Specially Designated Global Terrorist by the Department of the Treasury under Executive Order 13224 of September 23, 2001 (66 FR 49079);

(D) A specially designated terrorist as that term is defined in 31 CFR 595.311 (or any successor thereto);

(E) A terrorist organization as that term is defined in section 212(a)(3)(B)(vi) of the Immigration and Nationality Act (8 U.S.C. 1182(a)(3)(B)(vi));

(F) Committing or attempting to commit a crime of terrorism, as that offense is described in 18 U.S.C. 2331(5) or 2332b(g)(5);

(G) Committing or attempting the crime of providing material support or resources to terrorists, as that offense is defined in 18 U.S.C. 2339A; or

(H) Aiding, abetting, or conspiring in illegal activity with a person or organization described in paragraphs (b)(1)(ii)(A) through (G) of this section.

(2) Covered law enforcement tools and records.

(i) The policy governs the use by law enforcement authorities of subpoenas or, in civil matters, other similar compulsory process such as a civil investigative demand (collectively "subpoenas") to obtain information from members of the news media, including documents, testimony, and other materials; and the use by law enforcement authorities of subpoenas, or court orders issued pursuant to 18 U.S.C. 2703(d) ("2703(d) order") or 18 U.S.C. 3123 ("3123 order"), to obtain from third parties "communications records" or "business records" of members of the news media.

(ii) The policy also governs applications for warrants to search the premises or property of members of the news media, pursuant to Federal Rule of Criminal Procedure 41; or to obtain from third-party "communication service providers" the communications records or business records of members of the news media, pursuant to 18 U.S.C. 2703(a) and (b).

(3) Definitions.

(i) (A)"Communications records" include the contents of electronic communications as well as source and destination information associated with communications, such as email transaction logs and local and long distance telephone connection records, stored or transmitted by a third-party communication service provider with which the member of the news media has a contractual relationship.

(B) Communications records do not include information described in 18 U.S.C. 2703(c)(2)(A), (B), (D), (E), and (F).

(ii) A "communication service provider" is a provider of an electronic communication service or remote computing service as defined, respectively, in 18 U.S.C. 2510(15) and 18 U.S.C. 2711(2).

(iii)(A) "Business records" include work product and other documentary materials, and records of the activities, including the financial transactions, of a member of the news media related to the coverage, investigation, or reporting of news. Business records are limited to those generated or maintained by a third party with which the member of the news media has a contractual relationship, and which could provide information about the newsgathering techniques or sources of a member of the news media.

(B) Business records do not include records unrelated to newsgathering activities, such as those related to the purely commercial, financial, administrative, or technical, operations of a news media entity.

(C) Business records do not include records that are created or maintained either by the government or by a contractor on behalf of the government.

(c) Issuing subpoenas to members of the news media, or using subpoenas or court orders issued pursuant to 18 U.S.C. 2703(d) or 3123 to obtain from third parties communications records or business records of a member of the news media.

(1) Except as set forth in paragraph (c)(3) of this section, members of the Department must obtain the authorization of the Attorney General to issue a subpoena to a member of the news media; or to use a subpoena, 2703(d) order, or 3123 order to obtain from a third party communications records or business records of a member of the news media.

(2) Requests for the authorization of the Attorney General for the issuance of a subpoena to a member of the news media, or to use a subpoena, 2703(d) order, or 3123 order to obtain communications records or business records of a member of the news media, must be personally endorsed by the United States Attorney or Assistant Attorney General responsible for the matter.

(3) Exceptions to the Attorney General authorization requirement.

   (i) (A) A United States Attorney or Assistant Attorney General responsible for the matter may authorize the issuance of a subpoena to a member of the news media (e.g., for documents, video or audio recordings, testimony, or other materials) if the member of the news media expressly agrees to provide the requested information in response to a subpoena. This exception applies, but is not limited, to both published and unpublished materials and aired and unaired recordings.

   (B) In the case of an authorization under paragraph (c)(3)(i)(A) of this section, the United States Attorney or Assistant Attorney General responsible for the matter shall provide notice to the Director of the Criminal Division's Office of Enforcement Operations within 10 business days of the authorization of the issuance of the subpoena.

   (ii) In light of the intent of this policy to protect freedom of the press, newsgathering activities, and confidential news media sources, authorization of the Attorney General will not be required of members of the Department in the following circumstances:

(A) To issue subpoenas to news media entities for purely commercial, financial, administrative, technical, or other information unrelated to newsgathering activities; or for information or records relating to personnel not involved in newsgathering activities.

(B) To issue subpoenas to members of the news media for information related to public comments, messages, or postings by readers, viewers, customers, or subscribers, over which the member of the news media does not exercise editorial control prior to publication.

(C) To use subpoenas to obtain information from, or to use subpoenas, 2703(d) orders, or 3123 orders to obtain communications records or business records of, members of the news media who may be perpetrators or victims of, or witnesses to, crimes or other events, when such status (as a perpetrator, victim, or witness) is not based on, or within the scope of, newsgathering activities.

(iii) In the circumstances identified in paragraphs (c)(3)(ii)(A) through (C) of this section, the United States Attorney or Assistant Attorney General responsible for the matter must—

(A) Authorize the use of the subpoena or court order;

(B) Consult with the Criminal Division regarding appropriate review and safeguarding protocols; and

(C) Provide a copy of the subpoena or court order to the Director of the Office of Public Affairs and to the Director of the Criminal Division's Office of Enforcement Operations within 10 business days of the authorization.

(4) Considerations for the Attorney General in determining whether to authorize the issuance of a subpoena to a member of the news media.

(i) In matters in which a member of the Department determines that a member of the news media is a subject or target of an investigation relating to an offense committed in the course of, or arising out of, newsgathering activities, the member of the Department requesting Attorney General authorization to issue a subpoena to a member of the news media shall provide all facts necessary for determinations by the Attorney General regarding both whether the member of the news media is a subject or target of the investigation and whether to authorize the issuance of such subpoena. If the Attorney General determines that the member of the news media is a subject or target of an investigation relating to an offense committed in the course of, or arising out of, newsgathering activities, the Attorney General's determination regarding the issuance of the proposed subpoena should take into account the principles reflected in paragraph (a) of this section, but need not take into account the considerations identified in paragraphs (c)(4)(ii) through (viii) of this section.

(ii)   (A) In criminal matters, there should be reasonable grounds to believe, based on public information, or information from non-media sources, that a crime has occurred, and that the information sought is essential to a successful investigation or prosecution. The subpoena should not be used to obtain peripheral, nonessential, or speculative information.

(B) In civil matters, there should be reasonable grounds to believe, based on public information or information from non-media sources, that the information sought is essential to the successful completion of the investigation or litigation in a case of substantial importance. The subpoena should not be used to obtain peripheral, nonessential, cumulative, or speculative information.

(iii) The government should have made all reasonable attempts to obtain the information from alternative, non-media sources.

(iv)   (A) The government should have pursued negotiations with the affected member of the news media, unless the Attorney General determines that, for compelling reasons, such negotiations would pose a clear and substantial threat to the integrity of the investigation, risk grave harm to national security, or present an imminent risk of death or serious bodily harm. Where the nature of the investigation permits, the government should have explained to the member of the news media the government's needs in a particular investigation or prosecution, as well as its willingness to address the concerns of the member of the news media.

(B) The obligation to pursue negotiations with the affected member of the news media, unless excused by the Attorney General, is not intended to conflict with the requirement that members of the Department secure authorization from the Attorney General to question a member of the news media as required in paragraph (f)(1) of this section. Accordingly, members of the Department do not need to secure authorization from the Attorney General to pursue negotiations.

(v) The proposed subpoena generally should be limited to the verification of published information and to such surrounding circumstances as relate to the accuracy of the published information.

(vi) In investigations or prosecutions of unauthorized disclosures of national defense information or of classified information, where the Director of National Intelligence, after consultation with the relevant Department or agency head(s), certifies to the Attorney General the significance of the harm raised by the unauthorized disclosure and that the information disclosed was properly classified and reaffirms the intelligence community's continued support for the investigation or prosecution, the Attorney General may authorize members of the Department, in such investigations, to issue subpoenas to members of the news media. The certification, which the Attorney General should take into account along with other considerations identified in paragraphs (c)(4)(ii) through (viii) of this section, will be sought not more than 30 days prior to the submission of the approval request to the Attorney General.

(vii) Requests should be treated with care to avoid interference with newsgathering activities and to avoid claims of harassment.

(viii) The proposed subpoena should be narrowly drawn. It should be directed at material and relevant information regarding a limited subject matter, should cover a reasonably limited period of time, should avoid requiring production of a large volume of material, and should give reasonable and timely notice of the demand.

(5) Considerations for the Attorney General in determining whether to authorize the use of a subpoena, 2703(d) order, or 3123 order to obtain from third parties the communications records or business records of a member of the news media.

(i) In matters in which a member of the Department determines that a member of the news media is a subject or target of an investigation relating to an offense committed in the course of, or arising out of, newsgathering activities, the member of the Department requesting Attorney General authorization to use a subpoena, 2703(d) order, or 3123 order to obtain from a third party the communications records or business records of a member of the news media shall provide all facts necessary for determinations by the Attorney General regarding both whether the member of the news media is a subject or target of the investigation and whether to authorize the use of such subpoena or order. If the Attorney General determines that the member of the news media is a subject or target of an investigation relating to an offense committed in the course of, or arising out of, newsgathering activities, the Attorney

General's determination regarding the use of the proposed subpoena or order should take into account the principles reflected in paragraph (a) of this section, but need not take into account the considerations identified in paragraphs (c)(5)(ii) through (viii) of this section.

(ii)   (A) In criminal matters, there should be reasonable grounds to believe, based on public information, or information from non-media sources, that a crime has been committed, and that the information sought is essential to the successful investigation or prosecution of that crime. The subpoena or court order should not be used to obtain peripheral, nonessential, cumulative, or speculative information.

(B) In civil matters, there should be reasonable grounds to believe, based on public information, or information from non-media sources, that the information sought is essential to the successful completion of the investigation or litigation in a case of substantial importance. The subpoena should not be used to obtain peripheral, nonessential, cumulative, or speculative information.

(iii) The use of a subpoena or court order to obtain from a third party communications records or business records of a member of the news media should be pursued only after the government has made all reasonable attempts to obtain the information from alternative sources.

(iv)   (A) The government should have pursued negotiations with the affected member of the news media unless the Attorney General determines that, for compelling reasons, such negotiations would pose a clear and substantial threat to the integrity of the investigation, risk grave harm to national security, or present an imminent risk of death or serious bodily harm.

(B) The obligation to pursue negotiations with the affected member of the news media, unless excused by the Attorney General, is not intended to conflict with the requirement that members of the Department secure authorization from the Attorney General to question a member of the news media as set forth in paragraph (f)(1) of this section. Accordingly, members of the Department do not need to secure authorization from the Attorney General to pursue negotiations.

(v) In investigations or prosecutions of unauthorized disclosures of national defense information or of classified information, where the Director of National Intelligence, after consultation with the relevant Department or agency head(s), certifies to the Attorney General the significance of the harm raised by the unauthorized disclosure and that the information disclosed was properly classified and reaffirms the intelligence community's continued support for the investigation or prosecution, the Attorney General may authorize members of the Department, in such investigations, to use subpoenas or court orders issued pursuant to 18 U.S.C. 2703(d) or 3123 to obtain communications records or business records of a member of the news media. The certification, which the Attorney General should take into account along with the other considerations identified in paragraph (c)(5) of this section, will be sought not more than 30 days prior to the submission of the approval request to the Attorney General.

(vi) Requests should be treated with care to avoid interference with newsgathering activities and to avoid claims of harassment.

(vii) The proposed subpoena or court order should be narrowly drawn. It should be directed at material and relevant information regarding a limited subject matter, should cover a reasonably limited period of time, and should avoid requiring production of a large volume of material.

(viii) If appropriate, investigators should propose to use search protocols designed to minimize intrusion into potentially protected materials or newsgathering activities unrelated to the investigation, including but not limited to keyword searches (for electronic searches) and filter teams (reviewing teams separate from the prosecution and investigative teams).

(6) When the Attorney General has authorized the issuance of a subpoena to a member of the news media; or the use of a subpoena, 2703(d) order, or 3123 order to obtain from a third party communications records or business records of a member of the news media, members of the Department must consult with the Criminal Division before moving to compel compliance with any such subpoena or court order.

(d) Applying for warrants to search the premises, property, communications records, or business records of members of the news media.

(1) Except as set forth in paragraph (d)(4) of this section, members of the Department must obtain the authorization of the Attorney General to apply for a warrant to search the premises, property, communications records, or business records of a member of the news media.

(2) All requests for authorization of the Attorney General to apply for a warrant to search the premises, property, communications records,

or business records of a member of the news media must be personally endorsed by the United States Attorney or Assistant Attorney General responsible for the matter.

(3) In determining whether to authorize an application for a warrant to search the premises, property, communications records, or business records of a member of the news media, the Attorney General should take into account the considerations identified in paragraph (c)(5) of this section.

(4) Members of the Department may apply for a warrant to obtain work product materials or other documentary materials of a member of the news media pursuant to the "suspect exception" of the Privacy Protection Act ("PPA suspect exception"), 42 U.S.C. 2000aa(a)(1), (b)(1), when the member of the news media is a subject or target of a criminal investigation for conduct not based on, or within the scope of, newsgathering activities. In such instances, members of the Department must secure authorization from a Deputy Assistant Attorney General for the Criminal Division.

(5) Members of the Department should not be authorized to apply for a warrant to obtain work product materials or other documentary materials of a member of the news media under the PPA suspect exception, 42 U.S.C. 2000aa(a)(1), (b)(1), if the sole purpose is to further the investigation of a person other than the member of the news media.

(6) A Deputy Assistant Attorney General for the Criminal Division may authorize, under an applicable PPA exception, an application for a warrant to search the premises, property, communications records, or business records of an individual other than a member of the news media, but who is reasonably believed to have "a purpose to disseminate to the public a newspaper, book, broadcast, or other similar form of public communication." 42 U.S.C. 2000aa(a), (b).

(7) In executing a warrant authorized by the Attorney General or by a Deputy Assistant Attorney General for the Criminal Division investigators should use search protocols designed to minimize intrusion into potentially protected materials or newsgathering activities unrelated to the investigation, including but not limited to keyword searches (for electronic searches) and filter teams.

(e) Notice to affected member of the news media.

(1) (i) In matters in which the Attorney General has both determined that a member of the news media is a subject or target of an investigation relating to an offense committed in the course of, or arising out of, newsgathering activities, and authorized the use of a subpoena, court order, or warrant to obtain from a third party the communications records or business records of a member of the

news media pursuant to paragraph (c)(4)(i), (c)(5)(i), or (d)(1) of this section, members of the Department are not required to provide notice of the Attorney General's authorization to the affected member of the news media. The Attorney General nevertheless may direct that notice be provided.

(ii) If the Attorney General does not direct that notice be provided, the United States Attorney or Assistant Attorney General responsible for the matter shall provide to the Attorney General every 90 days an update regarding the status of the investigation, which update shall include an assessment of any harm to the investigation that would be caused by providing notice to the affected member of the news media. The Attorney General shall consider such update in determining whether to direct that notice be provided.

(2) (i) Except as set forth in paragraph (e)(1) of this section, when the Attorney General has authorized the use of a subpoena, court order, or warrant to obtain from a third party communications records or business records of a member of the news media, the affected member of the news media shall be given reasonable and timely notice of the Attorney General's determination before the use of the subpoena, court order, or warrant, unless the Attorney General determines that, for compelling reasons, such notice would pose a clear and substantial threat to the integrity of the investigation, risk grave harm to national security, or present an imminent risk of death or serious bodily harm.

(ii) The mere possibility that notice to the affected member of the news media, and potential judicial review, might delay the investigation is not, on its own, a compelling reason to delay notice.

(3) When the Attorney General has authorized the use of a subpoena, court order, or warrant to obtain communications records or business records of a member of the news media, and the affected member of the news media has not been given notice, pursuant to paragraph (e)(2) of this section, of the Attorney General's determination before the use of the subpoena, court order, or warrant, the United States Attorney or Assistant Attorney General responsible for the matter shall provide to the affected member of the news media notice of the order or warrant as soon as it is determined that such notice will no longer pose a clear and substantial threat to the integrity of the investigation, risk grave harm to national security, or present an imminent risk of death or serious bodily harm. In any event, such notice shall occur within 45 days of the government's receipt of any return made pursuant to the subpoena, court order, or warrant, except that the Attorney General may authorize delay of notice for an additional 45 days if he or she determines that, for compelling reasons, such notice would pose a clear and substantial threat to the integrity of the investigation, risk grave

harm to national security, or present an imminent risk of death or serious bodily harm. No further delays may be sought beyond the 90-day period.

(4) The United States Attorney or Assistant Attorney General responsible for the matter shall provide to the Director of the Office of Public Affairs and to the Director of the Criminal Division's Office of Enforcement Operations a copy of any notice to be provided to a member of the news media whose communications records or business records were sought or obtained at least 10 business days before such notice is provided to the affected member of the news media, and immediately after such notice is, in fact, provided to the affected member of the news media.

(f) Questioning, arresting, or charging members of the news media.

(1) No member of the Department shall subject a member of the news media to questioning as to any offense that he or she is suspected of having committed in the course of, or arising out of, newsgathering activities without first providing notice to the Director of the Office of Public Affairs and obtaining the express authorization of the Attorney General. The government need not view the member of the news media as a subject or target of an investigation, or have the intent to prosecute the member of the news media, to trigger the requirement that the Attorney General must authorize such questioning.

(2) No member of the Department shall seek a warrant for an arrest, or conduct an arrest, of a member of the news media for any offense that he or she is suspected of having committed in the course of, or arising out of, newsgathering activities without first providing notice to the Director of the Office of Public Affairs and obtaining the express authorization of the Attorney General.

(3) No member of the Department shall present information to a grand jury seeking a bill of indictment, or file an information, against a member of the news media for any offense that he or she is suspected of having committed in the course of, or arising out of newsgathering activities, without first providing notice to the Director of the Office of Public Affairs and obtaining the express authorization of the Attorney General.

(4) In requesting the Attorney General's authorization to question, to seek an arrest warrant for or to arrest, or to present information to a grand jury seeking an indictment or to file an information against, a member of the news media as provided in paragraphs (f)(1) through (3) of this section, members of the Department shall provide all facts necessary for a determination by the Attorney General.

(5) In determining whether to grant a request for authorization to question, to seek an arrest warrant for or to arrest, or to present information to a grand jury seeking an indictment or to file an information against, a member of the news media, the Attorney General should take into account the considerations reflected in the Statement of Principles in paragraph (a) of this section.

(g) Exigent circumstances.

(1) (i) A Deputy Assistant Attorney General for the Criminal Division may authorize the use of a subpoena or court order, as described in paragraph (c) of this section, or the questioning, arrest, or charging of a member of the news media, as described in paragraph (f) of this section, if he or she determines that the exigent use of such law enforcement tool or technique is necessary to prevent or mitigate an act of terrorism; other acts that are reasonably likely to cause significant and articulable harm to national security; death; kidnapping; substantial bodily harm; conduct that constitutes a specified offense against a minor (for example, as those terms are defined in section 111 of the Adam Walsh Child Protection and Safety Act of 2006, 42 U.S.C. 16911), or an attempt or conspiracy to commit such a criminal offense; or incapacitation or destruction of critical infrastructure (for example, as defined in section 1016(e) of the USA PATRIOT Act, 42 U.S.C. 5195c(e)).

(ii) A Deputy Assistant Attorney General for the Criminal Division may authorize an application for a warrant, as described in paragraph (d) of this section, if there is reason to believe that the immediate seizure of the materials at issue is necessary to prevent the death of, or serious bodily injury to, a human being, as provided in 42 U.S.C. 2000aa(a)(2) and (b)(2).

(2) Within 10 business days of the approval by a Deputy Assistant Attorney General for the Criminal Division of a request under paragraph (g) of this section, the United States Attorney or Assistant Attorney General responsible for the matter shall provide to the Attorney General and to the Director of the Office of Public Affairs a statement containing the information that would have been provided in a request for prior authorization.

(h) Safeguarding. Any information or records obtained from members of the news media or from third parties pursuant to this policy shall be closely held so as to prevent disclosure of the information to unauthorized persons or for improper purposes. Members of the Department should consult the United States Attorneys' Manual for specific guidance regarding the safeguarding of information or records obtained from members of the news media or from third parties pursuant to this policy.

(i) Failure to comply with policy. Failure to obtain the prior approval of the Attorney General, as required by this policy, may constitute grounds for an administrative reprimand or other appropriate disciplinary action.

(j) General provision. This policy is not intended to, and does not, create any right or benefit, substantive or procedural, enforceable at law or in equity by any party against the United States, its departments, agencies, or entities, its officers, employees, or agents, or any other person.

GUIDELINES ON METHODS OF OBTAINING DOCUMENTARY MATERIALS HELD BY THIRD PARTIES
28 C.F.R. Part 59.

§ 59.4 Procedures.[1]

(a) Provisions governing the use of search warrants generally.

(1) A search warrant should not be used to obtain documentary materials believed to be in the private possession of a disinterested third party unless it appears that the use of a subpoena, summons, request, or other less intrusive alternative means of obtaining the materials would substantially jeopardize the availability or usefulness of the materials sought, and the application for the warrant has been authorized as provided in paragraph (a)(2) of this section.

(2) No federal officer or employee shall apply for a warrant to search for and seize documentary materials believed to be in the private possession of a disinterested third party unless the application for the warrant has been authorized by an attorney for the government. Provided, however, that in an emergency situation in which the immediacy of the need to seize the materials does not permit an opportunity to secure the authorization of an attorney for the government, the application may be authorized by a supervisory law enforcement officer in the applicant's department or agency, if the appropriate U.S. Attorney (or where the case is not being handled by a U.S. Attorney's Office, the appropriate supervisory official of the Department of Justice) is notified of the authorization and the basis for justifying such authorization under this part within 24 hours of the authorization.

---

[1] Notwithstanding the provisions of this section, any application for a warrant to search for evidence of a criminal tax offense under the jurisdiction of the Tax Division must be specifically approved in advance by the Tax Division pursuant to section 6-2.330 of the U.S. Attorneys' Manual.

(b) Provisions governing the use of search warrants which may intrude upon professional, confidential relationships.

(1) A search warrant should not be used to obtain documentary materials believed to be in the private possession of a disinterested third party physician,[2] lawyer, or clergyman, under circumstances in which the materials sought, or other materials likely to be reviewed during the execution of the warrant, contain confidential information on patients, clients, or parishioners which was furnished or developed for the purposes of professional counseling or treatment, unless--

(i) It appears that the use of a subpoena, summons, request or other less intrusive alternative means of obtaining the materials would substantially jeopardize the availability or usefulness of the materials sought;

(ii) Access to the documentary materials appears to be of substantial importance to the investigation or prosecution for which they are sought; and

(iii) The application for the warrant has been approved as provided in paragraph (b)(2) of this section.

(2) No federal officer or employee shall apply for a warrant to search for and seize documentary materials believed to be in the private possession of a disinterested third party physician, lawyer, or clergyman under the circumstances described in paragraph (b)(1) of this section, unless, upon the recommendation of the U.S. Attorney (or where a case is not being handled by a U.S. Attorney's Office, upon the recommendation of the appropriate supervisory official of the Department of Justice), an appropriate Deputy Assistant Attorney General has authorized the application for the warrant. Provided, however, that in an emergency situation in which the immediacy of the need to seize the materials does not permit an opportunity to secure the authorization of a Deputy Assistant Attorney General, the application may be authorized by the U.S. Attorney (or where the case is not being handled by a U.S. Attorney's Office, by the appropriate supervisory official of the Department of Justice) if an appropriate Deputy Assistant Attorney General is notified of the authorization and the basis for justifying such authorization under this part within 72 hours of the authorization.

---

[2]Documentary materials created or compiled by a physician, but retained by the physician as a matter of practice at a hospital or clinic shall be deemed to be in the private possession of the physician, unless the clinic or hospital is a suspect in the offense.

(3) Whenever possible, a request for authorization by an appropriate Deputy Assistant Attorney General of a search warrant application pursuant to paragraph (b)(2) of this section shall be made in writing and shall include:

(i) The application for the warrant; and

(ii) A brief description of the facts and circumstances advanced as the basis for recommending authorization of the application under this part.

If a request for authorization of the application is made orally or if, in an emergency situation, the application is authorized by the U.S. Attorney or a supervisory official of the Department of Justice as provided in paragraph (b)(2) of this section, a written record of the request including the materials specified in paragraphs (b)(3)(i) and (ii) of this section shall be transmitted to an appropriate Deputy Assistant Attorney General within 7 days. The Deputy Assistant Attorneys General shall keep a record of the disposition of all requests for authorizations of search warrant applications made under paragraph (b) of this section.

(4) A search warrant authorized under paragraph (b)(2) of this section shall be executed in such a manner as to minimize, to the greatest extent practicable, scrutiny of confidential materials.

(5) Although it is impossible to define the full range of additional doctor- like therapeutic relationships which involve the furnishing or development of private information, the U.S. Attorney (or where a case is not being handled by a U.S. Attorney's Office, the appropriate supervisory official of the Department of Justice) should determine whether a search for documentary materials held by other disinterested third party professionals involved in such relationships (e.g. psychologists or psychiatric social workers or nurses) would implicate the special privacy concerns which are addressed in paragraph (b) of this section. If the U.S. Attorney (or other supervisory official of the Department of Justice) determines that such a search would require review of extremely confidential information furnished or developed for the purposes of professional counseling or treatment, the provisions of this subsection should be applied. Otherwise, at a minimum, the requirements of paragraph (a) of this section must be met.

(c) Considerations bearing on choice of methods. In determining whether, as an alternative to the use of a search warrant, the use of a subpoena or other less intrusive means of obtaining documentary materials would substantially jeopardize the availability or usefulness of the materials sought, the following factors, among others, should be considered:

(1) Whether it appears that the use of a subpoena or other alternative which gives advance notice of the government's interest in obtaining the materials would be likely to result in the destruction, alteration, concealment, or transfer of the materials sought; considerations, among others, bearing on this issue may include:

(i) Whether a suspect has access to the materials sought;

(ii) Whether there is a close relationship of friendship, loyalty, or sympathy between the possessor of the materials and a suspect;

(iii) Whether the possessor of the materials is under the domination or control of a suspect;

(iv) Whether the possessor of the materials has an interest in preventing the disclosure of the materials to the government;

(v) Whether the possessor's willingness to comply with a subpoena or request by the government would be likely to subject him to intimidation or threats of reprisal;

(vi) Whether the possessor of the materials has previously acted to obstruct a criminal investigation or judicial proceeding or refused to comply with or acted in defiance of court orders; or

(vii) Whether the possessor has expressed an intent to destroy, conceal, alter, or transfer the materials;

(2) The immediacy of the government's need to obtain the materials; considerations, among others, bearing on this issue may include:

(i) Whether the immediate seizure of the materials is necessary to prevent injury to persons or property;

(ii) Whether the prompt seizure of the materials is necessary to preserve their evidentiary value;

(iii) Whether delay in obtaining the materials would significantly jeopardize an ongoing investigation or prosecution; or

(iv) Whether a legally enforceable form of process, other than a search warrant, is reasonably available as a means of obtaining the materials.

The fact that the disinterested third party possessing the materials may have grounds to challenge a subpoena or other legal process is not in itself a legitimate basis for the use of a search warrant.

Ethical Standards for
Attorneys for the Government
28 C.F.R., Part 77

§ 77.1 Purpose and authority.

(a) The Department of Justice is committed to ensuring that its attorneys perform their duties in accordance with the highest ethical standards. The purpose of this part is to implement 28 U.S.C. 530B and to provide guidance to attorneys concerning the requirements imposed on Department attorneys by 28 U.S.C. 530B.

(b) Section 530B requires Department attorneys to comply with state and local federal court rules of professional responsibility, but should not be construed in any way to alter federal substantive, procedural, or evidentiary law or to interfere with the Attorney General's authority to send Department attorneys into any court in the United States.

(c) Section 530B imposes on Department attorneys the same rules of professional responsibility that apply to non-Department attorneys, but should not be construed to impose greater burdens on Department attorneys than those on non-Department attorneys or to alter rules of professional responsibility that expressly exempt government attorneys from their application.

(d) The regulations set forth in this part seek to provide guidance to Department attorneys in determining the rules with which such attorneys should comply.

§ 77.2 Definitions.

As used in this part, the following terms shall have the following meanings, unless the context indicates otherwise:

(a) The phrase attorney for the government means the Attorney General; the Deputy Attorney General; the Solicitor General; the Assistant Attorneys General for, and any attorney employed in, the Antitrust Division, Civil Division, Civil Rights Division, Criminal Division, Environment and Natural Resources Division, and Tax Division; the Chief Counsel for the DEA and any attorney employed in that office; the Chief Counsel for ATF and any attorney employed in that office; the General Counsel of the FBI and any attorney employed in that office or in the (Office of General Counsel) of the FBI; any attorney employed in, or head of, any other legal office in a Department of Justice agency; any United States Attorney; any Assistant United States Attorney; any Special Assistant to the Attorney General or Special Attorney duly appointed pursuant to 28 U.S.C. 515; any Special Assistant United States Attorney duly appointed pursuant to 28 U.S.C. 543 who is authorized to conduct criminal or civil law enforcement investigations or proceedings on behalf of the United States; and any other attorney employed by the

Department of Justice who is authorized to conduct criminal or civil law enforcement proceedings on behalf of the United States. The phrase attorney for the government also includes any independent counsel, or employee of such counsel, appointed under chapter 40 of title 28, United States Code. The phrase attorney for the government does not include attorneys employed as investigators or other law enforcement agents by the Department of Justice who are not authorized to represent the United States in criminal or civil law enforcement litigation or to supervise such proceedings.

(b) The term case means any proceeding over which a state or federal court has jurisdiction, including criminal prosecutions and civil actions. This term also includes grand jury investigations and related proceedings (such as motions to quash grand jury subpoenas and motions to compel testimony), applications for search warrants, and applications for electronic surveillance.

(c) The phrase civil law enforcement investigation means an investigation of possible civil violations of, or claims under, federal law that may form the basis for a civil law enforcement proceeding.

(d) The phrase civil law enforcement proceeding means a civil action or proceeding before any court or other tribunal brought by the Department of Justice under the authority of the United States to enforce federal laws or regulations, and includes proceedings related to the enforcement of an administrative subpoena or summons or civil investigative demand.

(e) The terms conduct and activity means any act performed by a Department attorney that implicates a rule governing attorneys, as that term is defined in paragraph (h) of this section.

(f) The phrase Department attorney[s] is synonymous with the phrase "attorney [s] for the government" as defined in this section.

(g) The term person means any individual or organization.

(h) The phrase state laws and rules and local federal court rules governing attorneys means rules enacted or adopted by any State or Territory of the United States or the District of Columbia or by any federal court, that prescribe ethical conduct for attorneys and that would subject an attorney, whether or not a Department attorney, to professional discipline, such as a code of professional responsibility. The phrase does not include:

(1) Any statute, rule, or regulation which does not govern ethical conduct, such as rules of procedure, evidence, or substantive law, whether or not such rule is included in a code of professional responsibility for attorneys;

(2) Any statute, rule, or regulation that purports to govern the conduct of any class of persons other than attorneys, such as rules that govern the conduct of all litigants and judges, as well as attorneys; or

(3) A statute, rule, or regulation requiring licensure or membership in a particular state bar.

(i) The phrase state of licensure means the District of Columbia or any State or Territory where a Department attorney is duly licensed and authorized to practice as an attorney. This term shall be construed in the same manner as it has been construed pursuant to the provisions of Pub.L. 96-132, 93 Stat. 1040, 1044 (1979), and Sec. 102 of the Departments of Commerce, Justice and State, the Judiciary, and Related Agency Appropriations Act, 1999, Pub.L. 105-277.

(j)(1) The phrase where such attorney engages in that attorney's duties identifies which rules of ethical conduct a Department attorney should comply with, and means, with respect to particular conduct:

(i) If there is a case pending, the rules of ethical conduct adopted by the local federal court or state court before which the case is pending; or

(ii) If there is no case pending, the rules of ethical conduct that would be applied by the attorney's state of licensure.

(2) A Department attorney does not "engage[ ] in that attorney's duties" in any states in which the attorney's conduct is not substantial and continuous, such as a jurisdiction in which an attorney takes a deposition (related to a case pending in another court) or directs a contact to be made by an investigative agent, or responds to an inquiry by an investigative agent. Nor does the phrase include any jurisdiction that would not ordinarily apply its rules of ethical conduct to particular conduct or activity by the attorney.

(k) The phrase to the same extent and in the same manner as other attorneys means that Department attorneys shall only be subject to laws and rules of ethical conduct governing attorneys in the same manner as such rules apply to non-Department attorneys. The phrase does not, however, purport to eliminate or otherwise alter state or federal laws and rules and federal court rules that expressly exclude some or all government attorneys from particular limitations or prohibitions.

§ 77.3 Application of 28 U.S.C. 530B.

In all criminal investigations and prosecutions, in all civil investigations and litigation (affirmative and defensive), and in all civil law enforcement investigations and proceedings, attorneys for the government shall conform their conduct and activities to the state rules and laws, and federal local court rules, governing attorneys in each State where such attorney engages in that attorney's duties, to the same extent and in the same manner as other attorneys in that State, as these terms are defined in § 77.2 of this part.

§ 77.4 Guidance.

(a) Rules of the court before which a case is pending. A government attorney shall, in all cases, comply with the rules of ethical conduct of the court before which a particular case is pending.

(b) Inconsistent rules where there is a pending case.

(1) If the rule of the attorney's state of licensure would prohibit an action that is permissible under the rules of the court before which a case is pending, the attorney should consider:

(i) Whether the attorney's state of licensure would apply the rule of the court before which the case is pending, rather than the rule of the state of licensure;

(ii) Whether the local federal court rule preempts contrary state rules; and

(iii) Whether application of traditional choice-of-law principles directs the attorney to comply with a particular rule.

(2) In the process of considering the factors described in paragraph (b)(1) of this section, the attorney is encouraged to consult with a supervisor or Professional Responsibility Officer to determine the best course of conduct.

(c) Choice of rules where there is no pending case.

(1) Where no case is pending, the attorney should generally comply with the ethical rules of the attorney's state of licensure, unless application of traditional choice-of-law principles directs the attorney to comply with the ethical rule of another jurisdiction or court, such as the ethical rule adopted by the court in which the case is likely to be brought.

(2) In the process of considering the factors described in paragraph (c)(1) of this section, the attorney is encouraged to consult with a supervisor or Professional Responsibility Officer to determine the best course of conduct.

(d) Rules that impose an irreconcilable conflict. If, after consideration of traditional choice-of-law principles, the attorney concludes that multiple rules may apply to particular conduct and that such rules impose irreconcilable obligations on the attorney, the attorney should consult with a supervisor or Professional Responsibility Officer to determine the best course of conduct.

(e) Supervisory attorneys. Each attorney, including supervisory attorneys, must assess his or her ethical obligations with respect to particular conduct.

Department attorneys shall not direct any attorney to engage in conduct that violates section 530B. A supervisor or other Department attorney who, in good faith, gives advice or guidance to another Department attorney about the other attorney's ethical obligations should not be deemed to violate these rules.

(f) Investigative Agents. A Department attorney shall not direct an investigative agent acting under the attorney's supervision to engage in conduct under circumstances that would violate the attorney's obligations under section 530B. A Department attorney who in good faith provides legal advice or guidance upon request to an investigative agent should not be deemed to violate these rules.

§ 77.5 No private remedies.

The principles set forth herein, and internal office procedures adopted pursuant hereto, are intended solely for the guidance of attorneys for the government. They are not intended to, do not, and may not be relied upon to create a right or benefit, substantive or procedural, enforceable at law by a party to litigation with the United States, including criminal defendants, targets or subjects of criminal investigations, witnesses in criminal or civil cases (including civil law enforcement proceedings), or plaintiffs or defendants in civil investigations or litigation; or any other person, whether or not a party to litigation with the United States, or their counsel; and shall not be a basis for dismissing criminal or civil charges or proceedings or for excluding relevant evidence in any judicial or administrative proceeding. Nor are any limitations placed on otherwise lawful litigative prerogatives of the Department of Justice as a result of this part.

UNITED STATES ATTORNEY'S MANUAL

Organization and Functions

1-1.100 Purpose

The United States Attorneys' Manual is designed as a quick and ready reference for United States Attorneys, Assistant United States Attorneys, and Department attorneys responsible for the prosecution of violations of federal law. It contains general policies and some procedures relevant to the work of the United States Attorneys' offices and to their relations with the legal divisions, investigative agencies, and other components within the Department of Justice. It is available on the Internet at http://www. justice.gov/usao/eousa/foia_reading_room/usam/.

The Manual provides only internal Department of Justice guidance. It is not intended to, does not, and may not be relied upon to create any rights, substantive or procedural, enforceable at law by any party in any matter civil or criminal. Nor are any limitations hereby placed on otherwise lawful litigative prerogatives of the Department of Justice.

1-1.200 Authority

The United States Attorneys' Manual was prepared under the general supervision of the Attorney General and under the direction of the Deputy Attorney General, by the United States Attorneys, represented by the Attorney General's Advisory Committee of United States Attorneys, the Litigating Divisions, the Executive Office for United States Attorneys, and the Justice Management Division. See A.G. Order 665-76. The Executive Office for United States Attorneys coordinates the periodic revision of the Manual in consultation with the Attorney General, Deputy Attorney General and Associate Attorney General.

This Manual is intended to be comprehensive. When the Manual conflicts with earlier Department statements, except for Attorney General's statements, the Manual will control. Should a situation arise in which a Department policy statement predating the Manual relates to a subject not addressed in the Manual, the prior statement controls, but this situation should be brought to the attention of the Executive Office for United States Attorneys, Manual Staff, Department of Justice, Room 2262, 950 Pennsylvania Avenue, N.W., Washington, D.C. 20530.

1-1.300 Disclosure

The Manual is available on the Internet at http://www.justice.gov /usao/eousa/foia_reading_room/usam/.

1-1.600 Revisions -- Policy (Bluesheets)/Procedures

Substantive changes to the Manual are submitted by the Attorney General, Deputy Attorney General, Associate Attorney General, a litigating division or the Executive Office for United States Attorneys (EOUSA). Substantive changes submitted by an Assistant Attorney General for a litigating division or the Director EOUSA must be reviewed by the Attorney General's Advisory Committee (AGAC) before being incorporated into the Manual. If the AGAC objects to the proposed change, it will meet with the litigating division or EOUSA to resolve. Unresolved issues will be resolved by the Deputy Attorney General or Attorney General. Policy changes issued by the Attorney General, Deputy Attorney General, and Associate Attorney General are effective upon issuance. For guidance in preparing a substantive change, contact the Manual Staff at 202-514-4633.

Clerical changes to the Manual do not require review by the Advisory Committee and can be incorporated directly into the Manual. Clerical changes should be sent to the USAM staff through the Director, EOUSA.

Office of Professional Responsibility

1-4.140 Office of Professional Responsibility Procedures

Preliminary Review. Upon receiving an allegation within its jurisdiction, DOJ OPR shall conduct an immediate preliminary review. DOJ OPR shall open an investigation only if it concludes that further investigation is warranted.

Review of Judicial Findings. If a judge makes a finding of misconduct by a Department employee or requests an inquiry by the Department into possible misconduct, DOJ OPR shall conduct an expedited inquiry without awaiting further judicial or appellate proceedings.

Notification at Conclusion of Investigation. Upon the completion of an investigation, DOJ OPR shall promptly notify the subject of the allegation, the employee's supervisor, and the complainant of the results.

Bad Faith Complaints. If DOJ OPR determines that an allegation made by an attorney was made in bad faith, as a result of gross negligence, or in reckless disregard for the truth, it shall report the complainant's misconduct to the appropriate entity established by the local authorities to handle attorney misconduct.

Former Employees. DOJ OPR shall obtain the approval of the Deputy Attorney General Before declining to investigate or terminate an investigation on the ground that an employee has left the Department. The decision whether to conduct an investigation under such circumstances will be made on a case-by-case basis.

Public Disclosure of OPR Findings. DOJ OPR will determine whether to publish a summary of one of its reports in accordance with a memorandum to OPR from the Deputy Attorney General dated December 13, 1993. For a copy, please contact the Legal Counsel staff at 202-514-4024.

Grand Jury

9-11.150 Subpoenaing Targets of the Investigation

A grand jury may properly subpoena a subject or a target of the investigation and question the target about his or her involvement in the crime under investigation. See United States v. Wong, 431 U.S. 174, 179 n. 8 (1977); United States v. Washington, 431 U.S. 181, 190 n. 6 (1977); United States v. Mandujano, 425 U.S. 564, 573-75 and 584 n. 9 (1976); United States v. Dionisio, 410 U.S. 1, 10 n. 8 (1973). However, in the context of particular cases such a subpoena may carry the appearance of unfairness. Because the potential for misunderstanding is great, before a known "target" (as defined in USAM 9-11.151) is subpoenaed to testify before the grand jury about his or her involvement in the crime under investigation, an effort should be made to secure the target's voluntary appearance. If a voluntary appearance cannot be obtained, the target should be subpoenaed only after the grand jury and the United States A ttorney or the responsible Assistant Attorney General have approved the subpoena. In determining whether to approve a subpoena for a "target," careful attention will be paid to the following considerations:

- The importance to the successful conduct of the grand jury's investigation of the testimony or other information sought;

- Whether the substance of the testimony or other information sought could be provided by other witnesses; and

- Whether the questions the prosecutor and the grand jurors intend to ask or the other information sought would be protected by a valid claim of privilege.

9-11.151 Advice of "Rights" of Grand Jury Witnesses

It is the policy of the Department of Justice to advise a grand jury witness of his or her rights if such witness is a "target" or "subject" of a grand jury investigation. See the Criminal Resource Manual at 160 for a sample target letter.

A "target" is a person as to whom the prosecutor or the grand jury has substantial evidence linking him or her to the commission of a crime and who, in the judgment of the prosecutor, is a putative defendant. An officer or employee of an organization which is a target is not automatically considered a target even if such officer's or employee's conduct contributed to the commission of the crime by the target organization. The same lack of automatic target status holds true for organizations which employ, or employed, an officer or employee who is a target.

A "subject" of an investigation is a person whose conduct is within the scope of the grand jury's investigation.

The Supreme Court declined to decide whether a grand jury witness must be warned of his or her Fifth Amendment privilege against compulsory self-incrimination before the witness's grand jury testimony can be used against the witness. See United States v. Washington, 431 U.S. 181, 186 and 190-191 (1977); United States v. Wong, 431 U.S. 174 (1977); United States v. Mandujano, 425 U.S. 564, 582 n. 7. (1976). In Mandujano the Court took cognizance of the fact that Federal prosecutors customarily warn "targets" of their Fifth Amendment rights before grand jury questioning begins. Similarly, in Washington, the Court pointed to the fact that Fifth Amendment warnings were administered as negating "any possible compulsion to self-incrimination which might otherwise exist" in the grand jury setting. See Washington, at 188.

Notwithstanding the lack of a clear constitutional imperative, it is the policy of the Department that an "Advice of Rights" form be appended to all grand jury subpoenas to be served on any "target" or "subject" of an investigation. See advice of rights below.

In addition, these "warnings" should be given by the prosecutor on the record before the grand jury and the witness should be asked to affirm that the witness understands them.

Although the Court in Washington, supra, held that "targets" of the grand jury's investigation are entitled to no special warnings relative to their status as "potential defendant(s)," the Department of Justice continues its longstanding policy to advise witnesses who are known "targets" of the investigation that their conduct is being investigated for possible violation of Federal criminal law. This supplemental advice of status of the witness as a target should be repeated on the record when the target witness is advised of the matters discussed in the preceding paragraphs.

When a district court insists that the notice of rights not be appended to a grand jury subpoena, the advice of rights may be set forth in a separate letter and mailed to or handed to the witness when the subpoena is served.

Advice of Rights

The grand jury is conducting an investigation of possible violations of Federal criminal laws involving: (State here the general subject matter of inquiry, e.g., conducting an illegal gambling business in violation of 18 U.S.C. § 1955).

•You may refuse to answer any question if a truthful answer to the question would tend to incriminate you.

• Anything that you do say may be used against you by the grand jury or in a subsequent legal proceeding.

• If you have retained counsel, the grand jury will permit you a reasonable opportunity to step outside the grand jury room to consult with counsel if you so desire.

Additional Advice to be Given to Targets: If the witness is a target, the above advice should also contain a supplemental warning that the witness's conduct is being investigated for possible violation of federal criminal law.

160 Sample Target Letter (Criminal Justice Manual)

This letter is supplied to a witness scheduled to appear before the federal Grand Jury in order to provide helpful background information about the Grand Jury. The Grand Jury consists of from sixteen to twenty-three persons from the District of ___. It is their responsibility to inquire into federal crimes which may have been committed in this District.

As a Grand Jury witness you will be asked to testify and answer questions, and to produce records and documents. Only the members of the Grand Jury, attorneys for the United States and a stenographer are permitted in the Grand Jury room while you testify.

We advise you that the Grand Jury is conducting an investigation of possible violations of federal criminal laws involving, but not necessarily limited to *. You are advised that the destruction or alteration of any document required to be produced before the grand jury constitutes serious violation of federal law, including but not limited to Obstruction of Justice.

You are advised that you are a target of the Grand Jury's investigation. You may refuse to answer any question if a truthful answer to the question would tend to incriminate you. Anything that you do or say may be used against you in a subsequent legal proceeding. If you have retained counsel, who represents you personally, the Grand Jury will permit you a reasonable opportunity to step outside the Grand Jury room and confer with counsel if you desire.

9-11.152 Requests by Subjects and Targets to Testify Before the Grand Jury

It is not altogether uncommon for subjects or targets of the grand jury's investigation, particularly in white-collar cases, to request or demand the opportunity to tell the grand jury their side of the story. While the prosecutor has no legal obligation to permit such witnesses to testify, United States v. Leverage Funding System, Inc., 637 F.2d 645 (9th Cir. 1980), cert. denied, 452 U.S. 961 (1981); United States v. Gardner, 516 F.2d 334 (7th Cir. 1975), cert. denied, 423 U.S. 861 (1976)), a refusal to do so can create the appearance of unfairness. Accordingly, under normal circumstances, where no burden upon the grand jury or delay of its proceedings is involved, reasonable requests by a "subject" or "target" of an investigation, as defined above, to testify personally before the grand jury ordinarily should be given favorable consideration, provided that such witness explicitly waives his or her privilege against self-incrimination, on the record before the grand jury, and is represented by counsel or voluntarily and knowingly appears without counsel and consents to full examination under oath.

Such witnesses may wish to supplement their testimony with the testimony of others. The decision whether to accommodate such requests or to reject them after listening to the testimony of the target or the subject, or to seek statements from the suggested witnesses, is a matter left to the sound discretion of the grand jury. When passing on such requests, it must be kept in mind that the grand jury was never intended to be and is not properly either an adversary proceeding or the arbiter of guilt or innocence. See, e.g., United States v. Calandra, 414 U.S. 338, 343 (1974).

9-11.153 Notification of Targets

When a target is not called to testify pursuant to USAM 9-11.150, and does not request to testify on his or her own motion (see USAM 9-11.152), the prosecutor, in appropriate cases, is encouraged to notify such person a reasonable time before seeking an indictment in order to afford him or her an opportunity to testify before the grand jury, subject to the conditions set forth in USAM 9-11.152. Notification would not be appropriate in routine clear cases or when such action might jeopardize the investigation or prosecution because of the likelihood of flight, destruction or fabrication of evidence, endangerment of other witnesses, undue delay or otherwise would be inconsistent with the ends of justice.

9-11.154 Advance Assertions of an Intention to Claim the Fifth Amendment Privilege Against Compulsory Self-Incrimination

A question frequently faced by Federal prosecutors is how to respond to an assertion by a prospective grand jury witness that if called to testify the witness will refuse to testify on Fifth Amendment grounds. If a "target" of the investigation and his or her attorney state in a writing, signed by both, that the "target" will refuse to testify on Fifth Amendment grounds, the witness ordinarily should be excused from testifying unless the grand jury and the United States Attorney agree to insist on the appearance. In determining the desirability of insisting on the appearance of such a person, consideration should be given to the factors which justified the subpoena in the first place, i.e., the importance of the testimony or other information sought, its unavailability from other sources, and the applicability of the Fifth Amendment privilege to the likely areas of inquiry.

Some argue that unless the prosecutor is prepared to seek an order pursuant to 18 U.S.C. § 6003, the witness should be excused from testifying. However, such a broad rule would be improper and make it too convenient for witnesses to avoid testifying truthfully to their knowledge of relevant facts. Moreover, once compelled to appear, the witness may be willing and able to answer some or all of the grand jury's questions without incriminating himself or herself.

9-11.155 Notification to Targets when Target Status Ends

The United States Attorney has the discretion to notify an individual, who has been the target of a grand jury investigation, that the individual is no longer considered to be a target by the United States Attorney's Office. Such a notification should be provided only by the United States Attorney having cognizance over the grand jury investigation.

Discontinuation of target status may be appropriate when:

• The target previously has been notified by the government that he or she was a target of the investigation; and,

• The criminal investigation involving the target has been discontinued without an indictment being returned charging the target, or the government receives evidence in a continuing investigation that conclusively establishes that target status has ended as to this individual.

• The target previously has been notified by the government that he or she was a target of the investigation; and,

The criminal investigation involving the target has been discontinued without an indictment being returned charging the target, or the government receives evidence in a continuing investigation that conclusively establishes that target status has ended as to this individual.

The United States Attorney may decline to issue such notification if the notification would adversely affect the integrity of the investigation or the grand jury process, or for other appropriate reasons. No explanation need be provided for declining such a request.

If the United States Attorney concludes that the notification is appropriate, the language of the notification may be tailored to the particular case. In a particular case, for example, the language of the notification may be drafted to preclude the target from using the notification as a "clean bill of health" or testimonial.

The delivering of such a notification to a target or the attorney for the target shall not preclude the United States Attorney's Office or the grand jury having cognizance over the investigation (or any other grand jury) from reinstituting such an investigation without notification to the target, or the attorney for the target, if, in the opinion of that or any other grand jury, or any United States Attorney's Office, circumstances warrant such a reinstitution.

9-11.160 Limitation on Resubpoenaing Contumacious Witnesses Before Successive Grand Juries

Witnesses who refuse to answer questions properly put to them by the grand jury may be held in contempt and either fined or imprisoned until they comply with the directions of the grand jury. The contempt may extend for the life of the grand jury.

While the Supreme Court in Shillitani v. United States, 384 U.S. 364, 371 n. 8 (1963), appears to approve the reimposition of civil contempt sanctions in successive grand juries, it is the policy of the Department of Justice generally not to resubpoena a contumacious witness before successive grand juries for the purpose of instituting further contempt proceedings. Resubpoenaing a contumacious witness may be justified in certain circumstances, however, such as when the questions to be asked the witness relate to matters not covered in the previous proceedings or when there is an indication from the witness or the witness's counsel that the witness will testify if called before the new grand jury. If the prosecutor believes that the witness possesses information essential to the investigation, resubpoenaing the witness may also be justified when the witness himself or herself is involved to a significant degree in the criminality about which the witness can testify. Prio r authorization must be obtained from the Assistant Attorney General, Criminal Division, to resubpoena a witness before the successive grand jury as well as to seek civil contempt sanctions should the witness persist in his or her refusal to testify. To obtain approval, the prosecutor must show either: (a) that the witness is prepared to testify; or (b) that the appearance of the witness is justified since the witness possesses information essential to the investigation.

If the grand jury's term is about to expire, the Department recommends that a subpoena ordinarily should not be issued to a witness who has advised the prosecutor that he or she will refuse to testify before such grand jury. The coercive effect of a civil contempt adjudication is substantially diluted if a grand jury is approaching its expiration date. This is a matter within the discretion of the United States Attorney and there may well be situations when it is necessary to subpoena a witness and institute contempt proceedings for recalcitrance in such circumstances. In most situations, however, it would seem preferable to subpoena the witness before a new grand jury.

9-11.233 Presentation of Exculpatory Evidence

In United States v. Williams, 112 S.Ct. 1735 (1992), the Supreme Court held that the Federal courts' supervisory powers over the grand jury did not include the power to make a rule allowing the dismissal of an otherwise valid indictment where the prosecutor failed to introduce substantial exculpatory evidence to a grand jury. It is the policy of the Department of Justice, however, that when a prosecutor conducting a grand jury inquiry is personally aware of substantial evidence that directly negates the guilt of a subject of the investigation, the prosecutor must present or otherwise disclose such evidence to the grand jury before seeking an indictment against such a person. While a failure to follow the Department's policy should not result in dismissal of an indictment, appellate courts may refer violations of the policy to the Office of Professional Responsibility for review.

9-11.255 Prior Department of Justice Approval Requirements -- Grand Jury Subpoenas to Lawyers and Members of the News Media

Prior approval of the Assistant Attorney General of the Criminal Division is required before a grand jury subpoena may be issued to an attorney for information relating to the representation of a client or the fees paid by such client. See USAM 9-13.410.

Prior approval of the Attorney General is required before a grand jury subpoena may be issued to members of the news media for information relating to the news gathering function. See 28 C.F.R. § 50.10(e); USAM 9-13.400. However, such approval is not required if the news media organization has expressly agreed to provide the subpoenaed materials which have been previously published or broadcast and the United States Attorney or responsible Assistant Attorney General is satisfied that the requirements of 28 C.F.R. § 50.10 have been satisfied.

Obtaining Evidence

9-13.400 News Media Subpoenas -- Subpoenas for News Media Telephone Toll Records -- Interrogation, Indictment, or Arrest of Members of the News Media

In recognition of the importance of freedom of the press to a free and democratic society, it is the Department's policy that the prosecutorial power of the Government should not be used in such a way that it impairs a reporter's responsibility to cover as broadly as possible controversial public issues. Accordingly, Government attorneys should ordinarily refrain from imposing upon members of the news media forms of compulsory process which might impair the news gathering function. In all cases, members of the Department must balance the public's interest in the free dissemination of ideas and information with the public's interest in effective law enforcement and the fair administration of justice. The policies, procedures and standards governing the issuance of subpoenas to members of the news media, subpoenas for the telephone toll records of members of the news media, and the interrogation, indictment, or arrest of members of the news media are set forth in 28 C.F.R. § 50.10.

The Attorney General's authorization is normally required before the issuance of any subpoena to a member of the news media or for the telephone toll records of a member of the news media. However, in those cases where the media member or his or her representative agrees to provide the material sought and that material has been published or broadcast, the United States Attorney or the responsible Assistant Attorney General may authorize issuance of the subpoena, thereafter submitting a report to the Office of Public Affairs detailing the circumstances surrounding the issuance of the subpoena. 28 C.F.R. § 50(e).

Before considering issuing a subpoena to a member of the news media, or for telephone toll records of a member of the news media, Department attorneys should take all reasonable steps to attempt to obtain the information through alternative sources or means. 28 C.F.R. § 50.10(b). In addition, Department attorneys contemplating issuing a subpoena to a member of the news media must first attempt negotiations with the media aimed at accommodating the interests of the trial or grand jury with the interests of the media. 28 C.F.R. § 50.10(c). Negotiations with the affected media member must also precede any request to subpoena the telephone toll records of any member of the news media, so long as the responsible Assistant Attorney General determines that such negotiations would not pose a substantial threat to the investigation at issue. 28 C.F.R. § 50.10(d).

Department attorneys seeking the Attorney General's authorization to issue a subpoena to a member of the news media, or for telephone toll records of a media member, must submit a written request summarizing the facts of the prosecution or investigation, explaining the essentiality of the information sought to the investigation or prosecution, describing attempts to obtain the voluntary cooperation of the news media through negotiation and explaining how the proposed subpoena will be fashioned as narrowly as possible to obtain the necessary information in a manner as minimally intrusive and burdensome as possible. Specific principles applicable to authorization requests for subpoenas to members of the news media are set forth in 28 C.F.R. § 50.10(f)(1)-(6), and for subpoenas for telephone toll records of members of the news media in 28 C.F.R. § 50.10(g)(1)-(4). The Department considers the requirements of 28 C.F.R. § 50.10 applicable to the issuance of subpoenas for the journalistic materials and telephone toll records of deceased journalists.

Except in cases involving exigent circumstances, Department attorneys must also obtain the express approval of the Attorney General prior to the interrogation or arrest of a member of the news media for an offense which he or she is suspected of having committed during the course of, or arising out of, his or her coverage or investigation of a news story, or while he or she was engaged in the performance of his or her official duties as a member of the news media. The Attorney General's authorization must also precede the presentment of an indictment to a grand jury or the filing of an information against a member of the news media for any such offense. 28 C.F.R. § 50.10(h)-(l).

In cases or matters under the supervision of the Criminal Division, any request for the Attorney General's authorization pursuant to 28 C.F.R. § 50.10, and any related questions or concerns, should be directed to the Policy and Statutory Enforcement Unit of the Office of Enforcement Operations. See the form in the Criminal Resource Manual at 299. In cases or matters under the supervision of other Divisions of the Department of Justice, the appropriate Division should be contacted.

In light of the intent of the regulation to protect freedom of the press, news gathering functions, and news media sources, the requirements of 28 C.F.R. § 50.10 do not apply to demands for purely commercial or financial information unrelated to the news gathering function. 28 C.F.R. § 50.10(m).

9-13.410 Guidelines for Issuing Grand Jury or Trial Subpoena to Attorneys for Information Relating to the Representation of Clients

A. *Clearance with the Criminal Division.* Because of the potential effects upon an attorney-client relationship that may result from the issuance of a subpoena to an attorney for information relating to the attorney's representation of a client, the Department exercises close control over such subpoenas. Such subpoenas (for both criminal and civil matters) must first be authorized by the Assistant Attorney General for the Criminal Division before they may issue, unless the information sought falls into one of the exceptions set forth below. Unless one of the specified exceptions applies, authorization must be obtained even for a "friendly subpoena" for client-related information, that is, even in situations where the attorney witness is willing to provide the information but requests the formality of a subpoena.

B. *Preliminary Steps.* When determining whether to issue a subpoena to an attorney for information relating to the attorney's representation of a client, the Assistant United States Attorney must strike a balance between an individual's right to the effective assistance of counsel and the public's interest in the fair administration of justice and effective law enforcement. To that end, all reasonable attempts shall be made to obtain the information from alternative sources before issuing the subpoena to the attorney, unless such efforts would compromise the investigation or case. These attempts shall include reasonable efforts to first obtain the information voluntarily from the attorney, unless such efforts would compromise the investigation or case, or would impair the ability to subpoena the information from the attorney in the event that the attempt to obtain the information voluntarily proves unsuccessful.

C. *Evaluation of the Request.* In considering a request to approve the issuance of a subpoena to an attorney for information relating to the representation of a client, the Assistant Attorney General of the Criminal Division applies the following principles:

- The information sought shall not be protected by a valid claim of privilege.

- All reasonable attempts to obtain the information from alternative sources shall have proved to be unsuccessful.

- In a criminal investigation or prosecution, there must be reasonable grounds to believe that a crime has been or is being committed, and that the information sought is reasonably needed for the successful completion of the investigation or prosecution. The subpoena must not be used to obtain peripheral or speculative information.

- In a civil case, there must be reasonable grounds to believe that the information sought is reasonably necessary to the successful completion of the litigation.

- The need for the information must outweigh the potential adverse effects upon the attorney-client relationship. In particular, the need for the information must outweigh the risk that the attorney may be disqualified from representation of the client as a result of having to testify against the client.

- The subpoena shall be narrowly drawn and directed at material information regarding a limited subject matter and shall cover a reasonable, limited period of time.

D. *Common Factual Settings Outside of the Authorization Requirement.* The authorization requirement applies only to proposed subpoenas to attorneys for testimony or documents relating to the attorney's representation of a client, and not to all subpoenas involving attorneys. For example:

- A subpoena directed to a bank for the records of an attorney's trust account does not require authorization because the subpoena is not directed to the attorney, and the information maintained at the bank is not a privileged attorney- client communication.

- While a subpoena which seeks client billing records requires authorization, a subpoena which seeks internal law office business documents (pay records of law office employees, law firm tax returns, etc.) does not, because it relates to the day-to-day business operations of the law firm, and not to the representation of a client.

- A subpoena seeking information regarding the attorney's personal activities, and not regarding his/her representation of a client, does not require authorization.

• A subpoena which seeks corporate business information, and which is directed to an attorney who serves as a corporate officer, does not require authorization. To make clear that the attorney is being subpoenaed in his/her capacity as a corporate officer, and that no attorney-client information is being sought, the subpoena should be addressed to "John Doe, in his capacity as secretary of the XYZ Corporation."

E. *Exceptions to the Authorization Requirement.* Authorization is not required where the contemplated subpoena is limited to seeking one or more of the following categories of information, since such subpoenas do not raise concerns regarding the potential application of the attorney-client privilege or the potential for negative impact upon the attorney-client relationship:

1. records of property transactions, including real estate closing statements, sales contracts, and payment records;

2. publicly filed documents, including bankruptcy records, unavailable from other sources;

3. testimony or documents necessary to respond to a claim of ineffective assistance of counsel, including, but not limited to, petitions filed pursuant to 28 U.S.C. § 2255 and D.C. Code § 23-110; and

4. materials within the scope of an explicit and unchallenged waiver by the attorney's client.

F. *Submitting the Request.* Requests for authorization should be submitted to the Policy and Statutory Enforcement Unit (PSEU), Office of Enforcement Operations, Criminal Division, through the form set out in the Criminal Resource Manual at 264. When documents are sought in addition to the testimony of the attorney witness, a draft of the subpoena duces tecum, listing the documents sought, must accompany the completed form. Send the completed auto-email form and draft subpoena by email to PSEU@usdoj.gov or, if email is unavailable, fax it to (202) 305-0562.

G. *No Rights Created by Guidelines*: These guidelines are set forth solely for the purpose of internal Department of Justice guidance. They are not intended to, do not, and may not be relied upon to create any rights, substantive or procedural, enforceable at law by any party in any matter, civil or criminal, nor do they place any limitations on otherwise lawful investigative or litigative prerogatives of the Department of Justice.

9-13.420 Searches of Premises of Subject Attorneys

NOTE: For purposes of this policy only, "subject" includes an attorney who is a "suspect, subject or target," or an attorney who is related by blood or marriage to a suspect, or who is believed to be in possession of contraband or the fruits or instrumentalities of a crime. This policy also applies to searches of business organizations where such searches involve materials in the possession of individuals serving in the capacity of legal advisor to the organization. Search warrants for "documentary materials" held by an attorney who is a "disinterested third party" (that is, any attorney who is not a subject) are governed by 28 C.F.R. 59.4 and USAM 9-19.221 et seq. See also 42 U.S.C. Section 2000aa-11(a)(3).

There are occasions when effective law enforcement may require the issuance of a search warrant for the premises of an attorney who is a subject of an investigation, and who also is or may be engaged in the practice of law on behalf of clients. Because of the potential effects of this type of search on legitimate attorney-client relationships and because of the possibility that, during such a search, the government may encounter material protected by a legitimate claim of privilege, it is important that close control be exercised over this type of search. Therefore, the following guidelines should be followed with respect to such searches:

A. *Alternatives to Search Warrants*. In order to avoid impinging on valid attorney-client relationships, prosecutors are expected to take the least intrusive approach consistent with vigorous and effective law enforcement when evidence is sought from an attorney actively engaged in the practice of law. Consideration should be given to obtaining information from other sources or through the use of a subpoena, unless such efforts could compromise the criminal investigation or prosecution, or could result in the obstruction or destruction of evidence, or would otherwise be ineffective.

> NOTE: Prior approval must be obtained from the Assistant Attorney General for the Criminal Division to issue a subpoena to an attorney relating to the representation of a client. See USAM 9-13.410.

B. *Authorization by United States Attorney or Assistant Attorney General*. No application for such a search warrant may be made to a court without the express approval of the United States Attorney or pertinent Assistant Attorney General. Ordinarily, authorization of an application for such a search warrant is appropriate when there is a strong need for the information or material and less intrusive means have been considered and rejected.

C. *Prior Consultation*. In addition to obtaining approval from the United States Attorney or the pertinent Assistant Attorney General, and before seeking judicial authorization for the search warrant, the federal prosecutor must consult with the Criminal Division.

> NOTE: Attorneys are encouraged to consult with the Criminal Division as early as possible regarding a possible search of an attorney's office. Telephone No. (202) 305-4023; Fax No. (202) 305-0562.

To facilitate the consultation, the prosecutor should submit the attached form (see Criminal Resource Manual at 265) containing relevant information about the proposed search along with a draft copy of the proposed search warrant, affidavit in support thereof, and any special instructions to the searching agents regarding search procedures and procedures to be followed to ensure that the prosecution team is not "tainted" by any privileged material inadvertently seized during the search. This information should be submitted to the Criminal Division through the Office of Enforcement Operations. This procedure does not preclude any United States Attorney or Assistant Attorney General from discussing the matter personally with the Assistant Attorney General of the Criminal Division.

If exigent circumstances prevent such prior consultation, the Criminal Division should be notified of the search as promptly as possible. In all cases, the Criminal Division should be provided as promptly as possible with a copy of the judicially authorized search warrant, search warrant affidavit, and any special instructions to the searching agents.

The Criminal Division is committed to ensuring that consultation regarding attorney search warrant requests will not delay investigations. Timely processing will be assisted if the Criminal Division is provided as much information about the search as early as possible. The Criminal Division should also be informed of any deadlines.

D. *Safeguarding Procedures and Contents of the Affidavit.* Procedures should be designed to ensure that privileged materials are not improperly viewed, seized or retained during the course of the search. While the procedures to be followed should be tailored to the facts of each case and the requirements and judicial preferences and precedents of each district, in all cases a prosecutor must employ adequate precautions to ensure that the materials are reviewed for privilege claims and that any privileged documents are returned to the attorney from whom they were seized.

E. *Conducting the Search.* The search warrant should be drawn as specifically as possible, consistent with the requirements of the investigation, to minimize the need to search and review privileged material to which no exception applies.

While every effort should be made to avoid viewing privileged material, the search may require limited review of arguably privileged material to ascertain whether the material is covered by the warrant. Therefore, to protect the attorney-client privilege and to ensure that the investigation is not compromised by exposure to privileged material relating to the investigation or to defense strategy, a "privilege team" should be designated, consisting of agents and lawyers not involved in the underlying investigation.

Instructions should be given and thoroughly discussed with the privilege team prior to the search. The instructions should set forth procedures designed to minimize the intrusion into privileged material, and should ensure that the privilege team does not disclose any information to the investigation/prosecution team unless and until so instructed by the attorney in charge of the privilege team. Privilege team lawyers should be available either on or off-site, to advise the agents during the course of the search, but should not participate in the search itself.

The affidavit in support of the search warrant may attach any written instructions or, at a minimum, should generally state the government's intention to employ procedures designed to ensure that attorney-client privileges are not violated.

If it is anticipated that computers will be searched or seized, prosecutors are expected to follow the procedures set forth in the current edition of Searching and Seizing Computers, published by CCIPS.

F. *Review Procedures*. The following review procedures should be discussed prior to approval of any warrant, consistent with the practice in your district, the circumstances of the investigation and the volume of materials seized.

• Who will conduct the review, i.e., a privilege team, a judicial officer, or a special master.

• Whether all documents will be submitted to a judicial officer or special master or only those which a privilege team has determined to be arguably privileged or arguably subject to an exception to the privilege.

• Whether copies of all seized materials will be provided to the subject attorney (or a legal representative) in order that: a) disruption of the law firm's operation is minimized; and b) the subject is afforded an opportunity to participate in the process of submitting disputed documents to the court by raising specific claims of privilege. To the extent possible, providing copies of seized records is encouraged, where such disclosure will not impede or obstruct the investigation.

• Whether appropriate arrangements have been made for storage and handling of electronic evidence and procedures developed for searching computer data (i.e., procedures which recognize the universal nature of computer seizure and are designed to avoid review of materials implicating the privilege of innocent clients).

These guidelines are set forth solely for the purpose of internal Department of Justice guidance. They are not intended to, do not, and may not be relied upon to create any rights, substantive or procedural, enforceable at law by any party in any matter, civil or criminal, nor do they place any limitations on otherwise lawful investigative or litigative prerogatives of the Department of Justice.

Witness Immunity

9-23.210 Decision to Request Immunity -- The Public Interest

Section 6003(b) of Title 18, United States Code, authorizes a United States Attorney to request immunity when, in his/her judgment, the testimony or other information that is expected to be obtained from the witness "may be necessary to the public interest." Some of the factors that should be weighed in making this judgment include:

A. The importance of the investigation or prosecution to effective enforcement of the criminal laws;

B. The value of the person's testimony or information to the investigation or prosecution;

C. The likelihood of prompt and full compliance with a compulsion order, and the effectiveness of available sanctions if there is no such compliance;

D. The person's relative culpability in connection with the offense or offenses being investigated or prosecuted, and his or her criminal history;

E. The possibility of successfully prosecuting the person prior to compelling his or her testimony;

F. The likelihood of adverse collateral consequences to the person if he or she testifies under a compulsion order.

These factors are not intended to be all-inclusive or to require a particular decision in a particular case. They are, however, representative of the kinds of factors that should be considered when deciding whether to seek immunity.

9-23.211 Decision to Request Immunity -- Close-Family Exception

When determining whether to request immunity for a witness, consideration should be given to whether the witness is a close family relative of the person against whom the testimony is sought. A close family relative is a spouse, parent, child, grandparent, grandchild or sibling of the witness. Absent specific justification, the Department will ordinarily avoid seeking to compel the testimony of a witness who is a close family relative of the defendant on trial or of the person upon whose conduct grand jury scrutiny is focusing. Such specific justification exists, among other circumstances, where (i) the witness and the relative participated in a common business enterprise and the testimony to be elicited relates to that enterprise or its activities; (ii) the testimony to be elicited relates to illegal conduct in which there is reason to believe that both the witness and the relative were active participants; or (iii) testimony to be elicited relates to a crime involving overriding prosecutorial concerns.

9-23.212 Decision to Request Immunity -- Conviction Prior to Compulsion

It is preferable as a matter of policy to punish offenders for their criminal conduct prior to compelling them to testify. While this is not feasible in all cases, a successful prosecution of the witness, or obtaining a plea of guilty to at least some of the charges against the witness, will avoid or mitigate arguments of co-defendants made to the court or jury that the witness "cut a deal" with the government to avoid the witness's own conviction and punishment.

9-23.214 Granting Immunity to Compel Testimony on Behalf of a Defendant

As a matter of policy, 18 U.S.C. § 6002 will not be used to compel the production of testimony or other information on behalf of a defendant except in extraordinary circumstances where the defendant plainly would be deprived of a fair trial without such testimony or other information. This policy is not intended to preclude compelling a defense witness to testify if the prosecutor believes that to do so is necessary to a successful prosecution.

9-23.250 Immunity for the Act of Producing Records

The Supreme Court has interpreted the Fifth Amendment privilege against self-incrimination to include the act of producing business records of a sole proprietorship. United States v. Doe, 465 U.S. 605 (1984). The act of producing records concedes the existence and possession of the records called for by the subpoena as well as the respondent's belief that such records are those described in the subpoena. Requests for immunity for the limited purpose of obtaining records pursuant to Doe should clearly state this fact in the application.

The same letter of authority is issued by DOJ for the production of records as for testimony. See the Criminal Resource Manual at 722 (Letter of Authority). Therefore, prosecutors should draft the court order to clearly limit the grant of immunity to the act of producing records pursuant to Doe, supra.

9-23.400 Authorization to Prosecute after Compulsion

After a person has testified or provided information pursuant to a compulsion order--except in the case of act-of-production immunity--an attorney for the government shall not initiate or recommend prosecution of the person for an offense or offenses first disclosed in, or closely related to, such testimony or information without the express written authorization of the Attorney General. Such requests for authorization should be sent to the Assistant Attorney General for the division that issued the letter of authority for requesting the original compulsion order.

The request to prosecute should indicate the circumstances justifying prosecution and the method by which the government will be able to establish that the evidence it will use against the witness will meet the government's burden under Kastigar v. United States, 406 U.S. 441 (1972).

Principles of Federal Prosecution

9-27.220 Grounds for Commencing or Declining Prosecution

The attorney for the government should commence or recommend Federal prosecution if he/she believes that the person's conduct constitutes a Federal offense and that the admissible evidence will probably be sufficient to obtain and sustain a conviction, unless, in his/her judgment, prosecution should be declined because:

1. No substantial Federal interest would be served by prosecution;

2. The person is subject to effective prosecution in another jurisdiction; or

3. There exists an adequate non-criminal alternative to prosecution.

Comment. USAM 9-27.220 expresses the principle that, ordinarily, the attorney for the government should initiate or recommend Federal prosecution if he/she believes that the person's conduct constitutes a Federal offense and that the admissible evidence probably will be sufficient to obtain and sustain a conviction. Evidence sufficient to sustain a conviction is required under Rule 29(a), Fed. R. Crim. P., to avoid a judgment of acquittal. Moreover, both as a matter of fundamental fairness and in the interest of the efficient administration of justice, no prosecution should be initiated against any person unless the government believes that the person probably will be found guilty by an unbiased trier of fact. In this connection, it should be noted that, when deciding whether to prosecute, the government attorney need not have in hand all the evidence upon which he/she intends to rely at trial: it is sufficient that he/she have a reasonable be lief that such evidence will be available and admissible at the time of trial. Thus, for example, it would be proper to commence a prosecution though a key witness is out of the country, so long as the witness's presence at trial could be expected with reasonable certainty.

The potential that--despite the law and the facts that create a sound, prosecutable case--the factfinder is likely to acquit the defendant because of the unpopularity of some factor involved in the prosecution or because of the overwhelming popularity of the defendant or his/her cause, is not a factor prohibiting prosecution. For example, in a civil rights case or a case involving an extremely popular political figure, it might be clear that the evidence of guilt--viewed objectively by an unbiased factfinder--would be sufficient to obtain and sustain a conviction, yet the prosecutor might reasonably doubt whether the jury would convict. In such a case, despite his/her negative assessment of the likelihood of a guilty verdict (based on factors extraneous to an objective view of the law and the facts), the prosecutor may properly conclude that it is necessary and desirable to commence or recommend prosecution and allow the criminal process to operate in accordance with its principles.

Merely because the attorney for the government believes that a person's conduct constitutes a Federal offense and that the admissible evidence will be sufficient to obtain and sustain a conviction, does not mean that he/she necessarily should initiate or recommend prosecution: USAM 9-27.220 notes three situations in which the prosecutor may property decline to take action nonetheless: when no substantial Federal interest would be served by prosecution; when the person is subject to effective prosecution in another jurisdiction; and when there exists an adequate non-criminal alternative to prosecution. It is left to the judgment of the attorney for the government whether such a situation exists. In exercising that judgment, the attorney for the government should consult USAM 9-27.230, 9-27.240, or 9-27.250, as appropriate.

9-27.230 Initiating and Declining Charges -- Substantial Federal Interest

A. In determining whether prosecution should be declined because no substantial Federal interest would be served by prosecution, the attorney for the government should weigh all relevant considerations, including:

1. Federal law enforcement priorities;

2. The nature and seriousness of the offense;

3. The deterrent effect of prosecution;

4. The person's culpability in connection with the offense;

5. The person's history with respect to criminal activity;

6. The person's willingness to cooperate in the investigation or prosecution of others; and

7. The probable sentence or other consequences if the person is convicted.

B. *Comment.* USAM 9-27.230 lists factors that may be relevant in determining whether prosecution should be declined because no substantial Federal interest would be served by prosecution in a case in which the person is believed to have committed a Federal offense and the admissible evidence is expected to be sufficient to obtain and sustain a conviction. The list of relevant considerations is not intended to be all-inclusive. Obviously, not all of the factors will be applicable to every case, and in any particular case one factor may deserve more weight than it might in another case.

1. *Federal Law Enforcement Priorities.* Federal law enforcement resources and Federal judicial resources are not sufficient to permit prosecution of every alleged offense over which Federal jurisdiction exists. Accordingly, in the interest of allocating its limited resources so as to achieve an effective nationwide law enforcement program, from time to time the Department establishes national investigative and prosecutorial priorities. These priorities are designed to focus Federal law enforcement efforts on those matters within the Federal jurisdiction that are most deserving of Federal attention and are most likely to be handled effectively at the Federal level. In addition, individual United States Attorneys may establish their own priorities, within the national priorities, in order to concentrate their resources on problems of particular local or regional significance. In weighing the Federal interest in a particular prosecution, the attorney for the government s hould give careful consideration to the extent to which prosecution would accord with established priorities.

2. *Nature and Seriousness of Offense.* It is important that limited Federal resources not be wasted in prosecuting inconsequential cases or cases in which the violation is only technical. Thus, in determining whether a substantial Federal interest exists that requires prosecution, the attorney for the government should consider the nature and seriousness of the offense involved. A number of factors may be relevant. One factor that is obviously of primary importance is the actual or potential impact of the offense on the community and on the victim.

The impact of an offense on the community in which it is committed can be measured in several ways: in terms of economic harm done to community interests; in terms of physical danger to the citizens or damage to public property; and in terms of erosion of the inhabitants' peace of mind and sense of security. In assessing the seriousness of the offense in these terms, the prosecutor may properly weigh such questions as whether the violation is technical or relatively inconsequential in nature and what the public attitude is toward prosecution under the circumstances of the case. The public may be indifferent, or even opposed, to enforcement of the controlling statute whether on substantive grounds, or because of a history of nonenforcement, or because the offense involves essentially a minor matter of private concern and the victim is not interested in having it pursued. On the other hand, the nature and circumstances of the offense, the identity of the offender or the victim, or t he attendant publicity, may be such as to create strong public sentiment in favor of prosecution. While public interest, or lack thereof, deserves the prosecutor's careful attention, it should not be used to justify a decision to prosecute, or to take other action, that cannot be supported on other grounds. Public and professional responsibility sometimes will require the choosing of a particularly unpopular course.

Economic, physical, and psychological considerations are also important in assessing the impact of the offense on the victim. In this connection, it is appropriate for the prosecutor to take into account such matters as the victim's age or health, and whether full or partial restitution has been made. Care should be taken in weighing the matter of restitution, however, to ensure against contributing to an impression that an offender can escape prosecution merely by returning the spoils of his/her crime.

3. *Deterrent Effect of Prosecution*. Deterrence of criminal conduct, whether it be criminal activity generally or a specific type of criminal conduct, is one of the primary goals of the criminal law. This purpose should be kept in mind, particularly when deciding whether a prosecution is warranted for an offense that appears to be relatively minor; some offenses, although seemingly not of great importance by themselves, if commonly committed would have a substantial cumulative impact on the community.

4. *The Person's Culpability*. Although the prosecutor has sufficient evidence of guilt, it is nevertheless appropriate for him/her to give consideration to the degree of the person's culpability in connection with the offenses, both in the abstract and in comparison with any others involved in the offense. If for example, the person was a relatively minor participant in a criminal enterprise conducted by others, or his/her motive was worthy, and no other circumstances require prosecution, the prosecutor might reasonably conclude that some course other than prosecution would be appropriate.

5. *The Person's Criminal History*. If a person is known to have a prior conviction or is reasonably believed to have engaged in criminal activity at an earlier time, this should, be considered in determining whether to initiate or recommend Federal prosecution. In this connection particular attention should be given to the nature of the person's prior criminal involvement, when it occurred, its relationship if any to the present offense, and whether he/she previously avoided prosecution as a result of an agreement not to prosecute in return for cooperation or as a result of an order compelling his/her testimony. By the same token, a person's lack of prior criminal involvement or his/her previous cooperation with the law enforcement officials should be given due consideration in appropriate cases.

6. *The Person's Willingness to Cooperate*. A person's willingness to cooperate in the investigation or prosecution of others is another appropriate consideration in the determination whether a Federal

prosecution should be undertaken. Generally speaking, a willingness to cooperate should not by itself relieve a person of criminal liability. There may be some cases, however, in which the value of a person's cooperation clearly outweighs the Federal interest in prosecuting him/her. These matters are discussed more fully below, in connection with plea agreements and non-prosecution agreements in return for cooperation.

7. *The Person's Personal Circumstances.* In some cases, the personal circumstances of an accused may be relevant in determining whether to prosecute or to take other action. Some circumstances peculiar to the accused, such as extreme youth, advanced age, or mental or physical impairment, may suggest that prosecution is not the most appropriate response to his/her offense; other circumstances, such as the fact that the accused occupied a position of trust or responsibility which he/she violated in committing the offense, might weigh in favor of prosecution.

8. *The Probable Sentence.* In assessing the strength of the Federal interest in prosecution, the attorney for the government should consider the sentence, or other consequence, that is likely to be imposed if prosecution is successful, and whether such a sentence or other consequence would justify the time and effort of prosecution. If the offender is already subject to a substantial sentence, or is already incarcerated, as a result of a conviction for another offense, the prosecutor should weigh the likelihood that another conviction will result in a meaningful addition to his/her sentence, might otherwise have a deterrent effect, or is necessary to ensure that the offender's record accurately reflects the extent of his/her criminal conduct. For example, it might be desirable to commence a bail-jumping prosecution against a person who already has been convicted of another offense so that law enforcement personnel and judicial officers who encounter him/her in the future wil l be aware of the risk of releasing him/her on bail. On the other hand, if the person is on probation or parole as a result of an earlier conviction, the prosecutor should consider whether the public interest might better be served by instituting a proceeding for violation of probation or revocation of parole, than by commencing a new prosecution. The prosecutor should also be alert to the desirability of instituting prosecution to prevent the running of the statute of limitations and to preserve the availability of a basis for an adequate sentence if there appears to be a chance that an offender's prior conviction may be reversed on appeal or collateral attack. Finally, if a person previously has been prosecuted in another jurisdiction for the same offense or a closely related offense, the attorney for the government should consult existing departmental policy statements on the subject of "successive prosecution" or "dual prosecution," depending on whether the earlier prosecution w as Federal or nonfederal. See USAM 9-2.031 (Petite Policy).

Just as there are factors that are appropriate to consider in determining whether a substantial Federal interest would be served by prosecution in a particular case, there are considerations that deserve no weight and should not influence the decision. These include the time and resources expended in Federal investigation of the case. No amount of investigative effort warrants commencing a Federal prosecution that is not fully justified on other grounds.

9-27.240 Initiating and Declining Charges -- Prosecution in Another Jurisdiction

A. In determining whether prosecution should be declined because the person is subject to effective prosecution in another jurisdiction, the attorney for the government should weigh all relevant considerations, including:

1. The strength of the other jurisdiction's interest in prosecution;

2. The other jurisdictions ability and willingness to prosecute effectively; and

3. The probable sentence or other consequences if the person is convicted in the other jurisdiction.

B. Comment. In many instances, it may be possible to prosecute criminal conduct in more than one jurisdiction. Although there may be instances in which a Federal prosecutor may wish to consider deferring to prosecution in another Federal district, in most instances the choice will probably be between Federal prosecution and prosecution by state or local authorities. USAM 9-27.240 sets forth three general considerations to be taken into account in determining whether a person is likely to be prosecuted effectively in another jurisdiction: the strength of the jurisdiction's interest in prosecution; its ability and willingness to prosecute effectively; and the probable sentence or other consequences if the person is convicted. As indicated with respect to the considerations listed in paragraph 3, these factors are illustrative only, and the attorney for the government should also consider any others that appear relevant to his/her in a particular case.

1. The Strength of the Jurisdiction's Interest. The attorney for the government should consider the relative Federal and state characteristics of the criminal conduct involved. Some offenses, even though in violation of Federal law, are of particularly strong interest to the authorities of the state or local jurisdiction in which they occur, either because of the nature of the offense, the identity of the offender or victim, the fact that the investigation was conducted primarily by state or local investigators, or some other circumstance. Whatever the reason, when it appears that the Federal interest in prosecution is less substantial than the interest of state or local authorities, consideration should be given to referring the case to those authorities rather than commencing or recommending a Federal prosecution.

2. Ability and Willingness to Prosecute Effectively. In assessing the likelihood of effective prosecution in another jurisdiction, the attorney for the government should also consider the intent of the authorities in that jurisdiction and whether that jurisdiction has the prosecutorial and judicial resources necessary to undertake prosecution promptly and effectively. Other relevant factors might be legal or evidentiary problems that might attend prosecution in the other jurisdiction. In addition, the Federal prosecutor should be alert to any local conditions, attitudes, relationships, or other circumstances that might cast doubt on the likelihood of the state or local authorities conducting a thorough and successful prosecution.

3. Probable Sentence Upon Conviction. The ultimate measure of the potential for effective prosecution in another jurisdiction is the sentence, or other consequence, that is likely to be imposed if the person is convicted. In considering this factor, the attorney for the government should bear in mind not only the statutory penalties in the jurisdiction and sentencing patterns in similar cases, but also, the particular characteristics of the offense or, of the offender that might be relevant to sentencing. He/she should also be alert to the possibility that a conviction under state law may, in some cases result in collateral consequences for the defendant, such as disbarment, that might not follow upon a conviction under Federal law.

9-27.250 Non-Criminal Alternatives to Prosecution

A. In determining whether prosecution should be declined because there exists an adequate, non-criminal alternative to prosecution, the attorney for the government should consider all relevant factors, including:

1. The sanctions available under the alternative means of disposition;

2. The likelihood that an effective sanction will be imposed; and

3. The effect of non-criminal disposition on Federal law enforcement interests.

B. Comment. When a person has committed a Federal offense, it is important that the law respond promptly, fairly, and effectively. This does not mean, however, that a criminal prosecution must be initiated. In recognition of the fact that resort to the criminal process is not necessarily the only appropriate response to serious forms of antisocial activity, Congress and state legislatures have provided civil and administrative remedies for many types of conduct that may also be subject to criminal sanction. Examples of such non-criminal approaches include civil tax proceedings; civil actions under the securities, customs, antitrust, or other regulatory laws; and reference of complaints to licensing authorities or to professional organizations such as bar associations. Another potentially useful alternative to prosecution in some cases is pretrial diversion. See USAM 9-22.000.

Attorneys for the government should familiarize themselves with these alternatives and should consider pursuing them if they are available in a particular case. Although on some occasions they should be pursued in addition to the criminal law procedures, on other occasions they can be expected to provide an effective substitute for criminal prosecution. In weighing the adequacy of such an alternative in a particular case, the prosecutor should consider the nature and severity of the sanctions that could be imposed, the likelihood that an adequate sanction would in fact be imposed, and the effect of such a non-criminal disposition on Federal law enforcement interests. It should be noted that referrals for non-criminal disposition may not include the transfer of grand jury material unless an order under Rule 6(e), Federal Rules of Criminal Procedure, has been obtained. See United States v. Sells Engineering, Inc., 463 U.S. 418 (1983).

9-27.260　Initiating and Declining Charges -- Impermissible Considerations

A. In determining whether to commence or recommend prosecution or take other action against a person, the attorney for the government should not be influenced by:

1. The person's race, religion, sex, national origin, or political association, activities or beliefs;

2. The attorney's own personal feelings concerning the person, the person's associates, or the victim; or

3. The possible affect of the decision on the attorney's own professional or personal circumstances.

B. Comment. USAM 9-27.260 sets forth various matters that plainly should not influence the determination whether to initiate or recommend prosecution or take other action. They are listed here not because it is anticipated that any attorney for the government might allow them to affect his/her judgment, but in order to make clear that Federal prosecutors will not be influenced by such improper considerations. Of course, in a case in which a particular characteristic listed in subparagraph (1) is pertinent to the offense (for example, in an immigration case the fact that the offender is not a United States national, or in a civil rights case the fact that the victim and the offender are of different races), the provision would not prohibit the prosecutor from considering it for the purpose intended by the Congress.

9-27.400　Plea Agreements Generally

A. The attorney for the government may, in an appropriate case, enter into an agreement with a defendant that, upon the defendant's plea of guilty or nolo contendere to a charged offense or to a lesser or related offense, he/she will move for dismissal of other charges, take a certain position with respect to the sentence to be imposed, or take other action. Plea agreements, and the role of the courts in such agreements, are addressed in Chapter Six of the Sentencing Guidelines. See also USAM 9-27.300 which discusses the individualized assessment by prosecutors of the extent to which particular charges fit the specific circumstances of the case, are consistent with the purposes of the Federal criminal code, and maximize the impact of Federal resources on crime.

B. Comment. USAM 9-27.400 permits, in appropriate cases, the disposition of Federal criminal charges pursuant to plea agreements between defendants and government attorneys. Such negotiated dispositions should be distinguished from situations in which a defendant pleads guilty or nolo contendere to fewer than all counts of an information or indictment in the absence of any agreement with the government. Only the former type of disposition is covered by the provisions of USAM 9-27.400 et seq.

Negotiated plea dispositions are explicitly sanctioned by Rule 11(e)(1), Fed. R. Crim. P., which provides that:

The attorney for the government and the attorney for the defendant or the defendant when acting pro se may engage in discussions with a view toward reaching an agreement that upon the entering of a plea of guilty or nolo contendere to a charged offense or to a lesser or related offense, the attorney for the government will do any of the following:

A. Move for dismissal of other charges; or

B. Make a recommendation, or agree not to oppose, the defendant's request for a particular sentence, with the understanding that such recommendation or request shall not be binding upon the court; or

C. Agree that a specific sentence is the appropriate disposition of the case.

Three types of plea agreements are encompassed by the language of USAM 9-27.400, agreements whereby in return for the defendant's plea to a charged offense or to a lesser or related offense, other charges are dismissed ("charge agreements"); agreements pursuant to which the government takes a certain position regarding the sentence to be imposed ("sentence agreements"); and agreements that combine a plea with a dismissal of charges and an undertaking by the prosecutor concerning the government's position at sentencing ("mixed agreements").

Once prosecutors have indicted, they should find themselves bargaining about charges which they have determined are readily provable and reflect the seriousness of the defendant's conduct. Charge agreements envision dismissal of counts in exchange for a plea. As with the indictment decision, the prosecutor should seek a plea to the most serious readily provable offense charged. Should a prosecutor determine in good faith after indictment that, as a result of a change in the evidence or for another reason (e.g., a need has arisen to protect the identity of a particular witness until he or she testifies against a more significant defendant), a charge is not readily provable or that an indictment exaggerates the seriousness of an offense or offenses, a plea bargain may reflect the prosecutor's reassessment. There should be documentation, however, in a case in which charges originally brought are dropped.

The language of USAM 9-27.400 with respect to sentence agreements is intended to cover the entire range of positions that the government might wish to take at the time of sentencing. Among the options are: taking no position regarding the sentence; not opposing the defendant's request; requesting a specific type of sentence (e.g., a fine or probation), a specific fine or term of imprisonment, or not more than a specific fine or term of imprisonment; and requesting concurrent rather than consecutive sentences. Agreement to any such option must be consistent with the guidelines.

There are only two types of sentence bargains. Both are permissible, but one is more complicated than the other. First, prosecutors may bargain for a sentence that is within the specified United States Sentencing Commission's guideline range. This means that when a guideline range is 18 to 24 months, the prosecutor has discretion to agree to recommend a sentence of 18 to 20 months rather than to argue for a sentence at the top of the range. Such a plea does not require that the actual sentence range be determined in advance. The plea agreement may have wording to the effect that once the range is determined by the court, the United States will recommend a low point in that range. Similarly, the prosecutor may agree to recommend a downward adjustment for acceptance of responsibility if he or she concludes in good faith that the defendant is entitled to the adjustment. Second, the prosecutor may seek to depart from the guidelines. This is more complicated than a bargain invo lving a sentence within a guideline range. Departures are discussed more generally below.

Department policy requires honesty in sentencing; Federal prosecutors are expected to identify for the court departures when they agree to support them. For example, it would be improper for a prosecutor to agree that a departure is in order, but to conceal the agreement in a charge bargain that is presented to a court as a fait accompli so that there is neither a record of nor judicial review of the departure.

Plea bargaining, both charge bargaining and sentence bargaining, must honestly reflect the totality and seriousness of the defendant's conduct and any departure to which the prosecutor is agreeing, and must be accomplished through appropriate guideline provisions.

The basic policy is that charges are not to be bargained away or dropped, unless the prosecutor has a good faith doubt as to the government's ability readily to prove a charge for legal or evidentiary reasons. There are, however, two exceptions.

First, if the applicable guideline range from which a sentence may be imposed would be unaffected, readily provable charges may be dismissed or dropped as part of a plea bargain. It is important to know whether dropping a charge may affect a sentence. For example, the multiple offense rules in Part D of Chapter 3 of the guidelines and the relevant conduct standard set forth in Sentencing Guideline 1B1.3(a)(2) will mean that certain dropped charges will be counted for purposes of determining the sentence, subject to the statutory maximum for the offense or offenses of conviction. It is vital that Federal prosecutors understand when conduct that is not charged in an indictment or conduct that is alleged in counts that are to be dismissed pursuant to a bargain may be counted for sentencing purposes and when it may not be. For example, in the case of a defendant who could be charged with five bank robberies, a decision to charge only one or to dismiss four counts pursuant to a bar gain precludes any consideration of the four uncharged or dismissed robberies in determining a guideline range, unless the plea agreement included a stipulation as to the other robberies. In contrast, in the case of a defendant who could be charged with five counts of fraud, the total amount of money involved in a fraudulent scheme will be considered in determining a guideline range even if the defendant pleads guilty to a single count and there is no stipulation as to the other counts.

Second, Federal prosecutors may drop readily provable charges with the specific approval of the United States Attorney or designated supervisory level official for reasons set forth in the file of the case. This exception recognizes that the aims of the Sentencing Reform Act must be sought without ignoring other, critical aspects of the Federal criminal justice system. For example, approvals to drop charges in a particular case might be given because the United States Attorney's office is particularly over-burdened, the case would be time-consuming to try, and proceeding to trial would significantly reduce the total number of cases disposed of by the office.

In Chapter 5, Part K of the Sentencing Guidelines, the Commission has listed departures that may be considered by a court in imposing a sentence. Moreover, Guideline 5K2.0 recognizes that a sentencing court may consider a ground for departure that has not been adequately considered by the Commission. A departure requires approval by the court. It violates the spirit of the guidelines and Department policy for prosecutor to enter into a plea bargain which is based upon the prosecutor's and the defendant's agreement that a departure is warranted, but that does not reveal to the court the existence of the departure and thereby afford the court an opportunity to reject it.

The Commission has recognized those bases for departure that are commonly justified. Accordingly, before the government may seek a departure based on a factor other than one set forth in Chapter 5, Part X, approval of the United States Attorney or designated supervisory officials is required. This approval is required whether or not a case is resolved through a negotiated plea.

Section 5K1.1 of the Sentencing Guidelines allows the United States to file a pleading with the sentencing court which permits the court to depart below the indicated guideline, on the basis that the defendant provided substantial assistance in the investigation or prosecution of another. Authority to approve such pleadings is limited to the United States Attorney, the Chief Assistant United States Attorney, and supervisory criminal Assistant United States Attorneys, or a committee including at least one of these individuals. Similarly, for Department of Justice attorneys, approval authority should be vested in a Section Chief or Office Director, or such official's deputy, or in a committee which includes at least one of these individuals.

Every United States Attorney or Department of Justice Section Chief or Office Director shall maintain documentation of the facts behind and justification for each substantial assistance pleading. The repository or repositories of this documentation need not be the case file itself. Freedom of Information Act considerations may suggest that a separate form showing the final decision be maintained.

The procedures described above shall also apply to Motions filed pursuant to Rule 35(b), Federal Rules of Criminal Procedure, where the sentence of a cooperating defendant is reduced after sentencing on motion of the United States. Such a filing is deemed for sentencing purposes to be the equivalent of a substantial assistance pleading.

The concession required by the government as part of a plea agreement, whether it be a "charge agreement," a "sentence agreement," or a "mixed agreement," should be weighed by the responsible government attorney in the light of the probable advantages and disadvantages of the plea disposition proposed in the particular case. Particular care should be exercised in considering whether to enter into a plea agreement pursuant to which the defendant will enter a nolo contendere plea. As discussed in USAM 9-27.500 and USAM 9-16.000, there are serious objections to such pleas and they should be opposed unless the responsible Assistant Attorney General concluded that the circumstances are so unusual that acceptance of such a plea would be in the public interest.

9-27.420 Plea Agreements -- Considerations to be Weighed

In determining whether it would be appropriate to enter into a plea agreement, the attorney for the government should weigh all relevant considerations, including:

   1. The defendant's willingness to cooperate in the investigation or prosecution of others;

   2. The defendant's history with respect to criminal activity;

   3. The nature and seriousness of the offense or offenses charged;

4. The defendant's remorse or contrition and his/her willingness to assume responsibility for his/her conduct;

5. The desirability of prompt and certain disposition of the case;

6. The likelihood of obtaining a conviction at trial;

7. The probable effect on witnesses;

8. The probable sentence or other consequences if the defendant is convicted;

9. The public interest in having the case tried rather than disposed of by a guilty plea;

10. The expense of trial and appeal;

11. The need to avoid delay in the disposition of other pending cases; and

12. The effect upon the victim's right to restitution.

B. Comment. USAM 9-27.420 sets forth some of the appropriate considerations to be weighed by the attorney for the government in deciding whether to enter into a plea agreement with a defendant pursuant to the provisions of Rule 11(e), Fed. R. Crim. P. The provision is not intended to suggest the desirability or lack of desirability of a plea agreement in any particular case or to be construed as a reflection on the merits of any plea agreement that actually may be reached; its purpose is solely to assist attorneys for the government in exercising their judgement as to whether some sort of plea agreement would be appropriate in a particular case. Government attorneys should consult the investigating agency involved and the victim, if appropriate or required by law, in any case in which it would be helpful to have their views concerning the relevance of particular factors or the weight they deserve.

1. *Defendant's Cooperation.* The defendant's willingness to provide timely and useful cooperation as part of his/her plea agreement should be given serious consideration. The weight it deserves will vary, of course, depending on the nature and value of the cooperation offered and whether the same benefit can be obtained without having to make the charge or sentence concession that would be involved in a plea agreement. In many situations, for example, all necessary cooperation in the form of testimony can be obtained through a compulsion order under 18 U.S.C.§§ 6001-6003. In such cases, that approach should be attempted unless, under the circumstances, it would seriously interfere with securing the person's conviction. If the defendant's cooperation is sufficiently substantial to justify the filing of a 5K1.1 Motion for a downward departure, the procedures set out in USAM 9-27.400 (B) shall be followed.

2. *Defendant's Criminal History*. One of the principal arguments against the practice of plea bargaining is that it results in leniency that reduces the deterrent impact of the law and leads to recidivism on the part of some offenders. Although this concern is probably most relevant in non-federal jurisdictions that must dispose of large volumes of routine cases with inadequate resources, nevertheless it should be kept in mind by Federal prosecutors, especially when dealing with repeat offenders or "career criminals." Particular care should be taken in the case of a defendant with a prior criminal record to ensure that society's need for protection is not sacrificed in the process of arriving at a plea disposition. In this connection, it is proper for the government attorney to consider not only the defendant's past, but also facts of other criminal involvement not resulting in conviction. By the same token, of course, it is also proper to consider a defendant's absence of past criminal involvement and his/her past cooperation with law enforcement officials. Note that 18 U.S.C. § 924(e), as well as Sentencing Guidelines 4B1.1 and 4B1.4 address "career criminals" and "armed career criminals." 18 U.S.C. § 3559(c) --the so-called "three strikes" statute--addresses serious violent recidivist offenders. The application of these provisions to a particular case may affect the plea negotiation posture of the parties.

3. *Nature and Seriousness of Offense Charged*. Important considerations in determining whether to enter into a plea agreement may be the nature and seriousness of the offense or offenses charged. In weighing those factors, the attorney for the government should bear in mind the interests sought to be protected by the statute defining the offense (e.g., the national defense, constitutional rights, the governmental process, personal safety, public welfare, or property), as well as nature and degree of harm caused or threatened to those interests and any attendant circumstances that aggravate or mitigate the seriousness of the offense in the particular case.

4. *Defendant's Attitude*. A defendant may demonstrate apparently genuine remorse or contrition, and a willingness to take responsibility for his/her criminal conduct by, for example, efforts to compensate the victim for injury or loss, or otherwise to ameliorate the consequences of his/her acts. These are factors that bear upon the likelihood of his/her repetition of the conduct involved and that may properly be considered in deciding whether a plea agreement would be appropriate. Sentencing Guideline 3E1.1 allows for a downward adjustment upon acceptance of responsibility by the defendant. It is permissible for a prosecutor to enter a plea agreement which approves such an adjustment if the defendant otherwise meets the requirements of the section.

It is particularly important that the defendant not be permitted to enter a guilty plea under circumstances that will allow him/her later to proclaim lack of culpability or even complete innocence. Such consequences can be avoided only if the court and the public are adequately informed of the nature and scope of the illegal activity and of the defendant's complicity and culpability. To this end, the attorney for the government is strongly encouraged to enter into a plea agreement only with the defendant's assurance that he/she will admit, the facts of the offense and of his/her culpable participation therein. A plea agreement may be entered into in the absence of such an assurance, but only if the defendant is willing to accept without contest a statement by the government in open court of the facts it could prove to demonstrate his/her guilt beyond a reasonable doubt. Except as provided in USAM 9-27.440, the attorney for the government should not enter into a plea agreement with a defendant who admits his/her guilt but disputes an essential element of the government's case.

5. *Prompt Disposition.* In assessing the value of prompt disposition of a criminal case, the attorney for the government should consider the timing of a proffered plea. A plea offer by a defendant on the eve of trial after the case has been fully prepared is hardly as advantageous from the standpoint of reducing public expense as one offered months or weeks earlier. In addition, a last minute plea adds to the difficulty of scheduling cases efficiently and may even result in wasting the prosecutorial and Judicial time reserved for the aborted trial. For these reasons, governmental attorneys should make clear to defense counsel at an early stage in the proceedings that, if there are to be any plea discussions, they must be concluded prior to a certain date well in advance of the trial date. See USSG § 3E1.1(b)(1). However, avoidance of unnecessary trial preparation and scheduling disruptions are not the only benefits to be gained from prompt disposition of a case by means of a guilty plea. Such a disposition also saves the government and the court the time and expense of trial and appeal. In addition, a plea agreement facilitates prompt imposition of sentence, thereby promoting the overall goals of the criminal justice system. Thus, occasionally it may be appropriate to enter into a plea agreement even after the usual time for making such agreements has passed.

6. *Likelihood of Conviction.* The trial of a criminal case inevitably involves risks and uncertainties, both for the prosecution and for the defense. Many factors, not all of which can be anticipated, can affect the outcome. To the extent that these factors can be identified, they should be considered in deciding whether to accept a plea or go to trial. In this connection, the prosecutor should weigh the strength of the government's case relative to the anticipated defense case, bearing in mind legal and evidentiary problems that might be expected, as well as the importance of the credibility of witnesses. However, although it is proper to consider factors bearing upon the likelihood of conviction in deciding whether to enter into a plea agreement, it obviously is improper for the prosecutor to attempt to dispose of a case by means of a plea agreement if he/she is not satisfied that the legal standards for guilt are met.

7. *Effect on Witnesses.* Attorneys for the government should bear in mind that it is often burdensome for witnesses to appear at trial and that sometimes to do so may cause them serious embarrassment or even place

them in jeopardy of physical or economic retaliation. The possibility of such adverse consequences to witnesses should not be overlooked in determining whether to go to trial or attempt to reach a plea agreement. Another possibility that may have to be considered is revealing the identity of informants. When an informant testifies at trial, his/her identity and relationship to the government become matters of public record. As a result, in addition to possible adverse consequences to the informant, there is a strong likelihood that the informant's usefulness in other investigations will be seriously diminished or destroyed. These are considerations that should be discussed with the investigating agency involved, as well as with any other agencies known to have an interest in using the informant in their investigations.

8. *Probable Sentence.* In determining whether to enter into a plea agreement, the attorney for the government may properly consider the probable outcome of the prosecution in terms of the sentence or other consequences for the defendant in the event that a plea agreement is reached. If the proposed agreement is a "sentence agreement" or a "mixed agreement," the prosecutor should realize that the position he/she agrees to take with respect to sentencing may have a significant effect on the sentence that is actually imposed. If the proposed agreement is a "charge agreement," the prosecutor should bear in mind the extent to which a plea to fewer or lesser offenses may reduce the sentence that otherwise could be imposed. In either event, it is important that the attorney for the government be aware of the need to preserve the basis for an appropriate sentence under all the circumstances of the case. Thorough knowledge of the Sentencing Guidelines, any applicable statutory minim um sentences, and any applicable sentence enhancements is clearly necessary to allow the prosecutor to accurately and adequately evaluate the effect of any plea agreement.

9. *Trial Rather Than Plea.* There may be situations in which the public interest might better be served by having a case tried rather than by having it disposed of by means of a guilty plea. These include situations in which it is particularly important to permit a clear public understanding that "justice is done" through exposing the exact nature of the defendant's wrongdoing at trial, or in which a plea agreement might be misconstrued to the detriment of public confidence in the criminal justice system. For this reason, the prosecutor should be careful not to place undue emphasis on factors which favor disposition of a case pursuant to a plea agreement.

10. *Expense of Trial and Appeal.* In assessing the expense of trial and appeal that would be saved by a plea disposition, the attorney for the government should consider not only such monetary costs as juror and witness fees, but also the time spent by judges, prosecutors, and law enforcement personnel who may be needed to testify or provide other assistance at trial. In this connection, the prosecutor should bear in mind the complexity of the case, the number of trial days and witnesses

required, and any extraordinary expenses that might be incurred such as the cost of sequestering the jury.

11. *Prompt Disposition of Other Cases.* A plea disposition in one case may facilitate the prompt disposition of other cases, including cases in which prosecution might otherwise be declined. This may occur simply because prosecutorial, judicial, or defense resources will become available for use in other cases, or because a plea by one of several defendants may have a "domino effect," leading to pleas by other defendants. In weighing the importance of these possible consequences, the attorney for the government should consider the state of the criminal docket and the speedy trial requirements in the district, the desirability of handling a larger volume of criminal cases, and the work loads of prosecutors, judges, and defense attorneys in the district.

9-27.430 Selecting Plea Agreement Charges

A. If a prosecution is to be concluded pursuant to a plea agreement, the defendant should be required to plead to a charge or charges:

1. That is the most serious readily provable charge consistent with the nature and extent of his/her criminal conduct;

2. That has an adequate factual basis;

3. That makes likely the imposition of an appropriate sentence and order of restitution, if appropriate, under all the circumstances of the case; and

4. That does not adversely affect the investigation or prosecution of others.

B. Comment. USAM 9-27.430 sets forth the considerations that should be taken into account in selecting the charge or charges to which a defendant should be required to plead guilty once it has been decided to dispose of the case pursuant to a plea agreement. The considerations are essentially the same as those governing the selection of charges to be included in the original indictment or information. See USAM 9-27.300.

1. *Relationship to Criminal Conduct.* The charge or charges to which a defendant pleads guilty should be consistent with the defendant's criminal conduct, both in nature and in scope. Except in unusual circumstances, this charge will be the most serious one, as defined in USAM 9-27.300. This principle governs the number of counts to which a plea should be required in cases involving different offenses, or in cases involving a series of familiar offenses. Therefore the prosecutor must be familiar with the Sentencing Guideline rules applicable to grouping offenses (Guideline 3D) and to relevant conduct (USSG § 1B1.3) among others. In regard to the seriousness of the offense, the guilty plea should assure that the public record of conviction provides an adequate indication of the defendant's

conduct. With respect to the number of counts, the prosecutor should take care to assure that no impression is given that multiple offenses are likely to result in no greater a potential penalty than is a single offense. The requirement that a defendant plead to a charge, that is consistent with the nature and extent of his/her criminal conduct is not inflexible. Although cooperation is usually acknowledged through a Sentencing Guideline 5K1.1 filing, there may be situations involving cooperating defendants in which considerations such as those discussed in USAM 9-27.600, take precedence. Such situations should be approached cautiously, however. Unless the government has strong corroboration for the cooperating defendant's testimony, his/her credibility may be subject to successful impeachment if he/she is permitted to plead to an offense that appears unrelated in seriousness or scope to the charges against the defendants on trial. It is also doubly important in such situations for the prosecutor to ensure that the public record of the plea demonstrates, the full extent of the defendant's involvement in the criminal activity, giving rise to the prosecution.

2. *Factual Basis.* The attorney for the government should also bear in mind the legal requirement that there be a factual basis for the charge or charges to which a guilty plea is entered. This requirement is intended to assure against conviction after a guilty plea of. a person who is not in fact guilty. Moreover, under Rule 11(f) of the Fed. R. Crim. P., a court may not enter a judgment upon a guilty plea "without making such inquiry as shall satisfy it that, there is a factual basis for the plea." For this reason, it is essential that the charge or charges selected as the subject of a plea agreement be such as could be prosecuted independently of the plea under these principles. However, as noted, in cases in which Alford or nolo contendere pleas are tendered, the attorney for the government may wish to make a stronger factual showing. In such cases there may remain some doubt as to the defendant's guilt even after the entry of his/her plea. Consequently, in order to a void such a misleading impression, the government should ask leave of the court to make a proffer of the facts available to it that show the defendant's guilt beyond a reasonable doubt.

In addition, the Department's policy is only to stipulate to facts that accurately represent the defendant's conduct. If a prosecutor wishes to support a departure from the guidelines, he or she should candidly do so and not stipulate to facts that are untrue. Stipulations to untrue facts are unethical. If a prosecutor has insufficient facts to contest a defendant's effort to seek a downward departure or to claim an adjustment, the prosecutor can say so. If the presentence report states facts that are inconsistent with a stipulation in which a prosecutor has joined, the prosecutor should object to the report or add a statement explaining the prosecutor's understanding of the facts or the reason for the stipulation.

Recounting the true nature of the defendant's involvement in a case will not always lead to a higher sentence. Where a defendant agrees to cooperate with the government by providing information concerning unlawful activities of others and the government agrees that self-incriminating information so provided will not be used against the defendant, Sentencing Guideline 1B1.8 provides that the information shall not be used in determining the applicable guideline range, except to the extent provided in the agreement. The existence of an agreement not to use information should be clearly reflected in the case file, the applicability of Guideline 1B1.8 should be documented, and the incriminating information must be disclosed to the court or the probation officer, even though it may not be used in determining a guideline sentence. Note that such information may still be used by the court in determining whether to depart from the guidelines and the extent of the departure. See US SG § 1B1.8.

3. *Basis for Sentencing.* In order to guard against inappropriate restriction of the court's sentencing options, the plea agreement should provide adequate scope for sentencing under all the circumstances of the case. To the extent that the plea agreement requires the government to take a position with respect to the sentence to be imposed, there should be little danger since the court will not be bound by the government's position. When a "charge agreement" is involved, however, the court will be limited to imposing the maxim term authorized by statue as well as the Sentencing Guideline range for the offense, to which the guilty plea is entered. Thus, as noted in USAM 9-27.320 above the prosecutor should take care to avoid a "charge agreement" that would unduly restrict the court's sentencing authority. In this connection, as in the initial selection of charges, the prosecutor should take into account the purposes of sentencing, the penalti es provided in the applicable statutes (including mandatory minimum penalties), the gravity of the offense, any aggravating or mitigating factors, and any post conviction consequences to which the defendant may be subject. In addition, if restitution is appropriate under the circumstances of the case, the plea agreement should specify the amount of restitution. See 18 U.S.C. § 3663 et seq.; 18 U.S.C. §§ 2248, 2259, 2264 and 2327; United States v. Arnold, 947 F.2d 1236, 1237-38 (5th Cir. 1991); and USAM 9-16.320.

4. *Effect on Other Cases.* In a multiple-defendant case, care must be taken to ensure that the disposition of the charges against one defendant does not adversely affect the investigation or prosecution of co-defendants. Among the possible adverse consequences to be avoided are the negative jury appeal that may result when relatively less culpable defendants are tried in the absence of a more culpable defendant or when a principal prosecution witness appears to be equally culpable as the defendants but has been permitted to plead to a significantly less serious offense; the possibility that one defendant's absence from the case will render useful evidence inadmissible at the trial of co-defendants; and the giving of questionable exculpatory testimony on behalf of the other defendants by the defendant who has pled guilty.

9-27.600 Entering into Non-prosecution Agreements in Return for Cooperation -- Generally

A. Except as hereafter provided, the attorney for the government may, with supervisory approval, enter into a non-prosecution agreement in exchange for a person's cooperation when, in his/her judgment, the person's timely cooperation appears to be necessary to the public interest and other means of obtaining the desired cooperation are unavailable or would not be effective.

B. Comment.

1. In many cases, it may be important to the success of an investigation or prosecution to obtain the testimonial or other cooperation of a person who is himself/herself implicated in the criminal conduct being investigated or prosecuted. However, because of his/her involvement, the person may refuse to cooperate on the basis of his/her Fifth Amendment privilege against compulsory self-incrimination. In this situation, there are several possible approaches the prosecutor can take to render the privilege inapplicable or to induce its waiver.

a. First, if time permits, the person may be charged, tried, and convicted before his/her cooperation is sought in the investigation or prosecution of others. Having already been convicted himself/herself, the person ordinarily will no longer have a valid privilege to refuse to testify and will have a strong incentive to reveal the truth in order to induce the sentencing judge to impose a lesser sentence than that which otherwise might be found appropriate.

b. Second, the person may be willing to cooperate if the charges or potential charge against him/her are reduced in number or degree in return for his/her cooperation and his/her entry of a guilty plea to the remaining charges. An agreement to file a motion pursuant to Sentencing Guideline 5K1.1 or Rule 35 of the Federal Rules of Criminal Procedure after the defendant gives full and complete cooperation is the preferred method for securing such cooperation. Usually such a concession by the government will be all that is necessary, or warranted, to secure the cooperation sought. Since it is certainly desirable as a matter of policy that an offender be required to incur at least some liability for his/her criminal conduct, government attorneys should attempt to secure this result in all appropriate cases, following the principles set forth in USAM 9-27.430 to the extent practicable.

c. The third method for securing the cooperation of a potential defendant is by means of a court order under 18 U.S.C. §§ 6001-6003. Those statutory provisions govern the conditions under which uncooperative witnesses may be compelled to testify or provide information notwithstanding their invocation of the privilege against compulsory self incrimination. In brief, under the so-called "use immunity" provisions of those statutes, the court may order the person to testify or provide other information, but neither his/her testimony nor the information he/she provides may be used against him/her, directly or indirectly, in any criminal case except a prosecution for perjury or other failure to comply with the order. Ordinarily, these "use immunity" provisions should be relied on in cases in which attorneys for the government need to obtain sworn testimony or the production of information before a grand jury or at trial, and in which there is reason to believe that the person will refuse to testify or provide the information on the basis of his/her privilege against compulsory self-incrimination. See USAM 9-23.000. Offers of immunity and immunity agreements should be in writing. Consideration should be given to documenting the evidence available prior to the immunity offer.

d. Finally, there may be cases in which it is impossible or impractical to employ the methods described above to secure the necessary information or other assistance, and in which the person is willing to cooperate only in return for an agreement that he/she will not be prosecuted at all for what he/she has done. The provisions set forth hereafter describe the conditions that should be met before such an agreement is made, as well as the procedures recommended for such cases.

It is important to note that these provisions apply only if the case involves an agreement with a person who might otherwise be prosecuted. If the person reasonably is viewed only as a potential witness rather than a potential defendant, and the person is willing to cooperate, there is no need to consult these provisions.

USAM 9-27.600 describes three circumstances that should exist before government attorneys enter into non-prosecution agreements in return for cooperation: the unavailability or ineffectiveness of other means of obtaining the desired cooperation; the apparent necessity of the cooperation to the public interest; and the approval of such a course of action by an appropriate supervisory official.

2. *Unavailability or Ineffectiveness of Other Means.* As indicated above, non-prosecution agreements are only one of several methods by which the prosecutor can obtain the cooperation of a person whose criminal involvement makes him/her a potential subject of prosecution. Each of the other methods--seeking cooperation after trial and conviction, bargaining for cooperation as part of a plea agreement, and compelling cooperation under a "use immunity" order--involves prosecuting the person or at least leaving open the possibility of prosecuting him/her on the basis of independently obtained evidence. Since these outcomes are clearly preferable to permitting an offender to avoid any liability for his/her conduct, the possible use of an

alternative to a non-prosecution agreement should be given serious consideration in the first instance.

Another reason for using an alternative to a non-prosecution agreement to obtain cooperation concerns the practical advantage in terms of the person's credibility if he/she testifies at trial. If the person already has been convicted, either after trial or upon a guilty plea, for participating in the events about which he/she testifies, his/her testimony is apt to be far more credible than if it appears to the trier of fact that he/she is getting off "scot free." Similarly, if his/her testimony is compelled by a court order, he/she cannot properly be portrayed by the defense as a person who has made a "deal" with the government and whose testimony is, therefore, suspect; his/her testimony will have been forced from him/her, not bargained for.

In some cases, however, there may be no effective means of obtaining the person's timely cooperation short of entering into a non-prosecution agreement. The person may be unwilling to cooperate fully in return for a reduction of charges, the delay involved in bringing him/her to trial might prejudice the investigation or prosecution in connection with which his/her cooperation is sought and it may be impossible or impractical to rely on the statutory provisions for compulsion of testimony or production of evidence. One example of the latter situation is a case in which the cooperation needed does not consist of testimony under oath or the production of information before a grand jury or at trial. Other examples are cases in which time is critical, or where use of the procedures of 18 U.S.C. §?-6003 would unreasonably disrupt the presentation of evidence to the grand jury or the expeditious development of an investigation, or where compliance with the statute of limitations or the Speedy Trial Act precludes timely application for a court order.

Only when it appears that the person's timely cooperation cannot be obtained by other means, or cannot be obtained effectively, should the attorney for the government consider entering into a non-prosecution agreement.

3. *Public Interest.* If he/she concludes that a non-prosecution agreement would be the only effective method for obtaining cooperation, the attorney for the government should consider whether, balancing the cost of foregoing prosecution against the potential benefit of the person's cooperation, the cooperation sought appears necessary to the public interest. This "public interest" determination is one of the conditions precedent to an application under 18 U.S.C. § 6003 for a court order compelling testimony. Like a compulsion order, a non-prosecution agreement limits the government's ability to undertake a subsequent prosecution of the witness. Accordingly, the same "public interest" test should be applied in this situation as well. Some of the considerations that may be relevant to the application of this test are set forth in USAM 9-27.620.

4. *Supervisory Approval.* Finally, the prosecutor should secure supervisory approval before entering into a non-prosecution agreement. Prosecutors

working under the direction of a United States Attorney must seek the approval of the United States Attorney or a supervisory Assistant United States Attorney. Departmental attorneys not supervised by a United States Attorney should obtain the approval of the appropriate Assistant Attorney General or his/her designee, and should notify the United States Attorney or Attorneys concerned. The requirement of approval by a superior is designed to provide review by an attorney experienced in such matters, and to ensure uniformity of policy and practice with respect to such agreements. This section should be read in conjunction with USAM 9-27.640, concerning particular types of cases in which an Assistant Attorney General or his/her designee must concur in or approve an agreement not to prosecute in ret urn for cooperation.

9-27.620 - Entering into Non-prosecution Agreements in Return for Cooperation—Considerations to be Weighed

A. In determining whether, a person's cooperation may be necessary to the public interest, the attorney for the government, and those whose approval is necessary, should weigh all relevant considerations, including:

  1. The importance of the investigation or prosecution to an effective program of law enforcement;

  2. The value of the person's cooperation to the investigation or prosecution; and

  3. The person's relative culpability in connection with the offense or offenses being investigated or prosecuted and his/her history with respect to criminal activity.

B. Comment. This paragraph is intended to assist Federal prosecutors, and those whose approval they must secure, in deciding whether a person's cooperation appears to be necessary to the public interest. The considerations listed here are not intended to be all-inclusive or to require a particular decision in a particular case. Rather they are meant to focus the decision-maker's attention on factors that probably will be controlling in the majority of cases.

  1. *Importance of Case.* Since the primary function of a Federal prosecutor is to enforce the criminal law, he/she should not routinely or indiscriminately enter into non-prosecution agreements, which are, in essence, agreements not to enforce the law under particular conditions. Rather, he/she should reserve the use of such agreements for cases in which the cooperation sought concerns the commission of a serious offense or in which successful prosecution is otherwise important in achieving effective enforcement of the criminal laws. The relative importance or unimportance of the contemplated case is therefore a significant threshold consideration.

2. *Value of Cooperation.* An agreement not to prosecute in return for a person's cooperation binds the government to the extent that the person carries out his/her part of the bargain. See Santobello v. New York 404 U.S. 257 (1971); Wade v. United States, 112 S. Ct. 1840 (1992). Since such an agreement forecloses enforcement of the criminal law against a person who otherwise may be liable to prosecution, it should not be entered into without a clear understanding of the nature of the quid pro quo and a careful assessment of its probable value to the government. In order to be in a position adequately to assess the potential value of a person's cooperation, the prosecutor should insist on an "offer of proof" or its equivalent from the person or his/her attorney. The prosecutor can then weigh the offer in terms of the investigation or prosecution in connection with which cooperation is sought. In doing so, he/she should consider such questions as whether the cooperation will in fact be forthcoming, whether the testimony or other information provided will be credible, whether it can be corroborated by other evidence, whether it will materially assist the investigation or prosecution, and whether substantially the same benefit can be obtained from someone else without an agreement not to prosecute. After assessing all of these factors, together with any others that may be relevant, the prosecutor can judge the strength of his/her case with and without the person's cooperation, and determine whether it may be in the public interest to agree to forego prosecution under the circumstances.

3. *Relative Culpability and Criminal History.* In determining whether it may be necessary to the public interest to agree to forego prosecution of a person who may have violated the law in return for that person's cooperation, it is also important to consider the degree of his/her apparent culpability relative to others who are subjects of the investigation or prosecution as well as his/her history of criminal involvement. Of course, ordinarily it would not be in the public interest to forego prosecution of a high-ranking member of a criminal enterprise in exchange for his/her cooperation against one of his/her subordinates, nor would the public interest be served by bargaining away the opportunity to prosecute a person with a long history of serious criminal involvement in order to obtain the conviction of someone else on less serious charges. These are matters with regard to which the attorney for the government may find it helpful to consult with the investigating agency or with other prosecuting authorities who may have an interest in the person or his/her associates.

It is also important to consider whether the person has a background of cooperation with law enforcement officials, either as a witness or an informant, and whether he/she has previously been the subject of a compulsion order under 18 U.S.C. §§ 6001-6003 or has escaped prosecution by virtue of an agreement not to prosecute. The information regarding compulsion orders may be available by telephone from the Policy and Statutory Enforcement Unit in the Office of Enforcement Operations of the Criminal Division.

9-27.630 Entering into Non-prosecution Agreements in Return for Cooperation-- Limiting the Scope of Commitment

A. In entering into a non-prosecution agreement, the attorney for the government should, if practicable, explicitly limit the scope of the government's commitment to:

  1. Non-prosecution based directly or indirectly on the testimony or other information provided; or

  2. Non-prosecution within his/her district with respect to a pending charge, or to a specific offense then known to have been committed by the person.

B. Comment. The attorney for the government should exercise extreme caution to ensure that his/her non-prosecution agreement does not confer "blanket" immunity on the witness. To this end, he/she should, in the first instance, attempt to limit his/her agreement to non-prosecution based on the testimony or information provided. Such an "informal use immunity" agreement has two advantages over an agreement not to prosecute the person in connection with a particular transaction: first, it preserves the prosecutor's option to prosecute on the basis of independently obtained evidence if it later appears that the person's criminal involvement was more serious than it originally appeared to be; and second, it encourages the witness to be as forthright as possible since the more he/she reveals the more protection he/she will have against a future prosecution. To further encourage full disclosure by the witness, it should be made clear in the agreement that the government's forbearance from prosecution is conditioned upon the witness's testimony or production of information being complete and truthful, and that failure to testify truthfully may result in a perjury prosecution.

Even if it is not practicable to obtain the desired cooperation pursuant to an "informal use immunity" agreement, the attorney for the government should attempt to limit the scope of the agreement in terms of the testimony and transactions covered, bearing in mind the possible effect of his/her agreement on prosecutions in other districts.

It is important that non-prosecution agreements be drawn in terms that will not bind other Federal prosecutors or agencies without their consent. Thus, if practicable, the attorney for the government should explicitly limit the scope of his/her agreement to non-prosecution within his/her district. If such a limitation is not practicable and it can reasonably be anticipated that the agreement may affect prosecution of the person in other districts, the attorney for the government contemplating such an agreement shall communicate the relevant facts to the Assistant Attorney General with supervisory responsibility for the subject matter. United States Attorneys may not make agreements which prejudice civil or tax liability without the express agreement of all affected Divisions and/or agencies. See also 9-16.000 et seq. for more information regarding plea agreements.

Finally, the attorney for the government should make it clear that his/her agreement relates only to non-prosecution and that he/she has no independent authority to promise that the witness will be admitted into the Department's Witness Security program or that the Marshal's Service will provide any benefits to the witness in exchange for his/her cooperation. This does not mean, of course, that the prosecutor should not cooperate in making arrangements with the Marshal's Service necessary for the protection of the witness in appropriate cases. The procedures to be followed in such cases are set forth in USAM 9-21.000.

Principles of Federal Prosecution of Business Organizations

9-28.100   Duties of Federal Prosecutors and Duties of Corporate Leaders

The prosecution of corporate crime is a high priority for the Department of Justice. By investigating allegations of wrongdoing and by bringing charges where appropriate for criminal misconduct, the Department promotes critical public interests. These interests include, to take just a few examples: (1) protecting the integrity of our free economic and capital markets; (2) protecting consumers, investors, and business entities that compete only through lawful means; and (3) protecting the American people from misconduct that would violate criminal laws safeguarding the environment.

In this regard, federal prosecutors and corporate leaders typically share common goals. For example, directors and officers owe a fiduciary duty to a corporation's shareholders, the corporation's true owners, and they owe duties of honest dealing to the investing public in connection with the corporation's regulatory filings and public statements. The faithful execution of these duties by corporate leadership serves the same values in promoting public trust and confidence that our criminal cases are designed to serve.

A prosecutor's duty to enforce the law requires the investigation and prosecution of criminal wrongdoing if it is discovered. In carrying out this mission with the diligence and resolve necessary to vindicate the important public interests discussed above, prosecutors should be mindful of the common cause we share with responsible corporate leaders. Prosecutors should also be mindful that confidence in the Department is affected both by the results we achieve and by the real and perceived ways in which we achieve them. Thus, the manner in which we do our job as prosecutors—including the professionalism we demonstrate, our willingness to secure the facts in a manner that encourages corporate compliance and self- regulation, and also our appreciation that corporate prosecutions can potentially harm blameless investors, employees, and others—affects public perception of our mission. Federal prosecutors recognize that they must maintain public confidence in the way in which they exercise their charging discretion. This endeavor requires the thoughtful analysis of all facts and circumstances presented in a given case. As always, professionalism and civility play an important part in the Department's discharge of its responsibilities in all areas, including the area of corporate investigations and prosecutions.

9-28.200 General Considerations of Corporate Liability

A. *General Principle:* Corporations should not be treated leniently because of their artificial nature nor should they be subject to harsher treatment. Vigorous enforcement of the criminal laws against corporate wrongdoers, where appropriate, results in great benefits for law enforcement and the public, particularly in the area of white collar crime. Indicting corporations for wrongdoing enables the government to be a force for positive change of corporate culture, and a force to prevent, discover, and punish serious crimes.

B. *Comment:* In all cases involving corporate wrongdoing, prosecutors should consider the factors discussed further below. In doing so, prosecutors should be aware of the public benefits that can flow from indicting a corporation in appropriate cases. For instance, corporations are likely to take immediate remedial steps when one is indicted for criminal misconduct that is pervasive throughout a particular industry, and thus an indictment can provide a unique opportunity for deterrence on a broad scale. In addition, a corporate indictment may result in specific deterrence by changing the culture of the indicted corporation and the behavior of its employees. Finally, certain crimes that carry with them a substantial risk of great public harm—e.g., environmental crimes or sweeping financial frauds—may be committed by a business entity, and there may therefore be a substantial federal interest in indicting a corporation under such circumstances.

In certain instances, it may be appropriate, upon consideration of the factors set forth herein, to resolve a corporate criminal case by means other than indictment. Non-prosecution and deferred prosecution agreements, for example, occupy an important middle ground between declining prosecution and obtaining the conviction of a corporation. These agreements are discussed further in USAM 9-28.1000. Likewise, civil and regulatory alternatives may be appropriate in certain cases, as discussed in USAM 9-28.1100.

Where a decision is made to charge a corporation, it does not necessarily follow that individual directors, officers, employees, or shareholders should not also be charged. Prosecution of a corporation is not a substitute for the prosecution of criminally culpable individuals within or without the corporation. Because a corporation can act only through individuals, imposition of individual criminal liability may provide the strongest deterrent against future corporate wrongdoing. Only rarely should provable individual culpability not be pursued, particularly if it relates to high-level corporate officers, even in the face of an offer of a corporate guilty plea or some other disposition of the charges against the corporation.

Corporations are "legal persons," capable of suing and being sued, and capable of committing crimes. Under the doctrine of respondeat superior, a corporation may be held criminally liable for the illegal acts of its directors, officers, employees, and agents. To hold a corporation liable for these actions, the government must establish that the corporate agent's actions (i) were within the scope of his duties and (ii) were intended, at least in part, to benefit the corporation. In all cases involving wrongdoing by corporate agents, prosecutors should not limit their focus solely to individuals or the corporation, but should consider both as potential targets.

Agents may act for mixed reasons—both for self-aggrandizement (both direct and indirect) and for the benefit of the corporation, and a corporation may be held liable as long as one motivation of its agent is to benefit the corporation. See United States v. Potter, 463 F.3d 9, 25 (1st Cir. 2006) (stating that the test to determine whether an agent is acting within the scope of employment is "whether the agent is performing acts of the kind which he is authorized to perform, and those acts are motivated, at least in part, by an intent to benefit the corporation."). In United States v. Automated Medical Laboratories, Inc., 770 F.2d 399 (4th Cir. 1985), for example, the Fourth Circuit affirmed a corporation's conviction for the actions of a subsidiary's employee despite the corporation's claim that the employee was acting for his own benefit, namely his "ambitious nature and his desire to ascend the corporate ladder." Id. at 407. The court stated, "Partucci was clearly acting in part to benefit AML since his advancement within the corporation depended on AML's well-being and its lack of difficulties with the FDA." Id.; see also United States v. Cincotta, 689 F.2d 238, 241-42 (1st Cir. 1982) (upholding a corporation's conviction, notwithstanding the substantial personal benefit reaped by its miscreant agents, because the fraudulent scheme required money to pass through the corporation's treasury and the fraudulently obtained goods were resold to the corporation's customers in the corporation's name).

Moreover, the corporation need not even necessarily profit from its agent's actions for it to be held liable. In Automated Medical Laboratories, the Fourth Circuit stated:

> [B]enefit is not a "touchstone of criminal corporate liability; benefit at best is an evidential, not an operative, fact." Thus, whether the agent's actions ultimately redounded to the benefit of the corporation is less significant than whether the agent acted with the intent to benefit the corporation. The basic purpose of requiring that an agent have acted with the intent to benefit the corporation, however, is to insulate the corporation from criminal liability for actions of its agents which may be inimical to the interests of the corporation or which may have been undertaken solely to advance the interests of that agent or of a party other than the corporation.

770 F.2d at 407 (internal citation omitted) (quoting Old Monastery Co. v. United States, 147 F.2d 905, 908 (4th Cir. 1945)).

9-28.300 Factors to Be Considered

A. *General Principle*: Generally, prosecutors apply the same factors in determining whether to charge a corporation as they do with respect to individuals. See USAM 9-27.220 et seq. Thus, the prosecutor must weigh all of the factors normally considered in the sound exercise of prosecutorial judgment: the sufficiency of the evidence; the likelihood of success at trial; the probable deterrent, rehabilitative, and other consequences of conviction; and the adequacy of noncriminal approaches. See id. However, due to the nature of the corporate "person," some additional factors are present. In conducting an investigation, determining whether to bring charges, and negotiating plea or other agreements, prosecutors should consider the following factors in reaching a decision as to the proper treatment of a corporate target:

1. the nature and seriousness of the offense, including the risk of harm to the public, and applicable policies and priorities, if any, governing the prosecution of corporations for particular categories of crime (see USAM 9-28.400);

2. the pervasiveness of wrongdoing within the corporation, including the complicity in, or the condoning of, the wrongdoing by corporate management (see USAM 9-28.500);

3. the corporation's history of similar misconduct, including prior criminal, civil, and regulatory enforcement actions against it (see USAM 9-28.600);

4. the corporation's timely and voluntary disclosure of wrongdoing and its willingness to cooperate in the investigation of its agents (see USAM 9-28.700);

5. the existence and effectiveness of the corporation's pre-existing compliance program (see USAM 9-28.800);

6. the corporation's remedial actions, including any efforts to implement an effective corporate compliance program or to improve an existing one, to replace responsible management, to discipline or terminate wrongdoers, to pay restitution, and to cooperate with the relevant government agencies (see USAM 9-28.900);

7. collateral consequences, including whether there is disproportionate harm to shareholders, pension holders, employees, and others not proven personally culpable, as well as impact on the public arising from the prosecution (see USAM 9-28.1000);

8. the adequacy of the prosecution of individuals responsible for the corporation's malfeasance; and

9. the adequacy of remedies such as civil or regulatory enforcement actions (see USAM 9-28.1100).

B. *Comment:* The factors listed in this section are intended to be illustrative of those that should be evaluated and are not an exhaustive list of potentially relevant considerations. Some of these factors may not apply to specific cases, and in some cases one factor may override all others. For example, the nature and seriousness of the offense may be such as to warrant prosecution regardless of the other factors. In most cases, however, no single factor will be dispositive. In addition, national law enforcement policies in various enforcement areas may require that more or less weight be given to certain of these factors than to others. Of course, prosecutors must exercise their thoughtful and pragmatic judgment in applying and balancing these factors, so as to achieve a fair and just outcome and promote respect for the law.

In making a decision to charge a corporation, the prosecutor generally has substantial latitude in determining when, whom, how, and even whether to prosecute for violations of federal criminal law. In exercising that discretion, prosecutors should consider the following statements of principles that summarize the considerations they should weigh and the practices they should follow in discharging their prosecutorial responsibilities. In doing so, prosecutors should ensure that the general purposes of the criminal law—assurance of warranted punishment, deterrence of further criminal conduct, protection of the public from dangerous and fraudulent conduct, rehabilitation of offenders, and restitution for victims and affected communities—are adequately met, taking into account the special nature of the corporate "person."

9-28.400 Special Policy Concerns

A. *General Principle:* The nature and seriousness of the crime, including the risk of harm to the public from the criminal misconduct, are obviously primary factors in determining whether to charge a corporation. In addition, corporate conduct, particularly that of national and multi-national corporations, necessarily intersects with federal economic, tax, and criminal law enforcement policies. In applying these Principles, prosecutors must consider the practices and policies of the appropriate Division of the Department, and must comply with those policies to the extent required by the facts presented.

B. *Comment:* In determining whether to charge a corporation, prosecutors should take into account federal law enforcement priorities as discussed above. See USAM 9-27.230. In addition, however, prosecutors must be aware of the specific policy goals and incentive programs established by the respective Divisions and regulatory agencies. Thus, whereas natural persons may be given incremental degrees of credit (ranging from immunity to lesser charges to sentencing considerations) for turning themselves in, making statements against their penal interest, and cooperating in the government's investigation of their own and others' wrongdoing, the same approach may not be appropriate in all circumstances with respect to corporations. As an example, it is entirely proper in many investigations for a prosecutor to consider the corporation's pre-indictment conduct, e.g., voluntary disclosure, cooperation, remediation or restitution, in determining whether to seek an indictment. However, this would not necessarily be appropriate in an antitrust investigation, in which antitrust violations, by definition, go to the heart of the corporation's business. With this in mind, the Antitrust Division has established a firm policy, understood in the business community, that credit should not be given at the charging stage for a compliance program and that amnesty is available only to the first corporation to make full disclosure to the government. As another example, the Tax Division has a strong preference for prosecuting responsible individuals, rather than entities, for corporate tax offenses. Thus, in determining whether or not to charge a corporation, prosecutors must consult with the Criminal, Antitrust, Tax, Environmental and Natural Resources, and National Security Divisions, as appropriate.

9-28.500 Pervasiveness of Wrongdoing Within the Corporation

A. *General Principle:* A corporation can only act through natural persons, and it is therefore held responsible for the acts of such persons fairly attributable to it. Charging a corporation for even minor misconduct may be appropriate where the wrongdoing was pervasive and was undertaken by a large number of employees, or by all the employees in a particular role within the corporation, or was condoned by upper management. On the other hand, it may not be appropriate to impose liability upon a corporation, particularly one with a robust compliance program in place, under a strict respondeat superior theory for the single isolated act of a rogue employee. There is, of course, a wide spectrum between these two extremes, and a prosecutor should exercise sound discretion in evaluating the pervasiveness of wrongdoing within a corporation.

B. *Comment*: Of these factors, the most important is the role and conduct of management. Although acts of even low-level employees may result in criminal liability, a corporation is directed by its management and management is responsible for a corporate culture in which criminal conduct is either discouraged or tacitly encouraged. As stated in commentary to the Sentencing Guidelines:

> Pervasiveness [is] case specific and [will] depend on the number, and degree of responsibility, of individuals [with] substantial authority ... who participated in, condoned, or were willfully ignorant of the offense. Fewer individuals need to be involved for a finding of pervasiveness if those individuals exercised a relatively high degree of authority.

Pervasiveness can occur either within an organization as a whole or within a unit of an organization.

USSG § 8C2.5, cmt. (n. 4).

9-28.600 The Corporation's Past History

A. *General Principle*: Prosecutors may consider a corporation's history of similar conduct, including prior criminal, civil, and regulatory enforcement actions against it, in determining whether to bring criminal charges and how best to resolve cases.

B. *Comment*: A corporation, like a natural person, is expected to learn from its mistakes. A history of similar misconduct may be probative of a corporate culture that encouraged, or at least condoned, such misdeeds, regardless of any compliance programs. Criminal prosecution of a corporation may be particularly appropriate where the corporation previously had been subject to non-criminal guidance, warnings, or sanctions, or previous criminal charges, and it either had not taken adequate action to prevent future unlawful conduct or had continued to engage in the misconduct in spite of the warnings or enforcement actions taken against it. The corporate structure itself (e.g., the creation or existence of subsidiaries or operating divisions) is not dispositive in this analysis, and enforcement actions taken against the corporation or any of its divisions, subsidiaries, and affiliates may be considered, if germane. See USSG § 8C2.5(c), cmt. (n. 6).

9-28.700 The Value of Cooperation

Cooperation is a potential mitigating factor, by which a corporation—just like any other subject of a criminal investigation—can gain credit in a case that otherwise is appropriate for indictment and prosecution. Of course, the decision not to cooperate by a corporation (or individual) is not itself evidence of misconduct, at least where the lack of cooperation does not involve criminal misconduct or demonstrate consciousness of guilt (e.g., suborning perjury or false statements, or refusing to comply with lawful discovery requests). Thus, failure to cooperate, in and of itself, does not support or require the filing of charges with respect to a corporation any more than with respect to an individual.

A. *General Principle*: In determining whether to charge a corporation and how to resolve corporate criminal cases, the corporation's timely and voluntary disclosure of wrongdoing and its cooperation with the government's investigation may be relevant factors. In gauging the extent of the corporation's cooperation, the prosecutor may consider, among other things, whether the corporation made a voluntary and timely disclosure, and the corporation's willingness to provide relevant information and evidence and identify relevant actors within and outside the corporation, including senior executives.

B. *Comment*: In investigating wrongdoing by or within a corporation, a prosecutor is likely to encounter several obstacles resulting from the nature of the corporation itself. It will often be difficult to determine which individual took which action on behalf of the corporation. Lines of authority and responsibility may be shared among operating divisions or departments, and records and personnel may be spread throughout the United States or even among several countries. Where the criminal conduct continued over an extended period of time, the culpable or knowledgeable personnel may have been promoted, transferred, or fired, or they may have quit or retired. Accordingly, a corporation's cooperation may be critical in identifying potentially relevant actors and locating relevant evidence, among other things, and in doing so expeditiously.

This dynamic—i.e., the difficulty of determining what happened, where the evidence is, and which individuals took or promoted putatively illegal corporate actions—can have negative consequences for both the government and the corporation that is the subject or target of a government investigation. More specifically, because of corporate attribution principles concerning actions of corporate officers and employees (see, e.g., supra section II), uncertainty about exactly who authorized or directed apparent corporate misconduct can inure to the detriment of a corporation. For example, it may not matter under the law which of several possible executives or leaders in a chain of command approved of or authorized criminal conduct; however, that information if known might bear on the propriety of a particular disposition short of indictment of the corporation. It may not be in the interest of a corporation or the government for a charging decision to be made in the absence of such information, which might occur if, for example, a statute of limitations were relevant and authorization by any one of the officials were enough to justify a charge under the law. Moreover, and at a minimum, a protracted government investigation of such an issue could, as a collateral consequence, disrupt the corporation's business operations or even depress its stock price.

For these reasons and more, cooperation can be a favorable course for both the government and the corporation. Cooperation benefits the government—and ultimately shareholders, employees, and other often blameless victims—by allowing prosecutors and federal agents, for example, to avoid protracted delays, which compromise their ability to quickly uncover and address the full extent of widespread corporate crimes. With cooperation by the corporation, the government may be able to reduce tangible losses, limit damage to reputation, and preserve assets for restitution. At the same time, cooperation may benefit the corporation by enabling the government to focus its investigative resources in a manner that will not unduly disrupt the corporation's legitimate business operations. In addition, and critically, cooperation may benefit the corporation by presenting it with the opportunity to earn credit for its efforts.

9-28.710 Attorney-Client and Work Product Protections

The attorney-client privilege and the attorney work product protection serve an extremely important function in the American legal system. The attorney-client privilege is one of the oldest and most sacrosanct privileges under the law. See Upjohn v. United States, 449 U.S. 383, 389 (1981). As the Supreme Court has stated, "[i]ts purpose is to encourage full and frank communication between attorneys and their clients and thereby promote broader public interests in the observance of law and administration of justice." Id. The value of promoting a corporation's ability to seek frank and comprehensive legal advice is particularly important in the contemporary global business environment, where corporations often face complex and dynamic legal and regulatory obligations imposed by the federal government and also by states and foreign governments. The work product doctrine serves similarly important goals.

For these reasons, waiving the attorney-client and work product protections has never been a prerequisite under the Department's prosecution guidelines for a corporation to be viewed as cooperative. Nonetheless, a wide range of commentators and members of the American legal community and criminal justice system have asserted that the Department's policies have been used, either wittingly or unwittingly, to coerce business entities into waiving attorney-client privilege and work-product protection. Everyone agrees that a corporation may freely waive its own privileges if it chooses to do so; indeed, such waivers occur routinely when corporations are victimized by their employees or others, conduct an internal investigation, and then disclose the details of the investigation to law enforcement officials in an effort to seek prosecution of the offenders. However, the contention, from a broad array of voices, is that the Department's position on attorney-client privilege and work product protection waivers has promoted an environment in which those protections are being unfairly eroded to the detriment of all.

The Department understands that the attorney-client privilege and attorney work product protection are essential and long- recognized components of the American legal system. What the government seeks and needs to advance its legitimate (indeed, essential) law enforcement mission is not waiver of those protections, but rather the facts known to the corporation about the putative criminal misconduct under review. In addition, while a corporation remains free to convey non-factual or "core" attorney-client communications or work product—if and only if the corporation voluntarily chooses to do so—prosecutors should not ask for such waivers and are directed not to do so. The critical factor is whether the corporation has provided the facts about the events, as explained further herein.

9-28.720 Cooperation: Disclosing the Relevant Facts

Eligibility for cooperation credit is not predicated upon the waiver of attorney-client privilege or work product protection. Instead, the sort of cooperation that is most valuable to resolving allegations of misconduct by a corporation and its officers, directors, employees, or agents is disclosure of the relevant facts concerning such misconduct. In this regard, the analysis parallels that for a non-corporate defendant, where cooperation typically requires disclosure of relevant factual knowledge and not of discussions between an individual and his attorneys.

Thus, when the government investigates potential corporate wrongdoing, it seeks the relevant facts. For example, how and when did the alleged misconduct occur? Who promoted or approved it? Who was responsible for committing it? In this respect, the investigation of a corporation differs little from the investigation of an individual. In both cases, the government needs to know the facts to achieve a just and fair outcome. The party under investigation may choose to cooperate by disclosing the facts, and the government may give credit for the party's disclosures. If a corporation wishes to receive credit for such cooperation, which then can be considered with all other cooperative efforts and circumstances in evaluating how fairly to proceed, then the corporation, like any person, must disclose the relevant facts of which it has knowledge.[1]

(a) Disclosing the Relevant Facts—Facts Gathered Through Internal Investigation

Individuals and corporations often obtain knowledge of facts in different ways. An individual knows the facts of his or others' misconduct through his own experience and perceptions. A corporation is an artificial construct that cannot, by definition, have personal knowledge of the facts. Some of those facts may be reflected in documentary or electronic media like emails, transaction or accounting documents, and other records. Often, the corporation gathers facts through an internal investigation. Exactly how and by whom the facts are gathered is for the corporation to decide. Many corporations choose to collect information about potential misconduct through lawyers, a process that may confer attorney-client privilege or attorney work product protection on at least some of the information collected. Other corporations may choose a method of fact- gathering that does not have that effect—for example, having employee or other witness statements collected

---

[1] There are other dimensions of cooperation beyond the mere disclosure of facts, of course. These can include, for example, providing non-privileged documents and other evidence, making witnesses available for interviews, and assisting in the interpretation of complex business records. This section of the Principles focuses solely on the disclosure of facts and the privilege issues that may be implicated thereby.

after interviews by non-attorney personnel. Whichever process the corporation selects, the government's key measure of cooperation must remain the same as it does for an individual: has the party timely disclosed the relevant facts about the putative misconduct? That is the operative question in assigning cooperation credit for the disclosure of information—not whether the corporation discloses attorney-client or work product materials. Accordingly, a corporation should receive the same credit for disclosing facts contained in materials that are not protected by the attorney- client privilege or attorney work product as it would for disclosing identical facts contained in materials that are so protected.[2] On this point the Report of the House Judiciary Committee, submitted in connection with the attorney-client privilege bill passed by the House of Representatives (H.R. 3013), comports with the approach required here:

> [A]n ... attorney of the United States may base cooperation credit on the facts that are disclosed, but is prohibited from basing cooperation credit upon whether or not the materials are protected by attorney-client privilege or attorney work product. As a result, an entity that voluntarily discloses should receive the same amount of cooperation credit for disclosing facts that happen to be contained in materials not protected by attorney-client privilege or attorney work product as it would receive for disclosing identical facts that are contained in materials protected by attorney-client privilege or attorney work product. There should be no differentials in an assessment of cooperation (i.e., neither a credit nor a penalty) based upon whether or not the materials disclosed are protected by attorney-client privilege or attorney work product.

H.R. Rep. No. 110-445 at 4 (2007).

In short, so long as the corporation timely discloses relevant facts about the putative misconduct, the corporation may receive due credit for such cooperation, regardless of whether it chooses to waive privilege or work product protection in the process.[3] Likewise, a corporation that does not

---

[2] By way of example, corporate personnel are typically interviewed during an internal investigation. If the interviews are conducted by counsel for the corporation, certain notes and memoranda generated from the interviews may be subject, at least in part, to the protections of attorney-client privilege and/or attorney work product. To receive cooperation credit for providing factual information, the corporation need not produce, and prosecutors may not request, protected notes or memoranda generated by the lawyers' interviews. To earn such credit, however, the corporation does need to produce, and prosecutors may request, relevant factual information—including relevant factual information acquired through those interviews, unless the identical information has otherwise been provided—as well as relevant non-privileged evidence such as accounting and business records and emails between non-attorney employees or agents.

[3] In assessing the timeliness of a corporation's disclosures, prosecutors should apply a standard of reasonableness in light of the totality of circumstances.

disclose the relevant facts about the alleged misconduct—for whatever reason—typically should not be entitled to receive credit for cooperation.

Two final and related points bear noting about the disclosure of facts, although they should be obvious. First, the government cannot compel, and the corporation has no obligation to make, such disclosures (although the government can obviously compel the disclosure of certain records and witness testimony through subpoenas). Second, a corporation's failure to provide relevant information does not mean the corporation will be indicted. It simply means that the corporation will not be entitled to mitigating credit for that cooperation. Whether the corporation faces charges will turn, as it does in any case, on the sufficiency of the evidence, the likelihood of success at trial, and all of the other factors identified in Section III above. If there is insufficient evidence to warrant indictment, after appropriate investigation has been completed, or if the other factors weigh against indictment, then the corporation should not be indicted, irrespective of whether it has earned cooperation credit. The converse is also true: The government may charge even the most cooperative corporation pursuant to these Principles if, in weighing and balancing the factors described herein, the prosecutor determines that a charge is required in the interests of justice. Put differently, even the most sincere and thorough effort to cooperate cannot necessarily absolve a corporation that has, for example, engaged in an egregious, orchestrated, and widespread fraud. Cooperation is a relevant potential mitigating factor, but it alone is not dispositive.

(b) Legal Advice and Attorney Work Product

Separate from (and usually preceding) the fact-gathering process in an internal investigation, a corporation, through its officers, employees, directors, or others, may have consulted with corporate counsel regarding or in a manner that concerns the legal implications of the putative misconduct at issue. Communications of this sort, which are both independent of the fact-gathering component of an internal investigation and made for the purpose of seeking or dispensing legal advice, lie at the core of the attorney-client privilege. Such communications can naturally have a salutary effect on corporate behavior—facilitating, for example, a corporation's effort to comply with complex and evolving legal and regulatory regimes.[4] Except as noted in subparagraphs (b)(i) and (b)(ii) below, a corporation need not disclose and prosecutors may not request the disclosure of such

---

[4] These privileged communications are not necessarily limited to those that occur contemporaneously with the underlying misconduct. They would include, for instance, legal advice provided by corporate counsel in an internal investigation report. Again, the key measure of cooperation is the disclosure of factual information known to the corporation, not the disclosure of legal advice or theories rendered in connection with the conduct at issue (subject to the two exceptions noted in USAM 9-28.720(b)(i-ii)).

communications as a condition for the corporation's eligibility to receive cooperation credit.

Likewise, non-factual or core attorney work product—for example, an attorney's mental impressions or legal theories—lies at the core of the attorney work product doctrine. A corporation need not disclose, and prosecutors may not request, the disclosure of such attorney work product as a condition for the corporation's eligibility to receive cooperation credit.

(i) Advice of Counsel Defense in the Instant Context

Occasionally a corporation or one of its employees may assert an advice-of-counsel defense, based upon communications with in- house or outside counsel that took place prior to or contemporaneously with the underlying conduct at issue. In such situations, the defendant must tender a legitimate factual basis to support the assertion of the advice-of-counsel defense. See, e.g., Pitt v. Dist. of Columbia, 491 F.3d 494, 504-05 (D.C. Cir. 2007); United States v. Wenger, 427 F.3d 840, 853-54 (10th Cir. 2005); United States v. Cheek, 3 F.3d 1057, 1061-62 (7th Cir. 1993). The Department cannot fairly be asked to discharge its responsibility to the public to investigate alleged corporate crime, or to temper what would otherwise be the appropriate course of prosecutive action, by simply accepting on faith an otherwise unproven assertion that an attorney—perhaps even an unnamed attorney—approved potentially unlawful practices. Accordingly, where an advice-of-counsel defense has been asserted, prosecutors may ask for the disclosure of the communications allegedly supporting it.

(ii) Communications in Furtherance of a Crime or Fraud

Communications between a corporation (through its officers, employees, directors, or agents) and corporate counsel that are made in furtherance of a crime or fraud are, under settled precedent, outside the scope and protection of the attorney- client privilege. See United States v. Zolin, 491 U.S. 554, 563 (1989); United States v. BDO Seidman, LLP, 492 F.3d 806, 818 (7th Cir. 2007). As a result, the Department may properly request such communications if they in fact exist.

9-28.730 Obstructing the Investigation

Another factor to be weighed by the prosecutor is whether the corporation has engaged in conduct intended to impede the investigation. Examples of such conduct could include: inappropriate directions to employees or their counsel, such as directions not to be truthful or to conceal relevant facts; making representations or submissions that contain misleading assertions or material omissions; and incomplete or delayed production of records.

In evaluating cooperation, however, prosecutors should not take into account whether a corporation is advancing or reimbursing attorneys' fees or providing counsel to employees, officers, or directors under investigation or indictment. Likewise, prosecutors may not request that a corporation refrain from taking such action. This prohibition is not meant to prevent a prosecutor from asking questions about an attorney's representation of a corporation or its employees, officers, or directors, where otherwise appropriate under the law.[5] Neither is it intended to limit the otherwise applicable reach of criminal obstruction of justice statutes such as 18 U.S.C. § 1503. If the payment of attorney fees were used in a manner that would otherwise constitute criminal obstruction of justice—for example, if fees were advanced on the condition that an employee adhere to a version of the facts that the corporation and the employee knew to be false—these Principles would not (and could not) render inapplicable such criminal prohibitions.

Similarly, the mere participation by a corporation in a joint defense agreement does not render the corporation ineligible to receive cooperation credit, and prosecutors may not request that a corporation refrain from entering into such agreements. Of course, the corporation may wish to avoid putting itself in the position of being disabled, by virtue of a particular joint defense or similar agreement, from providing some relevant facts to the government and thereby limiting its ability to seek such cooperation credit. Such might be the case if the corporation gathers facts from employees who have entered into a joint defense agreement with the corporation, and who may later seek to prevent the corporation from disclosing the facts it has acquired. Corporations may wish to address this situation by crafting or participating in joint defense agreements, to the extent they choose to enter them, that provide such flexibility as they deem appropriate.

Finally, it may on occasion be appropriate for the government to consider whether the corporation has shared with others sensitive information about the investigation that the government provided to the corporation. In appropriate situations, as it does with individuals, the government may properly request that, if a corporation wishes to receive credit for cooperation, the information provided by the government to the corporation not be transmitted to others—for example, where the disclosure of such information could lead to flight by individual subjects, destruction of evidence, or dissipation or concealment of assets.

9-28.740 Offering Cooperation: No Entitlement to Immunity

A corporation's offer of cooperation or cooperation itself does not automatically entitle it to immunity from prosecution or a favorable resolution of its case. A corporation should not be able to escape liability

---

[5] Routine questions regarding the representation status of a corporation and its employees, including how and by whom attorneys' fees are paid, sometimes arise in the course of an investigation under certain circumstances—to take one example, to assess conflict-of-interest issues. Such questions can be appropriate and this guidance is not intended to prohibit such limited inquiries.

merely by offering up its directors, officers, employees, or agents. Thus, a corporation's willingness to cooperate is not determinative; that factor, while relevant, needs to be considered in conjunction with all other factors.

9-28.750 Qualifying for Immunity, Amnesty, or Reduced Sanctions Through Voluntary Disclosures

In conjunction with regulatory agencies and other executive branch departments, the Department encourages corporations, as part of their compliance programs, to conduct internal investigations and to disclose the relevant facts to the appropriate authorities. Some agencies, such as the Securities and Exchange Commission and the Environmental Protection Agency, as well as the Department's Environmental and Natural Resources Division, have formal voluntary disclosure programs in which self-reporting, coupled with remediation and additional criteria, may qualify the corporation for amnesty or reduced sanctions. Even in the absence of a formal program, prosecutors may consider a corporation's timely and voluntary disclosure in evaluating the adequacy of the corporation's compliance program and its management's commitment to the compliance program. However, prosecution and economic policies specific to the industry or statute may require prosecution notwithstanding a corporation's willingness to cooperate. For example, the Antitrust Division has a policy of offering amnesty only to the first corporation to agree to cooperate. Moreover, amnesty, immunity, or reduced sanctions may not be appropriate where the corporation's business is permeated with fraud or other crimes.

9-28.760 Oversight Concerning Demands for Waivers of Attorney-Client Privilege or Work Product Protection By Corporations Contrary to This Policy

The Department underscores its commitment to attorney practices that are consistent with Department policies like those set forth herein concerning cooperation credit and due respect for the attorney-client privilege and work product protection. Counsel for corporations who believe that prosecutors are violating such guidance are encouraged to raise their concerns with supervisors, including the appropriate United States Attorney or Assistant Attorney General. Like any other allegation of attorney misconduct, such allegations are subject to potential investigation through established mechanisms.

9-28.800 Corporate Compliance Programs

A. *General Principle*: Compliance programs are established by corporate management to prevent and detect misconduct and to ensure that corporate activities are conducted in accordance with applicable criminal and civil laws, regulations, and rules. The Department encourages such corporate self-policing, including voluntary disclosures to the government of any problems that a corporation discovers on its own. However, the existence of a compliance program is not sufficient, in and of itself, to justify not charging a corporation for criminal misconduct undertaken by its officers, directors, employees, or agents. In addition, the nature of some crimes, e.g., antitrust violations, may be such that national law enforcement policies mandate prosecutions of corporations notwithstanding the existence of a compliance program.

B. *Comment*: The existence of a corporate compliance program, even one that specifically prohibited the very conduct in question, does not absolve the corporation from criminal liability under the doctrine of respondeat superior. See United States v. Basic Constr. Co., 711 F.2d 570, 573 (4th Cir. 1983) ("[A] corporation may be held criminally responsible for antitrust violations committed by its employees if they were acting within the scope of their authority, or apparent authority, and for the benefit of the corporation, even if ... such acts were against corporate policy or express instructions."). As explained in United States v. Potter, 463 F.3d 9 (1st Cir. 2006), a corporation cannot "avoid liability by adopting abstract rules" that forbid its agents from engaging in illegal acts, because "[e]ven a specific directive to an agent or employee or honest efforts to police such rules do not automatically free the company for the wrongful acts of agents." Id. at 25-26. See also United States v. Hilton Hotels Corp., 467 F.2d 1000, 1007 (9th Cir. 1972) (noting that a corporation "could not gain exculpation by issuing general instructions without undertaking to enforce those instructions by means commensurate with the obvious risks"); United States v. Beusch, 596 F.2d 871, 878 (9th Cir. 1979) ("[A] corporation may be liable for acts of its employees done contrary to express instructions and policies, but ...the existence of such instructions and policies may be considered in determining whether the employee in fact acted to benefit the corporation.").

While the Department recognizes that no compliance program can ever prevent all criminal activity by a corporation's employees, the critical factors in evaluating any program are whether the program is adequately designed for maximum effectiveness in preventing and detecting wrongdoing by employees and whether corporate management is enforcing the program or is tacitly encouraging or pressuring employees to engage in misconduct to achieve business objectives. The Department has no formulaic requirements regarding corporate compliance programs. The fundamental questions any prosecutor should ask are: Is the corporation's compliance program well designed? Is the program being applied earnestly and in good faith? Does the corporation's compliance program work? In answering these questions, the prosecutor should consider the comprehensiveness of the compliance program; the extent and pervasiveness of the criminal misconduct; the number and level of the corporate employees involved; the seriousness, duration, and frequency of the misconduct; and any remedial actions taken by the corporation, including, for example, disciplinary action against past violators uncovered by the prior compliance program, and revisions to corporate compliance programs in light of lessons learned.[6] Prosecutors should also consider the promptness of any disclosure of wrongdoing to the government. In evaluating compliance programs, prosecutors may consider whether the corporation has established corporate governance mechanisms that can effectively detect and prevent misconduct. For example, do the corporation's directors exercise independent review over proposed corporate actions rather than unquestioningly ratifying officers' recommendations; are internal audit functions conducted at a level sufficient to ensure their independence and accuracy; and have the directors established an information and reporting system in the organization reasonably designed to provide management and directors with timely and accurate information sufficient to allow them to reach an informed decision regarding the organization's compliance with the law. See, e.g., In re Caremark Int'l Inc. Derivative Litig., 698 A.2d 959, 968-70 (Del. Ch. 1996).

Prosecutors should therefore attempt to determine whether a corporation's compliance program is merely a "paper program" or whether it was designed, implemented, reviewed, and revised, as appropriate, in an effective manner. In addition, prosecutors should determine whether the corporation has provided for a staff sufficient to audit, document, analyze, and utilize the results of the corporation's compliance efforts. Prosecutors also should determine whether the corporation's employees are adequately informed about the compliance program and are convinced of the corporation's commitment to it. This will enable the prosecutor to make an informed decision as to whether the corporation has adopted and implemented a truly effective compliance program that, when consistent with other federal law enforcement policies, may result in a decision to charge only the corporation's employees and agents or to mitigate charges or sanctions against the corporation.

Compliance programs should be designed to detect the particular types of misconduct most likely to occur in a particular corporation's line of business. Many corporations operate in complex regulatory environments outside the normal experience of criminal prosecutors. Accordingly, prosecutors should consult with relevant federal and state agencies with the expertise to evaluate the adequacy of a program's design and implementation. For instance, state and federal banking, insurance, and medical boards, the Department of Defense, the Department of Health and Human Services, the Environmental Protection Agency, and the Securities and Exchange Commission have considerable experience with compliance programs and can be helpful to a prosecutor in evaluating such programs. In addition, the Fraud Section of the Criminal Division, the Commercial Litigation Branch of the Civil Division, and the Environmental Crimes Section of the Environment

---

[6] For a detailed review of these and other factors concerning corporate compliance programs, see USSG § 8B2.1.

and Natural Resources Division can assist United States Attorneys' Offices in finding the appropriate agency office(s) for such consultation.

9-28.900 Restitution and Remediation

A. *General Principle*: Although neither a corporation nor an individual target may avoid prosecution merely by paying a sum of money, a prosecutor may consider the corporation's willingness to make restitution and steps already taken to do so. A prosecutor may also consider other remedial actions, such as improving an existing compliance program or disciplining wrongdoers, in determining whether to charge the corporation and how to resolve corporate criminal cases.

B. *Comment*: In determining whether or not to prosecute a corporation, the government may consider whether the corporation has taken meaningful remedial measures. A corporation's response to misconduct says much about its willingness to ensure that such misconduct does not recur. Thus, corporations that fully recognize the seriousness of their misconduct and accept responsibility for it should be taking steps to implement the personnel, operational, and organizational changes necessary to establish an awareness among employees that criminal conduct will not be tolerated.

Among the factors prosecutors should consider and weigh are whether the corporation appropriately disciplined wrongdoers, once those employees are identified by the corporation as culpable for the misconduct. Employee discipline is a difficult task for many corporations because of the human element involved and sometimes because of the seniority of the employees concerned. Although corporations need to be fair to their employees, they must also be committed, at all levels of the corporation, to the highest standards of legal and ethical behavior. Effective internal discipline can be a powerful deterrent against improper behavior by a corporation's employees. Prosecutors should be satisfied that the corporation's focus is on the integrity and credibility of its remedial and disciplinary measures rather than on the protection of the wrongdoers.

In addition to employee discipline, two other factors used in evaluating a corporation's remedial efforts are restitution and reform. As with natural persons, the decision whether or not to prosecute should not depend upon the target's ability to pay restitution. A corporation's efforts to pay restitution even in advance of any court order is, however, evidence of its acceptance of responsibility and, consistent with the practices and policies of the appropriate Division of the Department entrusted with enforcing specific criminal laws, may be considered in determining whether to bring criminal charges. Similarly, although the inadequacy of a corporate compliance program is a factor to consider when deciding whether to charge a corporation, that corporation's quick recognition of the flaws in the program and its efforts to improve the program are also factors to consider as to appropriate disposition of a case.

9-28.1000 Collateral Consequences

A. *General Principle*: Prosecutors may consider the collateral consequences of a corporate criminal conviction or indictment in determining whether to charge the corporation with a criminal offense and how to resolve corporate criminal cases.

B. *Comment*: One of the factors in determining whether to charge a natural person or a corporation is whether the likely punishment is appropriate given the nature and seriousness of the crime. In the corporate context, prosecutors may take into account the possibly substantial consequences to a corporation's employees, investors, pensioners, and customers, many of whom may, depending on the size and nature of the corporation and their role in its operations, have played no role in the criminal conduct, have been unaware of it, or have been unable to prevent it. Prosecutors should also be aware of non-penal sanctions that may accompany a criminal charge, such as potential suspension or debarment from eligibility for government contracts or federally funded programs such as health care programs. Determining whether or not such non-penal sanctions are appropriate or required in a particular case is the responsibility of the relevant agency, and is a decision that will be made based on the applicable statutes, regulations, and policies.

Virtually every conviction of a corporation, like virtually every conviction of an individual, will have an impact on innocent third parties, and the mere existence of such an effect is not sufficient to preclude prosecution of the corporation. Therefore, in evaluating the relevance of collateral consequences, various factors already discussed, such as the pervasiveness of the criminal conduct and the adequacy of the corporation's compliance programs, should be considered in determining the weight to be given to this factor. For instance, the balance may tip in favor of prosecuting corporations in situations where the scope of the misconduct in a case is widespread and sustained within a corporate division (or spread throughout pockets of the corporate organization). In such cases, the possible unfairness of visiting punishment for the corporation's crimes upon shareholders may be of much less concern where those shareholders have substantially profited, even unknowingly, from widespread or pervasive criminal activity. Similarly, where the top layers of the corporation's management or the shareholders of a closely-held corporation were engaged in or aware of the wrongdoing, and the conduct at issue was accepted as a way of doing business for an extended period, debarment may be deemed not collateral, but a direct and entirely appropriate consequence of the corporation's wrongdoing.

On the other hand, where the collateral consequences of a corporate conviction for innocent third parties would be significant, it may be appropriate to consider a non-prosecution or deferred prosecution agreement with conditions designed, among other things, to promote compliance with applicable law and to prevent recidivism. Such agreements are a third option, besides a criminal indictment, on the one hand, and a declination, on the other. Declining prosecution may allow a corporate criminal to escape without consequences. Obtaining a conviction may produce a result that seriously harms innocent third parties who played no role in the criminal conduct. Under appropriate circumstances, a deferred prosecution or non-prosecution agreement can help restore the integrity of a company's operations and preserve the financial viability of a corporation that has engaged in criminal conduct, while preserving the government's ability to prosecute a recalcitrant corporation that materially breaches the agreement. Such agreements achieve other important objectives as well, like prompt restitution for victims.[7] Ultimately, the appropriateness of a criminal charge against a corporation, or some lesser alternative, must be evaluated in a pragmatic and reasoned way that produces a fair outcome, taking into consideration, among other things, the Department's need to promote and ensure respect for the law.

9-28.1100 Other Civil or Regulatory Alternatives

A. *General Principle*: Non-criminal alternatives to prosecution often exist and prosecutors may consider whether such sanctions would adequately deter, punish, and rehabilitate a corporation that has engaged in wrongful conduct. In evaluating the adequacy of non-criminal alternatives to prosecution—e.g., civil or regulatory enforcement actions—the prosecutor may consider all relevant factors, including:

1. the sanctions available under the alternative means of disposition;

2. the likelihood that an effective sanction will be imposed; and

3. the effect of non-criminal disposition on federal law enforcement interests.

B. *Comment*: The primary goals of criminal law are deterrence, punishment, and rehabilitation. Non-criminal sanctions may not be an appropriate response to a serious violation, a pattern of wrongdoing, or prior non-criminal sanctions without proper remediation. In other cases, however, these goals may be satisfied through civil or regulatory actions. In determining whether a federal criminal resolution is appropriate, the prosecutor should consider the same factors (modified appropriately for the regulatory context) considered when determining whether to leave prosecution of a natural person to another jurisdiction or to seek non-criminal alternatives to prosecution. These factors include: the strength of the regulatory authority's interest; the regulatory authority's ability and willingness to take effective enforcement action; the probable sanction if the regulatory authority's

---

[7] Prosecutors should note that in the case of national or multi-national corporations, multi-district or global agreements may be necessary. Such agreements may only be entered into with the approval of each affected district or the appropriate Department official. See USAM 9-27.641.

enforcement action is upheld; and the effect of a non-criminal disposition on federal law enforcement interests. See USAM 9-27.240, 9-27.250.

9-28.1200 Selecting Charges

A. *General Principle*: Once a prosecutor has decided to charge a corporation, the prosecutor at least presumptively should charge, or should recommend that the grand jury charge, the most serious offense that is consistent with the nature of the defendant's misconduct and that is likely to result in a sustainable conviction.

B. *Comment*: Once the decision to charge is made, the same rules as govern charging natural persons apply. These rules require "a faithful and honest application of the Sentencing Guidelines" and an "individualized assessment of the extent to which particular charges fit the specific circumstances of the case, are consistent with the purposes of the Federal criminal code, and maximize the impact of Federal resources on crime." See USAM 9-27.300. In making this determination, "it is appropriate that the attorney for the government consider, inter alia, such factors as the [advisory] sentencing guideline range yielded by the charge, whether the penalty yielded by such sentencing range ...is proportional to the seriousness of the defendant's conduct, and whether the charge achieves such purposes of the criminal law as punishment, protection of the public, specific and general deterrence, and rehabilitation." Id.

9-28.1300 Plea Agreements with Corporations

A. *General Principle*: In negotiating plea agreements with corporations, as with individuals, prosecutors should generally seek a plea to the most serious, readily provable offense charged. In addition, the terms of the plea agreement should contain appropriate provisions to ensure punishment, deterrence, rehabilitation, and compliance with the plea agreement in the corporate context. Although special circumstances may mandate a different conclusion, prosecutors generally should not agree to accept a corporate guilty plea in exchange for non-prosecution or dismissal of charges against individual officers and employees.

B. *Comment*: Prosecutors may enter into plea agreements with corporations for the same reasons and under the same constraints as apply to plea agreements with natural persons. See USAM 9-27.400-530. This means,inter alia, that the corporation should generally be required to plead guilty to the most serious, readily provable offense charged. In addition, any negotiated departures or recommended variances from the advisory Sentencing Guidelines must be justifiable under the Guidelines or 18 U.S.C. § 3553 and must be disclosed to the sentencing court. A corporation should be made to realize that pleading guilty to criminal charges constitutes an admission of guilt and not merely a resolution of an inconvenient distraction from its business. As with natural persons, pleas should be structured so that the corporation may not later "proclaim lack of culpability or even complete innocence." See USAM 9-27.420(b)(4), 9-27.440, 9-27.500. Thus, for instance, there should be placed upon the record a sufficient factual basis for the plea to prevent later corporate assertions of innocence.

A corporate plea agreement should also contain provisions that recognize the nature of the corporate "person" and that ensure that the principles of punishment, deterrence, and rehabilitation are met. In the corporate context, punishment and deterrence are generally accomplished by substantial fines, mandatory restitution, and institution of appropriate compliance measures, including, if necessary, continued judicial oversight or the use of special masters or corporate monitors. See USSG §§ 8B1.1, 8C2.1, et seq. In addition, where the corporation is a government contractor, permanent or temporary debarment may be appropriate. Where the corporation was engaged in fraud against the government (e.g., contracting fraud), a prosecutor may not negotiate away an agency's right to debar or delist the corporate defendant.

In negotiating a plea agreement, prosecutors should also consider the deterrent value of prosecutions of individuals within the corporation. Therefore, one factor that a prosecutor may consider in determining whether to enter into a plea agreement is whether the corporation is seeking immunity for its employees and officers or whether the corporation is willing to cooperate in the investigation of culpable individuals as outlined herein. Prosecutors should rarely negotiate away individual criminal liability in a corporate plea.

Rehabilitation, of course, requires that the corporation undertake to be law-abiding in the future. It is, therefore, appropriate to require the corporation, as a condition of probation, to implement a compliance program or to reform an existing one. As discussed above, prosecutors may consult with the appropriate state and federal agencies and components of the Justice Department to ensure that a proposed compliance program is adequate and meets industry standards and best practices. See USAM 9-28.800.

In plea agreements in which the corporation agrees to cooperate, the prosecutor should ensure that the cooperation is entirely truthful. To do so, the prosecutor may request that the corporation make appropriate disclosures of relevant factual information and documents, make employees and agents available for debriefing, file appropriate certified financial statements, agree to governmental or third-party audits, and take whatever other steps are necessary to ensure that the full scope of the corporate wrongdoing is disclosed and that the responsible personnel are identified and, if appropriate, prosecuted. See generally USAM 9-28.700. In taking such steps, Department prosecutors should recognize that attorney-client communications are often essential to a corporation's efforts to comply with complex regulatory and legal regimes, and that, as discussed at length above, cooperation is not measured by the waiver of attorney-client privilege and work product protection, but rather is measured by the disclosure of facts and other considerations identified herein such as making witnesses available for interviews and assisting in the interpretation of complex documents or business records.

These Principles provide only internal Department of Justice guidance. They are not intended to, do not, and may not be relied upon to create any rights, substantive or procedural, enforceable at law by any party in any matter civil or criminal. Nor are any limitations hereby placed on otherwise lawful litigative prerogatives of the Department of Justice.

Organized Crime and Racketeering

9-110.200 RICO Guidelines Preface

The decision to institute a federal criminal prosecution involves balancing society's interest in effective law enforcement against the consequences for the accused. Utilization of the RICO statute, more so than most other federal criminal sanctions, requires particularly careful and reasoned application, because, among other things, RICO incorporates certain state crimes. One purpose of these guidelines is to reemphasize the principle that the primary responsibility for enforcing state laws rests with the state concerned. Despite the broad statutory language of RICO and the legislative intent that the statute ". . . shall be liberally construed to effectuate its remedial purpose," it is the policy of the Criminal Division that RICO be selectively and uniformly used. It is the purpose of these guidelines to make it clear that not every proposed RICO charge that meets the technical requirements of a RICO violation will be approved. Further, the Criminal Division will not appro ve "imaginative" prosecutions under RICO which are far afield from the congressional purpose of the RICO statute. A RICO count which merely duplicates the elements of proof of traditional Hobbs Act, Travel Act, mail fraud, wire fraud, gambling or controlled substances cases, will not be approved unless it serves some special RICO purpose. Only in exceptional circumstances will approval be granted when RICO is sought merely to serve some evidentiary purpose.

These guidelines provide only internal Department of Justice guidance. They are not intended to, do not, and may not be relied upon to create any rights, substantive or procedural, enforceable at law by any party in any matter civil or criminal. Nor are any limitations hereby placed on otherwise lawful litigative prerogatives of the Department of Justice.

9-110.210 Authorization of RICO Prosecution—The Review Process

The review and approval function for all RICO matters has been centralized within the Organized Crime and Gang Section of the Criminal Division. To commence the review process, the final draft of the proposed indictment or information and a RICO prosecution memorandum shall be forwarded to the Organized Crime and Gang Section. Separate approval is required for superseding indictments or indictments based upon a previously approved information. Attorneys are encouraged to seek guidance from the Organized Crime and Gang Section by telephone prior to the time an investigation is undertaken and well before a final indictment and prosecution memorandum are submitted for review. Guidance on preparing the RICO prosecution memorandum is in the Criminal Resource Manual at 2071 et seq.

RICO reviews are handled on a first-in-first-out basis. Accordingly, the submitting attorney must allocate sufficient lead time to permit review, revision, conferences, and the scheduling of the grand jury. Unless there is a backlog, 15 working days is usually sufficient. The review process will not be dispensed with because a grand jury, which is about to expire, has been scheduled to meet to return a RICO indictment. Therefore, submitting attorneys are cautioned to budget their time and to await receipt of approval before scheduling the presentation of the indictment to a grand jury.

If modifications in the indictment are required, they must be made by the submitting attorney before the indictment is returned by the grand jury. Once the modifications have been made and the indictment has been returned, a copy of the indictment filed with the clerk of the court shall be forwarded to Organized Crime and Gang Section. If, however, it is determined that the RICO count is inappropriate, the submitting attorney will be advised of the Section's disapproval of the proposed indictment. The submitting attorney may wish to redraft the indictment based upon the Section's review and submit a revised indictment and/or prosecution memorandum at a later date.

9-110.300 RICO Guidelines Policy

It is the purpose of these guidelines to centralize the RICO review and policy implementation functions in the section of the Criminal Division having supervisory responsibility for this statute.

9-110.310 Considerations Prior to Seeking Indictment

Except as hereafter provided, a government attorney should seek approval for a RICO charge only if one or more of the following requirements is present:

1. RICO is necessary to ensure that the indictment adequately reflects the nature and extent of the criminal conduct involved in a way that prosecution only on the underlying charges would not;

2. A RICO prosecution would provide the basis for an appropriate sentence under all the circumstances of the case in a way that prosecution only on the underlying charges would not;

3. A RICO charge could combine related offenses which would otherwise have to be prosecuted separately in different jurisdictions;

4. RICO is necessary for a successful prosecution of the government's case against the defendant or a codefendant;

5. Use of RICO would provide a reasonable expectation of forfeiture which is proportionate to the underlying criminal conduct;

6. The case consists of violations of State law, but local law enforcement officials are unlikely or unable to successfully prosecute the case, in which the federal government has a significant interest;

7. The case consists of violations of State law, but involves prosecution of significant or government individuals, which may pose special problems for the local prosecutor.

The last two requirements reflect the principle that the prosecution of state crimes is primarily the responsibility of state authorities. RICO should be used to prosecute what are essentially violations of state law only if there is a compelling reason to do so. See also the Criminal Resource Manual at 2070.

9-110.320 Approval of Organized Crime and Racketeering Section Necessary

A RICO prosecution memorandum and draft indictment, felony information, civil complaint, or civil investigative demand shall be forwarded to the Organized Crime and Gang Section, Criminal Division, 1301 New York Ave., NW, Suite 700, Washington, DC 20005, at least 15 working days prior to the anticipated date of the proposed filing or the seeking of an indictment from the grand jury.

No criminal or civil prosecution or civil investigative demand shall be commenced or issued under the RICO statute without the prior approval of the Organized Crime and Gang Section, Criminal Division. Prior authorization from the Criminal Division to conduct a grand jury investigation based upon possible violations of 18 U.S.C. § 1962 is not required.

A RICO prosecution memorandum and draft pleading or civil investigative demand shall be forwarded to the Organized Crime and Gang Section. It is essential to the careful review which these factually and legally complex cases require that the attorney handling the case in the field not wait to submit the case until the grand jury or the statute of limitations is about to expire. Authorizations based on oral presentations will not be given. See the Criminal Resource Manual at 2071 et seq. for specific guidance.

These guidelines do not limit the authority of the Federal Bureau of Investigation to conduct investigations of suspected violations of RICO. The authority to conduct such investigations is governed by the FBI Guidelines on the Investigation of General Crimes. However, the factors identified here are the criteria by which the Department of Justice will determine whether to approve the proposed RICO. The fact that an investigation was authorized, or that substantial resources were committed to it, will not influence the Department in determining whether an indictment under the RICO statute is appropriate.

Use of RICO in a prosecution, like every other federal criminal statute, is also governed by the Principles of Federal Prosecution. See USAM 9-27.000, et seq. Inclusion of a RICO count in an indictment solely or even primarily to create a bargaining tool for later plea negotiations on lesser counts is not appropriate and would violate the Principles of Federal Prosecution.

9-110.330 Charging RICO Counts

A RICO charge where the predicate acts consist only of state offenses will not be approved except in the following circumstances:

A. Local law enforcement officials are unlikely to investigate and prosecute otherwise meritorious cases in which the Federal government has significant interest;

B. Significant organized crime involvement exists; or

C. The prosecution of significant political or governmental individuals may pose special problems for local prosecutors.

Deferred Prosecution Agreement

1.   Bristol-Myers Squibb Company ("BMS" or the "Company") by its undersigned attorneys, pursuant to authority granted by its Board of Directors, and the United States Attorney's Office for the District of New Jersey (the "Office"), enter into this Deferred Prosecution Agreement (the "Agreement"). Except as specifically provided below, the Agreement shall be in effect for a period of two years from the date it is fully executed.

2.   The Office has informed BMS that it will file, on or shortly after the date this Agreement is fully executed, a criminal complaint in the United States District Court for the District of New Jersey charging BMS with conspiracy to commit securities fraud, contrary to Title 15, United States Code, Sections 78j(b) & 78ff and Title 17, Code of Federal Regulations, Section 240.10b-5, in violation of Title 18, United States Code, Section 37 1, during the period of 2000 through 2001.

3.   BMS and the Office agree that, upon filing of the criminal complaint in accordance with the preceding paragraph, this Agreement shall be publicly filed in the United States District Court for the District of New Jersey, and BMS agrees to post the Agreement prominently on its website.

4.   In light of BMS's remedial actions to date and its willingness to

        (a) undertake additional remediation;

        (b) acknowledge responsibility for its behavior;

        (c) continue its cooperation with the Office and other governmental regulatory agencies;

        (d) demonstrate its future good conduct and full compliance with the securities laws and Generally Accepted Accounting Principles; and

        (e) consent to payment of additional restitution as set forth in paragraph 21, the Office shall recommend to the Court that prosecution of BMS on the criminal complaint filed pursuant to paragraph 2 be deferred for a period of twenty-four (24) months from the filing date of the criminal complaint. If the Court declines to defer prosecution for any reason, this Agreement shall be null and void, and the parties will revert to their pre-Agreement positions.

5.   BMS has undertaken extensive reforms and remedial actions in response to the conduct at BMS that is and has been the subject of

the investigation by the Office. These reforms and remedial actions have included:

(a) Retaining the Honorable Frederick B. Lacey as Independent Advisor, to conduct a comprehensive review of the implementation and effectiveness of the internal controls, financial reporting, disclosure, planning, budget and projection processes and related compliance actions of the Company, as well as to serve additional supervisory and monitoring functions described herein;

(b) Entering a Consent filed in the United States District Court for the District of New Jersey in United States Securities Exchange Commission v. Bristol-Myers Squibb Com~any, Civ. Action No. 04-3680 (FSH) (the "D.N.J. Action") providing for, among other things, the payment of a $100 million Civil Penalty and an additional $50 million Shareholder Fund payment, both of which amounts are to be distributed pursuant to the Fair Fund provisions of Section 308(a) of the Sarbanes-Oxley Act of 2002, as well as incorporating an array of remedial measures to be undertaken by BMS together with extensive supervisory and monitoring responsibilities to be carried out by the Independent Advisor during a review period extending through the filing of the Company's Form 10-K for the year ended 2005;

(c) Making a payment of an additional $300 million to compensate present and former BMS shareholders in connection with lawsuits filed and consolidated in In re Bristol- Myers Squibb Securities Litigation, Master File No. 02-CV-2251 (LAP) (S.D.N.Y.) (the "Consolidated Shareholder Litigation");

(d) Making significant personnel changes after April 2002 and after the Office commenced its investigation including:

(i) replacing the former Chief Financial Officer (CFO);
(ii) replacing the former President of the Worldwide Medicines Group;
(iii) replacing the former Controller;
(iv) establishing the position of Assistant Controller for Financial Compliance and Control;
(v) establishing the position of Chief Compliance Officer;
(vi) establishing a position for an experienced securities regulation and disclosure lawyer who has

a significant role in all BMS disclosure responsibilities;

(e) Changing its budget process, to assure that appropriate consideration is given to input and analysis from the bottom to top, and not exclusively from top to bottom, and adequately documenting that process;

(f) Forming a business risk and disclosure group that includes senior management, the Independent Advisor and counsel to the Independent Advisor;

(g) Identifying and implementing actions to improve the effectiveness of its disclosure controls and procedures and internal controls, including enhancing its resources and training with respect to financial reporting and disclosure responsibilities, and reviewing such actions with its Audit Committee and independent auditors;

(h) Implementing a formal review and certification process of its annual and quarterly reports filed with the Securities and Exchange Commission (SEC); and

(i) Providing an effective mechanism in the form of a confidential hotline and e-mail address, of which BMS employees are informed and can use to notify BMS of any concerns about wholesaler inventory levels or the integrity of the financial disclosures, books and records of BMS.

6.   BMS shall maintain and continue to implement any remedial measures already undertaken or mandated as part of agreements BMS has reached in the following matters: Bristol-Myers Squibb Derivative Litigation, Master File No. 02-CV-8571 (LAP) (S.D.N.Y.) (the "Shareholder Derivative Action"); the "D.N.J. Action"; and the "Consolidated Shareholder Litigation."

7.   In addition to the extensive remedial actions that it has taken to date, BMS agrees to undertake additional remedial actions and corporate reforms as set forth herein.

8.   BMS shall establish the position of non-executive Chairman of the BMS Board of Directors (the "Non-Executive Chairman"), to advance and underscore the Company's commitment to exemplary corporate citizenship, to best practices of effective corporate governance and the highest principles of integrity and professionalism, and to fostering a culture of openness, accountability and compliance throughout the Company. BMS shall retain the position of Non-Executive Chairman at least throughout the term of this Agreement.

9.   BMS agrees to appoint an additional non-executive Director acceptable to the Office to the BMS Board of Directors within sixty (60) days of the execution of this Agreement.

10.   The Company's CFO, General Counsel, and Chief Compliance Officer regularly shall brief and provide information to the Non-Executive Chairman, in a manner to be determined by the Non-Executive Chairman. In addition, the Non-Executive Chairman shall have the authority to meet with, and require reports on any subject from, any officer or employee of the Company.

11.   BMS agrees that until at least the date of the filing of the Company's Form 10-K for the year ended 2006, it will retain an outside, independent individual or entity (the "Monitor"), selected by BMS and approved by the Office. BMS may employ as the Monitor the Honorable Frederick B. Lacey. It shall be a condition of the Monitor's retention that the Monitor is independent of BMS and that no attorney-client relationship shall be formed between the Monitor and BMS.

12.   The Monitor shall:

(a) Monitor BMS's compliance with this Agreement, and have authority to require BMS to take any steps he believes are necessary to comply with the terms of this Agreement;

(b) Continue the review, reforms and other functions undertaken as the Independent Advisor;

(c) Report to the Office, on at least a quarterly basis and between thirty and forty-five calendar days after the filing of the Company's Form 10-K for the year ended 2006, as to BMS's compliance with this Agreement and the implementation and effectiveness of the internal controls, financial reporting, disclosure processes and related compliance functions of the Company. The first report to the Office shall be due within forty-five (45) days after the close of the second quarter 2005, and subsequent quarterly reports (other than the final report) shall be due by the close of the quarter. The reporting function of the Monitor shall extend until forty-five (45) days subsequent to the filing of the Company's Form 10-K for the year ended 2006 in order to facilitate the submission of the Monitor's final report to the Office;

(d) Cooperate with the SEC and provide information about BMS as requested by that agency;

(e) Monitor BMS's compliance with applicable federal securities laws, and in his quarterly reports make recommendations necessary to ensure that the Company complies with applicable federal securities laws;

(f) Monitor BMS's compliance with agreements BMS has reached in the Shareholder Derivative Action, the D.N.J. Action, and the Consolidated Shareholder Litigation; and

(g) Monitor the information received by the confidential hotline and e-mail address described in paragraph 5(i).

13.   BMS agrees that the Chief Executive Officer (CEO), Non-Executive Chairman, and General Counsel will meet quarterly with the Office and the Monitor, in conjunction with the Monitor's quarterly reports.

14.   BMS shall adopt all recommendations contained in each report submitted by the Monitor to the Office unless BMS objects to the recommendation and the Office agrees that adoption of the recommendation should not be required. The Monitor's reports to the Office shall not be received or reviewed by BMS prior to submission to the Office; such reports will be preliminary until senior management of BMS is given the opportunity, within ten (1 0) days after the submission of the report to the Office, to comment to the Monitor and the Office in writing upon such reports, and the Monitor has reviewed and provided to the Office responses to such comments, upon which such reports shall be considered final.

15.   BMS agrees that the Monitor may also disclose his reports, as directed by the Office, to any other federal, state or foreign law enforcement or regulatory agency in furtherance of an investigation of any other matters discovered by, or brought to the attention of, the Office in connection with the Office's investigation of BMS or the implementation of this Agreement.

16.   BMS agrees that if the Monitor resigns or is unable to serve the balance of his term, a successor shall be selected by BMS and approved by the Office within forty-five (45) days. BMS agrees that all provisions in this Agreement that apply to the Monitor shall apply to any successor Monitor.

17.   The Non-Executive Chairman and the Compensation Committee of the Board of Directors shall set goals and objectives relevant to compensation of the CEO, evaluate the CEO's performance in light of those goals and objectives, and recommend to the Board of Directors compensation based on this evaluation.

18.   BMS agrees that it will establish and maintain a training and education program, which shall be reviewed and approved by the

Board of Directors, designed to advance and underscore the Company's commitment to exemplary corporate citizenship, to best practices of effective corporate governance and the highest principles of integrity and professionalism, and to fostering a culture of openness, accountability and compliance throughout the Company. Completion of such training shall be mandatory for: (a) all BMS officers, executives and employees who are involved in accounting and financial reporting functions, or the oversight thereof, whether at the corporate or the division level, including but not limited to each officer or employee responsible for closing the books within his or her area of responsibility at the end of a quarterly or annual reporting period; (b) all employees of the BMS legal division with responsibility for finance, business risk or disclosure issues; and (c) other senior officers and executives at BMS, at both the corporate and operating levels, as proposed by BMS and approved by the Office (collectively the "Mandatory Participants"). Such training and education program will cover, at a minimum, the following subjects: (a) the obligations imposed by the federal securities laws, including disclosure obligations; (b) proper internal accounting controls and procedures; (c) discovering and recognizing accounting practices that do not conform to Generally Accepted Accounting Principles or that are otherwise improper; and (d) the obligations assumed by, and responses expected of, the Mandatory Participants upon learning of improper, illegal or potentially illegal acts relating to BMS's accounting and financial reporting. The Board of Directors shall communicate to the Mandatory Participants, in writing or by video, its review and endorsement of the training and education program.

19.   BMS shall commence providing the training mandated by paragraph 18 within ninety (90) days after the date of the execution of this Agreement and shall, at that time, submit to the Office a written description of the content and planned implementation of the training and education program. BMS shall thereafter provide such training and education on an annual basis for all those who become Mandatory Participants during the preceding twelve months.

20.   BMS shall endow a chair at Seton Hall University School of Law dedicated to the teaching of business ethics and corporate governance, which position shall include conducting one or more seminars per year on business ethics and corporate governance at Seton Hall University School of Law that members of BMS's executive and management staff, along with representatives of the executive and management staffs of other companies in the New Jersey area, may attend.

21.   BMS shall make an additional payment of $300 million into the shareholder compensation fund established pursuant to the consent judgment in the D.N.J. Action. This payment shall be administered according to the terms of such fund. Together with this payment, B

MS will have paid a total of $839 million in compensation to its shareholders and former shareholders. This sum includes payments already made by BMS of $300 million in the Consolidated Shareholder Litigation, $1 50 million in the D.N.J. Action, and $89 million in actions by shareholders who requested to be excluded from the settlement in the Consolidated Shareholder Litigation, as well as the additional $300 million that BMS shall pay pursuant to this Agreement. BMS may make the additional payment of $300 million in a single payment at or before the close of the third quarter of 2005, or in four approximately equal quarterly installments, with the first installment due at the close of the third quarter of 2005. None of the proceeds of the payment required by this Agreement shall be payable as attorney's fees. Any costs of administering the distribution of the additional payment called for by this agreement shall be borne by BMS. To the extent that any money paid into the D.N.J. shareholder compensation fund pursuant to this Agreement is not claimed by shareholders or former shareholders within three years, the remaining amount shall be paid to the United States Treasury.

22.   Within thirty (30) days of the execution of this Agreement, BMS agrees to call a meeting, on a date mutually agreed upon by BMS and the Office, of its senior executives and any senior financial personnel, and any other BMS employees who the Company desires to attend, such meeting to be attended by the United States Attorney and other representatives of the Office for the purpose of communicating the goals and expected effect of this Agreement.

23.   For a period of one year from the execution of this Agreement, the Non-Executive Chairman, CEO, and General Counsel shall contemporaneously monitor either in person or telephonically BMS's quarterly conference calls for analysts ("analyst calls"), and the Non-Executive Chairman shall attend and participate in any preparatory meetings held among the CEO, the CFO, the General Counsel and other members of BMS senior management in anticipation of the analyst calls. The General Counsel shall ensure that representatives of the BMS legal division are informed and consulted regarding, at a minimum, issues relating to disclosure or securities law that may arise in the course of preparing for the analyst calls.

24.   The CEO and CFO shall prepare and submit to the Non-Executive Chairman, Chief Compliance Officer and the Monitor described in paragraph 11 written reports on the following subjects: (a) all non-standard transactions with major U.S. wholesalers, such written report to be submitted within fifteen (1 5) days of such transaction; (b) an overview and analysis of BMS's annual budget process for its major business units, including description of significant instances of any top-down changes to business unit submissions, such written report to be submitted together with the proposed budget submitted

for approval to the Board of Directors; (c) sales and earnings forecasts or projections at the corporate or major business unit level which indicate a quarterly target will not be met, together with a description of steps subsequently taken, if any, to achieve the budget target, such written report to be submitted quarterly and at least ten (10) business days prior to the Company's scheduled quarterly analyst call; (d) description of significant instances in which the preliminary quarterly closing of the books of any major business unit indicated that the business unit would not meet its budget target for any sales or earnings measure.

25.   BMS agrees that it shall include in its quarterly and annual public filings with the SEC and its annual report to shareholders financial disclosures concerning the following: (a)(i) for the Company's U.S. Pharmaceuticals business, estimated wholesaler/direct-customer inventory levels of the top fifteen (1 5) products sold by such business and (ii) for major non-U.S. countries, estimated aggregate wholesaler/direct-customer inventory levels of the top fifteen (15) pharmaceutical products sold in such countries taken as a whole measured by aggregate annual sales in such countries; (b) arrangements with and policies concerning wholesalers/direct customers and other distributors of such products, including but not limited to efforts by BMS to control and monitor wholesaler/distributor inventory levels; (c) data concerning prescriptions or other measures of end-user demand for such top fifteen (15) BMS pharmaceutical products sold within the U.S. and in major non-U.S. countries; (d) acquisition, divestiture, and restructuring reserve policies and activity; and (e) rebate accrual policies and activity. The CEO shall, at the annual BMS shareholder meeting, report to the shareholders on these topics.

26.   BMS agrees that it will continue to review and improve, where necessary, the content of its public financial and non-financial public disclosures, including periodic SEC filings, annual and other shareholder reports, press releases, and disclosures during analyst conference calls, as well as during meetings with investors and credit ratings agencies. BMS agrees that it will at all times strive for openness and transparency in its public reporting and disclosures.

27.   BMS shall encourage the free flow of information between its employees and its external auditor, and encourage its CFO and senior finance personnel to seek advice from the external auditor. The CEO, CFO, General Counsel, and Chief Compliance Officer shall meet quarterly with the Company's external auditors, such meeting to occur following the closing of the Company's books for the quarter and prior to the Company's scheduled quarterly analyst call. At the quarterly meeting, the BMS attendees shall discuss business and financial reporting developments, issues and trends with the external auditor, as well as provide information to the external auditor

concerning the subjects described in paragraph 24 above, and shall respond to inquiries from the external auditor.

28.   BMS accepts and acknowledges responsibility for the facts set forth in the Statement of Facts attached as Appendix A (the "Statement of Facts") and incorporated by reference herein by entering into this Agreement and by, among other things, (a) the extensive remedial actions that it has taken to date, (b) its continuing commitment to full cooperation with the Office and other governmental agencies, and (c) and the other undertakings it has made as set forth in this Agreement.

29.   BMS agrees that in the event that future criminal proceedings are brought by the Office in accordance with paragraphs 4 and 36 through 39 of this Agreement, BMS will not contest the admissibility of the Statement of Facts in any such proceedings. Nothing in this Agreement shall be construed as an acknowledgment by BMS that the Agreement, including the Statement of Facts, is admissible or may be used in any proceeding other than in a proceeding brought by the Office.

30.   BMS expressly agrees that it shall not, through its present or future attorneys, Board of Directors, agents, officers or employees, make any public statement contradicting any statement of fact contained in the Statement of Facts. Any such contradictory public statement by BMS, its present or future attorneys, Board of Directors, agents, officers or employees, shall constitute a breach of this Agreement as governed by paragraphs 36 and 37 of this Agreement, and BMS would thereafter be subject to prosecution pursuant to the terms of this Agreement. The decision of whether any public statement by any such person contradicting a fact contained in the Statement of Facts will be imputed to BMS for the purpose of determining whether BMS has committed a knowing and material breach of this Agreement shall be at the sole discretion of the Office. Should the Office notify BMS of a public statement by any such person that in whole or in part contradicts a statement of fact contained in the Statement of Facts, BMS may avoid breach of this Agreement by publicly repudiating such statement within forty-eight (48) hours after such notification. This paragraph is not intended to apply to any statement by any former BMS employee, officer or director, or any BMS employee, officer or director testifying in any proceeding in an individual capacity and not on behalf of BMS.

31.   BMS agrees that its continuing cooperation during the term of this Agreement shall include, but shall not be not limited to, the following:

          (a) Not engaging in or attempting to engage in any criminal conduct as defined in paragraph 34.

(b) Completely, truthfully and promptly disclosing all information concerning all matters about which the Office and other government agencies designated by the Office may inquire, and continuing to provide the Office, upon request, all documents and other materials relating to matters about which the Office inquires, and analysis or other work product as may be requested by the Office, as promptly as is practicable. Cooperation under this paragraph shall include identification of documents that may be relevant to the matters under investigation.

(c) Consenting to any order sought by the Office permitting disclosure of any materials that constitute "matters occurring before the grand jury" within the meaning of Rule 6(e) of the Federal Rules of Criminal Procedure.

(d) Not asserting, in relation to any request of the Office, any claims of attorney-client privilege or attorney work-product doctrine as to any documents, records, information or testimony requested by the Office related to: (i) factual internal investigations undertaken by the Company or its counsel relating to the matters under investigation by the Office; (ii) legal advice given contemporaneously with, and related to, such matters. Such materials are referred to hereinafter as the "Confidential Materials." By producing the Confidential Materials pursuant to this Agreement, BMS does not intend to waive the protection of the attorney-client privilege or the attorney work-product doctrine, or any other applicable privilege, as to third parties. The Office will maintain the confidentiality of the Confidential Materials pursuant to this Agreement and will not disclose them to any third party, except to the extent that the Office determines, in its sole discretion, that disclosure is otherwise required by law or would be in furtherance of the discharge of the duties and responsibilities of the Office.

(e) Making available BMS officers, directors, and employees and using its best efforts to make available former BMS officers, directors, and employees to provide information and/or testimony at all reasonable times as requested by the Office, including sworn testimony before a federal grand jury or in federal trials, as well as interviews with federal law enforcement authorities. Cooperation under this paragraph shall include identification of witnesses who, to BMS's knowledge, may have material information regarding the matters under investigation.

(f) Providing testimony, certifications, and other information deemed necessary by the Office or a court to identify or establish the original location, authenticity, or other evidentiary foundation necessary to admit into evidence documents in any criminal or other proceeding as requested by the Office.

32.   BMS has provided extensive cooperation to the Office in connection with its investigation. BMS acknowledges and understands that its prior, ongoing and future cooperation are important factors in the decision of the Office to enter into this Agreement, and BMS agrees to continue to cooperate fully with the Office, and with any other governmental agency designated by the Office, regarding any issue about which BMS has knowledge or information.

33.   BMS authorizes the Office and the SEC to share information from and about BMS with each other and hereby waives any confidentiality accorded to that information by law, agreement or otherwise that would, absent authorization by BMS, prohibit or limit such sharing. No other waivers of confidentiality shall be required in that regard.

34.   BMS will inform the Office of any credible evidence of criminal conduct at BMS occurring after the date of the Agreement, including making available internal audit reports, letters threatening litigation, "whistleblower" complaints, civil complaints, and documents produced in civil litigation so evidencing such criminal conduct. For purposes of this Agreement, "criminal conduct" is defined as (a) any crime related to BMS's business activities committed by one or more BMS executive officers or directors; (b) securities fraud, accounting fraud, financial fraud or other business fraud materially affecting the books, records or publicly-filed reports of BMS; and (c) obstruction of justice.

35.   The Office may continue to investigate current and former BMS employees. Nothing in this Agreement restricts in any way the ability of the Office to investigate and prosecute any BMS employee or former BMS employee.

36.   Should the Office determine during the term of this Agreement that BMS has committed any criminal conduct as defined in paragraph 34 commenced subsequent to the date of this Agreement, or otherwise in any other respect knowingly and materially breached this Agreement, BMS shall, in the discretion of the Office, thereafter be subject to prosecution for any federal crimes of which the Office has knowledge, including crimes relating to the matters set forth in the Statement of Facts. Except in the event of a breach of this Agreement, it is the intention of the parties to this Agreement that all investigations of BMS relating to the matters set forth in the Statement of Facts that have been, or could have been, conducted by

the Office prior to the date of this Agreement shall not be pursued further as to BMS.

37.   Should the Office determine that BMS has knowingly and materially breached any provision of this Agreement, the Office shall provide written notice to BMS of the alleged breach and provide BMS with a two-week period in which to make a presentation to the Office to demonstrate that no breach occurred, or, to the extent applicable, that the breach was not material or knowingly committed or has been cured. The parties understand and agree that should BMS fail to make a presentation to the Office within a two-week period after receiving written notice of an alleged breach, it shall be conclusively presumed that BMS is in breach of this Agreement. The parties further understand and agree that the determination whether BMS has breached this Agreement rests solely in the discretion of the Office, and the exercise of discretion by the Office under this paragraph is not subject to review in any court or tribunal outside the Department of Justice. In the event of a breach of this Agreement that results in a prosecution of BMS, such prosecution may be premised upon any information provided by or on behalf of BMS to the Office at any time, unless otherwise agreed when the information was provided.

38.   BMS shall expressly waive all rights to a speedy trial pursuant to the Sixth Amendment of the United States Constitution, Title 18, United States Code, Section 3 161, Federal Rule of Criminal Procedure 48(b), and any applicable Local Rules of the United States District Court for the District of New Jersey, for the period that this Agreement is in effect.

39.   In case of a knowing material breach of this Agreement, any prosecution of BMS relating to the facts set forth in Appendix A that are not time-barred by the applicable statute of limitations as of the execution of this Agreement may be commenced against BMS notwithstanding the expiration of any applicable statute of limitations during the deferred prosecution period. BMS agrees to waive the statute of limitations with respect to any crime that would otherwise expire during the two-year term of this Agreement, and this waiver is knowing and voluntary and in express reliance on the advice of counsel.

40.   This agreement expires twenty-four (24) months after the date of its execution, except that, in the event that the Office is conducting an ongoing investigation, prosecution or proceeding related to the facts set forth in the Statement of Facts, the provisions of paragraph 31(b)-(f) regarding the Company's cooperation shall remain in effect until such investigation, prosecution or proceeding is concluded.

41.   The Office agrees that if BMS is in full compliance with all of its obligations under this Agreement, the Office, within ten (10) days of the expiration of twenty-four (24) months from the execution of this Agreement, will seek dismissal with prejudice of the criminal complaint filed pursuant to paragraph 2. Except as otherwise provided herein, during and upon the conclusion of the term of this Agreement, the Office agrees that it will not prosecute BMS further for the matters that have been the subject of the Office's investigation relating to this Agreement.

42.   BMS agrees that, if it sells or merges all or substantially all of its business operations as they exist as of the date of this Agreement to or into a single purchaser or group of affiliated purchasers during the term of this Agreement, it shall include in any contract for sale or merger a provision binding the purchaser/successor to the obligations described in this Agreement.

43.   It is understood that this Agreement is limited to BMS and the Office on behalf of the U.S. Department of Justice and cannot bind other federal, state or local authorities. However, the Office will bring this Agreement and the cooperation of BMS and its compliance with its other obligations under this Agreement to the attention of other prosecuting offices, if requested to do so.

44.   This Agreement constitutes the full and complete agreement between BMS and the Office and supersedes any previous agreement between them. No additional promises, agreements, or conditions have been entered into other than those set forth in this Agreement, and none will be entered into unless in writing and signed by the Office, BMS's counsel, and a duly authorized representative of BMS. It is understood that the Office may permit exceptions to or excuse particular requirements set forth in this Agreement at the written request of BMS or the Monitor, but any such permission shall be in writing.

APPENDIX A – STATEMENT OF FACTS

Bristol-Myers Squibb Company ("BMS" or the "Company") is a Delaware corporation with offices in New Jersey and one of the world's leading producers of pharmaceuticals and health care products. For 2000, BMS reported sales of $18.216 billion and net earnings of $4.711 billion, For 2001, BMS reported sales of $19.423 billion and net earnings of $5.245 billion. The great majority of BMS's sales and earnings in 2000 and 2001 were from sales of pharmaceutical products.

BMS is a publicly traded corporation, the common stock of which is listed on the New York Stock Exchange. BMS's shareholders are located throughout the United States, including in the District of New Jersey.

Wholesaler Sales & Channel Stuffing

BMS manufactures pharmaceutical products and distributes those products through wholesalers. In 2000 to 2001, four U.S. wholesalers handled the distribution of approximately 85% of BMS's U.S. pharmaceutical products. These wholesalers delivered BMS pharmaceutical products to thousands of independent pharmacies, retail chains, hospitals and other health care providers across the country. Wholesalers generally purchased product at least sufficient to meet the demand of these retail businesses.

In 2000 to 2001, BMS regularly used financial incentives to spur wholesalers to buy product in excess of prescription demand, so that BMS could report higher sales and earnings. This practice, which is commonly known as "channel stuffing," was also referred to as "sales acceleration" or "trade loading."

BMS used a variety of financial incentives to spur wholesalers to buy and hold additional product in excess of prescription demand. The financial incentives included:

(a) pre-price increase buy-ins – allowing wholesalers to purchase product in advance of a BMS price increase for the product;

(b) "extended datings" of invoices – extending the due date for the wholesaler's payment beyond the usual thirty days;

(c) additional early payment discounts – discounts beyond those customarily offered to wholesalers for paying early for product; and

(d) "future file" purchases – allowing wholesalers to buy at an old, lower price, even after a price increase had become effective.

Growth of Excess Inventory

Channel stuffing in 2000 to 2001 resulted in "excess inventory" at the wholesalers, because the wholesalers took on more inventory than the amount needed to meet anticipated demand. In the absence of sales incentives or investment purchases, a wholesaler's "normal" inventory level was generally in the approximate range of three weeks' to one month's supply of a mature prescription drug. The process of reducing excess inventory to levels closer to normal was often called a "workdown," and generally involved selling less than demand during the workdown period. High levels of excess inventory were therefore likely to have an adverse effect on future sales.

Double-Double, Mega-Double and "TOP Down" Budgeting

In 1994, BMS announced what became known as the "Double-Double" goal: to double BMS's sales, earnings and earnings per share ("EPS") in a seven year period. The Double-Double required average compound annual growth of approximately 10%. The last year of the Double-Double was 2000, and at the end of the year BMS announced that it had achieved the doubling of earnings and EPS, and that it "virtually" doubled its sales since 1993.

In September 2000 EMS announced the "Strategy for Growth," which incorporated what became known as the "Mega-Double" goal, a plan to double year-end 2000 sales and earnings by the end of 2005, a five-year period. Achievement of the Mega-Double required average compound annual growth of nearly 15%.

The Double-Double and Mega-Double goals were accompanied by what was known as a "top-down" budget process. EMS set aggressive sales and earnings budget targets for the Company and its business units, consistent with the Double-Double and Mega-Double goals.

Earnings Guidance and Estimates

The management of many public companies, including BMS, provided "guidance" to the investing public regarding the expected performance of the business, including EPS, for upcoming quarters and years. In 2000 and at least until December 13, 2001, BMS advised the investing public through its guidance that it expected performance consistent with the Double-Double and Mega-Double.

Relying in part on a company's guidance, professional securities analysts then made public their own estimates of the company's expected performance. These "earnings estimates" or "analyst expectations" – which when averaged were referred to as the "consensus estimates – were closely followed by investors.

By 2000, EMS had met or exceeded analysts' consensus estimates for at least twenty-four (24) straight quarters, and this consistency was part of the company's public image. BMS understood that its failure to meet or exceed the consensus estimates for a quarter likely would result in a decrease in the company's stock price.

SEC Reporting

As a public company, BMS was required to comply with the rules and regulations of the United States Securities and Exchange Commission (SEC). The SEC is an independent agency of the United States government which was charged by law with maintaining honest and efficient markets in securities. The SEC's rules and regulations were designed to protect members of the investing public by, among other things, ensuring that a company's financial information was accurately disclosed to the investing public.

Under the SEC's rules and regulations, BMS and its officers were required to submit quarterly reports on Form 10-Q and annual reports on Form 10-K which included financial statements that accurately presented BMS's financial condition and the results of its business operations. Federal law further required the data in these reports to be truthful and consistent with the underlying facts and required the accounting treatments employed in these reports to be consistent with generally accepted accounting principles ("GAAP").

Federal law also required that the Forms 10-Q and 10-K include a section entitled Management's Discussion and Analysis ("MD&A") containing additional information about the company's financial condition and operations. MD&A must contain any material information necessary to make the accompanying financial statements not misleading. The purpose of MD&A was to give investors an opportunity to look at the company through the eyes of management, and understand the company's prospects for the future. MD&A is required to focus on material events and uncertainties known to management that would cause reported financial information not to be necessarily indicative of future operating results or of future financial condition.

Press Releases and Conference Calls

After the end of each quarter, BMS made public announcements about its sales, earnings and business operations generally. The company issued press releases which described sales performance, overall and by product, and held conference calls for analysts regarding the performance of the business. In preparation for the conference calls, senior BMS executives met and discussed issues expected to arise and how to respond to those issues.

The Scheme to Defraud

"Making the Numbers"

BMS promoted a corporate culture in which meeting or exceeding company budget targets and the consensus estimates was considered mandatory. Achieving these goals was known as "making the numbers" or "hitting the numbers." Meeting internal BMS budget targets generally also resulted in sales and earnings that met or exceeded the consensus estimates.

To this end, BMS set aggressive internal sales and earnings targets for 2000, 2001 and earlier periods that would enable the company to hit the widely-touted Double-Double and Mega-Double goals. Every quarter, and at year-end, BMS pressured lower-level employees to meet their budget targets. Certain employees who suggested that the company's budget targets were too aggressive or expressed doubts that they could make the numbers were transferred or demoted.

In the late 1990s, BMS's use of channel stuffing and the accompanying build-up of excess inventory at the wholesalers caused concern among several BMS executives, and during 1999 the Company made some effort to reduce or slow the growth of excess inventory. At the end of 1999, however, senior management refused to accept a proposed BMS budget that would have missed the Double-Double goal, and reassigned the senior executive responsible for the budget proposal. No serious or systematic effort to work down inventory was adopted or undertaken by BMS during the period 2000 to 2001.

Throughout 2000 and 2001, BMS used channel stuffing to boost its sales and artificially inflate its earnings, which enabled BMS to make its numbers and report results consistent with the Double-Double and Mega-Double. This use of channel stuffing to boost sales and earnings, and the resulting steadily increasing levels of excess inventory at the wholesalers, was concealed from the investing public, and was not disclosed to BMS's external auditors and Board of Directors. Without channel stuffing, BMS would have missed its budget targets and the consensus estimates.

Manipulation of Corporate Reserves

BMS regularly set aside funds in "reserve" accounts, to be used for costs related to events such as corporate acquisitions, divestitures or restructuring. Under GAAP, reserves were to be based on good-faith estimates of costs that were reasonably likely to occur. BMS was not permitted to establish reserves that were not based on good-faith estimates of reasonably likely future costs, or to carry excess amounts in its reserve accounts for future use. BMS was not permitted to use reserves to increase revenue in the future or for expenses not related to the purpose for which the funds were originally set aside.

BMS maintained a "reserve schedule" showing available funds from BMS's improperly-established reserves, as well as excess amounts from other reserves. BMS used funds from the reserve schedule for improper purposes, in particular to boost BMS revenue when the company needed additional income to hit the consensus estimates.

Deliberate Rebate Under-Accrual

BMS expected, at the time it sold its products, that at a later time it would have to pay rebates in connection with a portion of those sales. These rebates included Medicaid, "prime vendor" and "managed health care" rebates. Because BMS sold its products to wholesalers, there was a period of time – a "lag" – between the time of sale and when BMS received and paid the rebate claims. In keeping with GAAP, BMS was required to set aside funds to pay for expected rebates at the time it booked revenue from its sales.

As BMS's excess inventory at the wholesalers grew in 2000 and 2001, BMS imposed accounting policies and procedures which caused BMS not to accrue for the rebate liabilities for excess inventory. These policies were inconsistent with GAAP and resulted in an under-accrual in BMS's rebate accounts. Throughout 2000 and 2001 BMS finance staff used an artificially low lag period of six months to estimate accrual balances, even as the excess inventory at the wholesalers grew steadily. By deviating from GAAP and intentionally under-accruing in the Medicaid rebate account, BMS hid the growth of excess inventory and made BMS's sales figures look stronger than they actually were.

Closing Budget Gaps Through Channel Stuffing and Improper Accounting

In 2000 and 2001, BMS often approached the end of a quarter with a gap between actual sales and earnings and the level of sales necessary to hit the company's budget targets. BMS used channel stuffing to make up the company's sales and earnings shortfalls and close the gap. This practice led to a steady increase in excess inventory at the wholesalers.

At various times during a quarter or at quarter-end, in order to supplement the revenue from channel stuffing activity, BMS used funds from improperly-established reserves to bolster income and enable BMS to hit its earnings targets and the consensus estimates. In every quarter in 2000 and 2001, BMS publicly announced that it had met or exceeded the consensus estimates. BMS would not have been able to make its numbers without channel stuffing and improper accounting measures. BMS did not disclose to the investing public that its success in makings its numbers was due to channel stuffing and improper accounting measures.

False and Misleading Disclosure

In 2000 and 2001, BMS did not disclose the nature or extent of the company's channel stuffing in its 10Ks and 1OQs or in its quarterly press releases and analyst conference calls. For example, BMS did not disclose:

(a) the use of financial incentives to the wholesalers to generate sales in excess of demand;

(b) the use of sales in excess of demand to close budget gaps and hit budget targets;

(c) the level of excess inventory at the wholesalers; and

(d) the amount that excess inventory increased each quarter in 2000 and 2001.

Items (a) through (d) above constituted information reasonably likely to have a material effect on BMS's financial condition or results of its business operations. Failure to disclose this information deprived the investing public of information regarding BMS's past performance and future prospects. Further, in addition to omitting material information, BMS made or caused others to make or permitted false and misleading statements of material fact on the quarterly analyst conference calls and in the company's SEC filings.

U.S. Department of Justice
Criminal Division

Washington, DC 20530
September 21, 2007

Saul M. Pilchen, Esq.
Skadden Arps Slate Meagher & Flom LLP
1440 New York Ave., NW
Washington, DC 20005

Re: Paradigm B.Y.

Dear Mr. Pilchen:

On the understandings specified below, the United States Department of Justice, Criminal Division, Fraud Section ("this Office" or "the Department") will not criminally prosecute Paradigm B.V, and its subsidiaries and affiliates, (collectively, "PARADIGM") for any crimes (except for criminal tax violations, as to which this Office cannot and does not make any agreement) related to the making of and agreement to make improper payments by PARADIGM's employees and agents to government officials in China, Indonesia, Kazakhstan, Mexico, and Nigeria between 2002 and 2007, in order to assist in obtaining and retaining business with government entities, and PARADIGM's accounting and recordkeeping associated with these improper payments, as described in Appendix A to this letter, which is incorporated by reference herein.

It is understood that PARADIGM admits, accepts, and acknowledges responsibility for the conduct set forth in Appendix A, and agrees not to make any public statement contradicting Appendix A.

If PARADIGM fully complies with the understandings specified in this agreement,
including all Appendices hereto ("the Agreement"), no information given by or on behalf of PARADIGM at the request of this Office (or any other information directly or indirectly derived therefrom) will be used against PARADIGM in any criminal tax prosecution. This Agreement does not provide any protection against prosecution ior any crimes except as set forth above, and applies only to PARADIGM and not to any other entities or individuals except as set forth in this Agreement. PARADIGM expressly understands that the protections provided to PARADIGM shall not apply to any acquiror or successor entities unless and until such acquiror or successor formally adopts and executes this Agreement.

This Agreement shall have a term of eighteen (18) months from the date of this Agreement, except as specifically provided in the following paragraph. It is understood that for the eighteen (18) month term of the Agreement,

PARADIGM shall: (a) commit no crimes whatsoever; (b) truthfully and completely disclose all information with respect to the activities of PARADIGM, its officers and employees, and others concerning all matters about which this Office inquires of it, which information can be used for any purpose, except as otherwise limited in this Agreement; and (e) bring to this Office's attention all criminal conduct by, or criminal investigations of, PARADIGM or any of its senior managerial employees, that comes to the attention of PARADIGM or its senior management, as well as any administrative proceeding or civil action brought by any governmental authority that alleges fraud by or against PARADIGM.

Until the date upon which all investigations and prosecutions arising out of the conduct described in this Agreement are concluded, whether or not they are concluded within the eighteen (18) month term specified in the preceding paragraph, PARADIGM shall (a) cooperate fully with this Office, the Federal Bureau of Investigation, the Securities and Exchange Commission, and any other law enforcement agency designated by this Office, in connection with any investigation related to the matters described in Appendix A; (b) assist this Office in any investigation or prosecution arising out of the conduct described in this Agreement by providing logistical and technical support for any meeting, interview, grand jury proceeding, or any trial or other court proceeding; (c) use its best efforts to secure the attendance and truthful statements or testimony of any officer, agent or employee at any meeting or interview or before the grand jury or at any trial or other court proceeding; and (d) provide this Office, upon request, any document, record, or other tangible evidence about which this Office or any designated law enforcement agency inquires.

It is understood that any assistance PARADIGM may provide to federal criminal investigators shall be pursuant to the specific instructions and control of this Office and designated investigators.

It is understood that PARADIGM shall adopt a set of internal controls, including a compliance code and compliance standards and procedures, as set forth in Appendix B, and retain outside compliance counsel, as set forth in Appendix C.

It is understood that PARADIGM agrees to pay a monetary penalty of $1,000,000. PARADIGM must pay this sum to the United States within thirty (30) days of the date of this Agreement. PARADIGM agrees that no tax deduction will be sought in connection with this payment.

It is understood that, should this Office determine that PARADIGM has committed any crime during the term of this Agreement, has given false, incomplete, or misleading testimony or information, or has otherwise violated any provision of this Agreement, PARADIGM shall thereafter be subject to prosecution for any federal violation of which this Office has knowledge, including perjury and obstruction of justice. Any such prosecution that is not time-barred by the applicable statute of limitations on the date of the signing of this Agreement may be commenced against PARADIGM, notwithstanding the expiration of the statute of limitations between the signing of this Agreement and the expiration of the term of the Agreement plus one year. Thus, by signing this Agreement, PARADIGM agrees that the statute of limitations with respect to any prosecution that is not time-barred on the date of this Agreement shall be tolled for the term of the Agreement plus one year.

It is understood that, if this Office determines that PARADIGM has committed any crime during the term of this Agreement, has given false, incomplete, or misleading testimony or information, or has otherwise violated any provision of this Agreement: (a) all statements and admissions made by PARADIGM to this Office or other designated law enforcement agents, including Appendix A hereto, and any testimony given by PARADIGM before a grand jury or other tribunal, whether prior or subsequent to the signing of this Agreement, and any leads derived from such statements or testimony shall be admissible in evidence in any criminal proceeding brought against PARADIGM; and (b) PARADIGM shall assert no claim under the United States Constitution, any statute, Rule 410 of the Federal Rules of Evidence, or any other federal rule that such statements or any leads therefrom should be suppressed. By signing this Agreement, PARADIGM waives all rights in the foregoing respects.

It is further understood that this Agreement does not bind any federal, state or local prosecuting authority other than this Office. This Office will, however, bring the cooperation of PARADIGM to the attention of other prosecuting and other investigative authorities, if requested by PARADIGM.

It is further understood that PARADIGM and this Office may disclose this Agreement to the public.

With respect to this matter, from the date of this Agreement supersedes all prior, if any6, understandings, promises and/or conditions between this Office and PARADIGM. No additional promises, agreements, and conditions have been entered into other than those set forth in this letter and none will be entered into unless in writing and signed by all parties.

Very truly yours,

STEVEN A. TYRRELL
Chief, Fraud Section

By: _____
Mark F. Mendelsohn
Deputy Chief, Fraud Section

Robertson T. Park
Assistant Chief, Fraud Section

AGREED AND CONSENTED TO:
Paradigm B.V.

-----------------------------   ----------------------
John M. Allen, General Counsel   Date

APPROVED:

-----------------------------   ----------------------
Saul M. Pilchen, Esq.   Date
Skadden Arps Slate Meagher & Flom LLP
Attorney for Paradigm B.V.

APPENDIX A
STATEMENT OF FACTS

This Statement of Facts is incorporated by reference as part of the
Agreement, dated September 21, 2007, between the United States
Department of Justice, Criminal Division, Fraud Section ("this Office" or "the
Department") and Paradigm B.V. and its subsidiaries and affiliates
("Paradigm" or "the Company").

I. Background

1. At all times relevant to the facts described herein, Paradigm was a private
limited liability company registered in The Netherlands. Paradigm was a
provider of enterprise software solutions to the global oil and natural gas
exploration and production industry. Customers used Paradigm's integrated
software suite to create dynamic digital models of the Earth's subsurface by
analyzing and interpreting vast amounts of data. The software enabled
customers to locate new oil and natural gas reservoirs and optimize
production from new and existing reservoirs. Paradigm's revenue was
generated from the sale of software and providing related services,
consulting, and post-contract support.

2. During due diligence being conducted by Paradigm in connection with its
anticipated initial public offering, in or around January 2007, Paradigm
identified conduct that appeared to violate the Foreign Corrupt Practices Act
("FCPA") 15 U.S.C. § 78dd-1, et seq. In response, Paradigm conducted an
investigation through outside counsel. Further, the Company made a
voluntary disclosure to, and has cooperated fully with, the Department
through the course of the investigation. Paradigm also has instituted

extensive remedial compliance measures.

II. Paradigm Became A Domestic Concern

3. Since approximately August 2002. Paradigm was headquartered in The Netherlands, with its principal place of business in Herzliya, Israel, and with substantial operations in the Asia Pacific region, Latin America, and the Middle East.

4. On or about July 1, 2005, Paradigm became a "domestic concern," as that term is defined in the FCPA, 15 LLS.C. § 78dd-2(h)(l)(B), after gradually relocating its principal place of business from Herzliya, Israel to Houston, Texas. This consisted of, among other things: (a) retention of a Houston-based Chief Executive Officer; (b) moving key senior management positions from Herzliya, Israel to Houston; (c) retaining an outside auditor in Houston; (d) transitioning financial and accounting functions from Herzliya, Israel to Houston; and (e)
moving the coordination of operational business activities from Herzliya. Israel to Houston. The conduct described in this Statement of Facts took place after Paradigm became a domestic concern, unless otherwise noted.

III. The Improper Payments

A. Kazakhstan

5. In August 2005, KazMunaiGas, Kazakhstan's national oil company, issued a tender for geological software. During the tender process, an unidentified KazMunaiGas official recommended Paradigm retain Frontera Holding S.A. ("Frontera"), a company registered in the British West Indies, ostensibly to assist Paradigm in preparing tender documentation. Paradigm retained Frontera without conducting due diligence and without entering into a written agreement detailing the services to be provided.

6. After retaining Frontera, Paradigm submitted a bid to KazMunaiGas in the amount of $249,290 and won the tender in or about August 2005. On October 21, 2005,Paradigm entered into a contract with KazMunaiGas. Paradigm then received an invoice from Frontera requesting a "commission" in the amount of $22,250 in January 2006. On April 3, 2006, Paradigm wired payment in the amount of' $22,250 from an account in Glasgow, Scotland to an account at the Latvian Trade Bank in the name of Frontera. Documentary evidence showing that Frontera actually prepared any tender documentation or performed any other services for Paradigm is lacking.

B. China

7. Paradigm conducted its business in China through a representative office ("Paradigm China") and a wholly-owned foreign enterprise ("WOFE"). Paradigm China was responsible for software sales and post-contract support,

and the WOFE was responsible for services work. The vast majority of Paradigm China's customers were Chinese national oil companies or state-owned entities.

8. In July 2006, Paradigm China entered into an agent agreement with Tangshan Haitai Oil Technology Consulting Co. Ltd. ("Tangshan") in connection with a transaction involving Zhonghai Petroleum (China) Co., Ltd. ("Zhonghai"), a company owned by the China National Offshore Oil Company ("CNOOC"). Under the agreement, Tangshan was to receive a 5% commission. The agreement also contemplated commissions being passed on to representatives of Zhonghai, and that Paradigm China and Tangshan would split equally the cost of paying those commissions. The total amount of commissions paid to Tangshan could not be determined from the readily available documentation, but Paradigm China's Country Manager confirmed that at least one such commission was paid.

9. Paradigm China retained employees of Chinese national oil companies or state-owned entities as "internal consultants," and agreed to pay those consultants in cash to evaluate Paradigm's software. Paradigm China's payments to the internal consultants were intended to cause these technical workers to encourage their companies' procurement divisions to purchase Paradigm's software. Paradigm China also paid internal consultants for inspection and acceptance of Paradigm's products and services. These "inspection" and "acceptance" fees were paid in cash, at or around the time of business negotiations, and once the software was delivered and installed. The "inspection" and "acceptance" fees amounted to approximately $1 00-$200 per person, but the total amount paid could not be determined from the readily available documentation.

10. Paradigm China also paid travel and entertainments expenses for internal consultants and employees of Chinese national oil companies and state-owned entities, including customer "training" trips in connection with obtaining specific business. The expenses incurred in connection with the trips included airfare, hotel, meals, gifts, cash per diems, and entertainment - including sightseeing and cash payments for shopping. The total amount paid for these expenses could not be determined from the readily available documentation.

C. Mexico

11. Paradigm acquired a Mexican entity, AGI Mexicana S.A. de C.V. ("Paradigm Mexico"), in 2004. In that year, Paradigm Mexico entered into a subcontract with the Mexican Bureau of Geophysical Contracting ("BGP") valued at $1.48 million. Under the BGP contract, Paradigm Mexico was to perform work under a contract that BGP had entered into with Pemex, the Mexican national oil company. Paradigm Mexico used the services of an agent in connection with this business, but did not have a written agreement with him. The agent requested that his commission payments, totaling $206,698, be paid through five different entities. Paradigm Mexico did not conduct any

due diligence on the agent, or the five entities through which he requested payment.

12. Paradigm Mexico paid some, but not all, of the agent's invoices. When new Paradigm senior management learned the agent did not have a written contract with Paradigm Mexico, Paradigm suspended payments to the agent. The agent sued in a Mexican court seeking to collect on the unpaid invoices, but Paradigm Mexico ultimately prevailed in that lawsuit.

13. In 2005, Paradigm Mexico also entered into a subcontract with a U.S. oil services company, which had a contract with Pemex for processing work, In connection with both the BGP subcontract discussed above and this second subcontract, a governmental decision maker employed at Pemex was taken by Paradigm Mexico to Napa Valley, California for relationship building and client entertainment. The agent in the BGP deal accompanied the Pemex decision maker on the trip. The trip coincided with the birthday of the Pemex decision maker and involved visits to wineries and dinners. The total cost of the trip for all attendees was approximately $12,000. In 2005, Paradigm Mexico also spent approximately $10,000 entertaining the same Pemex decision maker in connection with obtaining or retaining business. The entertainment took the form of dinners, drinks, and other activities.

14. Further, during the same time frame as the second deal discussed above, the same Pemex decision maker requested that Paradigm Mexico hire his brother. Paradigm Mexico acquiesced to that demand and hired the decision maker's brother as a driver. While employed at Paradigm Mexico, the brother did perform some work as a driver.

15. Paradigm Mexico also entered into a third contract with another branch of Pemex, Central Seismic Processing Center ("CNPS"). The Pemex decision maker on the BGP deal and the second deal with the U.S. oil services company was the responsible official for this third contract. In close proximity to when the CNPS contract was signed, Paradigm Mexico leased a house from the wife of the CNPS tender official. The house was used by Paradigm Mexico's staff; and the rental fee appears to have been fair market value.

D. Nigeria

16. Paradigm operated in Nigeria through a subsidiary, Paradigm Geophysical Nigeria Ltd. ('Paradigm Nigeria"). In 2003, Paradigm began discussing the prospect of forming a service alliance with Integrated Data Services Limited ("IDSL") to perform services and processing work in Nigeria. IDSL was incorporated in 1988 as one of eleven subsidiary companies of the Nigerian National Petroleum Corporation ("NNPC"), a Nigerian governmental agency, IDSL is considered the services arm of NNPC. A meeting between former Paradigm representatives and an IDSL official concerning the proposed joint venture took place in Houston in 2003. Thereafter, in 2004, Paradigm submitted its bid for the IDSL joint venture.

17. in February 2004, Paradigm retained an agent to assist Paradigm Nigeria with its operations. After Paradigm submitted its IDSL bid, Paradigm amended its contract with the agent, authorizing an agent commission in the event Paradigm Nigeria received the IDSL contract.

18. In May 2005, former Paradigm representatives agreed to make corrupt payments of between $100,000 and $200,000 through its agent, in order to secure the IDSL award. The proposed payments were to be made to unidentified Nigerian politicians. After Paradigm learned it had not received the IDSL contract, Paradigm terminated the services of the agent.

E. Indonesia

19. Prior to April 1, 2004, Paradigm conducted its business in Indonesia through a subsidiary, PT Paradigm Geophysical Indonesia ("Paradigm Indonesia"). At that time, Paradigm Indonesia used an agent to facilitate sales. From April 1, 2004, Until January 1, 2007, Paradigm conducted its Indonesian business exclusively through the agent, who was funded via an account at a U.S. financial institution.

20. In April 2003, employees of Pertamina, Indonesia's national oil company, requested funds from Paradigm Indonesia for the purpose of obtaining or retaining business. Such payments were made. The agent was involved in making the payments. At the time, the agent received commission payments from Paradigm through a New York bank account. The total amount of any improper payments could not be determined from the readily available documentation, but Paradigm's Regional Controller confirmed that at least one such improper payment was made.

APPENDIX B
In order to address deficiencies in its internal controls, policies and procedures regarding compliance with the Foreign Corrupt Practices Act ("FCPA") and other applicable anticorruption laws, and in preparation for the registration of its securities pursuant to 15 U.S.C. § 781 and its listing on a United States exchange as a public company, Paradigm BY., on behalf of itself and its subsidiaries and affiliates (collectively referred to herein as 'Paradigm"), agrees to conduct, in a manner consistent with this Agreement, a review of its existing internal controls, policies and procedures.

Where necessary and appropriate, Paradigm further agrees to adopt new or to modify existing internal controls, policies and procedures in order to ensure that it maintains: (a) a system of internal accounting controls designed to ensure that Paradigm makes and keeps fair and accurate books, records and accounts; and (b) a rigorous anti-corruption compliance code, standards, and procedures designed to detect and deter violations of the FCPA and other applicable anti-corruption laws, At a minimum, this should include, but ought not be limited to, the following elements:

1. A clearly articulated corporate policy against violations of the FCPA and other applicable anti-corruption laws.

2. A system of financial and accounting procedures, including a system of internal accounting controls, designed to ensure the maintenance of fair and accurate books, records and accounts.

3. Promulgation of a compliance code, standards and procedures designed to reduce the prospect of violations of the FCPA, other applicable anti-corruption laws and Paradigm's compliance code. These standards and procedures should apply to all directors, officers, and employees and, where necessary and appropriate, outside parties acting on behalf of Paradigm in a foreign jurisdiction including agents, consultants, representatives, distributors, teaming partners, and joint venture partners (collectively referred to as "agents and business partners").

4. The assignment of responsibility to one or more senior corporate officials of Paradigm for the implementation of and oversight of compliance with policies, standards and procedures regarding the FCPA and other applicable anti-corruption laws. Such corporate official(s) shall have the authority to report matters directly to Paradigm's Audit Committee of the Board of Directors.

5. Mechanisms designed to ensure that Paradigm's policies, standards and procedures regarding the PCPA and other applicable anti-corruption laws are effectively communicated to all directors, officers, employees and, where necessary and appropriate, agents and business partners. This should include: (1) periodic training for all directors, officers, employees, agents and business partners; and (2) annual certifications by all directors, officers, employees, agents and business partners, certifying compliance therewith.

6. An effective system for reporting suspected criminal conduct and/or violations of the compliance policies, standards, and procedures regarding the FCPA and other applicable anti-corruption laws for directors, officers, employees, agents and business partners.

7. Appropriate disciplinary procedures to address, among other things, violations of the FCPA, other applicable anti-corruption laws, and Paradigm's compliance code, standards and procedures by Paradigm directors, officers, and employees.

8. Appropriate due diligence requirements pertaining to the retention and oversight of agents and business partners.

9. Standard provisions in agreements, contracts, and renewals thereof with alt agents and business partners that are designed to prevent violations of the FCPA and other applicable anti-corruption laws, which may, depending upon the circumstances, include: (I) anti-corruption representations and

undertakings relating to compliance with the FCPA and other applicable anti-corruption laws; (2) rights to conduct audits of the books and records of the agent or business partner to ensure compliance with the foregoing; and (3) rights to terminate an agent or business partner as a result of any breach of anti-corruption laws and regulations or representations and undertakings related to such matters.

APPENDIX C

COMMITMENT TO RETAIN OUTSIDE COMPLIANCE COUNSEL

Paradigm has retained the law firm of Skadden Arps Slate Meagher and Flom LLP as outside compliance counsel ("Compliance Counsel"). For the eighteen (18) month term of this Agreement, Compliance Counsel shall:

1. Review the implementation and effectiveness of Paradigm's compliance code, policies and procedures as they relate to the FCPA and other applicable anti-corruption laws.

2. Recommend, where necessary and appropriate, enhancements to Paradigm's compliance code, policies and procedures as they relate to the FCPA and other applicable anticorruption laws.

3. Review Paradigm's compliance with this Agreement

4. Recommend and, if appropriate, direct that internal investigations be conducted and voluntary disclosures be made to the Department of Justice and other relevant regulatory agencies.

5. Report periodically, as directed by the Department of Justice, regarding the foregoing.

West's Federal Forms
District Courts-Criminal
Honorable William A. Knox[1]

Chapter 84. Arraignment And Preparation For Trial
[Federal Rules Of Criminal Procedure, Rules 10 And 11]
Rule 10--Forms

§ 7394. **Joint Defense Agreement**

JOINT DEFENSE AGREEMENT

I. BACKGROUND

This Agreement, dated as of [*date*], concerns the joint defense of _____, its shareholders and employees (hereinafter "_____") and _____ (hereinafter "_____") with respect to the following matters: (1) a lawsuit filed by _____ against _____ and others as Civil Action _____ in the United States District Court for the District of _____ (hereinafter the "_____ Lawsuit"); (2) a lawsuit threatened to be filed by _____ against _____, _____ and others in the Circuit Court of _____, Missouri (hereinafter "_____ Lawsuit"); and (3) investigations being conducted by the Resolution Trust Corporation as Receiver for _____, the Federal Deposit Insurance Corporation as Receiver for _____ and _____, the United States Attorney for the District of _____ and the United States Attorney for the _____ District of _____ regarding the operation and practices of certain banks and savings and loans located in _____ and _____ (hereinafter the "Investigations"). By agreement of the parties, and with waiver of any conflicts or potential conflicts, the law firm of _____ represents one of the shareholders of _____ and other defendants, but does not represent _____ who appears *pro se*, in the _____ Lawsuit; it represents _____, but not _____, in the threatened _____ Lawsuit; and it represents _____ and _____ in connection with the Investigations.

II. MUTUALITY OF INTEREST

_____ and _____ believe that there is a mutuality of interest in a common and joint defense in regard to these matters and any related civil, criminal or administrative proceedings. In this regard, _____ and _____ wish to continue to pursue their separate but common interests, and to avoid any suggestions of waiver of the confidentiality of privileged communications, memoranda and documents. Accordingly, it is their intention and understanding that communications among them, either

---

[1] U.S. Magistrate Judge, Jefferson City, Missouri

through [*law firm*] or otherwise, and any joint interviews of prospective witnesses, are confidential and are protected from disclosure to any third party by attorney-client and attorneys' work- product privileges.

III. MAINTENANCE OF PRIVILEGE

In order to pursue that joint defense effectively, _____ and _____ have also concluded that, from time to time, their mutual interests will be best served by sharing documents, factual material, mental impressions, strategies, legal theories, memoranda, interview reports, and other information, including their confidences, all of which will hereinafter be referred to as "Defense Materials." In the absence of such sharing, these Defense Materials would be privileged from disclosure to adverse or other parties as a result of the attorney-client privilege, the attorney work-product privilege or other applicable privileges. It is the purpose of this Agreement to ensure that the exchanges and disclosures of Defense Materials contemplated herein do not diminish in any way the confidentiality of the Defense Materials and do not constitute a waiver of any privilege otherwise available.

IV. CONSENT AND OTHER RIGHTS

To this end, it is understood and agreed that information obtained by [*law firm*] from either _____ or _____ shall remain confidential and shall be protected from disclosure to any third party except as provided herein. It is further understood and agreed that any documents exchanged between them, either through [*law firm*] or otherwise, and the information contained therein, and any other confidences exchanged between them, shall be used solely in connection with the _____ Lawsuit, the threatened _____ Lawsuit, the Investigations, and any related civil, and criminal or administrative proceedings. _____ and _____ further agree that neither will disclose Defense Materials received from each other or through [*law firm*], or the contents thereof, to anyone except executive officers of _____, without first obtaining the consent of all parties who may be entitled to claim any privilege with respect to such materials.

V. DEMAND OR SUBPOENA OF MATERIAL

If any other person or entity requests or demands, by subpoena or otherwise, any Defense Materials received from the other, directly or through [*law firm*], or jointly obtained on behalf of both parties, the party receiving the request or demand will immediately notify the other party. The person or entity seeking such Defense Materials will be informed that these materials are only on loan and that demand should be made on the appropriate party. Each party will take all steps necessary to permit the assertion of all application rights and privileges with respect to said Defense Materials and shall cooperate fully with the other in any judicial proceeding relating to disclosure of the Defense Materials.

VI. JOINT DEFENSE DOCTRINE

It is understood that all work performed by [*law firm*], its attorneys, employees and agents with regard to its representations and communicated to either _____ or _____ or both in connection with these representations shall be accomplished pursuant to the work product and the attorney-client privilege and to the "joint defense doctrine" and all other applicable rights and privileges, including those recognized in *Continental Oil Company v. United States,* 330 F.2d 347 (9th Cir.1964); *Hunydee v. United States,* 355 F.2d 183 (9th Cir.1965), *In the Matter of a Grand Jury Subpoena Dated November 16, 1974,* 406 F.Supp. 381 (S.D.N.Y.1975), and *United States v. McPartlin,* 595 F.2d 1321 (7th Cir.1979).

VII. CHANGED CIRCUMSTANCES

In the event any party decides to withdraw from this Agreement for any reason, that party shall immediately notify [*law firm*] in writing, of that parties' withdrawal from this Agreement, which will thereupon be terminated as to that party; provided, however, that no such termination shall effect or impair the obligations of confidentiality with respect to materials previously furnished pursuant to this Agreement. Further, any party, upon withdrawal, shall return all materials provided by the other parties hereto, including any copies of Defense Materials.

VIII. CONFLICT OF INTEREST AND DISQUALIFICATION

_____ and _____ hereby further agree that in the event that either becomes a cooperating government witness, nothing in this Agreement shall create a conflict of interest so as to require the disqualification of [*law firm*] from the representation of the other and _____ and _____ hereby waive any such conflict of interest.

It is agreed, however, that [*law firm*] shall not be disqualified from examining or cross-examining either _____ or _____, if either testifies at any proceeding, whether under grant or immunity or otherwise, because of [*law firm*]'s participation in this Agreement.

IX. LIMITATION OF DUTIES AND CONFLICTS

_____ and _____ have been advised, and have agreed, that [*law firm*] does not represent _____ in the _____ Lawsuit or in the threatened _____ Lawsuit. _____ and _____ have been advised, and have agreed, that it will be acting only as the attorney for its client in each action and will owe a duty of loyalty only to its client. Each client has agreed to knowingly and intelligently waive any conflict of interest that may arise from [*law firm*] examining them at any proceeding.

X. INJUNCTIVE RELIEF

_____ and _____ acknowledge that disclosure of any communication in violation of this Agreement will cause the parties hereto to suffer irreparable harm for which there is no adequate legal remedy. Each party hereto acknowledges that immediate injunctive relief is an appropriate and necessary remedy for any violation or threatened violation of the Agreement.

XI. CONTINUANCE OF AGREEMENT

This Agreement shall continue in effect notwithstanding any conclusion or resolution as to either _____ or _____ of the _____ Lawsuit, the threatened _____ Lawsuit or the Investigations or any administrative, civil, or criminal proceedings arising from or relating to any of them. _____ and _____ agree that they will continue to be bound by this Agreement following any such conclusion or resolution.

XII. NON WAIVER

Any waiver in any particular instance of the rights and limitations contained herein shall not be deemed, and is not intended to be, a general waiver of any rights or limitations contained herein and shall not operate as a waiver beyond the particular instance.

XIII. EXPLANATION AND MODIFICATION

By signing this Agreement, _____ and _____ certify that the contents of this Joint Defense Agreement have been explained to them, and that they agree to abide by the understandings reflected in the Agreement. Any modifications of the Agreement must be in writing and signed by all parties.

The foregoing is agreed to by the following parties as of the date first written above.

[_SIGNATURE BLOCK FOR PARTIES_]

_____

By_____

APPROVED:

[_SIGNATURE BLOCK FOR LAW FIRM_]

SECURITIES AND EXCHANGE COMMISSION
Washington, D.C. 20549

Supplemental Information for Persons Requested to Supply Information Voluntarily or Directed to Supply Information Pursuant to a Commission Subpoena

A. False Statements and Documents

Section 1001 of Title 18 of the United States Code provides as follows:

> [W]hoever, in any matter within the jurisdiction of the executive, legislative, or judicial branch of the Government of the United States, knowingly and willfully--
>> (1) falsifies, conceals, or covers up by any trick, scheme, or device a material fact;
>> (2) makes any materially false, fictitious, or fraudulent statement or representation; or
>> (3) makes or uses any false writing or document knowing the same to contain any materially false, fictitious, or fraudulent statement or entry;
> shall be fined under this title, imprisoned not more than 5 years . . . or both.

B. Testimony

If your testimony is taken, you should be aware of the following:

1. *Record*. Your testimony will be transcribed by a reporter. If you desire to go off the record, please indicate this to the Commission employee taking your testimony, who will determine whether to grant your request. The reporter will not go off the record at your, or your counsel's, direction.

2. *Counsel*. You have the right to be accompanied, represented and advised by counsel of your choice. Your counsel may advise you before, during and after your testimony; question you briefly at the conclusion of your testimony to clarify any of the answers you give during testimony; and make summary notes during your testimony solely for your use. If you are accompanied by counsel, you may consult privately.

If you are not accompanied by counsel, please advise the Commission employee taking your testimony if, during the testimony, you desire to be accompanied, represented and advised by counsel. Your testimony will be adjourned once to afford you the opportunity to arrange to be so accompanied, represented or advised.

You may be represented by counsel who also represents other persons involved in the Commission's investigation. This multiple representation, however, presents a potential conflict of interest if one client's interests are or may be adverse to another's. If you are represented by counsel who also represents other persons involved in the investigation, the Commission will assume that you and counsel have discussed and resolved all issues concerning possible conflicts of interest. The choice of counsel, and the responsibility for that choice, is yours.

3. *Transcript Availability.* Rule 6 of the Commission's Rules Relating to Investigations, 17 CFR 203.6, states:

> A person who has submitted documentary evidence or testimony in a formal investigative proceeding shall be entitled, upon written request, to procure a copy of his documentary evidence or a transcript of his testimony on payment of the appropriate fees: *Provided, however,* That in a nonpublic formal investigative proceeding the Commission may for good cause deny such request. In any event, any witness, upon proper identification, shall have the right to inspect the official transcript of the witness' own testimony.

If you wish to purchase a copy of the transcript of your testimony, the reporter will provide you with a copy of the appropriate form. Persons requested to supply information voluntarily will be allowed the rights provided by this rule.

4. *Perjury.* Section 1621 of Title 18 of the United States Code provides as follows:

Whoever--

> (1) having taken an oath before a competent tribunal, officer, or person, in any case in which a law of the United States authorizes an oath to be administered, that he will testify, declare, depose, or certify truly, or that any written testimony, declaration, deposition, or certificate by him subscribed, is true, willfully and contrary to such oath states or subscribes any material matter which he does not believe to be true; or
>
> (2) in any declaration, certificate, verification, or statement under

penalty of perjury as permitted under section 1746 of title 28, United States Code, willfully subscribes as true any material matter which he does not believe to be true;

is guilty of perjury and shall, except as otherwise expressly provided by law, be fined under this title or imprisoned not more than five years, or both.

5. *Fifth Amendment and Voluntary Testimony*. Information you give may be used against you in any federal, state, local or foreign administrative, civil or criminal proceeding brought by the Commission or any other agency.

You may refuse, in accordance with the rights guaranteed to you by the Fifth Amendment to the Constitution of the United States, to give any information that may tend to incriminate you.

If your testimony is not pursuant to subpoena, your appearance to testify is voluntary, you need not answer any question, and you may leave whenever you wish. Your cooperation is, however, appreciated.

6. *Formal Order Availability*. If the Commission has issued a formal order of investigation, it will be shown to you during your testimony, at your request. If you desire a copy of the formal order, please make your request in writing.

C. Submissions and Settlements

Rule 5(c) of the Commission's Rules on Informal and Other Procedures, 17 CFR 202.5(c), states:

> Persons who become involved in . . . investigations may, on their own initiative, submit a written statement to the Commission setting forth their interests and position in regard to the subject matter of the investigation. Upon request, the staff, in its discretion, may advise such persons of the general nature of the investigation, including the indicated violations as they pertain to them, and the amount of time that may be available for preparing and submitting a statement prior to the presentation of a staff recommendation to the Commission for the commencement of an administrative or injunction proceeding. Submissions by interested persons should be forwarded to the appropriate Division Director or Regional Director with a copy to the staff members conducting the investigation and should be clearly referenced to the specific investigation to which they relate. In the event a recommendation for the commencement of

an enforcement proceeding is presented by the staff, any submissions by interested persons will be forwarded to the Commission in conjunction with the staff memorandum.

The staff of the Commission routinely seeks to introduce submissions made pursuant to Rule 5(c) as evidence in Commission enforcement proceedings, when the staff deems appropriate.

Rule 5(f) of the Commission's Rules on Informal and Other Procedures, 17 CFR 202.5(f), states:

> In the course of the Commission's investigations, civil lawsuits, and administrative proceedings, the staff, with appropriate authorization, may discuss with persons involved the disposition of such matters by consent, by settlement, or in some other manner. It is the policy of the Commission, however, that the disposition of any such matter may not, expressly or impliedly, extend to any criminal charges that have been, or may be, brought against any such person or any recommendation with respect thereto. Accordingly, any person involved in an enforcement matter before the Commission who consents, or agrees to consent, to any judgment or order does so solely for the purpose of resolving the claims against him in that investigative, civil, or administrative matter and not for the purpose of resolving any criminal charges that have been, or might be, brought against him. This policy reflects the fact that neither the Commission nor its staff has the authority or responsibility for instituting, conducting, settling, or otherwise disposing of criminal proceedings. That authority and responsibility are vested in the Attorney General and representatives of the Department of Justice.

D. Freedom of Information Act

The Freedom of Information Act, 5 U.S.C. 552 (the "FOIA"), generally provides for disclosure of information to the public. Rule 83 of the Commission's Rules on Information and Requests, 17 CFR 200.83, provides a procedure by which a person can make a written request that information submitted to the Commission not be disclosed under the FOIA. That rule states that no determination as to the validity of such a request will be made until a request for disclosure of the information under the FOIA is received. Accordingly, no response to a request that information not be disclosed under the FOIA is necessary or will be given until a request for disclosure under the FOIA is received. If you desire an acknowledgment of receipt of your written request that information not be disclosed under the FOIA, please provide a duplicate request, together with a stamped, self-addressed envelope.

E. Authority for Solicitation of Information

Persons Directed to Supply Information Pursuant to Subpoena. The authority for requiring production of information is set forth in the subpoena. Disclosure of the information to the Commission is mandatory, subject to the valid assertion of any legal right or privilege you might have.

Persons Requested to Supply Information Voluntarily. One or more of the following provisions authorizes the Commission to solicit the information requested: Sections 19 and/or 20 of the Securities Act of 1933; Section 21 of the Securities Exchange Act of 1934; Section 321 of the Trust Indenture Act of 1939; Section 42 of the Investment Company Act of 1940; Section 209 of the Investment Advisers Act of 1940; and 17 CFR 202.5. Disclosure of the requested information to the Commission is voluntary on your part.

F. Effect of Not Supplying Information

Persons Directed to Supply Information Pursuant to Subpoena. If you fail to comply with the subpoena, the Commission may seek a court order requiring you to do so. If such an order is obtained and you thereafter fail to supply the information, you may be subject to civil and/or criminal sanctions for contempt of court. In addition, if the subpoena was issued pursuant to the Securities Exchange Act of 1934, the Investment Company Act of 1940, and/or the Investment Advisers Act of 1940, and if you, without just cause, fail or refuse to attend and testify, or to answer any lawful inquiry, or to produce books, papers, correspondence, memoranda, and other records in compliance with the subpoena, you may be found guilty of a misdemeanor and fined not more than $1,000 or imprisoned for a term of not more than one year, or both.

Persons Requested to Supply Information Voluntarily. There are no direct sanctions and thus no direct effects for failing to provide all or any part of the requested information.

G. Principal Uses of Information

The Commission's principal purpose in soliciting the information is to gather facts in order to determine whether any person has violated, is violating, or is about to violate any provision of the federal securities laws or rules for which the Commission has enforcement authority, such as rules of securities exchanges and the rules of the Municipal Securities Rulemaking Board. Facts developed may, however, constitute violations of other laws or rules. Information provided may be used in Commission and other agency enforcement proceedings. Unless the Commission or its staff explicitly agrees to the contrary in writing, you should not assume that the Commission or its staff acquiesces in, accedes to, or concurs or agrees with, any position, condition, request, reservation of right, understanding, or any other statement that purports, or may be deemed, to be or to reflect a limitation upon the Commission's receipt, use, disposition, transfer, or retention, in accordance with applicable law, of information provided.

H. Routine Uses of Information

The Commission often makes its files available to other governmental agencies, particularly United States Attorneys and state prosecutors. There is a likelihood that information supplied by you will be made available to such agencies where appropriate. Whether or not the Commission makes its files available to other governmental agencies is, in general, a confidential matter between the Commission and such other governmental agencies.

Set forth below is a list of the routine uses which may be made of the information furnished.

1. To appropriate agencies, entities, and persons when (a) it is suspected or confirmed that the security or confidentiality of information in the system of records has been compromised; (b) the SEC has determined that, as a result of the suspected or confirmed compromise, there is a risk of harm to economic or property interests, identity theft or fraud, or harm to the security or integrity of this system or other systems or programs (whether maintained by the SEC or another agency or entity) that rely upon the compromised information; and (c) the disclosure made to such agencies, entities, and persons is reasonably necessary to assist in connection with the SEC's efforts to respond to the suspected or confirmed compromise and prevent, minimize, or remedy such harm.

2. To other federal, state, local, or foreign law enforcement agencies; securities self-regulatory organizations; and foreign financial regulatory authorities to assist in or coordinate regulatory or law enforcement activities with the SEC.

3. To national securities exchanges and national securities associations that are registered with the SEC, the Municipal Securities Rulemaking Board; the Securities Investor Protection Corporation; the Public Company Accounting Oversight Board; the federal banking authorities, including, but not limited to, the Board of Governors of the Federal Reserve System, the Comptroller of the Currency, and the Federal Deposit Insurance Corporation; state securities regulatory agencies or organizations; or regulatory authorities of a foreign government in connection with their regulatory or enforcement responsibilities.

4. By SEC personnel for purposes of investigating possible violations of, or to conduct investigations authorized by, the federal securities laws.

5. In any proceeding where the federal securities laws are in issue or in which the Commission, or past or present members of its staff, is a party or otherwise involved in an official capacity.

6. In connection with proceedings by the Commission pursuant to Rule 102(e) of its Rules of Practice, 17 CFR 201.102(e).

7. To a bar association, state accountancy board, or other federal, state, local, or foreign licensing or oversight authority; or professional association or self-regulatory authority to the extent that it performs similar functions (including the Public Company Accounting Oversight Board) for investigations or possible disciplinary action.

8. To a federal, state, local, tribal, foreign, or international agency, if necessary to obtain information relevant to the SEC's decision concerning the hiring or retention of an employee; the issuance of a security clearance; the letting of a contract; or the issuance of a license, grant, or other benefit.

9. To a federal, state, local, tribal, foreign, or international agency in response to its request for information concerning the hiring or retention of an employee; the issuance of a security clearance; the reporting of an investigation of an employee; the letting of a contract; or the issuance of a license, grant, or other benefit by the requesting agency, to the extent that the information is relevant and necessary to the requesting agency's decision on the matter.

10. To produce summary descriptive statistics and analytical studies, as a data source for management information, in support of the function for which the records are collected and maintained or for related personnel

management functions or manpower studies; may also be used to respond to general requests for statistical information (without personal identification of individuals) under the Freedom of Information Act.

11. To any trustee, receiver, master, special counsel, or other individual or entity that is appointed by a court of competent jurisdiction, or as a result of an agreement between the parties in connection with litigation or administrative proceedings involving allegations of violations of the federal securities laws (as defined in section 3(a)(47) of the Securities Exchange Act of 1934, 15 U.S.C. 78c(a)(47)) or pursuant to the Commission's Rules of Practice, 17 CFR 201.100 - 900 or the Commission's Rules of Fair Fund and Disgorgement Plans, 17 CFR 201.1100-1106, or otherwise, where such trustee, receiver, master, special counsel, or other individual or entity is specifically designated to perform particular functions with respect to, or as a result of, the pending action or proceeding or in connection with the administration and enforcement by the Commission of the federal securities laws or the Commission's Rules of Practice or the Rules of Fair Fund and Disgorgement Plans.

12. To any persons during the course of any inquiry, examination, or investigation conducted by the SEC's staff, or in connection with civil litigation, if the staff has reason to believe that the person to whom the record is disclosed may have further information about the matters related therein, and those matters appeared to be relevant at the time to the subject matter of the inquiry.

13. To interns, grantees, experts, contractors, and others who have been engaged by the Commission to assist in the performance of a service related to this system of records and who need access to the records for the purpose of assisting the Commission in the efficient administration of its programs, including by performing clerical, stenographic, or data analysis functions, or by reproduction of records by electronic or other means. Recipients of these records shall be required to comply with the requirements of the Privacy Act of 1974, as amended, 5 U.S.C. 552a.

14. In reports published by the Commission pursuant to authority granted in the federal securities laws (as such term is defined in section 3(a)(47) of the Securities Exchange Act of 1934, 15 U.S.C. 78c(a)(47)), which authority shall include, but not be limited to, section 21(a) of the Securities Exchange Act of 1934, 15 U.S.C. 78u(a)).

15. To members of advisory committees that are created by the Commission or by Congress to render advice and recommendations to the Commission or to Congress, to be used solely in connection with their official designated functions.

16. To any person who is or has agreed to be subject to the Commission's Rules of Conduct, 17 CFR 200.735-1 to 200.735-18, and who assists in the investigation by the Commission of possible violations of the federal securities laws (as such term is defined in section 3(a)(47) of the Securities Exchange Act of 1934, 15 U.S.C. 78c(a)(47)), in the preparation or conduct of enforcement actions brought by the Commission for such violations, or otherwise in connection with the Commission's enforcement or regulatory functions under the federal securities laws.

17. To a Congressional office from the record of an individual in response to an inquiry from the Congressional office made at the request of that individual.

18. To members of Congress, the press, and the public in response to inquiries relating to particular Registrants and their activities, and other matters under the Commission's jurisdiction.

19. To prepare and publish information relating to violations of the federal securities laws as provided in 15 U.S.C. 78c(a)(47)), as amended.

20. To respond to subpoenas in any litigation or other proceeding.

21. To a trustee in bankruptcy.

22. To any governmental agency, governmental or private collection agent, consumer reporting agency or commercial reporting agency, governmental or private employer of a debtor, or any other person, for collection, including collection by administrative offset, federal salary offset, tax refund offset, or administrative wage garnishment, of amounts owed as a result of Commission civil or administrative proceedings.

*****

Small Business Owners: The SEC always welcomes comments on how it can better assist small businesses. If you would like more information, or have questions or comments about federal securities regulations as they affect small businesses, please contact the Office of Small Business Policy, in the

SEC's Division of Corporation Finance, at 202- 551-3460. If you would prefer to comment to someone outside of the SEC, you can contact the Small Business Regulatory Enforcement Ombudsman at http://www.sba.gov/ombudsman or toll free at 888-REG-FAIR. The Ombudsman's office receives comments from small businesses and annually evaluates federal agency enforcement activities for their responsiveness to the special needs of small business.

AO110 (Rev. 04/07) Subpoena to Testify Before Grand Jury

UNITED STATES DISTRICT COURT

_____ DISTRICT OF _____

TO:

SUBPOENA TO TESTIFY
BEFORE GRAND JURY

SUBPOENA FOR:
☐ PERSON   ☐ DOCUMENT(S) OR OBJECT(S)

YOU ARE HEREBY COMMANDED to appear and testify before the Grand Jury of the United States District Court at the place, date, and time specified below.

PLACE	COURTROOM
	DATE AND TIME

YOU ARE ALSO COMMANDED to bring with you the following document(s) or object(s):*

☐ *Please see additional information on reverse.*

This subpoena shall remain in effect until you are granted leave to depart by the court or by an officer acting on behalf of the court.

CLERK	DATE
(By) Deputy Clerk	

This subpoena is issued on application of the United States of America	NAME, ADDRESS AND PHONE NUMBER OF ASSISTANT U.S. ATTORNEY

* If not applicable, enter "none".

AO110 (Rev. 04/07) Subpoena to Testify Before Grand Jury

RETURN OF SERVICE [1]			
RECEIVED BY SERVER	DATE	PLACE	
SERVED	DATE	PLACE	
SERVED ON (PRINT NAME)			
SERVED BY (PRINT NAME)		TITLE	

STATEMENT OF SERVICE FEES		
TRAVEL	SERVICES	TOTAL 0.00

DECLARATION OF SERVER [2]

I declare under penalty of perjury under the laws of the United States of America that the foregoing information contained in the Proof of Service is true and correct.

Executed on _____
DATE

SIGNATURE OF SERVER

ADDRESS OF SERVER

ADDITIONAL INFORMATION

(1)　As to who may serve a subpoena and the manner of its service see Rule 17(d), Federal Rules of Criminal Procedure, or Rule 45(b), Federal Rules of Civil Procedure.

(2)　"Fees and mileage need not be tendered to the witness upon service of a subpoena issued on behalf of the United States or an officer or agency thereof (Rule 45(b), Federal Rules of Civil Procedure; Rule 17(d), Federal Rules of Criminal Procedure) or on behalf of certain indigent parties and criminal defendants who are unable to pay such costs (28 USC 1825, Rule 17(b) Federal Rules of Criminal Procedure)".

UNITED STATES DISTRICT COURT

SOUTHERN DISTRICT OF TEXAS

INDICTMENT

Cr. No. _____

(T. 18, U.S.C., §§

1512(b)(2) and 3551

et

seq.)

------------------------x

UNITED STATES OF AMERICA

against

ARTHUR ANDERSEN, LLP
                Defendant.

THE GRAND JURY CHARGES:

I. <u>ANDERSEN AND ENRON</u>

1 . ARTHUR ANDERSEN, LLP ("ANDERSEN), is a partnership that performs, among other things, accounting and consulting services' for clients that operate businesses throughout the United States and the world. ANDERSEN is one of the so-called 'Big Five" accounting firms in the United States. ANDERSEN has its headquarters in Chicago, Illinois, and maintains offices throughout the world, including in Houston, Texas.

2. Enron Corp. ("Enron") was an Oregon corporation with its principal place of business in Houston, Texas. For most of 2001, Enron was considered the seventh largest corporation in the United States based on its reported revenues. In the previous ten years, Enron had evolved from a regional natural gas provider to, among other things, a trader of natural gas, electricity and other commodities, with retail operations in energy and other products.

3. For the past 16 years, up until it filed for bankruptcy in December 2001, Enron retained ANDERSEN to be its auditor. Enron was one of ANDERSEN's largest clients worldwide, and became ANDERSEN's largest client in ANDERSEN's Gulf Coast region. ANDERSEN earned tens of millions of dollars from Enron in annual auditing and other fees.

4. ANDERSEN performed both internal and external auditing work for Enron mainly in Houston, Texas. ANDERSEN established within Enron's offices in Houston a work space for the ANDERSEN team that had primary responsibility for performing audit work for Enron. In addition to Houston, ANDERSEN personnel performed work for Enron in, among other locations, Chicago, Illinois, Portland, Oregon, and London, England.

II. THE ANTICIPATION OF LITIGATION AGAINST ENRON AND ANDERSEN

5. In the summer and fall of 2001, a series of significant developments led to ANDERSEN's foreseeing imminent civil litigation against, and government investigations of, Enron and ANDERSEN.

6. On or about October 16, 2001, Enron issued a press release announcing a $618 million net loss for the third quarter of 2001. That same day, but not as part of the press release, Enron announced to analysts that it would reduce shareholder equity by approximately $1.2 billion. The market reacted immediately and the stock price of Enron shares plummeted.

7. The Securities and Exchange Commission ("SEC") , which investigates possible violations of the federal securities laws, opened an inquiry into Enron the very next day, requesting in writing information from Enron.

8. In addition to the negative financial information disclosed by Enron to the public and to analysts on October 16, 2001, ANDERSEN was aware by this time of additional significant facts unknown to the public.

- The approximately $1.2 billion reduction in shareholder equity disclosed to analysts on October 16, 2001, was necessitated by ANDERSEN and Enron having previously improperly categorized hundreds of millions of dollars as an increase, rather than a decrease, to Enron shareholder equity.

- The Enron October 16, 2001, press release characterized numerous charges against income for the third quarter as non-recurring" even though ANDERSEN believed the company did not have a basis for concluding that the charges would in fact be non-recurring. Indeed, ANDERSEN advised Enron against using that term, and documented its objections internally in the event of litigation, but did not report its objections or otherwise take steps to cure the public statement,

- ANDERSEN was put on direct notice of the allegations of Sherron Watkins, a. current Enron employee and former ANDERSEN employee, regarding possible fraud and other improprieties at Enron, and in particular, Enron' a use of off-balance-sheet "special purpose entities" that enabled the company to camouflage the true financial condition of the company. Watkins had reported her concerns to a partner at ANDERSEN, who thereafter disseminated them within ANDERSEN, including to the team working on the Enron audit. in addition, the team had received warnings about possible undisclosed side-agreements at Enron.

- The ANDERSEN team handling the Enron audit directly contravened the accounting methodology approved by ANDERSEN's own specialists working in its Professional Standards Group. In opposition to the views of its own experts, the ANDERSEN auditors had advised Enron in the spring of 2001 that it could use a favorable accounting method for its "special purpose entities."

• In 2000, an internal review conducted by senior management within ANDERSEN evaluated the ANDERSEN team assigned to audit Enron and rated the team as only a "2" on a scale of one to five, with five being the highest rating.

• On or about October 9, 2001, correctly anticipating litigation and government investigations, ANDERSEN, which had an internal department of lawyers for routine legal matters, retained an experienced New York law firm to handle future Enron-related litigation.

III. **THE WHOLESALE DESTRUCTION OF DOCUMENTS BY ANDERSEN**

9. By Friday, October 19, 2001, Enron alerted the ANDERSEN audit team that the SEC had begun an inquiry regarding the Enron "special purpose entities" and the involvement of Enron's Chief Financial Officer. The next morning, an emergency conference call among high-level ANDERSEN management was convened to address the SEC inquiry. During the call, it was decided that documentation that could assist Enron in responding to the SEC was to be assembled by the ANDERSEN auditors.

10. After spending Monday, October 22, 2001 at Enron, ANDERSEN partners assigned to the Enron engagement team launched on October' 23, 2001, a wholesale destruction of documents at ANDERSEN's offices in Houston, Texas. ANDERSEN personnel were called to urgent and mandatory meetings. Instead of being advised to preserve documentation so as to assist Enron and the SEC, ANDERSEN employees on the Enron engagement team were instructed by ANDERSEN partners and others to destroy immediately documentation relating to Enron, and told to work overtime if necessary to accomplish the destruction. During the next few weeks, an unparalleled initiative was undertaken to shred physical documentation and del6te computer files. Tons of paper relating to the Enron audit were promptly shredded as part of the orchestrated document destruction. The shredder at the ANDERSEN office at the Enron building was used virtually constantly and, to handle the overload, dozens of large trunks filled with Enron documents were sent to ANDERSEN's main Houston office to be shredded. A systematic effort was also undertaken and carried out to purge the computer hard-drives and E-mail system of Enron-related files.

11. In addition to shredding and deleting documents in Houston, Texas, instructions were given to ANDERSEN personnel working on Enron audit matters in Portland, Oregon, Chicago, Illinois, and London, England, to make sure that Enron documents were destroyed there as well. Indeed, in London,

a coordinated effort by ANDERSEN partners and others, similar to the initiative undertaken in Houston, was put into place to destroy Enron-related documents within days of notice of the SEC inquiry. Enron-related documents also were destroyed by ANDERSEN partners in Chicago.

12. On or about November 8, 2001, the SEC served ANDERSEN with the anticipated subpoena relating to its work for Enron. In response, members of the ANDERSEN team on the Enron audit were alerted finally that there could be "no more shredding" because the firm had been "officially served" for documents.

THE CHARGE: OBSTRUCTION OF JUSTICE

13. On or about and between October 10, 2001, and November 9, 2001, within the Southern District of Texas and elsewhere, including Chicago, Illinois, Portland, Oregon, and London, England, ANDERSEN, through its partners and others, did knowingly, intentionally and corruptly persuade and attempt to persuade other persons, to wit: ANDERSEN employees, with intent to cause and induce such persons to (a) withhold records, documents and other objects from official proceedings, namely: regulatory and criminal proceedings and investigations, and (b) alter, destroy, mutilate and conceal objects with intent to impair the objects, integrity and availability for use in such official proceedings.
(Title 18, United States code, Sections 1512 (b) (2) and 3551 et seq.)

A TRUE BILL

_____
FOREPERSON

JOSHUA R. HOCHBERG
ACTING UNITED STATES ATTORNEY
SOUTHERN DISTRICT OF TEXAS

LESLIE R. CALDWELL
DIRECTOR, ENRON TASK FORCE

By:_____
Samuel W. Buell
Andrew Weissmann
Special Attorneys
Department of Justice

UNITED STATES DISTRICT COURT
SOUTHERN DISTRICT OF NEW YORK

- - - - - - - - - - - - - - - - x

UNITED STATES OF AMERICA :

                                             SUPERSEDING

- v.   :

                                             INDICTMENT

MARTHA STEWART and   :   S1 03 Cr. 717
                                               (MGC)

PETER BACANOVIC,

                              :

Defendants.

                              :

- - - - - - - - - - - - - - - - x

COUNT ONE
(Conspiracy to Obstruct Justice,
Make False Statements, and Commit Perjury)

The Grand Jury charges:

Background

    1. At all times relevant to this Indictment, MARTHA STEWART, the defendant, was chairman of the board of directors and chief executive officer of Martha Stewart Living Omnimedia, Inc. ("MSLO"). MSLO was a corporation organized under the laws of Delaware with its principal executive and administrative offices located at 11 West 42nd Street, New York, New York. MSLO was engaged in businesses spanning four major areas: publishing of magazines and books; television production; merchandising; and internet and catalog sales. MSLO's products bear the "Martha Stewart" brand name. MSLO's common stock was listed and traded on the New York Stock Exchange ("NYSE"), a national securities exchange located in New York, New York, under the symbol "MSO."

    2. Prior to forming MSLO, MARTHA STEWART had been licensed by NASD, a national securities association, to sell securities and was employed as a securities broker from in or about 1968 through in or about 1973. On March 22, 2002, STEWART was nominated to serve on the board of directors of the NYSE. On June 6, 2002, STEWART was elected to the NYSE board of directors, a position which she held until she resigned on October 3, 2002.

    3. At all times relevant to this Indictment, PETER BACANOVIC, the defendant, was licensed by NASD to sell securities. BACANOVIC was employed as a securities broker with the title "Financial Advisor" at Merrill Lynch & Co., Inc. ("Merrill Lynch"), a broker-dealer headquartered in New York, New York, at a branch office located at 1251 Avenue of the Americas,

New York, New York.

4. At all times relevant to this Indictment, MARTHA STEWART maintained securities brokerage accounts at Merrill Lynch. PETER BACANOVIC was the registered representative for STEWART's Merrill Lynch accounts and had a close personal relationship with STEWART. Because of commissions generated from her accounts and accounts that BACANOVIC obtained as a result of his relationship with STEWART, as well as her high public profile, STEWART was one of BACANOVIC's most important brokerage clients.

5. At all times relevant to this Indictment, Douglas Faneuil, a co-conspirator not named as a defendant herein, was employed by Merrill Lynch as an assistant to PETER BACANOVIC.

<u>Merrill Lynch's Policies on Safeguarding</u>
<u>Client Information and Insider Trading</u>

6. At all times relevant to this Indictment, Merrill Lynch established and distributed to its employees, including to PETER BACANOVIC, policies regarding employees' duties to maintain in strict confidence information concerning Merrill Lynch's clients. The policies stated, in relevant part:

Confidentiality of Client Information
You may not discuss the business affairs of any client with anyone, including other employees except on a need-to-know basis. Information or records concerning the business of the Firm and/or its clients may not be released except to persons legally entitled to receive them.

Client Information Privacy Policy
Merrill Lynch protects the confidentiality and security of client information. Employees must understand the need for careful handling of this information. Merrill Lynch's client information privacy policy provides that –
. . .

• Employees may not discuss the business affairs of any client with any other employee, except on a strict need-to-know basis.

• We do not release client information, except upon a client's authorization or when permitted or required by law.

7. At all times relevant to this Indictment, Merrill Lynch specifically warned its employees, including PETER BACANOVIC, of the impropriety of so-called "piggybacking" –- buying or selling a security after a client bought or sold the same security in order to take advantage of that client's perceived knowledge or expertise. The directive stated, in pertinent part:

You should not "piggyback," that is, enter transactions after a client's trades to take advantage of perceived expertise or knowledge on the part of the client. If the client's successful trading pattern arose from an improper element such as inside information, you (and the Firm) could be subject to a regulatory or criminal investigation or proceeding.

8. At all times relevant to this Indictment, Merrill Lynch also distributed policies advising its employees, including PETER BACANOVIC, of their responsibilities under the federal securities laws, which stated in part:

Inside Information
Background and Definition
U.S. Federal and State securities laws and laws of certain other countries make it unlawful for anyone in possession of non- public material information to take advantage of such information in connection with purchasing or selling securities or recommending to others the purchase or sale of securities. Such information must not be disclosed to others who may, thereafter, take advantage of it in purchasing or selling securities.

Information is material if a reasonable person would want to consider it in determining whether to engage in a securities transaction or if it could reasonably be expected to affect the market price of a security if it becomes generally known. Information should be considered non-public if it has not been disclosed in the news media, research reports, corporate public filings or reports, or in some other similar public manner, Non-public information should generally be regarded as material unless it is clearly unimportant to investors.

BACANOVIC's Acquisition of Confidential, Nonpublic Information

9. At all times relevant to this Indictment, ImClone Systems Incorporated ("ImClone") was a corporation organized under the laws of the State of Delaware with its principal place of business in New York, New York. ImClone was engaged in the business of developing biologic medicines, including Erbitux, a biologic treatment for irinotecan-refractory colorectal cancer. ImClone publicly described Erbitux as its lead product candidate. ImClone's common stock was listed and traded on the NASDAQ National Market System, an electronic securities market system administered by NASD, under the symbol "IMCL."

10. At all times relevant to this Indictment, Samuel Waksal was the president, chief executive officer, and a director of ImClone. Waksal and several members of his family were clients of PETER BACANOVIC.

11. At all times relevant to this Indictment, MARTHA STEWART and Samuel Waksal were personal friends.

12. On or about October 31, 2001, ImClone submitted to the United States Food and Drug Administration (the "FDA") a Biologics Licensing Application ("BLA") for approval of Erbitux (the "Erbitux BLA"). Pursuant to FDA regulations, within 60 days following the submission of a BLA, the FDA must decide whether the BLA is administratively and scientifically complete to be accepted for FDA review. Only if a BLA is accepted for filing does the FDA review the application to determine whether the proposed treatment will be approved. It had been publicly reported that the FDA's decision whether to accept the Erbitux BLA for filing was expected by the end of December 2001.

13. On the morning of December 27, 2001, between 9:00 a.m. and 10:00 a.m. (EST), Douglas Faneuil informed PETER BACANOVIC that Samuel Waksal and a member of his family (the "Waksal Family Member") were seeking to sell all the ImClone shares they held at Merrill Lynch, then worth over $7.3 million (collectively referred to as the "Waksal Shares"). Faneuil advised BACANOVIC that the Waksal Family Member had placed an order to sell all of the Waksal Family Member's ImClone stock. By approximately 9:48 a.m., the Waksal Family Member's approximately 39,472 shares had been sold for approximately $2,472,837. Faneuil further advised BACANOVIC that Samuel Waksal had requested that all of the ImClone stock in Samuel Waksal's Merrill Lynch account, approximately 79,797 shares, then worth approximately $4.9 million, be transferred to the Waksal Family Member and then sold. Samuel Waksal's written direction to Merrill Lynch stated that the transfer request was "URGENT -IMMEDIATE ACTION REQUIRED" and that it was "imperative" that the transfer take place during the morning of December 27, 2001.

14. On December 27, 2001, information regarding efforts by ImClone's CEO, Samuel Waksal, to sell all of the ImClone shares that he held at Merrill Lynch constituted confidential, nonpublic information.

STEWART's Sale of ImClone Stock

15. In breach of the duties PETER BACANOVIC owed to Merrill Lynch and its clients to keep client information confidential, on or about December 27, 2001, BACANOVIC directed his assistant, Douglas Faneuil, to disclose to MARTHA STEWART information regarding the sale and attempted sale of the Waksal Shares -- information that BACANOVIC had misappropriated and stolen from Merrill Lynch and its clients.

16. On December 27, 2001, at approximately 10:04 a.m. (EST), within minutes after being informed of the sale and attempted sale of the Waksal Shares, PETER BACANOVIC called MARTHA STEWART. After being told that STEWART was in transit and unavailable, BACANOVIC left a message, memorialized by STEWART's assistant, that "Peter Bacanovic thinks

ImClone is going to start trading downward." At approximately 10:04 a.m., the price of ImClone stock was approximately $61.53 per share. BACANOVIC, who was on vacation, directed Douglas Faneuil to inform STEWART about the Waksal transactions when she returned the call.

17. On December 27, 2001, at approximately 1:39 p.m. (EST), MARTHA STEWART telephoned the office of PETER BACANOVIC and spoke to Douglas Faneuil, who informed her that Samuel Waksal was trying to sell all of the ImClone stock that Waksal held at Merrill Lynch. Upon hearing this news, STEWART directed Faneuil to sell all of her ImClone stock -- 3,928 shares. All 3,928 ImClone shares owned by STEWART were sold that day at approximately 1:52 p.m. (EST) at an average price of $58.43 per share, yielding proceeds of approximately $228,000.

18. As a client of Merrill Lynch and as a former securities broker, MARTHA STEWART knew that information regarding the sale and attempted sale of the Waksal Shares had been communicated to her in violation of the duties of trust and confidence owed to Merrill Lynch and its clients.

Public Announcement of the FDA Decision

19. After the close of business on December 28, 2001, ImClone issued a press release announcing that the FDA had refused to accept the Erbitux BLA for filing.

20. On December 28, 2001, prior to the public announcement of the FDA decision, the price of ImClone stock closed at $55.25 per share. On December 31, 2001, the first day that ImClone stock traded after the FDA's decision was publicly announced, the price of ImClone stock opened at $45.39, representing a decline of approximately 18%.

21. By selling a total of 3,928 shares of ImClone stock on the same day as the sale and attempted sale of the Waksal Shares, MARTHA STEWART avoided significant trading losses. If STEWART had sold at the price at which ImClone stock opened on December 31, 2001, STEWART would have lost $51,222. If STEWART had sold at the price at which ImClone stock closed on December 31, 2001, STEWART would have lost $45,673.

The Scheme to Obstruct Justice

22. In or about January 2002, the Northeast Regional Office of the United States Securities and Exchange Commission ("SEC"), an agency of the United States, the Federal Bureau of Investigation (the "FBI"), and the United States Attorney's Office for the Southern District of New York commenced investigations into trading in ImClone securities in advance of the public announcement of the FDA's negative decision, including into the trades conducted by Samuel Waksal and MARTHA STEWART. The investigations focused on whether such trades were made in violation of

federal securities laws and regulations that prohibit trading on the basis of material, nonpublic information. It was material to the investigations to determine, among other things, what was communicated to STEWART about ImClone on December 27, 2001 and the reasons for STEWART's December 27, 2001 sale of ImClone stock.

23. As described more fully below, after learning of the investigations, MARTHA STEWART and PETER BACANOVIC, and others known and unknown, entered into an unlawful conspiracy to obstruct the investigations; to make false statements and provide false and misleading information regarding STEWART's sale of ImClone stock; and to commit perjury, all to conceal and cover up that BACANOVIC had breached his duties of trust and confidence to Merrill Lynch and its clients and caused STEWART to be provided information regarding the sale and attempted sale of the Waksal Shares, and that STEWART had sold her ImClone stock while in possession of that information. Specifically, and among other things, STEWART and BACANOVIC agreed that rather than tell the truth about the communications with STEWART on December 27, 2001 and the reasons for STEWART's sale of ImClone stock on December 27, 2001, they would instead fabricate and attempt to deceive investigators with a fictitious explanation for her sale -- that STEWART sold her ImClone stock on December 27, 2001 because she and BACANOVIC had a pre-existing agreement to sell the stock if and when the price dropped to $60 per share.

BACANOVIC's False Statements on January 7, 2002

24. On or about January 7, 2002, in New York, New York, SEC staff attorneys interviewed PETER BACANOVIC by telephone. During the interview, the SEC staff attorneys questioned BACANOVIC regarding, among other things, the sale of ImClone stock on December 27, 2001 by MARTHA STEWART. In furtherance of the conspiracy, and with the intent and purpose to conceal and cover up that BACANOVIC had caused STEWART to be provided information regarding the sale and attempted sale of the Waksal Shares and that STEWART had sold her ImClone stock while in possession of that information, BACANOVIC made the following false statements, in substance and in part, and concealed and covered up the following facts that were material to the SEC's
investigation, among others:

a. BACANOVIC stated that in a conversation with STEWART on December 20, 2001, STEWART said that she had decided to sell her ImClone shares if ImClone's market price fell to $60 per share. This statement was false in that, as BACANOVIC well knew, STEWART did not inform him of such a decision to sell her shares.

b. BACANOVIC stated that on December 27, 2001, STEWART had spoken to BACANOVIC, that he told STEWART that ImClone's price had dropped below $60 per share, and that STEWART placed her order to sell her

ImClone stock with him. This statement was false in that, as BACANOVIC well knew, STEWART did not speak to BACANOVIC when she placed her order to sell ImClone stock, but rather spoke to Douglas Faneuil, and concealed and covered up that Faneuil conveyed information to STEWART regarding the sale and attempted sale of the Waksal Shares.

STEWART's Alteration of
BACANOVIC's December 27, 2001 Message

25. On or about January 25, 2002, the FBI and the U.S. Attorney's Office contacted the office of MARTHA STEWART and requested to interview STEWART. The interview was scheduled to occur on February 4, 2002.

26. On or about January 31, 2002, after learning that the FBI and the U.S. Attorney's Office had requested an interview with her, and immediately following a lengthy conversation with her attorney, MARTHA STEWART accessed the phone message log maintained on computer by her assistant and reviewed the phone message that PETER BACANOVIC had left for her on December 27, 2001. In furtherance of the conspiracy, and knowing that BACANOVIC's message for STEWART was based on information regarding the sale and attempted sale of the Waksal Shares that BACANOVIC subsequently caused to be conveyed to her, STEWART deleted the substance of BACANOVIC's phone message, changing the message from "Peter Bacanovic thinks ImClone is going to start trading downward," to "Peter Bacanovic re imclone." After altering the message, STEWART directed her assistant to return the message to its original wording.

STEWART's False Statements on February 4, 2002

27. On or about February 4, 2002, MARTHA STEWART, accompanied by her lawyers, was interviewed in New York, New York by the SEC, the FBI, and the U.S. Attorney's Office. In furtherance of the conspiracy, and with the intent and purpose to conceal and cover up that BACANOVIC had caused STEWART to be provided information regarding the sale and attempted sale of the Waksal Shares and that STEWART had sold her ImClone stock while in possession of that information, STEWART made the following false statements of facts, in substance and in part, and concealed and covered up the following material facts, among others:

a. STEWART stated that at a time when ImClone was trading at approximately $74 per share (which prior to December 27, 2001, had last occurred on December 6, 2001), STEWART and PETER BACANOVIC both decided that STEWART would sell her ImClone shares when ImClone started trading at $60 per share. This statement was false and misleading in that, as STEWART well knew, no such decision had been made.

b. STEWART stated that she did not know whether the phone message BACANOVIC left for STEWART on December 27, 2001 was recorded in the phone message log maintained by her assistant. This statement was false and misleading in that, as STEWART well knew but concealed and covered up, the message was recorded in the phone message log, the substance of which – "Peter Bacanovic thinks ImClone is going to start trading downward" -- STEWART had reviewed when she temporarily altered the message just four days before the interview.

c. STEWART stated that on December 27, 2001, STEWART spoke to BACANOVIC, who told her that ImClone was trading a little below $60 per share and asked STEWART if she wanted to sell. STEWART stated that after being informed of ImClone's stock price, she directed BACANOVIC to sell her ImClone shares that day because she did not want to be bothered over her vacation. These statements were false and misleading in that, as STEWART well knew but concealed and covered up, STEWART spoke to Faneuil, not BACANOVIC, on December 27, 2001, and STEWART sold her ImClone shares that day after Douglas Faneuil conveyed to her information regarding the sale and attempted sale of the Waksal Shares.

d. STEWART stated that before concluding their telephone conversation on December 27, 2001, BACANOVIC and STEWART discussed "how MSLO stock was doing" and Kmart. This statement was false and misleading in that, as STEWART well knew, STEWART spoke to Douglas Faneuil, not BACANOVIC, and had no such discussions that day with either BACANOVIC or Faneuil regarding MSLO or Kmart. STEWART provided these false details of her purported conversation with BACANOVIC to conceal and cover up the fact that STEWART spoke on December 27, 2001 to Douglas Faneuil, who conveyed to her information regarding the sale and attempted sale of the Waksal Shares.

e. STEWART stated that, during the period from December 28, 2001 to the date of the interview, February 4, 2002, STEWART had only one conversation with BACANOVIC regarding ImClone, in which only publicly disclosed matters in the "public arena" were discussed. STEWART further stated that although BACANOVIC mentioned that Merrill Lynch had been questioned by the SEC regarding trading in ImClone generally, BACANOVIC did not inform STEWART that he had been questioned by the SEC or that he had been questioned regarding STEWART's account. These statements were false and misleading in that, as STEWART well knew, during the period from December 28, 2001 through February 4, 2002, STEWART had conversations with BACANOVIC regarding STEWART's sale of ImClone shares and the investigation of that sale, and BACANOVIC had informed STEWART that he had been questioned by the SEC regarding her sale of ImClone. STEWART made these false statements to conceal and cover up that she and BACANOVIC had agreed to provide false information to the SEC, the FBI, and the U.S. Attorney's Office regarding STEWART's sale of ImClone stock and conceal and cover up that BACANOVIC had caused STEWART to be provided information regarding the sale and attempted sale of the Waksal Shares and that STEWART had sold her ImClone stock while in possession of that information.

BACANOVIC's Alteration of His "Worksheet"

28. On or about January 28, 2002, the SEC issued an Order Directing Private Investigations and Designating Officers to Take Testimony. On or about the same date, the SEC served upon Merrill Lynch a request for production of documents, requesting, among other things, documents relating to brokerage accounts maintained by MARTHA STEWART. On or about January 29, 2002, the SEC's request was communicated to PETER BACANOVIC by representatives of Merrill Lynch.

29. As described more fully below, in furtherance of the scheme to obstruct justice, PETER BACANOVIC altered a document in order to fabricate evidence that would purportedly corroborate BACANOVIC's and MARTHA STEWART's claims that STEWART had decided to sell her ImClone stock if the market price fell to $60 per share.

30. In or about December 2001, PETER BACANOVIC had discussions with MARTHA STEWART regarding engaging in "tax loss selling," i.e., selling stocks that had declined below the price at which they had been purchased in order to recognize losses from those sales to offset taxable gains realized during the same year from profitable sales of other securities. On December 21 and 24, 2001, BACANOVIC executed sales at a loss of stock in twenty-two companies that STEWART held in her Merrill Lynch portfolio.

31. On or about December 21, 2001, PETER BACANOVIC printed a "worksheet" that listed each of the stocks held by MARTHA STEWART at Merrill Lynch, including ImClone, as well as, among other things, the market value of each of the holdings as of the close of business on December 20, 2001, and STEWART's unrealized profit or loss in each stock as of the close of business on December 20, 2001 (the "Worksheet"). On or about December 21, 2001, BACANOVIC made handwritten notes in blue ballpoint ink on the Worksheet concerning transactions and planned transactions in STEWART's account. On or about December 21, 2001, BACANOVIC made no notes on the Worksheet regarding any purported decision to sell STEWART's ImClone shares at $60 per share.

32. In furtherance of the conspiracy, after learning of the SEC's investigation of STEWART's sale of ImClone stock and with the intent and purpose to mislead the SEC and others into believing that there existed documentary evidence corroborating BACANOVIC's and STEWART's false claim that they had an agreement to sell STEWART's ImClone shares if the market price fell to $60 per share, PETER BACANOVIC altered the Worksheet, using ink that was blue ballpoint, but was scientifically distinguishable from the ink used elsewhere on the Worksheet. BACANOVIC

added the notation "@ 60" near the entry for ImClone.

33. In furtherance of the conspiracy, on or about January 30, 2002, PETER BACANOVIC gave the altered Worksheet to a Merrill Lynch manager with the intent that the altered Worksheet be produced to the SEC in response to the SEC's request for documents. BACANOVIC falsely represented to the Merrill Lynch manager that the altered Worksheet was used in a "selling discussion" he had with MARTHA STEWART. On or about February 14, 2002, Merrill Lynch produced the altered Worksheet to the SEC pursuant to the SEC's request for production of documents.

BACANOVIC's Perjured Testimony Before the SEC

34. On or about February 4, 2002, the SEC issued a subpoena to PETER BACANOVIC directing BACANOVIC to provide testimony under oath.

35. On February 13, 2002, PETER BACANOVIC appeared before the SEC in New York, New York, pursuant to subpoena, and gave testimony under oath. In furtherance of the conspiracy, and with the intent and purpose to conceal and cover up that BACANOVIC had caused STEWART to be provided information regarding the sale and attempted sale of the Waksal Shares and that STEWART had sold her ImClone stock while in possession of that information, BACANOVIC falsely testified, in substance and in part, about the following matters, among others:

a. BACANOVIC testified that on December 20, 2001, after the close of business, BACANOVIC and MARTHA STEWART had a telephone conversation in which they decided that STEWART would sell her ImClone shares if ImClone fell to $60 per share. This testimony was false in that, as BACANOVIC well knew, they had made no such decision.

b. BACANOVIC testified that he had notes of his conversation with STEWART on December 20, 2001, that reflected their discussion regarding a decision to sell ImClone at $60 per share. This testimony was false in that, as BACANOVIC well knew, he had no notes that reflected any actual discussion on or about December 20, 2001 about a decision to sell ImClone at $60 per share. BACANOVIC also well knew that he had falsely added the notation "@ 60" to the Worksheet after STEWART's sale of ImClone stock and after he learned of the SEC's investigation, for the purpose of obstructing that investigation.

c. BACANOVIC testified that during the period from December 28, 2001 through the date of his testimony, February 13, 2002, BACANOVIC and STEWART did not discuss STEWART's December 27, 2001 sale of ImClone stock. BACANOVIC further testifed that he did not inform STEWART of any questions asked by anyone regarding that sale. This testimony was false in that, as BACANOVIC well knew, BACANOVIC had conversations with

STEWART in January and February 2002 regarding, among other matters, the investigations of STEWART's sale of ImClone stock.

STEWART's False Statements on April 10, 2002

36. On or about April 10, 2002, MARTHA STEWART was interviewed by telephone by the SEC, the FBI, and the U.S. Attorney's Office, the representatives of which were in New York, New York. In furtherance of the conspiracy, and with the intent and purpose to conceal and cover up that PETER BACANOVIC had caused STEWART to be provided information regarding the sale and attempted sale of the Waksal Shares and that STEWART had sold her ImClone stock while in possession of that information, STEWART made the following false and misleading statements, in substance and in part, and concealed and covered up the following material facts, among others:

a. STEWART stated that she did not recall if she and BACANOVIC discussed Samuel Waksal on December 27, 2001, nor did she recall being informed on December 27, 2001 that any of the Waksals were selling their ImClone stock. This statement was false and misleading in that STEWART in fact recalled that she was informed on December 27, 2001 that Samuel Waksal was attempting to sell all of his ImClone shares at Merrill Lynch.

b. STEWART stated that the conversation with PETER BACANOVIC that she had previously described in her February 4, 2002 interview (referenced in ¶ 27 above) -- the conversation in which BACANOVIC and STEWART purportedly decided that STEWART would sell her ImClone shares when ImClone started trading at $60 per share -- occurred sometime in November or December 2001, after she sold all of her ImClone shares from the Martha Stewart Defined Pension Fund (which occurred on or about October 26, 2001). This statement was false and misleading in that, as STEWART well knew, STEWART and BACANOVIC had made no such decision.

c. STEWART stated that on December 27, 2001, STEWART spoke to BACANOVIC, who told her that ImClone was trading below $60 per share and suggested that STEWART sell her ImClone shares. These statements were false and misleading in that, as STEWART well knew but concealed and covered up, STEWART spoke to Faneuil, not BACANOVIC, on December 27, 2001, and STEWART sold her ImClone shares that day after Douglas Faneuil conveyed to her information regarding the sale and attempted sale of the Waksal Shares.

The Conspiracy

37. From in or about January 2002 until in or about April 2002, in the Southern District of New York and elsewhere, PETER BACANOVIC and MARTHA STEWART, and others known and unknown, unlawfully, willfully,

and knowingly did combine, conspire, confederate and agree together and with each other to commit offenses against the United States, to wit: to obstruct justice, in violation of Section 1505 of Title 18, United States Code; to make false statements, in violation of Section 1001 of Title 18, United States Code; and to commit perjury, in violation of Section 1621 of Title 18, United States Code.

Objects of the Conspiracy
Obstruction of Justice

38. It was a part and an object of the conspiracy that MARTHA STEWART and PETER BACANOVIC, and others known and unknown, unlawfully, willfully and knowingly, would and did corruptly influence, obstruct and impede, and endeavor to influence, obstruct and impede the due and proper administration of the law under which a pending proceeding was being had before a department and agency of the United States, namely, an investigation by the SEC, in violation of Title 18, United States Code, Section 1505.

False Statements

39. It was further a part and an object of the conspiracy that MARTHA STEWART and PETER BACANOVIC, and others known and unknown, unlawfully, willfully and knowingly, in a matter within the jurisdiction of the executive branch of the Government of the United States, would and did falsify, conceal, and cover up by trick, scheme, and device material facts, and make materially false, fictitious, and fraudulent statements and representations, and make and use false writings and documents knowing the same to contain materially false, fictitious, and fraudulent statements and entries, in violation of Title 18, United States Code, Section 1001.

Perjury

40. It was further a part and an object of the conspiracy that PETER BACANOVIC, having taken an oath before a competent tribunal, officer and person, in a case in which the law of the United States authorizes an oath to be administered, namely, in testimony before the SEC, that he would testify, declare, depose and certify truly, and that any written testimony, declaration, deposition and certificate by him subscribed, would be true, unlawfully, willfully, knowingly, and contrary to such oath, would and did state and subscribe material matters which he did not believe to be true, in violation of Title 18, United States Code, Section 1621.

Overt Acts

41. In furtherance of the conspiracy and to effect the illegal objects thereof, the following overt acts, among others, were committed in the Southern District of New York and elsewhere:

a. On January 7, 2002, in New York, New York, PETER BACANOVIC provided false and misleading information to the SEC regarding the December 27, 2001 sale of ImClone stock by MARTHA STEWART.

b. In January 2002, PETER BACANOVIC in New York, New York, encouraged Douglas Faneuil to refrain from disclosing that Faneuil had informed MARTHA STEWART on December 27, 2001 of the sale and attempted sale of the Waksal Shares.

c. On January 25, 2002, after MARTHA STEWART learned that the FBI and the U.S. Attorney's Office requested to interview her, STEWART placed a call from her cellular telephone to PETER BACANOVIC's cellular telephone.

d. On or about January 30, 2002, in New York, New York, PETER BACANOVIC provided the altered Worksheet to a Merrill Lynch manager with the intent that the Worksheet be produced to the SEC.

e. At 7:09 a.m. on February 4, 2002, the morning of MARTHA STEWART's interview with the SEC, the FBI, and the U.S. Attorney's Office, PETER BACANOVIC placed a call from his cellular telephone to STEWART's cellular telephone.

f. On February 4, 2002, in New York, New York, MARTHA STEWART made false and misleading statements to the SEC, the FBI, and the U.S. Attorney's Office regarding her December 27, 2001 sale of ImClone stock.

g. On February 13, 2002, in New York, New York, PETER BACANOVIC gave false and misleading testimony regarding MARTHA STEWART's December 27, 2001 sale of ImClone stock.

h. On April 10, 2002, in New York, New York, MARTHA STEWART made false and misleading statements to the SEC, the FBI, and the U.S. Attorney's Office regarding her December 27, 2001 sale of ImClone stock.

(Title 18, United States Code, Section 371).

COUNT TWO

(False Statements by Peter Bacanovic)

The Grand Jury further charges:

42. The allegations of paragraphs 1 through 36 are repeated and realleged as though fully set forth herein.

43. On or about January 7, 2002, in the Southern District of New York, PETER BACANOVIC unlawfully, willfully, and knowingly, in a matter within the jurisdiction of the executive branch of the Government of the United States, falsified, concealed, and covered up by trick, scheme, and device material facts, and made materially false, fictitious, and fraudulent statements and representations, to wit, BACANOVIC participated in an interview by telephone with SEC staff attorneys in New York, New York, in which he made the following false statements and concealed and covered up facts that were material to the SEC's investigation:

Specification One

BACANOVIC falsely stated that on December 20, 2001, he had a conversation with STEWART in which she decided to sell her ImClone stock at $60 per share.

Specification Two

BACANOVIC falsely stated that he had a conversation with MARTHA STEWART on December 27, 2001, in which he told STEWART that ImClone's stock price had dropped and STEWART told him to sell her ImClone stock.

(Title 18, United States Code, Sections 1001(a)(1) and (2)).

COUNT THREE

(False Statements by Martha Stewart)

The Grand Jury further charges:

44. The allegations of paragraphs 1 through 36 and 41 are repeated and realleged as though fully set forth herein.

45. On or about February 4, 2002, in the Southern District of New York, MARTHA STEWART unlawfully, willfully, and knowingly, in a matter within the jurisdiction of the executive branch of the Government of the United States, falsified, concealed, and covered up by trick, scheme, and device material facts, and made materially false, fictitious, and fraudulent statements and representations, to wit, STEWART participated in an interview with the SEC, the FBI, and the U.S. Attorney's Office for the Southern District of New York in New York, New York, in which she made the following false statements and concealed and covered up facts that were material to the investigations:

Specification One

STEWART falsely stated that in a conversation that had occurred at a time when ImClone was trading at $74 per share, STEWART and BACANOVIC decided that STEWART would sell her shares when ImClone started trading at $60 per share.

Specification Two

STEWART falsely stated that on December 27, 2001, at approximately 1:30 p.m. (EST), STEWART spoke to BACANOVIC, who told STEWART that ImClone was trading a little below $60 per share and that he asked STEWART if she wanted to sell, and then STEWART told BACANOVIC to sell her shares.

Specification Three

STEWART falsely stated that she did not recall speaking to BACANOVIC's assistant on December 27, 2001.

Specification Four

STEWART falsely stated that before ending her call with BACANOVIC on December 27, 2001, STEWART and BACANOVIC had discussions regarding what MSLO stock was doing and regarding Kmart.

Specification Five

STEWART falsely stated that she decided to sell her ImClone stock on December 27, 2001 because she did not want to be bothered over her vacation.

Specification Six

STEWART falsely stated that she did not know if there was a phone message from BACANOVIC on December 27, 2001 in the log of telephone messages maintained by her assistant.

Specification Seven

STEWART falsely stated that since December 28, 2001, she had only one conversation with BACANOVIC regarding ImClone, in which they only discussed matters in the "public arena."

Specification Eight

STEWART falsely stated that since December 28, 2001, BACANOVIC mentioned to STEWART in a telephone conversation that Merrill Lynch had been questioned by the SEC regarding ImClone, but did not tell STEWART that he had been questioned by the SEC or that he had been questioned by the SEC regarding STEWART's account.

(Title 18, United States Code, Sections 1001(a)(1) and (2)).

COUNT FOUR
(False Statements by Martha Stewart)

The Grand Jury further charges:

46. The allegations of paragraphs 1 through 36 and 41 are repeated and realleged as though fully set forth herein.

47. On or about April 10, 2002, in the Southern District of New York, MARTHA STEWART unlawfully, willfully, and knowingly, in a matter within the jurisdiction of the executive branch of the Government of the United States, falsified, concealed, and covered up by trick, scheme, and device material facts, and made materially false, fictitious, and fraudulent statements and representations, to wit, STEWART participated in an interview with the SEC, the FBI, and the U.S. Attorney's Office for the Southern District of New York in New York, New York, in which she made the following false statements and concealed and covered up facts that were material to the investigations:

Specification One

STEWART falsely stated that she did not recall if she and BACANOVIC discussed Samuel Waksal on December 27, 2001, nor did she recall being informed on December 27, 2001 that any of the Waksals were selling their ImClone stock.

Specification Two

STEWART falsely stated that in a conversation that occurred sometime in November or December 2001, after she sold all of her ImClone shares from the Martha Stewart Defined Pension Fund, STEWART and BACANOVIC decided that STEWART would sell her shares when ImClone started trading at $60 per share.

Specification Three

STEWART falsely stated that on December 27, 2001, at approximately 1:30 p.m. (EST), STEWART spoke to BACANOVIC, who told her that ImClone was trading below $60 per share and suggested that STEWART sell her ImClone shares.

(Title 18, United States Code, Sections 1001(a)(1) and (2)).

COUNT FIVE
(Making and Using False Documents by Peter Bacanovic)

The Grand Jury further charges:

48. The allegations of paragraphs 1 through 36 and 41 are repeated and realleged as though fully set forth herein.

49. In or about January 2002, in the Southern District of New York and elsewhere, PETER BACANOVIC unlawfully, willfully, and knowingly, in a matter within the jurisdiction of the executive branch of the Government of the United States, made and used false writings and documents knowing the same to contain materially false, fictitious, and fraudulent statements and entries, to wit, BACANOVIC altered the Worksheet to add the notation "@ 60" and caused it to be produced to the SEC.

(Title 18, United States Code, Sections 1001(a)(3) and 2).

COUNT SIX
(Perjury by Peter Bacanovic)

The Grand Jury further charges:

50. The allegations of paragraphs 1 through 36 and 41 are repeated and realleged as though fully set forth herein.

51. On February 13, 2002, in the Southern District of New York, PETER BACANOVIC, having taken an oath before a competent tribunal, officer and person, in a case in which the law of the United States authorizes an oath to be administered, namely, in testimony before an officer of the SEC, that he would testify, declare, depose and certify truly, and that any written testimony, declaration, deposition and certificate by him subscribed, would be true, unlawfully, willfully, knowingly, and contrary to such oath, stated and subscribed material matters which he did not believe to be true, namely, the testimony on or about February 13, 2002, the underlined portions of which he believed to be materially false:

Specification One
(Page 14, Line 11 - Page 16, Line 7)

Q: And she [MARTHA STEWART's assistant] told you that Ms. Stewart was in transit?

A: Ms. Stewart was in transit, that she didn't know when she would be speaking with her, and that she would try to give her the message.

Q: And what was the message?

A: The message was to please call us back, and also to please advise her that ImClone stock was at whatever the price was at that time.
. . .

Q: And you specifically told [MARTHA STEWART's assistant] that ImClone stock was dropping?

A: No. We just gave her the price of the stock.
. . .

Q: When you called [MARTHA STEWART's assistant], can you just try and think, to be as specific as possible, when you asked her to ask Ms. Stewart to please call you back, did you say, "It's urgent, call me back immediately"? Something like that?

A: No. I said, "I would like to speak with her, if possible, today and regarding ImClone and the current price of the stock is. Understanding that she is in transit and that she sometimes is very, very difficult
to reach."

Specification Two
(Page 69, Line 2 - Page 72, Line 4)

Q: When was the last time you saw her?

A: In January.

Q: When in January?

A: I would be able to give you the exact date, it's in my office in my calendar. I saw her approximately in the middle of the month.
. . .

Q: Did ImClone come up in the meeting at all?

A: She had asked me if I had spoken to Sam, and I said, no, I had not. And that was it.
. . .

Q: Did her investment in ImClone come up at all?

A: No.
. . .

Q: In addition to that meeting, have you talked to her at all since December 28th? Besides that meeting?

A: Well, I spoke with her about the fact that I wanted to schedule the meeting. I spoke with her to confirm that I had received the second part of the transfer. And then she – and I spoke with her when she reconfirmed that these payments were going to be going out.

Q: And when you spoke with her in any of these conversations, did ImClone come up?

A: Did not.

Q: Did Sam Waksal come up?

A: No. Oh – I don't recall. Possibly. I don't recall if Sam Waksal – we might have made reference to a newspaper article.

Q: What newspaper article?

A: There have been so many, I don't really remember. One of the earlier ones that began to appear.

Q: Do you remember what it was about the article that you guys were discussing?

A: Just the publicity.

Q: The publicity involving her?

A: No. There was no publicity, this was not about her, this is about Sam.

Specification Three
(Page 77, Line 16 - Page 82, Line 21)

Q: Did there come a time when she wanted to sell the ImClone stock?

A: Well, it was at my solicitation.

Q: Tell me about that.

A: When we were doing her portfolio review for tax planning purposes that took place in the week prior to Christmas, it came to me as a great surprise, having felt that I had liquidated all ImClone shares from her accounts at that time, that the stock was still there.

Q: Let me just – you had a tax planning discussion with her?

A: Which was also a portfolio review — a comprehensive portfolio review with her.

Q: And this happened the week before Christmas?

A: Correct.

Q: So, approximately?

A: I believe the exact date was December 20th, I believe.

Q: And where did this take place?

A: On the telephone. And we reviewed each and every position in the account. And we discussed the fundamentals of all the positions. We discussed gains and losses for all the positions. We discussed the overall status of the portfolio, and included in that discussion was ImClone. And so we reviewed ImClone and discussed what her intentions were for ImClone at that time versus my recommendations.

Q: What were her desires for the ImClone stock?

A: She felt — that the time, the stock had already come off its highs a little bit. And she wanted to hold the stock, and I challenged that by saying, "The stock has [sic] clearly declining, why would you hold it? Why are you holding this, considering we sold 50,000 or 40,000 shares two months ago?" . . . And she goes — and at that point, we determined that if, in fact, it fell much further, then we would sell it. . . .

Q: So, going back, she didn't really want to sell it, you recommended that she sell it. You can continue on from there.

A: So, we made a deal. I said, "Okay, if you would not like to sell the stock now, how long are you going to wait before you sell this stock?"

Q: I'm sorry, on December 20th, when you had this conversation, do you remember what the price of the stock was?

A: It was in the mid 60s. And, at that point, we determined that $60 a share would be a suitable price, should it ever fall that low. Of course, she never thought it would.

Specification Four
(Page 104, Line 15 - Page 105, Line 8)

Q: Did you ever tell Martha Stewart that the SEC had been speaking with Merrill Lynch about sales in ImClone at the end of the year?

A: I said that we had had – we had been reviewing this internally. And that was all.

Q: In other words, you didn't mention that the SEC was looking into this?

A: No.

Q: Tell me about the conversation you had with her when you said, "We've been reviewing this internally."

A: I said, you know, "In light of the news, the disclosures and news and following the stock price, Merrill Lynch has been reviewing, you know, all our transactions in ImClone."

Q: Did you tell her that anyone was asking questions about her transactions specifically?

A: I did not.

Q: Did she ask you that?

A: She did not.

(Page 124, Line 22 - Page 125, Line 13)

Q: At any time, did you and she discuss the investigation – any investigation by the Securities and Exchange Commission?

A: No.

Q: Did you and she discuss any investigation by any entity at all into trading in ImClone stock or --

A: I believe I said earlier that Merrill Lynch itself was investigating the situation with ImClone without making reference to any transaction or any person and obliquely just referring to the company.

Q: Other than the Merrill Lynch investigation, did you and she discuss any other investigation into ImClone? . . . Can you just say that out loud --

A: No.

Q: – for the record?

A: No, we did not.

Specification Five
(Page 106, Line 13 - Page 107, Line 6)

Q: Did you say anything that would give her cause for concern, the fact that she sold on December 27th?

A: No. Because she had no cause for concern. Because we had reviewed this position, I have notes of the conversation, it was completely typical, and she would have had no cause for concern. So, no.

Q: And you have notes of what conversation?

A: Well, I mean, I have a worksheet that I worked from that day, that we did on the 20th, where all of this stuff, which is a printout of a screen, with all sorts of markings on it. And so, I mean, all of this was discussed at the time, long prior. And so she had no reason for concern.

Q: And the information about her selling – her possibly selling ImClone at 60 would be reflected on that worksheet?

A: Yeah, I mean, reflected on the worksheet in a very loose way. I mean, things are highlighted, marked for sales. Some things are circled. I mean, it's scribbled on.

Specification Six
(Page 114, Line 10 - Page 115, Line 3)

Q: Who came up with the $60 price for ImClone? To sell?

A: We quibbled over it. And so we came to this price together.

Q: What was the price you recommended? Did you recommend a price --?

A: I recommended an immediate sale.

Q: So you wanted her to sell about --

A: Right away.

Q: And what price did she come to you and say, "I'll sell it at."

A: She didn't really have a price. I said, "Listen, what will you settle for? How low does this have to go before you're prepared to part with this?" She said, "I don't know." I said, "Well, how about $60 a share? Does that sound reasonable?" And the conversation was something like that. She said, "Yes, sure, $60."

(Title 18, United States Code, Section 1621).

COUNT SEVEN
(Obstruction of Justice by Peter Bacanovic)

The Grand Jury further charges:

52. The allegations of paragraphs 1 through 36, 41 and 51 are repeated and realleged as though fully set forth herein.

53. From in or about January 2002 through in or about April 2002, in the Southern District of New York and elsewhere, PETER BACANOVIC unlawfully, willfully and knowingly, corruptly influenced, obstructed and impeded, and endeavored to influence, obstruct and impede the due and proper administration of the law under which a pending proceeding was being had before a department and agency of the United States, namely, the SEC, by providing and causing to be provided false and misleading information and documents to the SEC relating to the sale of ImClone stock by MARTHA STEWART.

(Title 18, United States Code, Sections 1505 and 2).

COUNT EIGHT
(Obstruction of Justice by Martha Stewart)

The Grand Jury further charges:

54. The allegations of paragraphs 1 through 36, 41 and 51 are repeated and realleged as though fully set forth herein.

55. From in or about January 2002 through in or about April 2002, in the Southern District of New York and elsewhere, MARTHA STEWART unlawfully, willfully and knowingly, corruptly influenced, obstructed and impeded, and endeavored to influence, obstruct and impede the due and proper administration of the law under which a pending proceeding was being had before a department and agency of the United States, namely, the SEC, by providing and causing to be provided false and misleading information to the SEC relating to STEWART's sale of ImClone stock.

(Title 18, United States Code, Sections 1505 and 2).

COUNT NINE
(Securities Fraud by Martha Stewart)

The Grand Jury further charges:

56. The allegations of paragraphs 1 through 36 and 41 are repeated and realleged as though fully set forth herein.

57. At all times relevant to this Indictment, MARTHA STEWART's reputation, as well as the likelihood of any criminal or regulatory action against STEWART, were material to MSLO's shareholders because of the negative impact that any such action or damage to her reputation could have on the company which bears her name, as STEWART well knew. In MSLO's 1999 prospectus the company stated, "Our continued success and the value of our brand name therefore depends, to a large degree, on the reputation of Martha Stewart."

58. During the evening of June 6, 2002, the Associated Press reported that MARTHA STEWART sold ImClone shares prior to the news of the FDA's rejection of the Erbitux application, a fact which had not previously been publicly reported. On June 7, 2002, following the public announcement that STEWART had sold ImClone shares on the same day as members of the family of Samuel Waksal, MSLO's market price began steadily to fall, from a closing price of $19.01 on June 6, 2002 to a closing price of $11.47 on June 28, 2002.

59. As of June 6, 2002, MARTHA STEWART held 30,713,475 shares of MSLO Class A common stock, which constituted 62.6% of the outstanding Class A common stock of MSLO. STEWART also held 100% of the outstanding 30,619,375 shares of MSLO Class B common stock. Each share of the Class B common stock was convertible on a one-for-one basis into Class A common stock at STEWART's option. Combined, these shares gave STEWART control over 94.4% of shareholders' voting power.

60. As set forth more fully below, in an effort to stop or at least slow the steady erosion of MSLO's stock price caused by investor concerns, STEWART made or caused to be made a series of false and misleading public statements during June 2002 regarding her sale of ImClone stock on December 27, 2001 that concealed and omitted that STEWART had been provided information regarding the sale and attempted sale of the Waksal Shares and that STEWART had sold her ImClone stock while in possession of that information. STEWART made these false and misleading statements with the intent to defraud and deceive purchasers and sellers of MSLO common stock and to maintain the value of her own MSLO stock by preventing a decline in the market price of MSLO's stock. These false and misleading statements were contained in: (a) statements made on behalf of STEWART by STEWART's attorney tothe Wall Street Journal, published on June 7, 2002; (b) written public statements issued by STEWART on June 12

and 18, 2002; and (c) statements made by STEWART at a conference for securitiesanalysts and investors on June 19, 2002.

The June 7 Statement

61. On or about June 6, 2002, MARTHA STEWART was advised that the Wall Street Journal intended to publish an article stating that STEWART sold ImClone shares on December 27, 2001, a fact that had not yet been publicly reported. With the intent and knowledge that false and misleading information would be publicly disseminated, STEWART caused her attorney in New York, New York to provide to the Wall Street Journal the following false and misleading information regarding the reason for STEWART's December 27, 2001 sale of ImClone stock (the "June 7 Statement") that concealed that STEWART had been provided information regarding the sale and attempted sale of the Waksal Shares and that STEWART had sold her ImClone stock while in possession of that information:

> The sale was executed because Ms. Stewart had a predetermined price at which she planned to sell the stock. That determination, made more than a month before that trade, was to sell if the stock ever went less than $60.

This false and misleading information was published in an article in the Wall Street Journal on June 7, 2002.

The June 12 Statement

62. On June 12, 2002, the news media widely reported that Samuel Waksal had been arrested and charged in a criminal complaint with insider trading. Following this announcement, the stock price of MSLO fell approximately 5.6%, from an opening price of $15.90 to a closing price of $15.

63. On June 12, 2002, after the close of trading on the NYSE, MARTHA STEWART in New York, New York, prepared and caused to be issued a public statement (the "June 12 Statement"), in which STEWART made the following false and misleading statements that concealed that STEWART had been provided information regarding the sale and attempted sale of the Waksal Shares and that STEWART had sold her ImClone stock while in possession of that information, among others:

a. STEWART falsely stated that she had agreed with her broker "several weeks" after a tender offer made by Bristol-Myers Squibb to ImClone shareholders in October 2001, at a time when the ImClone shares were trading at about $70, that "if the ImClone stock price were to fall below $60, we would sell my holdings";

b. STEWART falsely stated that on December 27, 2001, "I returned a call from my broker advising me that ImClone had fallen below $60 . . . and reiterated my instructions to sell the shares"; and

c. STEWART falsely stated that she "did not have any nonpublic information regarding ImClone when [she] sold [her] ImClone shares."

The June 18 Statement

64. As of June 18, 2002, MARTHA STEWART was scheduled to speak at a conference for securities analysts and investors (the "Conference"), at which she expected that questions could be asked about her sale of ImClone shares. In preparation for that Conference, STEWART prepared and approved another public statement about her ImClone sale. On June 18, 2002, after the close of trading on the NYSE, MARTHA STEWART in New York, New York, prepared and caused to be issued a public statement (the "June 18 Statement"), in which she made the following false and misleading statements that concealed that STEWART had been provided information regarding the sale and attempted sale of the Waksal Shares and that STEWART had sold her ImClone stock while in possession of that information, among others:

a. STEWART falsely stated that "[i]n my June 12, 2002 statement I explained what did happen";

b. STEWART falsely stated that her December 27, 2001 sale of ImClone stock "was based on information that was available to the public that day";

c. STEWART falsely stated that "[s]ince the stock had fallen below $60, I sold my shares, as I had previously agreed to do with my broker"; and

d. STEWART falsely stated that she had cooperated with the SEC and U.S. Attorney's Office "fully and to the best of my ability."

65. On the morning of June 19, 2002, MARTHA STEWART read the June 18 Statement at the Conference in New York, New York.

Statutory Allegations

66. In or about June 2002, in the Southern District of New York and elsewhere, MARTHA STEWART unlawfully, willfully and knowingly, directly and indirectly, by use of the means and instrumentalities of interstate commerce, the mails and the facilities of national securities exchanges, did use and employ manipulative and deceptive devices and contrivances, in violation of Title 17, Code of Federal Regulations, Section 240.10b-5, by (a) employing devices, schemes and artifices to defraud; (b) making untrue statements of material facts and omitting to state material facts necessary in order to make the statements made, in the light of the circumstances under which they were made, not misleading; and (c) engaging in acts, practices and

courses of business which operated and would operate as a fraud and deceit upon purchasers and sellers of MSLO common stock.

(Title 15, United States Code, Sections 78j(b) and 78ff; Title 17, Code of Federal Regulations, Section 240.10b-5; and Title 18, United States Code, Section 2.)

‾‾‾‾‾‾‾‾‾‾‾‾‾‾
FOREPERSON

‾‾‾‾‾‾‾‾‾‾‾‾‾‾‾‾‾‾‾‾‾‾
DAVID N. KELLEY
United States Attorney

IN THE UNITED STATES DISTRICT COURT
FOR THE SOUTHERN DISTRICT OF TEXAS
HOUSTON DIVISION

UNITED STATES OF AMERICA,	)
	)
Plaintiff,	)
	)
v.	) No. CR-H-
	04-25(S-2)
	)
RICHARD A. CAUSEY,	)
	)
Defendant.	)
_____	)

PLEA AGREEMENT

Pursuant to Rule 11(c)(1)(C) of the Federal Rules of Criminal Procedure, the United States Department of Justice by the Enron Task Force ("the Department") and Richard A. Causey ("Defendant") agree to the following:

1. Defendant will plead guilty to Count 19 of the Superseding Indictment, charging him with securities fraud, in violation of Title 17, Code of Federal Regulations, Section 240.10b-5, Title 15 United States Code, 78j(b) and 78ff. Defendant agrees that he is pleading guilty because he is guilty, and that the facts contained in Exhibit A (attached and incorporated herein) are true and supply a factual basis for his plea. At the time the offenses were committed by the Defendant, the offense of securities fraud carried the following statutory penalty:

Count 19 - Securities Fraud

   a.   Maximum term of imprisonment: 10 years
         (17 C.F.R. § 240.10b-5, Title 15 U.S.C. 78j(b) and 78ff)

   b.   Minimum term of imprisonment: 0 years
         (17 C.F.R. § 240.10b-5, Title 15 U.S.C. 78j(b) and 78ff)

   c.   Maximum supervised release term: 3 years, to follow any term of imprisonment; if a condition of release is violated, Defendant may be sentenced to up to two years without credit for pre-release imprisonment or time previously served on post-release supervision (18 U.S.C. §§ 3583 (b) & (e))

   d.   Maximum fine: $1,000,000 or twice the gain/loss (18 U.S.C. § 3571(b)(3))

e.   Restitution: As determined by the Court pursuant to statute. (18 U.S.C. §§ 3663 and 3663A)

f.   Special Assessment: $100 (18 U.S.C. § 3013)

Sentencing Guidelines

2.   The defendant understands that, in imposing the sentence, the Court will be guided by the United States Sentencing Guidelines (the "Guidelines"). The defendant understands that the Guidelines are advisory, not mandatory, but that the Court must consider the Guidelines in determining a reasonable sentence. The Department and the Defendant agree that the applicable Sentencing Guideline range exceeds 84 months.

3.   Pursuant to Rule 11(c)(1)(C) of the Federal Rules of Criminal Procedure, the Defendant and the Department agree to ask the Court to impose an agreed-upon sentence of 84 months incarceration and to order forfeiture in the amount of $1,250,000.00. The Defendant and the Department agree that if the Court refuses to accept the plea agreement with this agreed-upon sentence, the agreement will be null and void. The Defendant agrees that he will not seek a sentence below 84 months incarceration, and Defendant understands that except under the circumstances described in paragraph 4 below, the Court will be required to impose a sentence of 84 months and to order the agreed-upon forfeiture amount, or the plea agreement will be null and void.

4. If the Defendant provides truthful, complete, and accurate information to the Department, then the Department in its sole and exclusive discretion may move the Court, pursuant to Sentencing Guideline Section 5K1.1 and 18 U.S.C. § 3553(e), to depart downward from the 84-month agreed-upon sentence set forth in paragraph 3. Defendant understands and agrees that under the terms of this Agreement and Rule 11(c)(1)(C) and regardless of any such motion that the Department may make, Defendant cannot and will not be sentenced to a period of incarceration of less than 60 months. Defendant further agrees that he will not move for a downward departure on any grounds and that no such grounds are applicable.

5.   The parties further agree that the Defendant's forfeiture of $1,250,000.00 in criminal proceeds and his agreement to relinquish any claim he may have to deferred compensation, as described in paragraphs 11 and 12 below, fully satisfies the forfeiture, fine, and restitution provisions of the sentencing laws and Guidelines.

Waiver of Rights

6. If the Court accepts the plea agreement pursuant to Rule 11(c)(1)(C) and sentences Defendant to the agreed-upon sentence as set forth in paragraphs 3, 4, and 5, Defendant will not file an appeal or collaterally

attack his conviction, guilty plea, or sentence.

7. Defendant waives all defenses based on venue (but reserves the right to request a change of venue if his plea is vacated or plea withdrawn), speedy trial under the Constitution and Speedy Trial Act, and the statute of limitations with respect to any prosecution that is not time-barred on the date that this Agreement is signed, in the event that (a) Defendant's conviction is later vacated for any reason, (b) Defendant violates any provision of this Agreement, or (c)) Defendant's plea is later withdrawn.

8. Defendant understands that by pleading guilty he is waiving important rights including: (a) the right to persist in his previously entered plea of not guilty; (b) the right to a jury trial with respect to guilt or sentencing; (c) the right to be represented by counsel – and if necessary to have the court appoint counsel to represent him – at trial and at every other stage of the proceedings; (d) the right at trial to confront and cross-examine adverse witnesses, to be protected from compelled self-incrimination, to testify and present evidence, and to compel the attendance of witnesses; and (e) the right to additional discovery and disclosures from the Department. Defendant waives any right to additional disclosure from the Department in connection with his guilty plea.

Defendant's Obligations

9. Defendant agrees not to accept remuneration or compensation of any sort, directly or indirectly, for the dissemination through books, articles, speeches, interviews, or any other means, of information regarding his work at Enron or the investigation or prosecution of any civil or criminal cases against him.

Forfeiture and Monetary Penalties

10. Defendant agrees to pay the special assessment of $100.00 by check payable to the Clerk of the Court at or before sentencing. 18 U.S.C. § 3013(a)(2)(A); U.S.S.G. § 5E1.3.

11. Defendant agrees to forfeit to the government $1,250,000.00, to be satisfied from funds located within Wachovia Securities Account 2005-0471, which contains sufficient funds for this purpose and which constitutes proceeds of the offense to which Defendant will plead guilty pursuant to this Agreement. Defendant warrants that he and his wife, Elizabeth A. Causey, are the sole owners of all property listed above, and they agree to hold the United States, its agents and employees harmless from any claims whatsoever in connection with the seizure or forfeiture of property covered by this agreement. Defendant further agrees to waive all interest in the amount listed above for forfeiture in any administrative or judicial forfeiture proceeding, whether criminal or civil, state or federal. Defendant's wife, Elizabeth A. Causey, also agrees to waive her right, title, and interest in the Wachovia Securities Account 2005-0471 up to and including the forfeiture

amount, and her execution of the attached Stipulation and Waiver is a condition precedent of this Agreement. Defendant agrees to consent to the entry of orders of forfeiture for such property and waives the requirements of Federal Rules of Criminal Procedure 32.2 and 43(a) regarding notice of forfeiture in the charging instrument, announcement of the forfeiture at sentencing, and incorporation of the forfeiture in the judgment. Defendant acknowledges that he understands that the forfeiture of assets is part of the sentence that may be imposed in this case and waives any failure by the court to advise him of this, pursuant to Rule 11(b)(1)(J), at the time his guilty plea is accepted. Defendant further agrees to waive all constitutional and statutory challenges in any manner (including direct appeal, habeas corpus, or any other means) to any forfeiture carried out in accordance with this agreement on any grounds, including that the forfeiture constitutes an excessive fine or punishment. Defendant agrees to take all steps as requested by the United States to pass clear title to the forfeitable assets to the United States, and to testify truthfully in any related judicial proceeding. Defendant agrees not to seek a refund from the United States Treasury of the amount that he paid in taxes in connection with the receipt of $1,250,000.00 in proceeds from the offense to which he will plead guilty, and waives his right, title, and interest to the taxes paid on that amount.

12. Defendant further agrees to relinquish any claim he may have to deferred compensation, severance, or any other form of payment related to his employment by Enron or any related entity.

The Department's Obligations

13. The Department agrees that, except as provided for in this Agreement, no further criminal charges will be brought against Defendant for any act or offense in which he engaged in his capacity as an officer and/or employee of Enron Corporation, or arising out of such employment, and the Department will move after sentencing to dismiss the remaining counts of the Superseding Indictment against him with prejudice.

14. The Department further agrees that no statements made by Defendant during any debriefing meetings with the Department will be used against him in any criminal proceedings instituted by the Department, except as provided in paragraphs 1, 3, 4, and 5.

Hyde Amendment Waiver

15. Defendant agrees that with respect to all charges contained in the Superseding Indictment in the above-captioned action, he is not a "prevailing party" within the meaning of the "Hyde Amendment," Section 617, PL 105-119 (Nov. 26, 1997), and will not file any claim under that law.

<u>Scope</u>

16. This Agreement does not bind any federal, state, or local prosecuting authority other than the Department, and does not prohibit the Department or any other department, agency, or commission of the United States from initiating or prosecuting any civil, administrative, or tax proceedings directly or indirectly involving Defendant.

<u>Complete Agreement</u>

17. No promises, agreements or conditions have been entered into by the parties other than those set forth in this Agreement and none will be entered into unless memorialized in writing and signed by all parties. This Agreement supersedes any prior promises, agreements, or conditions between the parties, including any written proffer agreements. To become effective, this Agreement must be signed by all signatories listed below and in the addenda.

Dated: Houston, Texas
　　　　December ___, 2005

　　　　　　　　　　　　　　　　SEAN BERKOWITZ
　　　　　　　　　　　　　　　　Director, Enron Task Force

　　　　　　　　　　By:　　_____
　　　　　　　　　　　　　　Kathryn Ruemmler
　　　　　　　　　　　　　　Deputy Director, Enron Task
Force

UNITED STATES DISTRICT COURT
SOUTHERN DISTRICT OF TEXAS
HOUSTON DIVISION

UNITED STATES OF AMERICA	§	
	§	
v.	§	Cr. No. H-04-25 (S-2)
	§	(Lake, J.)
RICHARD A. CAUSEY,	§	
	§	
Defendant.	§	
_____	§	

Exhibit A to Plea Agreement

The following factual statement made by defendant Richard A. Causey is submitted to provide a factual basis for my plea of guilty to Count Nineteen (securities fraud) of the above captioned Superseding Indictment, charging me with securities fraud, in violation of Title 15, United States Code, Sections 78j(b) and 78ff.

1. I was the Chief Accounting Officer ("CAO") of Enron Corporation ("Enron") from 1998 through Enron's bankruptcy in December 2001. While CAO, I and other members of Enron's senior management fraudulently misled investors and others about the true financial position of Enron in order to inflate artificially the price of Enron's stock.

2. More specifically, I conspired with members of Enron's senior management to make false and misleading statements, in Enron's filings with the Securities and Exchange Commission ("SEC") and in analyst calls, about the financial condition of Enron, which did not fairly and accurately reflect Enron's actual financial condition and performance as I knew it.

3. Certain of the conduct, for which I accept responsibility, is detailed below.

False and Misleading Statements in SEC Filings

4. Along with others in senior management, I was responsible for the preparation and drafting of the financial statements that were included in Enron's annual reports filed with the SEC on Form 10-K and its quarterly reports on Form 10-Q. I, along with others in senior management, were responsible for ensuring that the financial statements contained in Enron's public filings fairly presented Enron's true financial condition. The financial statements were required to include a section entitled Management, Discussion and Analysis ("MD&A"), which required, among other things, that management disclose information necessary to an understanding of Enron's financial condition and results of operations. I reviewed drafts of Enron's quarterly and annual reports, and I signed these reports attesting to their

accuracy. As set forth below, I participated along with others in Enron's senior management in efforts to use Enron's public filings and public statements to mislead the investing public about the true nature of Enron's financial performance by making false and misleading statements, and omitting facts necessary to make certain statements not misleading.

5. For example, in the first quarter of 2000, Enron recorded $85 million in earnings from a partnership interest it held in a vehicle named JEDI, which held Enron stock. I and others reported these earnings as recurring earnings from operations when, as I and others knew, the earnings in fact came from a dramatic increase in Enron's stock price resulting from positive investor reaction to Enron's January 20, 2000 analyst conference. I and others understood that it would have been material information to investors and analysts that a significant portion of Enron's reported earnings from its Assets and Investments business came solely from an increase in its own stock price. I and others misled investors by describing the earnings as coming from the strong performance of Enron's portfolio of energy related and other investments. I and others intentionally failed to disclose the true nature of the earnings and the fact that Enron management was taking large positions in Enron stock.

6. Another example concerns disclosures in 2001 relating to Enron's retail business, Enron Energy Services ("EES"). During the first quarter of 2001, I became aware that EES had incurred hundreds of millions of dollars in losses resulting from California regulatory actions and the identification of significant valuation errors in EES contracts. These losses were in excess of EES's targeted earnings for the entire year of 2001. I understood that EES had been promoted by Enron management as a growth segment of the company that was a major contributor to Enron's stock price. I and others in senior management believed that had these losses been disclosed to Enron's shareholders and the analyst community, the reaction would have been severely negative and the stock price would have declined.

7. I and others in senior management made a decision to move the risk management function of EES into another business unit, Enron Wholesale Services ("EWS"). This reorganization allowed us to avoid reporting the losses in EES's results so that I and others in senior management could continue to tout EES as a growing and successful business. I and others in management intentionally failed to disclose to the investing public any reference to EES's losses, which we knew was material information.

8. On April 17, 2001, Enron issued its earnings release for its first quarter 2001 results, a copy of which I reviewed. I and others reported to Enron's shareholders and the investing public that EES had earned $40 million in recurring IBIT for the first quarter of 2001. We did not disclose that EES had in fact incurred hundreds of millions of dollars in losses during the first quarter of 2001 that through an accounting change we had concealed in EWS. By failing to disclose the true performance of EES, I and others

intentionally misled Enron's shareholders and the investing public.

10-Q for the First Quarter 2001

9. On or about May 15, 2001, Enron filed its Form 10-Q, which I reviewed and signed. While the 10-Q disclosed the transfer of risk management functions, the 10-Q did not disclose the losses that EES would otherwise have incurred, which was required in order to fairly present to Enron's shareholders and the investing public Enron's true financial condition. This information was material and would have been important to a reasonable investor. I and others in senior management failed to include this information in Enron's 10-Q because we were concerned that disclosing such information would have a negative effect on Enron's stock price.

10. On or about May 15, 2001, within the Southern District of Texas, Enron filed via electronic transmission its Form 10-Q for the first quarter 2001, with the Securities and Exchange Commission. As set forth above, in connection with Enron's Form 10-Q for the first quarter 2001, a copy of which I signed, I and others in Enron senior management did willfully and unlawfully use and employ manipulative and deceptive devices and contrivances and directly and indirectly (I) employ devices, schemes and artifices to defraud; (ii) make untrue statements of material facts and omit to state facts necessary in order to make the statements made, in light of the circumstances under which they were made, not misleading; and (iii) engage in acts, practices, and courses of conduct which would and did operate as a fraud and deceit upon members of the investing public, in connection with purchases and sales of Enron securities.

11. I understood that my conduct and the conduct of those with whom I conspired would have a material effect on Enron's financial statements which Enron shareholders and potential shareholders relied upon in making investment decisions. Enron's stock was traded on the New York Stock Exchange. I also understood that interstate wire transmissions, including fax transmissions, email and telephone calls, would be used and were used in furtherance of the scheme. Specifically, I knew that Enron's annual and quarterly reports were filed with the SEC via interstate wire transmissions.

12. The preceding is a summary of facts that make me guilty, which I make for the purpose of providing the Court with a factual basis for my guilty plea to Count 19 of the Superseding Indictment. It does not include all of the facts known to me concerning criminal activity in which I and other members of Enron senior management engaged. I make this statement knowingly and voluntarily because I am in fact guilty of the crime charged.

Richard A. Causey   December _____,
                                           2005

Defendant

CHAPTER ONE - INTRODUCTION
AND GENERAL APPLICATION PRINCIPLES

PART A - INTRODUCTION

1. Authority

The United States Sentencing Commission ("Commission") is an independent agency in the judicial branch composed of seven voting and two non-voting, ex officio members. Its principal purpose is to establish sentencing policies and practices for the federal criminal justice system that will assure the ends of justice by promulgating detailed guidelines prescribing the appropriate sentences for offenders convicted of federal crimes.

The guidelines and policy statements promulgated by the Commission are issued pursuant to Section 994(a) of Title 28, United States Code.

2. The Statutory Mission

The Sentencing Reform Act of 1984 (Title II of the Comprehensive Crime Control Act of 1984) provides for the development of guidelines that will further the basic purposes of criminal punishment: deterrence, incapacitation, just punishment, and rehabilitation. The Act delegates broad authority to the Commission to review and rationalize the federal sentencing process.

The Act contains detailed instructions as to how this determination should be made, the most important of which directs the Commission to create categories of offense behavior and offender characteristics. An offense behavior category might consist, for example, of "bank robbery/committed with a gun/$2500 taken." An offender characteristic category might be "offender with one prior conviction not resulting in imprisonment." The Commission is required to prescribe guideline ranges that specify an appropriate sentence for each class of convicted persons determined by coordinating the offense behavior categories with the offender characteristic categories. Where the guidelines call for imprisonment, the range must be narrow: the maximum of the range cannot exceed the minimum by more than the greater of 25 percent or six months. 28 U.S.C. § 994(b)(2).

Pursuant to the Act, the sentencing court must select a sentence from within the guideline range. If, however, a particular case presents atypical features, the Act allows the court to depart from the guidelines and sentence outside the prescribed range. In that case, the court must specify reasons for departure. 18 U.S.C. § 3553(b). If the court sentences within the guideline range, an appellate court may review the sentence to determine whether the guidelines were correctly applied. If the court departs from the guideline range, an appellate court may review the reasonableness of the departure.

18 U.S.C. § 3742. The Act also abolishes parole, and substantially reduces and restructures good behavior adjustments.

The Commission's initial guidelines were submitted to Congress on April 13, 1987. After the prescribed period of Congressional review, the guidelines took effect on November 1, 1987, and apply to all offenses committed on or after that date. The Commission has the authority to submit

guideline amendments each year to Congress between the beginning of a regular Congressional session and May 1. Such amendments automatically take effect 180 days after submission unless a law is enacted to the contrary. 28 U.S.C. § 994(p).

The initial sentencing guidelines and policy statements were developed after extensive hearings, deliberation, and consideration of substantial public comment. The Commission emphasizes, however, that it views the guideline-writing process as evolutionary. It expects, and the governing statute anticipates, that continuing research, experience, and analysis will result in modifications and revisions to the guidelines through submission of amendments to Congress. To this end, the Commission is established as a permanent agency to monitor sentencing practices in the federal courts.

3.   The Basic Approach (Policy Statement)

To understand the guidelines and their underlying rationale, it is important to focus on the three objectives that Congress sought to achieve in enacting the Sentencing Reform Act of 1984. The Act's basic objective was to enhance the ability of the criminal justice system to combat crime through an effective, fair sentencing system. To achieve this end, Congress first sought honesty in sentencing. It sought to avoid the confusion and implicit deception that arose out of the pre-guidelines sentencing system which required the court to impose an indeterminate sentence of imprisonment and empowered the parole commission to determine how much of the sentence an offender actually would serve in prison. This practice usually resulted in a substantial reduction in the effective length of the sentence imposed, with defendants often serving only about one-third of the sentence imposed by the court.

Second, Congress sought reasonable uniformity in sentencing by narrowing the wide disparity in sentences imposed for similar criminal offenses committed by similar offenders.   Third, Congress sought proportionality in sentencing through a system that imposes appropriately different sentences for criminal conduct of differing severity.

Honesty is easy to achieve: the abolition of parole makes the sentence imposed by the court the sentence the offender will serve, less approximately fifteen percent for good behavior. There is a tension, however, between the mandate of uniformity and the mandate of proportionality. Simple uniformity -- sentencing every offender to five years -- destroys proportionality. Having only a few simple categories of crimes would make the guidelines uniform and easy to administer, but might lump together offenses that are different in important respects. For example, a single category for robbery that included armed and unarmed robberies, robberies with and without injuries, robberies of a few dollars and robberies of millions, would be far too broad.

A sentencing system tailored to fit every conceivable wrinkle of each case would quickly become unworkable and seriously compromise the certainty of punishment and its deterrent effect. For example: a bank robber with (or without) a gun, which the robber kept hidden (or brandished), might have frightened (or merely warned), injured seriously (or less seriously), tied up (or simply pushed) a guard, teller, or customer, at night (or at noon), in an effort to obtain money for other crimes (or for other purposes), in the company of a few (or many) other robbers, for the first (or fourth) time.

The list of potentially relevant features of criminal behavior is long; the fact that they can occur in multiple combinations means that the list of possible permutations of factors is virtually endless. The appropriate relationships among these different factors are exceedingly difficult to establish, for they are often context specific. Sentencing courts do not treat the occurrence of a simple bruise identically in all cases, irrespective of whether that bruise occurred in the context of a bank robbery or in the context of a breach of peace. This is so, in part, because the risk that such a harm will occur differs depending on the underlying offense with which it is connected; and also because, in part, the relationship between punishment and multiple harms is not simply additive. The relation varies depending on how much other harm has occurred. Thus, it would not be proper to assign points for each kind of harm and simply add them up, irrespective of context and total amounts.

The larger the number of subcategories of offense and offender characteristics included in the guidelines, the greater the complexity and the less workable the system. Moreover, complex combinations of offense and offender characteristics would apply and interact in unforeseen ways to unforeseen situations, thus failing to cure the unfairness of a simple, broad category system. Finally, and perhaps most importantly, probation officers and courts, in applying a complex system having numerous subcategories, would be required to make a host of decisions regarding whether the underlying facts were sufficient to bring the case within a particular subcategory. The greater the number of decisions required and the greater their complexity, the greater the risk that different courts would apply the guidelines differently to situations that, in fact, are similar, thereby reintroducing the very disparity that the guidelines were designed to reduce.

In view of the arguments, it would have been tempting to retreat to the simple, broad category approach and to grant courts the discretion to select the proper point along a broad sentencing range. Granting such broad discretion, however, would have risked correspondingly broad disparity in sentencing, for different courts may exercise their discretionary powers in different ways. Such an approach would have risked a return to the wide disparity that Congress established the Commission to reduce and would have been contrary to the Commission's mandate set forth in the Sentencing Reform Act of 1984.

In the end, there was no completely satisfying solution to this problem. The Commission had to balance the comparative virtues and vices of broad, simple categorization and detailed, complex subcategorization, and within the constraints established by that balance, minimize the discretionary powers of the sentencing court. Any system will, to a degree, enjoy the benefits and suffer from the drawbacks of each approach.

A philosophical problem arose when the Commission attempted to reconcile the differing perceptions of the purposes of criminal punishment. Most observers of the criminal law agree that the ultimate aim of the law itself, and of punishment in particular, is the control of crime. Beyond this point, however, the consensus seems to break down. Some argue that appropriate punishment should be defined primarily on the basis of the principle of "just deserts." Under this principle, punishment should be scaled to the offender's culpability and the resulting harms. Others argue that punishment should be imposed primarily on the basis of practical "crime control" considerations. This theory calls for sentences that most effectively lessen the likelihood of future crime, either by deterring others or incapacitating the defendant.

Adherents of each of these points of view urged the Commission to choose between them and accord one primacy over the other. As a practical matter, however, this choice was unnecessary because in most sentencing decisions the application of either philosophy will produce the same or similar results.

In its initial set of guidelines, the Commission sought to solve both the practical and philosophical problems of developing a coherent sentencing system by taking an empirical approach that used as a starting point data estimating pre-guidelines sentencing practice. It analyzed data drawn from 10,000 presentence investigations, the differing elements of various crimes as distinguished in substantive criminal statutes, the United States Parole Commission's guidelines and statistics, and data from other relevant sources in order to determine which distinctions were important in pre-guidelines practice. After consideration, the Commission accepted, modified, or rationalized these distinctions.

This empirical approach helped the Commission resolve its practical problem by defining a list of relevant distinctions that, although of considerable length, was short enough to create a manageable set of guidelines. Existing categories are relatively broad and omit distinctions that some may believe important, yet they include most of the major distinctions that statutes and data suggest made a significant difference in sentencing decisions. Relevant distinctions not reflected in the guidelines probably will occur rarely and sentencing courts may take such unusual cases into account by departing from the guidelines.

The Commission's empirical approach also helped resolve its philosophical dilemma. Those who adhere to a just deserts philosophy may concede that the lack of consensus might make it difficult to say exactly what punishment is deserved for a particular crime. Likewise, those who subscribe to a philosophy of crime control may acknowledge that the lack of sufficient data might make it difficult to determine exactly the punishment that will best prevent that crime. Both groups might therefore recognize the wisdom of looking to those distinctions that judges and legislators have, in fact, made over the course of time. These established distinctions are ones that the community believes, or has found over time, to be important from either a just deserts or crime control perspective.

The Commission did not simply copy estimates of pre-guidelines practice as revealed by the data, even though establishing offense values on this basis would help eliminate disparity because the data represent averages. Rather, it departed from the data at different points for various important reasons. Congressional statutes, for example, suggested or required departure, as in the case of the Anti-Drug Abuse Act of 1986 that imposed increased and mandatory minimum sentences. In addition, the data revealed inconsistencies in treatment, such as punishing economic crime less severely than other apparently equivalent behavior.

Despite these policy-oriented departures from pre-guidelines practice, the guidelines represent an approach that begins with, and builds upon, empirical data. The guidelines will not please those who wish the Commission to adopt a single philosophical theory and then work deductively to establish a simple and perfect set of categorizations and distinctions. The guidelines may prove acceptable, however, to those who seek more modest, incremental improvements in the status quo, who believe the best is often the enemy of the good, and who recognize that these guidelines are, as the Act contemplates, but the first step in an evolutionary process. After spending considerable time and resources exploring alternative approaches, the Commission developed these guidelines as a practical effort toward the achievement of a more honest, uniform, equitable, proportional, and therefore effective sentencing system.

4.   The Guidelines' Resolution of Major Issues (Policy Statement)

The guideline-drafting process required the Commission to resolve a host of important policy questions typically involving rather evenly balanced sets of competing considerations. As an aid to understanding the guidelines, this introduction briefly discusses several of those issues; commentary in the guidelines explains others.

(a) Real Offense vs. Charge Offense Sentencing.

One of the most important questions for the Commission to decide was whether to base sentences upon the actual conduct in which the defendant engaged regardless of the charges for which he was indicted or convicted ("real offense" sentencing), or upon the conduct that constitutes the elements of the offense for which the defendant was charged and of which he was convicted ("charge offense" sentencing). A bank robber, for example, might have used a gun, frightened bystanders, taken $50,000, injured a teller, refused to stop when ordered, and raced away damaging property during his escape. A pure real offense system would sentence on the basis of all identifiable conduct. A pure charge offense system would overlook some of the harms that did not constitute statutory elements of the offenses of which the defendant was convicted.

The Commission initially sought to develop a pure real offense system. After all, the pre-guidelines sentencing system was, in a sense, this type of system. The sentencing court and the parole commission took account of the conduct in which the defendant actually engaged, as determined in a presentence report, at the sentencing hearing, or before a parole commission hearing officer. The Commission's initial efforts in this direction, carried out in the spring and early summer of 1986, proved unproductive, mostly for practical reasons. To make such a system work, even to formalize and rationalize the status quo, would have required the Commission to decide precisely which harms to take into account, how to add them up, and what kinds of procedures the courts should use to determine the presence or absence of disputed factual elements. The Commission found no practical way to combine and account for the large number of diverse harms arising in different circumstances; nor did it find a practical way to reconcile the need for a fair adjudicatory procedure with the need for a speedy sentencing process given the potential existence of hosts of adjudicated "real harm" facts in many typical cases. The effort proposed as a solution to these problems required the use of, for example, quadratic roots and other mathematical operations that the Commission considered too complex to be workable. In the Commission's view, such a system risked return to wide disparity in sentencing practice.

In its initial set of guidelines submitted to Congress in April 1987, the Commission moved closer to a charge offense system. This system, however, does contain a significant number of real offense elements. For one thing, the hundreds of overlapping and duplicative statutory provisions that make up the federal criminal law forced the Commission to write guidelines that are descriptive of generic conduct rather than guidelines that track purely statutory language. For another, the guidelines take account of a number of important, commonly occurring real offense elements such as role in the offense, the presence of a gun, or the amount of money actually taken, through alternative base offense levels, specific offense characteristics, cross references, and adjustments.

The Commission recognized that a charge offense system has drawbacks of its own. One of the most important is the potential it affords prosecutors to influence sentences by increasing or decreasing the number of counts in an indictment.   Of course, the defendant's actual conduct (that which the prosecutor can prove in court) imposes a natural limit upon the prosecutor's ability to increase a defendant's sentence.   Moreover, the Commission has written its rules for the treatment of multicount convictions with an eye toward eliminating unfair treatment that might flow from count manipulation.   For example, the guidelines treat a three-count indictment, each count of which charges sale of 100 grams of heroin or theft of $10,000, the same as a single-count indictment charging sale of 300 grams of heroin or theft of $30,000.   Furthermore, a sentencing court may control any inappropriate manipulation of the indictment through use of its departure power.   Finally, the Commission will closely monitor charging and plea agreement practices and will make appropriate adjustments should they become necessary.

(b) Departures.

The sentencing statute permits a court to depart from a guideline-specified sentence only when it finds "an aggravating or mitigating circumstance of a kind, or to a degree, not adequately taken into consideration by the Sentencing Commission in formulating the guidelines that should result in a sentence different from that described." 18 U.S.C. § 3553(b).   The Commission intends the sentencing courts to treat each guideline as carving out a "heartland," a set of typical cases embodying the conduct that each guideline describes.   When a court finds an atypical case, one to which a particular guideline linguistically applies but where conduct significantly differs from the norm, the court may consider whether a departure is warranted.   Section 5H1.10 (Race, Sex, National Origin, Creed, Religion, and Socio-Economic Status), §5H1.12 (Lack of Guidance as a Youth and Similar Circumstances), the third sentence of §5H1.4 (Physical Condition, Including Drug or Alcohol Dependence or Abuse), the last sentence of §5K2.12 (Coercion and Duress), and §5K2.19 (Post-Sentencing Rehabilitative Efforts) list several factors that the court cannot take into account as grounds for departure.   With those specific exceptions, however, the Commission does not intend to limit the kinds of factors, whether or not mentioned anywhere else in the guidelines, that could constitute grounds for departure in an unusual case.

The Commission has adopted this departure policy for two reasons. First, it is difficult to prescribe a single set of guidelines that encompasses the vast range of human conduct potentially relevant to a sentencing decision. The Commission also recognizes that the initial set of guidelines need not do so.   The Commission is a permanent body, empowered by law to write and rewrite guidelines, with progressive changes, over many years.   By monitoring when courts depart from the guidelines and by analyzing their stated reasons for doing so and court decisions with references thereto, the Commission, over time, will be able to refine the guidelines to specify more precisely when departures should and should not be permitted.

Second, the Commission believes that despite the courts' legal freedom to depart from the guidelines, they will not do so very often. This is because the guidelines, offense by offense, seek to take account of those factors that the Commission's data indicate made a significant difference in pre-guidelines sentencing practice. Thus, for example, where the presence of physical injury made an important difference in pre-guidelines sentencing practice (as in the case of robbery or assault), the guidelines specifically include this factor to enhance the sentence. Where the guidelines do not specify an augmentation or diminution, this is generally because the sentencing data did not permit the Commission to conclude that the factor was empirically important in relation to the particular offense. Of course, an important factor (e.g., physical injury) may infrequently occur in connection with a particular crime (e.g., fraud). Such rare occurrences are precisely the type of events that the courts' departure powers were designed to cover -- unusual cases outside the range of the more typical offenses for which the guidelines were designed.

It is important to note that the guidelines refer to two different kinds of departure. The first involves instances in which the guidelines provide specific guidance for departure by analogy or by other numerical or non-numerical suggestions. The Commission intends such suggestions as policy guidance for the courts. The Commission expects that most departures will reflect the suggestions and that the courts of appeals may prove more likely to find departures "unreasonable" where they fall outside suggested levels.

A second type of departure will remain unguided. It may rest upon grounds referred to in Chapter Five, Part K (Departures) or on grounds not mentioned in the guidelines. While Chapter Five, Part K lists factors that the Commission believes may constitute grounds for departure, the list is not exhaustive. The Commission recognizes that there may be other grounds for departure that are not mentioned; it also believes there may be cases in which a departure outside suggested levels is warranted. In its view, however, such cases will be highly infrequent.

(c) <u>Plea Agreements</u>.

Nearly ninety percent of all federal criminal cases involve guilty pleas and many of these cases involve some form of plea agreement. Some commentators on early Commission guideline drafts urged the Commission not to attempt any major reforms of the plea agreement process on the grounds that any set of guidelines that threatened to change pre-guidelines practice radically also threatened to make the federal system unmanageable. Others argued that guidelines that failed to control and limit plea agreements would leave untouched a "loophole" large enough to undo the good that sentencing guidelines would bring.

The Commission decided not to make major changes in plea agreement practices in the initial guidelines, but rather to provide guidance by issuing general policy statements concerning the acceptance of plea agreements in

Chapter Six, Part B (Plea Agreements). The rules set forth in Fed. R. Crim. P. 11(e) govern the acceptance or rejection of such agreements. The Commission will collect data on the courts' plea practices and will analyze this information to determine when and why the courts accept or reject plea agreements and whether plea agreement practices are undermining the intent of the Sentencing Reform Act. In light of this information and analysis, the Commission will seek to further regulate the plea agreement process as appropriate. Importantly, if the policy statements relating to plea agreements are followed, circumvention of the Sentencing Reform Act and the guidelines should not occur.

The Commission expects the guidelines to have a positive, rationalizing impact upon plea agreements for two reasons. First, the guidelines create a clear, definite expectation in respect to the sentence that a court will impose if a trial takes place. In the event a prosecutor and defense attorney explore the possibility of a negotiated plea, they will no longer work in the dark. This fact alone should help to reduce irrationality in respect to actual sentencing outcomes. Second, the guidelines create a norm to which courts will likely refer when they decide whether, under Rule 11(e), to accept or to reject a plea agreement or recommendation.

(d) Probation and Split Sentences.

The statute provides that the guidelines are to "reflect the general appropriateness of imposing a sentence other than imprisonment in cases in which the defendant is a first offender who has not been convicted of a crime of violence or an otherwise serious offense . . . ." 28 U.S.C. § 994(j). Under pre-guidelines sentencing practice, courts sentenced to probation an inappropriately high percentage of offenders guilty of certain economic crimes, such as theft, tax evasion, antitrust offenses, insider trading, fraud, and embezzlement, that in the Commission's view are "serious."

The Commission's solution to this problem has been to write guidelines that classify as serious many offenses for which probation previously was frequently given and provide for at least a short period of imprisonment in such cases. The Commission concluded that the definite prospect of prison, even though the term may be short, will serve as a significant deterrent, particularly when compared with pre-guidelines practice where probation, not prison, was the norm.

More specifically, the guidelines work as follows in respect to a first offender. For offense levels one through eight, the sentencing court may elect to sentence the offender to probation (with or without confinement conditions) or to a prison term. For offense levels nine and ten, the court may substitute probation for a prison term, but the probation must include confinement conditions (community confinement, intermittent confinement, or home detention). For offense levels eleven and twelve, the court must impose at least one-half the minimum confinement sentence in the form of prison confinement, the remainder to be served on supervised release with a condition of community confinement or home detention. The Commission, of course, has not dealt with the single acts of aberrant behavior that still may justify probation at higher offense levels through departures.

(e) Multi-Count Convictions.

The Commission, like several state sentencing commissions, has found it particularly difficult to develop guidelines for sentencing defendants convicted of multiple violations of law, each of which makes up a separate count in an indictment. The difficulty is that when a defendant engages in conduct that causes several harms, each additional harm, even if it increases the extent to which punishment is warranted, does not necessarily warrant a proportionate increase in punishment. A defendant who assaults others during a fight, for example, may warrant more punishment if he injures ten people than if he injures one, but his conduct does not necessarily warrant ten times the punishment. If it did, many of the simplest offenses, for reasons that are often fortuitous, would lead to sentences of life imprisonment -- sentences that neither just deserts nor crime control theories of punishment would justify.

Several individual guidelines provide special instructions for increasing punishment when the conduct that is the subject of that count involves multiple occurrences or has caused several harms. The guidelines also provide general rules for aggravating punishment in light of multiple harms charged separately in separate counts. These rules may produce occasional anomalies, but normally they will permit an appropriate degree of aggravation of punishment for multiple offenses that are the subjects of separate counts.

These rules are set out in Chapter Three, Part D (Multiple Counts). They essentially provide: (1) when the conduct involves fungible items (e.g., separate drug transactions or thefts of money), the amounts are added and the guidelines apply to the total amount; (2) when nonfungible harms are involved, the offense level for the most serious count is increased (according to a diminishing scale) to reflect the existence of other counts of conviction. The guidelines have been written in order to minimize the possibility that an arbitrary casting of a single transaction into several counts will produce a longer sentence. In addition, the sentencing court will have adequate power to prevent such a result through departures.

(f) Regulatory Offenses.

Regulatory statutes, though primarily civil in nature, sometimes contain criminal provisions in respect to particularly harmful activity. Such criminal provisions often describe not only substantive offenses, but also more technical, administratively-related offenses such as failure to keep accurate records or to provide requested information. These statutes pose two problems: first, which criminal regulatory provisions should the Commission initially consider, and second, how should it treat technical or administratively-related criminal violations?

In respect to the first problem, the Commission found that it could not comprehensively treat all regulatory violations in the initial set of guidelines. There are hundreds of such provisions scattered throughout the United States Code. To find all potential violations would involve examination of each individual federal regulation. Because of this practical difficulty, the Commission sought to determine, with the assistance of the Department of Justice and several regulatory agencies, which criminal regulatory offenses were particularly important in light of the need for enforcement of the general regulatory scheme. The Commission addressed these offenses in the initial guidelines.

In respect to the second problem, the Commission has developed a system for treating technical recordkeeping and reporting offenses that divides them into four categories. First, in the simplest of cases, the offender may have failed to fill out a form intentionally, but without knowledge or intent that substantive harm would likely follow. He might fail, for example, to keep an accurate record of toxic substance transport, but that failure may not lead, nor be likely to lead, to the release or improper handling of any toxic substance. Second, the same failure may be accompanied by a significant likelihood that substantive harm will occur; it may make a release of a toxic substance more likely. Third, the same failure may have led to substantive harm. Fourth, the failure may represent an effort to conceal a substantive harm that has occurred.

The structure of a typical guideline for a regulatory offense provides a low base offense level (e.g., 6) aimed at the first type of recordkeeping or reporting offense. Specific offense characteristics designed to reflect substantive harms that do occur in respect to some regulatory offenses, or that are likely to occur, increase the offense level. A specific offense characteristic also provides that a recordkeeping or reporting offense that conceals a substantive offense will have the same offense level as the substantive offense.

(g) Sentencing Ranges.

In determining the appropriate sentencing ranges for each offense, the Commission estimated the average sentences served within each category under the pre-guidelines sentencing system. It also examined the sentences specified in federal statutes, in the parole guidelines, and in other relevant, analogous sources. The Commission's Supplementary Report on the Initial Sentencing Guidelines (1987) contains a comparison between estimates of pre-guidelines sentencing practice and sentences under the guidelines.

While the Commission has not considered itself bound by pre-guidelines sentencing practice, it has not attempted to develop an entirely new system of sentencing on the basis of theory alone. Guideline sentences, in many instances, will approximate average pre-guidelines practice and adherence to the guidelines will help to eliminate wide disparity. For example, where a high percentage of persons received probation under pre-guidelines practice, a guideline may include one or more specific offense characteristics in an effort to distinguish those types of defendants who received probation from those who received more severe sentences. In some instances, short sentences of incarceration for all offenders in a category have been substituted for a pre-guidelines sentencing practice of very wide variability in which some defendants received probation while others received several years in prison for the same offense. Moreover, inasmuch as those who pleaded guilty under pre-guidelines practice often received lesser sentences, the guidelines permit the court to impose lesser sentences on those defendants who accept responsibility for their misconduct. For defendants who provide substantial assistance to the government in the investigation or prosecution of others, a downward departure may be warranted.

The Commission has also examined its sentencing ranges in light of their likely impact upon prison population. Specific legislation, such as the Anti-Drug Abuse Act of 1986 and the career offender provisions of the Sentencing Reform Act of 1984 (28 U.S.C. § 994(h)), required the Commission to promulgate guidelines that will lead to substantial prison population increases. These increases will occur irrespective of the guidelines. The guidelines themselves, insofar as they reflect policy decisions made by the Commission (rather than legislated mandatory minimum or career offender sentences), are projected to lead to an increase in prison population that computer models, produced by the Commission and the Bureau of Prisons in 1987, estimated at approximately 10 percent over a period of ten years.

(h) The Sentencing Table.

The Commission has established a sentencing table that for technical and practical reasons contains 43 levels. Each level in the table prescribes ranges that overlap with the ranges in the preceding and succeeding levels. By overlapping the ranges, the table should discourage unnecessary litigation. Both prosecution and defense will realize that the difference between one level and another will not necessarily make a difference in the sentence that the court imposes. Thus, little purpose will be served in protracted litigation trying to determine, for example, whether $10,000 or $11,000 was obtained as a result of a fraud. At the same time, the levels work to increase a sentence proportionately. A change of six levels roughly doubles the sentence irrespective of the level at which one starts. The guidelines, in keeping with the statutory requirement that the maximum of any range cannot exceed the minimum by more than the greater of 25 percent or six months (28 U.S.C. § 994(b)(2)), permit courts to exercise the greatest permissible range of sentencing discretion. The table overlaps offense levels meaningfully, works proportionately, and at the same time preserves the maximum degree of allowable discretion for the court within each level.

Similarly, many of the individual guidelines refer to tables that correlate amounts of money with offense levels. These tables often have many rather than a few levels. Again, the reason is to minimize the likelihood of unnecessary litigation. If a money table were to make only a few distinctions, each distinction would become more important and litigation over which category an offender fell within would become more likely. Where a table has many small monetary distinctions, it minimizes the likelihood of litigation because the precise amount of money involved is of considerably less importance.

5.   A Concluding Note

The Commission emphasizes that it drafted the initial guidelines with considerable caution. It examined the many hundreds of criminal statutes in the United States Code. It began with those that were the basis for a significant number of prosecutions and sought to place them in a rational order. It developed additional distinctions relevant to the application of these provisions and it applied sentencing ranges to each resulting category. In doing so, it relied upon pre-guidelines sentencing practice as revealed by its own statistical analyses based on summary reports of some 40,000 convictions, a sample of 10,000 augmented presentence reports, the parole guidelines, and policy judgments.

The Commission recognizes that some will criticize this approach as overly cautious, as representing too little a departure from pre-guidelines sentencing practice. Yet, it will cure wide disparity. The Commission is a permanent body that can amend the guidelines each year. Although the data available to it, like all data, are imperfect, experience with the guidelines will lead to additional information and provide a firm empirical basis for consideration of revisions.

Finally, the guidelines will apply to more than 90 percent of all felony and Class A misdemeanor cases in the federal courts. Because of time constraints and the nonexistence of statistical information, some offenses that occur infrequently are not considered in the guidelines. Their exclusion does not reflect any judgment regarding their seriousness and they will be addressed as the Commission refines the guidelines over time.

PART B - GENERAL APPLICATION PRINCIPLES

§1B1.6.   Structure of the Guidelines

The guidelines are presented in numbered chapters divided into alphabetical parts. The parts are divided into subparts and individual guidelines. Each guideline is identified by three numbers and a letter corresponding to the chapter, part, subpart and individual guideline.

The first number is the chapter, the letter represents the part of the chapter, the second number is the subpart, and the final number is the guideline. Section 2B1.1, for example, is the first guideline in the first subpart in Part B of Chapter Two. Or, §3A1.2 is the second guideline in the first subpart in Part A of Chapter Three. Policy statements are similarly identified.

To illustrate:

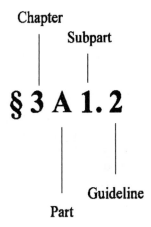

Historical Note: Effective November 1, 1987.

§1B1.7.   **Significance of Commentary**

The Commentary that accompanies the guideline sections may serve a number of purposes. First, it may interpret the guideline or explain how it is to be applied. Failure to follow such commentary could constitute an incorrect application of the guidelines, subjecting the sentence to possible reversal on appeal. See 18 U.S.C. § 3742. Second, the commentary may suggest circumstances which, in the view of the Commission, may warrant departure from the guidelines. Such commentary is to be treated as the legal equivalent of a policy statement. Finally, the commentary may provide background information, including factors considered in promulgating the guideline or reasons underlying promulgation of the guideline. As with a policy statement, such commentary may provide guidance in assessing the reasonableness of any departure from the guidelines.

Commentary

Portions of this document not labeled as guidelines or commentary also express the policy of the Commission or provide guidance as to the interpretation and application of the guidelines. These are to be construed as commentary and thus have the force of policy statements.

"[C]ommentary in the Guidelines Manual that interprets or explains a guideline is authoritative unless it violates the Constitution or a federal statute, or is inconsistent with, or a plainly erroneous reading of, that guideline." Stinson v. United States, 508 U.S. 36, 38 (1993).

<u>Historical Note</u>: Effective November 1, 1987. Amended effective November 1, 1993 (<u>see</u> Appendix C, amendment 498).

CHAPTER TWO–OFFENSE CONDUCT
PART B - BASIC ECONOMIC OFFENSES

§2B1.1. Larceny, Embezzlement, and Other Forms of Theft; Offenses Involving Stolen Property; Property Damage or Destruction; Fraud and Deceit; Forgery; Offenses Involving Altered or Counterfeit Instruments Other than Counterfeit Bearer Obligations of the United States

(Note: The November 2015 Amendments are included here)

(a) Base Offense Level:

   (1) **7**, if (A) the defendant was convicted of an offense referenced to this guideline; and (B) that offense of conviction has a statutory maximum term of imprisonment of 20 years or more; or

   (2) **6**, otherwise.

(b) Specific Offense Characteristics

   (1) If the loss exceeded $6,500, increase the offense level as follows:

<u>Loss</u>	(Apply the Greatest) <u>Increase in Level</u>
(A) $6,500 or less	no increase
(B) More than $6,500	add **2**
(C) More than $15,000	add **4**
(D) More than $40,000	add **6**
(E) More than $95,000	add **8**
(F) More than $150,000	add **10**
(G) More than $250,000	add **12**
(H) More than $550,000	add **14**
(I) More than $1,500,000	add **16**
(J) More than $3,500,000	add **18**
(K) More than $9,500,000	add **20**

(L) More than $25,000,000   add **22**

(M) More than $65,000,000   add **24**

(N) More than $150,000,000   add **26**

(O) More than $250,000,000   add **28**

(P) More than $550,000,000   add **30**.

(2) (Apply the greatest) If the offense–

    (A) (i) involved 10 or more victims; or (ii) was committed through mass-marketing, increase by **2** levels;

    (B) involved 50 or more victims, increase by **4** levels; or

    (C) involved 250 or more victims, increase by **6** levels.

(3) If the offense involved a theft from the person of another, increase by **2** levels.

(4) If the offense involved receiving stolen property, and the defendant was a person in the business of receiving and selling stolen property, increase by **2** levels.

(5) If the offense involved theft of, damage to, destruction of, or trafficking in, property from a national cemetery or veterans' memorial, increase by **2** levels.

(6) If (A) the defendant was convicted of an offense under 18 U.S.C. § 1037; and (B) the offense involved obtaining electronic mail addresses through improper means, increase by **2** levels.

(7) If (A) the defendant was convicted of a Federal health care offense involving a Government health care program; and (B) the loss under subsection (b)(1) to the Government health care program was (i) more than $1,000,000, increase by **2** levels; (ii) more than $7,000,000, increase by **3** levels; or (iii) more than $20,000,000, increase by **4** levels.

(8) (Apply the greater) If–

    (A) the offense involved conduct described in 18 U.S.C. § 670, increase by **2** levels; or

    (B) the offense involved conduct described in 18 U.S.C. § 670, and the defendant was employed by, or was an agent of, an organization in the supply chain for the pre-retail medical product, increase by **4** levels.

(9) If the offense involved (A) a misrepresentation that the defendant was acting on behalf of a charitable, educational, religious, or political organization, or a government agency; (B) a misrepresentation or other fraudulent action during the course of a bankruptcy proceeding; (C) a

violation of any prior, specific judicial or administrative order, injunction, decree, or process not addressed elsewhere in the guidelines; or (D) a misrepresentation to a consumer in connection with obtaining, providing, or furnishing financial assistance for an institution of higher education, increase by **2** levels. If the resulting offense level is less than level **10**, increase to level **10**.

(10) If (A) the defendant relocated, or participated in relocating, a fraudulent scheme to another jurisdiction to evade law enforcement or regulatory officials; (B) a substantial part of a fraudulent scheme was committed from outside the United States; or (C) the offense otherwise involved sophisticated means, increase by **2** levels. If the resulting offense level is less than level **12**, increase to level **12**.

(11) If the offense involved (A) the possession or use of any (i) device-making equipment, or (ii) authentication feature; (B) the production or trafficking of any (i) unauthorized access device or counterfeit access device, or (ii) authentication feature; or (C)(i) the unauthorized transfer or use of any means of identification unlawfully to produce or obtain any other means of identification, or (ii) the possession of 5 or more means of identification that unlawfully were produced from, or obtained by the use of, another means of identification, increase by **2** levels. If the resulting offense level is less than level **12**, increase to level **12**.

(12) If the offense involved conduct described in 18 U.S.C. § 1040, increase by **2** levels. If the resulting offense level is less than level **12**, increase to level **12**.

(13) (Apply the greater) If the offense involved misappropriation of a trade secret and the defendant knew or intended—

> (A) that the trade secret would be transported or transmitted out of the United States, increase by **2** levels; or
>
> (B) that the offense would benefit a foreign government, foreign instrumentality, or foreign agent, increase by **4** levels.

If subparagraph (B) applies and the resulting offense level is less than level **14**, increase to level **14**.

(14) If the offense involved an organized scheme to steal or to receive stolen (A) vehicles or vehicle parts; or (B) goods or chattels that are part of a cargo shipment, increase by **2** levels. If the resulting offense level is less than level **14**, increase to level **14**.

(15) If the offense involved (A) the conscious or reckless risk of death or serious bodily injury; or (B) possession of a dangerous weapon (including a firearm) in connection with the offense, increase by **2** levels. If the resulting offense level is less than level **14**, increase to level **14**.

(16) (Apply the greater) If–

(A) the defendant derived more than $1,000,000 in gross receipts from one or more financial institutions as a result of the offense, increase by **2** levels; or

(B) the offense (i) substantially jeopardized the safety and soundness of a financial institution; (ii) substantially endangered the solvency or financial security of an organization that, at any time during the offense, (I) was a publicly traded company; or (II) had 1,000 or more employees; or (iii) substantially endangered the solvency or financial security of 100 or more victims, increase by **4** levels.

(C) The cumulative adjustments from application of both subsections (b)(2) and (b)(15)(B) shall not exceed **8** levels, except as provided in subdivision (D).

(D) If the resulting offense level determined under subdivision (A) or (B) is less than level **24**, increase to level **24**.

(17) If (A) the defendant was convicted of an offense under 18 U.S.C. § 1030, and the offense involved an intent to obtain personal information, or (B) the offense involved the unauthorized public dissemination of personal information, increase by **2** levels.

(18) (A) (Apply the greatest) If the defendant was convicted of an offense under:

(i) 18 U.S.C. § 1030, and the offense involved a computer system used to maintain or operate a critical infrastructure, or used by or for a government entity in furtherance of the administration of justice, national defense, or national security, increase by **2** levels.

(ii) 18 U.S.C. § 1030(a)(5)(A), increase by **4** levels.

(iii) 18 U.S.C. § 1030, and the offense caused a substantial disruption of a critical infrastructure, increase by **6** levels.

(B) If subdivision (A)(iii) applies, and the offense level is less than level **24**, increase to level **24**.

(19) If the offense involved–

(A) a violation of securities law and, at the time of the offense, the defendant was (i) an officer or a director of a publicly traded company; (ii) a registered broker or dealer, or a person associated with a broker or dealer; or (iii) an investment adviser, or a person associated with an investment adviser; or

(B) a violation of commodities law and, at the time of the offense, the

defendant was (i) an officer or a director of a futures commission merchant or an introducing broker; (ii) a commodities trading advisor; or (iii) a commodity pool operator,

increase by **4** levels.

(c) Cross References

(1) If (A) a firearm, destructive device, explosive material, or controlled substance was taken, or the taking of any such item was an object of the offense; or (B) the stolen property received, transported, transferred, transmitted, or possessed was a firearm, destructive device, explosive material, or controlled substance, apply §2D1.1 (Unlawful Manufacturing, Importing, Exporting, or Trafficking (Including Possession with Intent to Commit These Offenses); Attempt or Conspiracy), §2D2.1 (Unlawful Possession; Attempt or Conspiracy), §2K1.3 (Unlawful Receipt, Possession, or Transportation of Explosive Materials; Prohibited Transactions Involving Explosive Materials), or §2K2.1 (Unlawful Receipt, Possession, or Transportation of Firearms or Ammunition; Prohibited Transactions Involving Firearms or Ammunition), as appropriate.

(2) If the offense involved arson, or property damage by use of explosives, apply §2K1.4 (Arson; Property Damage by Use of Explosives), if the resulting offense level is greater than that determined above.

(3) If (A) neither subdivision (1) nor (2) of this subsection applies; (B) the defendant was convicted under a statute proscribing false, fictitious, or fraudulent statements or representations generally (e.g., 18 U.S.C. § 1001, § 1341, § 1342, or § 1343); and (C) the conduct set forth in the count of conviction establishes an offense specifically covered by another guideline in Chapter Two (Offense Conduct), apply that other guideline.

(4) If the offense involved a cultural heritage resource or a paleontological resource, apply §2B1.5 (Theft of, Damage to, or Destruction of, Cultural Heritage Resources or Paleontological Resources; Unlawful Sale, Purchase, Exchange, Transportation, or Receipt of Cultural Heritage Resources or Paleontological Resources), if the resulting offense level is greater than that determined above.

Commentary

Statutory Provisions: 7 U.S.C. §§ 6, 6b, 6c, 6h, 6o, 13, 23; 15 U.S.C. §§ 50, 77e, 77q, 77x, 78j, 78ff, 80b-6, 1644, 6821; 18 U.S.C. §§ 38, 225, 285-289, 471-473, 500, 510, 553(a)(1), 641, 656, 657, 659, 662, 664, 1001-1008, 1010-1014, 1016-1022, 1025, 1026, 1028, 1029, 1030(a)(4)-(5), 1031, 1037, 1040, 1341-1344, 1348, 1350, 1361, 1363, 1369, 1702, 1703 (if vandalism or malicious mischief, including destruction of mail, is involved), 1708, 1831, 1832, 1992(a)(1), (a)(5), 2113(b), 2282A, 2282B, 2291, 2312-2317, 2332b(a)(1), 2701; 19 U.S.C. § 2401f; 29 U.S.C. § 501(c); 42 U.S.C. § 1011; 49 U.S.C. §§ 14915, 30170,

46317(a), 60123(b). For additional statutory provision(s), see Appendix A (Statutory Index).

Application Notes:

1. *Definitions.—For purposes of this guideline:*

"Cultural heritage resource" has the meaning given that term in Application Note 1 of the Commentary to §2B1.5 (Theft of, Damage to, or Destruction of, Cultural Heritage Resources or Paleontological Resources; Unlawful Sale, Purchase, Exchange, Transportation, or Receipt of Cultural Heritage Resources or Paleontological Resources).

"Equity securities" has the meaning given that term in section 3(a)(11) of the Securities Exchange Act of 1934 (15 U.S.C. § 78c(a)(11)).

"Federal health care offense" has the meaning given that term in 18 U.S.C. § 24.

"Financial institution" includes any institution described in 18 U.S.C. § 20, § 656, § 657, § 1005, § 1006, § 1007, or § 1014; any state or foreign bank, trust company, credit union, insurance company, investment company, mutual fund, savings (building and loan) association, union or employee pension fund; any health, medical, or hospital insurance association; brokers and dealers registered, or required to be registered, with the Securities and Exchange Commission; futures commodity merchants and commodity pool operators registered, or required to be registered, with the Commodity Futures Trading Commission; and any similar entity, whether or not insured by the federal government. "Union or employee pension fund" and "any health, medical, or hospital insurance association," primarily include large pension funds that serve many persons (e.g., pension funds of large national and international organizations, unions, and corporations doing substantial interstate business), and associations that undertake to provide pension, disability, or other benefits (e.g., medical or hospitalization insurance) to large numbers of persons.

"Firearm" and "destructive device" have the meaning given those terms in the Commentary to §1B1.1 (Application Instructions).

"Foreign instrumentality" and "foreign agent" have the meaning given those terms in 18 U.S.C. § 1839(1) and (2), respectively.

"Government health care program" means any plan or program that provides health benefits, whether directly, through insurance, or otherwise, which is funded directly, in whole or in part, by federal or state government. Examples of such programs are the Medicare program, the Medicaid program, and the CHIP program.

"Means of identification" has the meaning given that term in 18 U.S.C. § 1028(d)(7), except that such means of identification shall be of an actual (i.e.,

not fictitious) individual, other than the defendant or a person for whose conduct the defendant is accountable under §1B1.3 (Relevant Conduct).

"National cemetery" means a cemetery (A) established under section 2400 of title 38, United States Code; or (B) under the jurisdiction of the Secretary of the Army, the Secretary of the Navy, the Secretary of the Air Force, or the Secretary of the Interior.

"Paleontological resource" has the meaning given that term in Application Note 1 of the Commentary to §2B1.5 (Theft of, Damage to, or Destruction of, Cultural Heritage Resources or Paleontological Resources; Unlawful Sale, Purchase, Exchange, Transportation, or Receipt of Cultural Heritage Resources or Paleontological Resources).

"Personal information" means sensitive or private information involving an identifiable individual (including such information in the possession of a third party), including (A) medical records; (B) wills; (C) diaries; (D) private correspondence, including e-mail; (E) financial records; (F) photographs of a sensitive or private nature; or (G) similar information.

"Pre-retail medical product" has the meaning given that term in 18 U.S.C. § 670(e).

"Publicly traded company" means an issuer (A) with a class of securities registered under section 12 of the Securities Exchange Act of 1934 (15 U.S.C. § 78l); or (B) that is required to file reports under section 15(d) of the Securities Exchange Act of 1934 (15 U.S.C. § 78o(d)). "Issuer" has the meaning given that term in section 3 of the Securities Exchange Act of 1934 (15 U.S.C. § 78c).

"Supply chain" has the meaning given that term in 18 U.S.C. § 670(e).

"Theft from the person of another" means theft, without the use of force, of property that was being held by another person or was within arms' reach. Examples include pick-pocketing and non-forcible purse-snatching, such as the theft of a purse from a shopping cart.

"Trade secret" has the meaning given that term in 18 U.S.C. § 1839(3).

"Veterans' memorial" means any structure, plaque, statue, or other monument described in 18 U.S.C. § 1369(a).

"Victim" means (A) any person who sustained any part of the actual loss determined under subsection (b)(1); or (B) any individual who sustained bodily injury as a result of the offense. "Person" includes individuals, corporations, companies, associations, firms, partnerships, societies, and joint stock companies.

2. Application of Subsection (a)(1).—

(A) "Referenced to this Guideline".—For purposes of subsection (a)(1), an offense is "referenced to this guideline" if (i) this guideline is the applicable Chapter Two guideline determined under the provisions of §1B1.2 (Applicable Guidelines) for the offense of conviction; or (ii) in the case of a conviction for conspiracy, solicitation, or attempt to which §2X1.1 (Attempt, Solicitation, or Conspiracy) applies, this guideline is the appropriate guideline for the offense the defendant was convicted of conspiring, soliciting, or attempting to commit.

(B) Definition of "Statutory Maximum Term of Imprisonment".—For purposes of this guideline, "statutory maximum term of imprisonment" means the maximum term of imprisonment authorized for the offense of conviction, including any increase in that maximum term under a statutory enhancement provision.

(C) Base Offense Level Determination for Cases Involving Multiple Counts.—In a case involving multiple counts sentenced under this guideline, the applicable base offense level is determined by the count of conviction that provides the highest statutory maximum term of imprisonment.

3. Loss Under Subsection (b)(1).—This application note applies to the determination of loss under subsection (b)(1).

(A) General Rule.—Subject to the exclusions in subdivision (D), loss is the greater of actual loss or intended loss.

(i) Actual Loss.—"Actual loss" means the reasonably foreseeable pecuniary harm that resulted from the offense.

(ii) Intended Loss.—"Intended loss" (I) means the pecuniary harm that was intended to result from the offense; and (II) includes intended pecuniary harm that would have been impossible or unlikely to occur (e.g., as in a government sting operation, or an insurance fraud in which the claim exceeded the insured value).

(iii) Pecuniary Harm.—"Pecuniary harm" means harm that is monetary or that otherwise is readily measurable in money. Accordingly, pecuniary harm does not include emotional distress, harm to reputation, or other non-economic harm.

(iv) Reasonably Foreseeable Pecuniary Harm.—For purposes of this guideline, "reasonably foreseeable pecuniary harm" means pecuniary harm that the defendant knew or, under the circumstances, reasonably should have known, was a potential result of the offense.

(v) Rules of Construction in Certain Cases.—In the cases described in subdivisions (I) through (III), reasonably foreseeable pecuniary harm shall be considered to include the pecuniary harm specified for those cases as follows:

(I) Product Substitution Cases.—In the case of a product substitution offense, the reasonably foreseeable pecuniary harm includes the reasonably foreseeable costs of making substitute transactions and handling or disposing of the product delivered, or of retrofitting the product so that it can be used for its intended purpose, and the reasonably foreseeable costs of rectifying the actual or potential disruption to the victim's business operations caused by the product substitution.

(II) Procurement Fraud Cases.—In the case of a procurement fraud, such as a fraud affecting a defense contract award, reasonably foreseeable pecuniary harm includes the reasonably foreseeable administrative costs to the government and other participants of repeating or correcting the procurement action affected, plus any increased costs to procure the product or service involved that was reasonably foreseeable.

(III) Offenses Under 18 U.S.C. § 1030.—In the case of an offense under 18 U.S.C. § 1030, actual loss includes the following pecuniary harm, regardless of whether such pecuniary harm was reasonably foreseeable: any reasonable cost to any victim, including the cost of responding to an offense, conducting a damage assessment, and restoring the data, program, system, or information to its condition prior to the offense, and any revenue lost, cost incurred, or other damages incurred because of interruption of service.

(B) Gain.—The court shall use the gain that resulted from the offense as an alternative measure of loss only if there is a loss but it reasonably cannot be determined.

(C) Estimation of Loss.—The court need only make a reasonable estimate of the loss. The sentencing judge is in a unique position to assess the evidence and estimate the loss based upon that evidence. For this reason, the court's loss determination is entitled to appropriate deference. See 18 U.S.C. § 3742(e) and (f).

The estimate of the loss shall be based on available information, taking into account, as appropriate and practicable under the circumstances, factors such as the following:

(i) The fair market value of the property unlawfully taken, copied, or destroyed; or, if the fair market value is impracticable to determine or inadequately measures the harm, the cost to the victim of replacing that property.

(ii) In the case of proprietary information (e.g., trade secrets), the cost of developing that information or the reduction in the value of that information that resulted from the offense.

(iii) The cost of repairs to damaged property.

(iv) The approximate number of victims multiplied by the average loss to each victim.

(v) The reduction that resulted from the offense in the value of equity securities or other corporate assets.

(vi) More general factors, such as the scope and duration of the offense and revenues generated by similar operations.

(D) Exclusions from Loss.—Loss shall not include the following:

(i) Interest of any kind, finance charges, late fees, penalties, amounts based on an agreed-upon return or rate of return, or other similar costs.

(ii) Costs to the government of, and costs incurred by victims primarily to aid the government in, the prosecution and criminal investigation of an offense.

(E) Credits Against Loss.—Loss shall be reduced by the following:

(i) The money returned, and the fair market value of the property returned and the services rendered, by the defendant or other persons acting jointly with the defendant, to the victim before the offense was detected. The time of detection of the offense is the earlier of (I) the time the offense was discovered by a victim or government agency; or (II) the time the defendant knew or reasonably should have known that the offense was detected or about to be detected by a victim or government agency.

(ii) In a case involving collateral pledged or otherwise provided by the defendant, the amount the victim has recovered at the time of sentencing from disposition of the collateral, or if the collateral has not been disposed of by that time, the fair market value of the collateral at the time of sentencing.

(iii) Notwithstanding clause (ii), in the case of a fraud involving a mortgage loan, if the collateral has not been disposed of by the time of sentencing, use the fair market value of the collateral as of the date on which the guilt of the defendant has been established, whether by guilty plea, trial, or plea of nolo contendere.

In such a case, there shall be a rebuttable presumption that the most recent tax assessment value of the collateral is a reasonable estimate of the fair market value. In determining whether the most recent tax assessment value is a reasonable estimate of the fair market value, the court may consider, among other factors, the recency of the tax assessment and the extent to which the jurisdiction's tax assessment practices reflect factors not relevant to fair market value.

(F) Special Rules.—Notwithstanding subdivision (A), the following special rules shall be used to assist in determining loss in the cases indicated:

(i) Stolen or Counterfeit Credit Cards and Access Devices; Purloined Numbers and Codes.—In a case involving any counterfeit access device or unauthorized access device, loss includes any unauthorized charges made with the counterfeit access device or unauthorized access device and shall be not less

than $500 per access device. However, if the unauthorized access device is a means of telecommunica¬tions access that identifies a specific telecommunications instrument or telecommu¬nications account (including an electronic serial number/mobile identification number (ESN/MIN) pair), and that means was only possessed, and not used, during the commission of the offense, loss shall be not less than $100 per unused means. For purposes of this subdivision, "counterfeit access device" and "unauthorized access device" have the meaning given those terms in Application Note 10(A).

(ii) Government Benefits.—In a case involving government benefits (e.g., grants, loans, entitlement program payments), loss shall be considered to be not less than the value of the benefits obtained by unintended recipients or diverted to unintended uses, as the case may be. For example, if the defendant was the intended recipient of food stamps having a value of $100 but fraudulently received food stamps having a value of $150, loss is $50.

(iii) Davis-Bacon Act Violations.—In a case involving a Davis-Bacon Act violation (i.e., a violation of 40 U.S.C. § 3142, criminally prosecuted under 18 U.S.C. § 1001), the value of the benefits shall be considered to be not less than the difference between the legally required wages and actual wages paid.

(iv) Ponzi and Other Fraudulent Investment Schemes.—In a case involving a fraudulent investment scheme, such as a Ponzi scheme, loss shall not be reduced by the money or the value of the property transferred to any individual investor in the scheme in excess of that investor's principal investment (i.e., the gain to an individual investor in the scheme shall not be used to offset the loss to another individual investor in the scheme).

(v) Certain Other Unlawful Misrepresentation Schemes.—In a case involving a scheme in which (I) services were fraudulently rendered to the victim by persons falsely posing as licensed professionals; (II) goods were falsely represented as approved by a governmental regulatory agency; or (III) goods for which regulatory approval by a government agency was required but not obtained, or was obtained by fraud, loss shall include the amount paid for the property, services or goods transferred, rendered, or misrepresented, with no credit provided for the value of those items or services.

(vi) Value of Controlled Substances.—In a case involving controlled substances, loss is the estimated street value of the controlled substances.

(vii) Value of Cultural Heritage Resources or Paleontological Resources.—In a case involving a cultural heritage resource or paleontological resource, loss attributable to that resource shall be determined in accordance with the rules for determining the "value of the resource" set forth in Application Note 2 of the Commentary to §2B1.5.

(viii) Federal Health Care Offenses Involving Government Health Care Programs.—In a case in which the defendant is convicted of a Federal health care offense involving a Government health care program, the aggregate dollar amount of fraudulent bills submitted to the Government health care

program shall constitute prima facie evidence of the amount of the intended loss, i.e., is evidence sufficient to establish the amount of the intended loss, if not rebutted.

(ix) Fraudulent Inflation or Deflation in Value of Securities or Commodities.—In a case involving the fraudulent inflation or deflation in the value of a publicly traded security or commodity, there shall be a rebuttable presumption that the actual loss attributable to the change in value of the security or commodity is the amount determined by–

(I) calculating the difference between the average price of the security or commodity during the period that the fraud occurred and the average price of the security or commodity during the 90-day period after the fraud was disclosed to the market, and

(II) multiplying the difference in average price by the number of shares outstanding.

In determining whether the amount so determined is a reasonable estimate of the actual loss attributable to the change in value of the security or commodity, the court may consider, among other factors, the extent to which the amount so determined includes significant changes in value not resulting from the offense (e.g., changes caused by external market forces, such as changed economic circumstances, changed investor expectations, and new industry-specific or firm-specific facts, conditions, or events).

4. Application of Subsection (b)(2).–

(A) Definition.—For purposes of subsection (b)(2), "mass-marketing" means a plan, program, promotion, or campaign that is conducted through solicitation by telephone, mail, the Internet, or other means to induce a large number of persons to (i) purchase goods or services; (ii) participate in a contest or sweepstakes; or (iii) invest for financial profit. "Mass-marketing" includes, for example, a telemarketing campaign that solicits a large number of individuals to purchase fraudulent life insurance policies.

(B) Applicability to Transmission of Multiple Commercial Electronic Mail Messages.—For purposes of subsection (b)(2), an offense under 18 U.S.C. § 1037, or any other offense involving conduct described in 18 U.S.C. § 1037, shall be considered to have been committed through mass-marketing. Accordingly, the defendant shall receive at least a two-level enhancement under subsection (b)(2) and may, depending on the facts of the case, receive a greater enhancement under such subsection, if the defendant was convicted under, or the offense involved conduct described in, 18 U.S.C. § 1037.

(C) Undelivered United States Mail.—

(i) In General.—In a case in which undelivered United States mail was taken, or the taking of such item was an object of the offense, or in a case in which the stolen property received, transported, transferred, transmitted, or

possessed was undelivered United States mail, "victim" means (I) any victim as defined in Application Note 1; or (II) any person who was the intended recipient, or addressee, of the undelivered United States mail.

(ii) *Special Rule.*—A case described in subdivision (C)(i) of this note that involved–

(I) a United States Postal Service relay box, collection box, delivery vehicle, satchel, or cart, shall be considered to have involved at least 50 victims.

(II) a housing unit cluster box or any similar receptacle that contains multiple mailboxes, whether such receptacle is owned by the United States Postal Service or otherwise owned, shall, unless proven otherwise, be presumed to have involved the number of victims corresponding to the number of mailboxes in each cluster box or similar receptacle.

(iii) *Definition.*— "Undelivered United States mail" means mail that has not actually been received by the addressee or the addressee's agent (*e.g.*, mail taken from the addressee's mail box).

(D) *Vulnerable Victims.*—If subsection (b)(2)(B) or (C) applies, an enhancement under §3A1.1(b)(2) shall not apply.

(E) *Cases Involving Means of Identification.*—For purposes of subsection (b)(2), in a case involving means of identification "victim" means (i) any victim as defined in Application Note 1; or (ii) any individual whose means of identification was used unlawfully or without authority.

5. *Enhancement for Business of Receiving and Selling Stolen Property under Subsection (b)(4).*—For purposes of subsection (b)(4), the court shall consider the following non-exhaustive list of factors in determining whether the defendant was in the business of receiving and selling stolen property:

(A) The regularity and sophistication of the defendant's activities.

(B) The value and size of the inventory of stolen property maintained by the defendant.

(C) The extent to which the defendant's activities encouraged or facilitated other crimes.

(D) The defendant's past activities involving stolen property.

6. *Application of Subsection (b)(6).*–For purposes of subsection (b)(6), "improper means" includes the unauthorized harvesting of electronic mail addresses of users of a website, proprietary service, or other online public forum.

7. *Application of Subsection (b)(8)(B).*–If subsection (b)(8)(B) applies, do not apply an adjustment under §3B1.3 (Abuse of Position of Trust or Use of Special Skill).

8. *Application of Subsection (b)(9).*—

(A) *In General.*—The adjustments in subsection (b)(9) are alternative rather than cumulative. If, in a particular case, however, more than one of the enumerated factors applied, an upward departure may be warranted.

(B) *Misrepresentations Regarding Charitable and Other Institutions.*—Subsection (b)(9)(A) applies in any case in which the defendant represented that the defendant was acting to obtain a benefit on behalf of a charitable, educational, religious, or political organization, or a government agency (regardless of whether the defendant actually was associated with the organization or government agency) when, in fact, the defendant intended to divert all or part of that benefit (*e.g.*, for the defendant's personal gain). Subsection (b)(9)(A) applies, for example, to the following:

(i) A defendant who solicited contributions for a non-existent famine relief organization.

(ii) A defendant who solicited donations from church members by falsely claiming to be a fundraiser for a religiously affiliated school.

(iii) A defendant, chief of a local fire department, who conducted a public fundraiser representing that the purpose of the fundraiser was to procure sufficient funds for a new fire engine when, in fact, the defendant intended to divert some of the funds for the defendant's personal benefit.

(C) *Fraud in Contravention of Prior Judicial Order.*—Subsection (b)(9)(C) provides an enhancement if the defendant commits a fraud in contravention of a prior, official judicial or administrative warning, in the form of an order, injunction, decree, or process, to take or not to take a specified action. A defendant who does not comply with such a prior, official judicial or administrative warning demonstrates aggravated criminal intent and deserves additional punishment. If it is established that an entity the defendant controlled was a party to the prior proceeding that resulted in the official judicial or administrative action, and the defendant had knowledge of that prior decree or order, this enhancement applies even if the defendant was not a specifically named party in that prior case. For example, a defendant whose business previously was enjoined from selling a dangerous product, but who nonetheless engaged in fraudulent conduct to sell the product, is subject to this enhancement. This enhancement does not apply if the same conduct resulted in an enhancement pursuant to a provision found elsewhere in the guidelines (*e.g.*, a violation of a condition of release addressed in §3C1.3 (Commission of Offense While on Release) or a violation of probation addressed in §4A1.1 (Criminal History Category)).

(D) *College Scholarship Fraud.*—For purposes of subsection (b)(9)(D):

"Financial assistance" means any scholarship, grant, loan, tuition, discount, award, or other financial assistance for the purpose of financing an education.

"Institution of higher education" has the meaning given that term in section 101 of the Higher Education Act of 1954 (20 U.S.C. § 1001).

(E) *Non-Applicability of Chapter Three Adjustments.*—

(i) *Subsection (b)(9)(A).*—If the conduct that forms the basis for an enhancement under subsection (b)(9)(A) is the only conduct that forms the basis for an adjustment under §3B1.3 (Abuse of Position of Trust or Use of Special Skill), do not apply that adjustment under §3B1.3.

(ii) *Subsection (b)(9)(B) and (C).*—If the conduct that forms the basis for an enhancement under subsection (b)(9)(B) or (C) is the only conduct that forms the basis for an adjustment under §3C1.1 (Obstructing or Impeding the Administration of Justice), do not apply that adjustment under §3C1.1.

9. *Sophisticated Means Enhancement under Subsection (b)(10).*—

(A) *Definition of United States.*—For purposes of subsection (b)(10)(B), "United States" means each of the 50 states, the District of Columbia, the Commonwealth of Puerto Rico, the United States Virgin Islands, Guam, the Northern Mariana Islands, and American Samoa.

(B) *Sophisticated Means Enhancement.*—For purposes of subsection (b)(10)(C), "sophisticated means" means especially complex or especially intricate offense conduct pertaining to the execution or concealment of an offense. For example, in a tele-marketing scheme, locating the main office of the scheme in one jurisdiction but locating soliciting operations in another jurisdiction ordinarily indicates sophisticated means. Conduct such as hiding assets or transactions, or both, through the use of fictitious entities, corporate shells, or offshore financial accounts also ordinarily indicates sophisticated means.

(C) *Non-Applicability of Chapter Three Adjustment.*—If the conduct that forms the basis for an enhancement under subsection (b)(10) is the only conduct that forms the basis for an adjustment under §3C1.1, do not apply that adjustment under §3C1.1.

10. *Application of Subsection (b)(11).*—

(A) *Definitions.*—For purposes of subsection (b)(11):

"Authentication feature" has the meaning given that term in 18 U.S.C. § 1028(d)(1).

"Counterfeit access device" (i) has the meaning given that term in 18 U.S.C. § 1029(e)(2); and (ii) includes a telecommunications instrument that has been modified or altered to obtain unauthorized use of telecommunications service.

"Device-making equipment" (i) has the meaning given that term in 18 U.S.C. § 1029(e)(6); and (ii) includes (I) any hardware or software that has been configured as described in 18 U.S.C. § 1029(a)(9); and (II) a scanning receiver

referred to in 18 U.S.C. § 1029(a)(8). "Scanning receiver" has the meaning given that term in 18 U.S.C. § 1029(e)(8).

"Produce" includes manufacture, design, alter, authenticate, duplicate, or assemble. "Production" includes manufacture, design, alteration, authentication, duplication, or assembly.

"Telecommunications service" has the meaning given that term in 18 U.S.C. § 1029(e)(9).

"Unauthorized access device" has the meaning given that term in 18 U.S.C. § 1029(e)(3).

(B) Authentication Features and Identification Documents.—Offenses involving authentication features, identification documents, false identification documents, and means of identification, in violation of 18 U.S.C. § 1028, also are covered by this guideline. If the primary purpose of the offense, under 18 U.S.C. § 1028, was to violate, or assist another to violate, the law pertaining to naturalization, citizenship, or legal resident status, apply §2L2.1 (Trafficking in a Document Relating to Naturalization) or §2L2.2 (Fraudulently Acquiring Documents Relating to Naturalization), as appropriate, rather than this guideline.

(C) Application of Subsection (b)(11)(C)(i).—

(i) In General.—Subsection (b)(11)(C)(i) applies in a case in which a means of identification of an individual other than the defendant (or a person for whose conduct the defendant is accountable under §1B1.3 (Relevant Conduct)) is used without that individual's authorization unlawfully to produce or obtain another means of identification.

(ii) Examples.—Examples of conduct to which subsection (b)(11)(C)(i) applies are as follows:

(I) A defendant obtains an individual's name and social security number from a source (e.g., from a piece of mail taken from the individual's mailbox) and obtains a bank loan in that individual's name. In this example, the account number of the bank loan is the other means of identification that has been obtained unlawfully.

(II) A defendant obtains an individual's name and address from a source (e.g., from a driver's license in a stolen wallet) and applies for, obtains, and subsequently uses a credit card in that individual's name. In this example, the credit card is the other means of identification that has been obtained unlawfully.

(iii) Non-Applicability of Subsection (b)(11)(C)(i).—Examples of conduct to which subsection (b)(11)(C)(i) does not apply are as follows:

(I) A defendant uses a credit card from a stolen wallet only to make a purchase. In such a case, the defendant has not used the stolen credit card to obtain another means of identification.

(II) A defendant forges another individual's signature to cash a stolen check. Forging another individual's signature is not producing another means of identification.

(D) Application of Subsection (b)(11)(C)(ii).—Subsection (b)(11)(C)(ii) applies in any case in which the offense involved the possession of 5 or more means of identification that unlawfully were produced or obtained, regardless of the number of individuals in whose name (or other identifying information) the means of identification were so produced or so obtained.

11. Application of Subsection (b)(14).—Subsection (b)(14) provides a minimum offense level in the case of an ongoing, sophisticated operation (e.g., an auto theft ring or "chop shop") to steal or to receive stolen (A) vehicles or vehicle parts; or (B) goods or chattels that are part of a cargo shipment. For purposes of this subsection, "vehicle" means motor vehicle, vessel, or aircraft. A "cargo shipment" includes cargo transported on a railroad car, bus, steamboat, vessel, or airplane.

12. Gross Receipts Enhancement under Subsection (b)(16)(A).—

(A) In General.—For purposes of subsection (b)(16)(A), the defendant shall be considered to have derived more than $1,000,000 in gross receipts if the gross receipts to the defendant individually, rather than to all participants, exceeded $1,000,000.

(B) Definition.— "Gross receipts from the offense" includes all property, real or personal, tangible or intangible, which is obtained directly or indirectly as a result of such offense. See 18 U.S.C. § 982(a)(4).

13. Application of Subsection (b)(16)(B).—

(A) Application of Subsection (b)(16)(B)(i).—The following is a non-exhaustive list of factors that the court shall consider in determining whether, as a result of the offense, the safety and soundness of a financial institution was substantially jeopardized:

(i) The financial institution became insolvent.

(ii) The financial institution substantially reduced benefits to pensioners or insureds.

(iii) The financial institution was unable on demand to refund fully any deposit, payment, or investment.

(iv) The financial institution was so depleted of its assets as to be forced to merge with another institution in order to continue active operations.

(v) One or more of the criteria in clauses (i) through (iv) was likely to result from the offense but did not result from the offense because of federal government intervention, such as a "bailout".

(B) Application of Subsection (b)(16)(B)(ii).—

(i) Definition.—For purposes of this subsection, "organization" has the meaning given that term in Application Note 1 of §8A1.1 (Applicability of Chapter Eight).

(ii) In General.—The following is a non-exhaustive list of factors that the court shall consider in determining whether, as a result of the offense, the solvency or financial security of an organization that was a publicly traded company or that had more than 1,000 employees was substantially endangered:

(I) The organization became insolvent or suffered a substantial reduction in the value of its assets.

(II) The organization filed for bankruptcy under Chapters 7, 11, or 13 of the Bankruptcy Code (title 11, United States Code).

(III) The organization suffered a substantial reduction in the value of its equity securities or the value of its employee retirement accounts.

(IV) The organization substantially reduced its workforce.

(V) The organization substantially reduced its employee pension benefits.

(VI) The liquidity of the equity securities of a publicly traded company was substantially endangered. For example, the company was delisted from its primary listing exchange, or trading of the company's securities was halted for more than one full trading day.

(VII) One or more of the criteria in subclauses (I) through (VI) was likely to result from the offense but did not result from the offense because of federal government intervention, such as a "bailout".

14. Application of Subsection (b)(18).—

1.   *(A) Definitions.—For purposes of subsection (b)(18):*

"Critical infrastructure" means systems and assets vital to national defense, national security, economic security, public health or safety, or any combination of those matters. A critical infrastructure may be publicly or privately owned. Examples of critical infrastructures include gas and oil production, storage, and delivery systems, water supply systems, telecommunications networks, electrical power delivery systems, financing and banking systems, emergency services (including medical, police, fire, and rescue services), transportation systems and services (including highways, mass transit, airlines, and airports), and government operations that provide essential services to the public.

*"Government entity" has the meaning given that term in 18 U.S.C. §
1030(e)(9).*

*(B) Subsection (b)(18)(A)(iii).—If the same conduct that forms the basis for an
enhancement under subsection (b)(18)(A)(iii) is the only conduct that forms the
basis for an enhancement under subsection (b)(16)(B), do not apply the
enhancement under subsection (b)(16)(B).*

15. Application of Subsection (b)(19).—

(A) Definitions.—For purposes of subsection (b)(19):

*"Commodities law" means (i) the Commodity Exchange Act (7 U.S.C. § 1 et
seq.) and 18 U.S.C. § 1348; and (ii) includes the rules, regulations, and orders
issued by the Commodity Futures Trading Commission.*

*"Commodity pool operator" has the meaning given that term in section 1a(11)
of the Commodity Exchange Act (7 U.S.C. § 1a(11)).*

*"Commodity trading advisor" has the meaning given that term in section
1a(12) of the Commodity Exchange Act (7 U.S.C. § 1a(12)).*

*"Futures commission merchant" has the meaning given that term in section
1a(28) of the Commodity Exchange Act (7 U.S.C. § 1a(28)).*

*"Introducing broker" has the meaning given that term in section 1a(31) of the
Commodity Exchange Act (7 U.S.C. § 1a(31)).*

*"Investment adviser" has the meaning given that term in section 202(a)(11) of
the Investment Advisers Act of 1940 (15 U.S.C. § 80b-2(a)(11)).*

*"Person associated with a broker or dealer" has the meaning given that term
in section 3(a)(18) of the Securities Exchange Act of 1934 (15 U.S.C. §
78c(a)(18)).*

*"Person associated with an investment adviser" has the meaning given that
term in section 202(a)(17) of the Investment Advisers Act of 1940 (15 U.S.C.
§ 80b-2(a)(17)).*

*"Registered broker or dealer" has the meaning given that term in section
3(a)(48) of the Securities Exchange Act of 1934 (15 U.S.C. § 78c(a)(48)).*

*"Securities law" (i) means 18 U.S.C. §§ 1348, 1350, and the provisions of law
referred to in section 3(a)(47) of the Securities Exchange Act of 1934 (15 U.S.C.
§ 78c(a)(47)); and (ii) includes the rules, regulations, and orders issued by the
Securities and Exchange Commission pursuant to the provisions of law
referred to in such section.*

*(B) In General.—A conviction under a securities law or commodities law is not
required in order for subsection (b)(19) to apply. This subsection would apply
in the case of a defendant convicted under a general fraud statute if the*

defendant's conduct violated a securities law or commodities law. For example, this subsection would apply if an officer of a publicly traded company violated regulations issued by the Securities and Exchange Commission by fraudulently influencing an independent audit of the company's financial statements for the purposes of rendering such financial statements materially misleading, even if the officer is convicted only of wire fraud.

(C) Nonapplicability of §3B1.3 (Abuse of Position of Trust or Use of Special Skill).—If subsection (b)(19) applies, do not apply §3B1.3.

16. Cross Reference in Subsection (c)(3).—Subsection (c)(3) provides a cross reference to another guideline in Chapter Two (Offense Conduct) in cases in which the defendant is convicted of a general fraud statute, and the count of conviction establishes an offense involving fraudulent conduct that is more aptly covered by another guideline. Sometimes, offenses involving fraudulent statements are prosecuted under 18 U.S.C. § 1001, or a similarly general statute, although the offense involves fraudulent conduct that is also covered by a more specific statute. Examples include false entries regarding currency transactions, for which §2S1.3 (Structuring Transactions to Evade Reporting Requirements) likely would be more apt, and false statements to a customs officer, for which §2T3.1 (Evading Import Duties or Restrictions (Smuggling); Receiving or Trafficking in Smuggled Property) likely would be more apt. In certain other cases, the mail or wire fraud statutes, or other relatively broad statutes, are used primarily as jurisdictional bases for the prosecution of other offenses. For example, a state employee who improperly influenced the award of a contract and used the mails to commit the offense may be prosecuted under 18 U.S.C. § 1341 for fraud involving the deprivation of the intangible right of honest services. Such a case would be more aptly sentenced pursuant to §2C1.1 (Offering, Giving, Soliciting, or Receiving a Bribe; Extortion Under Color of Official Right; Fraud involving the Deprivation of the Intangible Right to Honest Services of Public Officials; Conspiracy to Defraud by Interference with Governmental Functions).

17. Continuing Financial Crimes Enterprise.—If the defendant is convicted under 18 U.S.C. § 225 (relating to a continuing financial crimes enterprise), the offense level is that applicable to the underlying series of offenses comprising the "continuing financial crimes enterprise".

18. Partially Completed Offenses.—In the case of a partially completed offense (e.g., an offense involving a completed theft or fraud that is part of a larger, attempted theft or fraud), the offense level is to be determined in accordance with the provisions of §2X1.1 (Attempt, Solicitation, or Conspiracy) whether the conviction is for the substantive offense, the inchoate offense (attempt, solicitation, or conspiracy), or both. See Application Note 4 of the Commentary to §2X1.1.

19. Multiple-Count Indictments.—Some fraudulent schemes may result in multiple-count indictments, depending on the technical elements of the offense. The cumulative loss produced by a common scheme or course of conduct should be used in determining the offense level, regardless of the number of counts of conviction. See *Chapter Three, Part D (Multiple Counts).*

20. *Departure Considerations.*—

(A) *Upward Departure Considerations.*—*There may be cases in which the offense level determined under this guideline substantially understates the seriousness of the offense. In such cases, an upward departure may be warranted. The following is a non-exhaustive list of factors that the court may consider in determining whether an upward departure is warranted:*

(i) *A primary objective of the offense was an aggravating, non-monetary objective. For example, a primary objective of the offense was to inflict emotional harm.*

(ii) *The offense caused or risked substantial non-monetary harm. For example, the offense caused physical harm, psychological harm, or severe emotional trauma, or resulted in a substantial invasion of a privacy interest (through, for example, the theft of personal information such as medical, educational, or financial records). An upward departure would be warranted, for example, in an 18 U.S.C. § 1030 offense involving damage to a protected computer, if, as a result of that offense, death resulted. An upward departure also would be warranted, for example, in a case involving animal enterprise terrorism under 18 U.S.C. § 43, if, in the course of the offense, serious bodily injury or death resulted, or substantial scientific research or information were destroyed. Similarly, an upward departure would be warranted in a case involving conduct described in 18 U.S.C. § 670 if the offense resulted in serious bodily injury or death, including serious bodily injury or death resulting from the use of the pre-retail medical product.*

(iii) *The offense involved a substantial amount of interest of any kind, finance charges, late fees, penalties, amounts based on an agreed-upon return or rate of return, or other similar costs, not included in the determination of loss for purposes of subsection (b)(1).*

(iv) *The offense created a risk of substantial loss beyond the loss determined for purposes of subsection (b)(1), such as a risk of a significant disruption of a national financial market.*

(v) *In a case involving stolen information from a "protected computer", as defined in 18 U.S.C. § 1030(e)(2), the defendant sought the stolen information to further a broader criminal purpose.*

(vi) *In a case involving access devices or unlawfully produced or unlawfully obtained means of identification:*

(I) *The offense caused substantial harm to the victim's reputation or credit record, or the victim suffered a substantial inconvenience related to repairing the victim's reputation or a damaged credit record.*

(II) An individual whose means of identification the defendant used to obtain unlawful means of identification is erroneously arrested or denied a job because an arrest record has been made in that individual's name.

(III) The defendant produced or obtained numerous means of identification with respect to one individual and essentially assumed that individual's identity.

(B) Upward Departure for Debilitating Impact on a Critical Infrastructure.—An upward departure would be warranted in a case in which subsection (b)(18)(A)(iii) applies and the disruption to the critical infrastructure(s) is so substantial as to have a debilitating impact on national security, national economic security, national public health or safety, or any combination of those matters.

(C) Downward Departure Consideration.—There may be cases in which the offense level determined under this guideline substantially overstates the seriousness of the offense. In such cases, a downward departure may be warranted.

For example, a securities fraud involving a fraudulent statement made publicly to the market may produce an aggregate loss amount that is substantial but diffuse, with relatively small loss amounts suffered by a relatively large number of victims. In such a case, the loss table in subsection (b)(1) and the victims table in subsection (b)(2) may combine to produce an offense level that substantially overstates the seriousness of the offense. If so, a downward departure may be warranted.

(D) Downward Departure for Major Disaster or Emergency Victims.—If (i) the minimum offense level of level 12 in subsection (b)(12) applies; (ii) the defendant sustained damage, loss, hardship, or suffering caused by a major disaster or an emergency as those terms are defined in 42 U.S.C. § 5122; and (iii) the benefits received illegally were only an extension or overpayment of benefits received legitimately, a downward departure may be warranted.

Background: This guideline covers offenses involving theft, stolen property, property damage or destruction, fraud, forgery, and counterfeiting (other than offenses involving altered or counterfeit bearer obligations of the United States).

Because federal fraud statutes often are broadly written, a single pattern of offense conduct usually can be prosecuted under several code sections, as a result of which the offense of conviction may be somewhat arbitrary. Furthermore, most fraud statutes cover a broad range of conduct with extreme variation in severity. The specific offense characteristics and cross references contained in this guideline are designed with these considerations in mind.

The Commission has determined that, ordinarily, the sentences of defendants convicted of federal offenses should reflect the nature and magnitude of the loss caused or intended by their crimes. Accordingly, along with other relevant factors under the guidelines, loss serves as a measure of the seriousness of the offense and the defendant's relative culpability and is a principal factor in determining the offense level under this guideline.

Theft from the person of another, such as pickpocketing or non-forcible purse-snatching, receives an enhanced sentence because of the increased risk of physical injury. This guideline does not include an enhancement for thefts from the person by means of force or fear; such crimes are robberies and are covered under §2B3.1 (Robbery).

A minimum offense level of level 14 is provided for offenses involving an organized scheme to steal vehicles or vehicle parts. Typically, the scope of such activity is substantial, but the value of the property may be particularly difficult to ascertain in individual cases because the stolen property is rapidly resold or otherwise disposed of in the course of the offense. Therefore, the specific offense characteristic of "organized scheme" is used as an alternative to "loss" in setting a minimum offense level.

Use of false pretenses involving charitable causes and government agencies enhances the sentences of defendants who take advantage of victims' trust in government or law enforcement agencies or the generosity and charitable motives of victims. Taking advantage of a victim's self-interest does not mitigate the seriousness of fraudulent conduct; rather, defendants who exploit victims' charitable impulses or trust in government create particular social harm. In a similar vein, a defendant who has been subject to civil or administrative proceedings for the same or similar fraudulent conduct demonstrates aggravated criminal intent and is deserving of additional punishment for not conforming with the requirements of judicial process or orders issued by federal, state, or local administrative agencies.

Offenses that involve the use of financial transactions or financial accounts outside the United States in an effort to conceal illicit profits and criminal conduct involve a particularly high level of sophistication and complexity. These offenses are difficult to detect and require costly investigations and prosecutions. Diplomatic processes often must be used to secure testimony and evidence beyond the jurisdiction of United States courts. Consequently, a minimum offense level of level 12 is provided for these offenses.

Subsection (b)(5) implements the instruction to the Commission in section 2 of Public Law 105–101 and the directive to the Commission in section 3 of Public Law 110–384.

Subsection (b)(7) implements the directive to the Commission in section 10606 of Public Law 111–148.

Subsection (b)(8) implements the directive to the Commission in section 7 of Public Law 112–186.

Subsection (b)(9)(D) implements, in a broader form, the directive in section 3 of the College Scholarship Fraud Prevention Act of 2000, Public Law 106–420.

Subsection (b)(10) implements, in a broader form, the instruction to the Commission in section 6(c)(2) of Public Law 105–184.

Subsections (b)(11)(A)(i) and (B)(i) implement the instruction to the Commission in section 4 of the Wireless Telephone Protection Act, Public Law 105–172.

Subsection (b)(11)(C) implements the directive to the Commission in section 4 of the Identity Theft and Assumption Deterrence Act of 1998, Public Law 105–318. This subsection focuses principally on an aggravated form of identity theft known as "affirmative identity theft" or "breeding", in which a defendant uses another individual's name, social security number, or some other form of identification (the "means of identification") to "breed" (i.e., produce or obtain) new or additional forms of identification. Because 18 U.S.C. § 1028(d) broadly defines "means of identification", the new or additional forms of identification can include items such as a driver's license, a credit card, or a bank loan. This subsection provides a minimum offense level of level 12, in part because of the seriousness of the offense. The minimum offense level accounts for the fact that the means of identification that were "bred" (i.e., produced or obtained) often are within the defendant's exclusive control, making it difficult for the individual victim to detect that the victim's identity has been "stolen." Generally, the victim does not become aware of the offense until certain harms have already occurred (e.g., a damaged credit rating or an inability to obtain a loan). The minimum offense level also accounts for the non-monetary harm associated with these types of offenses, much of which may be difficult or impossible to quantify (e.g., harm to the individual's reputation or credit rating, inconvenience, and other difficulties resulting from the offense). The legislative history of the Identity Theft and Assumption Deterrence Act of 1998 indicates that Congress was especially concerned with providing increased punishment for this type of harm.

Subsection (b)(12) implements the directive in section 5 of Public Law 110–179.

Subsection (b)(13) implements the directive in section 3 of Public Law 112–269.

Subsection (b)(15)(B) implements, in a broader form, the instruction to the Commission in section 110512 of Public Law 103–322.

Subsection (b)(16)(A) implements, in a broader form, the instruction to the Commission in section 2507 of Public Law 101–647.

Subsection (b)(16)(B)(i) implements, in a broader form, the instruction to the Commission in section 961(m) of Public Law 101–73.

Subsection (b)(17) implements the directive in section 209 of Public Law 110–326.

Subsection (b)(18) implements the directive in section 225(b) of Public Law 107–296. The minimum offense level of level 24 provided in subsection (b)(18)(B) for an offense that resulted in a substantial disruption of a critical infrastructure reflects the serious impact such an offense could have on national security, national economic security, national public health or safety, or a combination of any of these matters.

Historical Note: Effective November 1, 1987. Amended effective June 15, 1988 (see Appendix C, amendment 7); November 1, 1989 (see Appendix C, amendments 99-101 and 303); November 1, 1990 (see Appendix C, amendments 312, 317, and 361); November 1, 1991 (see Appendix C, amendments 364 and 393); November 1, 1993 (see Appendix C, amendments 481 and 482); November 1, 1995 (see Appendix C, amendment 512); November 1, 1997 (see Appendix C, amendment 551); November 1, 1998 (see Appendix C, amendment 576); November 1, 2000 (see Appendix C, amendment 596); November 1, 2001 (see Appendix C, amendment 617); November 1, 2002 (see Appendix C, amendments 637, 638, and 646); January 25, 2003 (see Appendix C, amendment 647); November 1, 2003 (see Appendix C, amendments 653, 654, 655, and 661); November 1, 2004 (see Appendix C, amendments 665, 666, and 674); November 1, 2005 (see Appendix C, amendment 679); November 1, 2006 (see Appendix C, amendments 685 and 696); November 1, 2007 (see Appendix C, amendments 699, 700, and 702); February 6, 2008 (see Appendix C, amendment 714); November 1, 2008 (see Appendix C, amendments 719 and 725); November 1, 2009 (see Appendix C, amendments 726, 733, and 737); November 1, 2010 (see Appendix C, amendments 745 and 747); November 1, 2011 (see Appendix C, amendment 749); November 1, 2012 (see Appendix C, amendment 761); November 1, 2013 (see Appendix C, amendments 771, 772, and 777).

PART C - OFFENSES INVOLVING PUBLIC OFFICIALS

§2C1.1. Offering, Giving, Soliciting, or Receiving a Bribe; Extortion Under Color of Official Right; Fraud Involving the Deprivation of the Intangible Right to Honest Services of Public Officials; Conspiracy to Defraud by Interference with Governmental Functions

(a) Base Offense Level:

    (1) **14**, if the defendant was a public official; or

    (2) **12**, otherwise.

(b) Specific Offense Characteristics

    (1) If the offense involved more than one bribe or extortion, increase by **2** levels.

(2) If the value of the payment, the benefit received or to be received in return for the payment, the value of anything obtained or to be obtained by a public official or others acting with a public official, or the loss to the government from the offense, whichever is greatest, exceeded $5,000, increase by the number of levels from the table in §2B1.1 (Theft, Property Destruction, and Fraud) corresponding to that amount.

(3) If the offense involved an elected public official or any public official in a high-level decision-making or sensitive position, increase by **4** levels. If the resulting offense level is less than level **18**, increase to level **18**.

(4) If the defendant was a public official who facilitated (A) entry into the United States for a person, a vehicle, or cargo; (B) the obtaining of a passport or a document relating to naturalization, citizenship, legal entry, or legal resident status; or (C) the obtaining of a government identification document, increase by **2** levels.

(c) Cross References

(1) If the offense was committed for the purpose of facilitating the commission of another criminal offense, apply the offense guideline applicable to a conspiracy to commit that other offense, if the resulting offense level is greater than that determined above.

(2) If the offense was committed for the purpose of concealing, or obstructing justice in respect to, another criminal offense, apply §2X3.1 (Accessory After the Fact) or §2J1.2 (Obstruction of Justice), as appropriate, in respect to that other offense, if the resulting offense level is greater than that determined above.

(3) If the offense involved a threat of physical injury or property destruction, apply §2B3.2 (Extortion by Force or Threat of Injury or Serious Damage), if the resulting offense level is greater than that determined above.

(d) Special Instruction for Fines - Organizations

(1) In lieu of the pecuniary loss under subsection (a)(3) of §8C2.4 (Base Fine), use the greatest of: (A) the value of the unlawful payment; (B) the value of the benefit received or to be received in return for the unlawful payment; or (C) the consequential damages resulting from the unlawful payment.

Commentary

Statutory Provisions: 15 U.S.C. §§ 78dd-1, 78dd-2, 78dd-3; 18 U.S.C. §§ 201(b)(1), (2), 226, 227, 371 (if conspiracy to defraud by interference with governmental functions), 872, 1341 (if the scheme or artifice to defraud was to deprive another of the intangible right of honest services of a public official), 1342 (if the scheme or artifice to defraud was to deprive another of the intangible right of honest services of a public official), 1343 (if the scheme or artifice to defraud was to deprive another of the intangible right of honest services of a public official), 1951. For additional statutory provision(s), see Appendix A (Statutory Index).

Application Notes:

1. *Definitions.*—*For purposes of this guideline:*

"Government identification document" means a document made or issued by or under the authority of the United States Government, a State, or a political subdivision of a State, which, when completed with information concerning a particular individual, is of a type intended or commonly accepted for the purpose of identification of individuals.

"Payment" means anything of value. A payment need not be monetary.

"Public official" shall be construed broadly and includes the following:

(A) "Public official" as defined in 18 U.S.C. § 201(a)(1).

(B) A member of a state or local legislature. "State" means a State of the United States, and any commonwealth, territory, or possession of the United States.

(C) An officer or employee or person acting for or on behalf of a state or local government, or any department, agency, or branch of government thereof, in any official function, under or by authority of such department, agency, or branch of government, or a juror in a state or local trial.

(D) Any person who has been selected to be a person described in subdivisions (A), (B), or (C), either before or after such person has qualified.

(E) An individual who, although not otherwise covered by subdivisions (A) through (D): (i) is in a position of public trust with official responsibility for carrying out a government program or policy; (ii) acts under color of law or official right; or (iii) participates so substantially in government operations as to possess de facto authority to make governmental decisions (e.g., which may include a leader of a state or local political party who acts in the manner described in this subdivision).

2. *More than One Bribe or Extortion.*—*Subsection (b)(1) provides an adjustment for offenses involving more than one incident of either bribery or extortion. Related payments that, in essence, constitute a single incident of bribery or extortion (e.g., a number of installment payments for a single action) are to be treated as a single bribe or extortion, even if charged in separate counts.*

In a case involving more than one incident of bribery or extortion, the applicable amounts under subsection (b)(2) (i.e., the greatest of the value of the payment, the benefit received or to be received, the value of anything obtained or to be obtained by a public official or others acting with a public official, or the loss to the government) are determined separately for each incident and then added together.

3. *Application of Subsection (b)(2).–"Loss", for purposes of subsection (b)(2), shall be determined in accordance with Application Note 3 of the Commentary to §2B1.1 (Theft, Property Destruction, and Fraud). The value of "the benefit received or to be received" means the net value of such benefit. Examples: (A) A government employee, in return for a $500 bribe, reduces the price of a piece of surplus property offered for sale by the government from $10,000 to $2,000; the value of the benefit received is $8,000. (B) A $150,000 contract on which $20,000 profit was made was awarded in return for a bribe; the value of the benefit received is $20,000. Do not deduct the value of the bribe itself in computing the value of the benefit received or to be received. In the preceding examples, therefore, the value of the benefit received would be the same regardless of the value of the bribe.*

4. *Application of Subsection (b)(3).—*

(A) Definition.— "High-level decision-making or sensitive position" means a position characterized by a direct authority to make decisions for, or on behalf of, a government department, agency, or other government entity, or by a substantial influence over the decision-making process.

(B) Examples.—Examples of a public official in a high-level decision-making position include a prosecuting attorney, a judge, an agency administrator, and any other public official with a similar level of authority. Examples of a public official who holds a sensitive position include a juror, a law enforcement officer, an election official, and any other similarly situated individual.

5. *Application of Subsection (c).—For the purposes of determining whether to apply the cross references in this section, the "resulting offense level" means the final offense level (i.e., the offense level determined by taking into account both the Chapter Two offense level and any applicable adjustments from Chapter Three, Parts A-D). See §1B1.5(d); Application Note 2 of the Commentary to §1B1.5 (Interpretation of References to Other Offense Guidelines).*

6. *Inapplicability of §3B1.3.—Do not apply §3B1.3 (Abuse of Position of Trust or Use of Special Skill).*

7. *Upward Departure Provisions.—In some cases the monetary value of the unlawful payment may not be known or may not adequately reflect the seriousness of the offense. For example, a small payment may be made in exchange for the falsification of inspection records for a shipment of defective parachutes or the destruction of evidence in a major narcotics case. In part, this issue is addressed by the enhancements in §2C1.1(b)(2) and (c)(1), (2), and (3). However, in cases in which the seriousness of the offense is still not adequately reflected, an upward departure is warranted. See Chapter Five, Part K (Departures).*

In a case in which the court finds that the defendant's conduct was part of a systematic or pervasive corruption of a governmental function, process, or office that may cause loss of public confidence in government, an upward departure may be warranted. See §5K2.7 (Disruption of Governmental Function).

Background: This section applies to a person who offers or gives a bribe for a corrupt purpose, such as inducing a public official to participate in a fraud or to influence such individual's official actions, or to a public official who solicits or accepts such a bribe.

The object and nature of a bribe may vary widely from case to case. In some cases, the object may be commercial advantage (e.g., preferential treatment in the award of a government contract). In others, the object may be issuance of a license to which the recipient is not entitled. In still others, the object may be the obstruction of justice. Consequently, a guideline for the offense must be designed to cover diverse situations.

In determining the net value of the benefit received or to be received, the value of the bribe is not deducted from the gross value of such benefit; the harm is the same regardless of value of the bribe paid to receive the benefit. In a case in which the value of the bribe exceeds the value of the benefit, or in which the value of the benefit cannot be determined, the value of the bribe is used because it is likely that the payer of such a bribe expected something in return that would be worth more than the value of the bribe. Moreover, for deterrence purposes, the punishment should be commensurate with the gain to the payer or the recipient of the bribe, whichever is greater.

Under §2C1.1(b)(3), if the payment was for the purpose of influencing an official act by certain officials, the offense level is increased by 4 levels.

Under §2C1.1(c)(1), if the payment was to facilitate the commission of another criminal offense, the guideline applicable to a conspiracy to commit that other offense will apply if the result is greater than that determined above. For example, if a bribe was given to a law enforcement officer to allow the smuggling of a quantity of cocaine, the guideline for conspiracy to import cocaine would be applied if it resulted in a greater offense level.

Under §2C1.1(c)(2), if the payment was to conceal another criminal offense or obstruct justice in respect to another criminal offense, the guideline from §2X3.1 (Accessory After the Fact) or §2J1.2 (Obstruction of Justice), as appropriate, will apply if the result is greater than that determined above. For example, if a bribe was given for the purpose of concealing the offense of espionage, the guideline for accessory after the fact to espionage would be applied.

Under §2C1.1(c)(3), if the offense involved forcible extortion, the guideline from §2B3.2 (Extortion by Force or Threat of Injury or Serious Damage) will apply if the result is greater than that determined above.

Section 2C1.1 also applies to offenses under 15 U.S.C. §§ 78dd-1, 78dd-2, and 78dd-3. Such offenses generally involve a payment to a foreign public official, candidate for public office, or agent or intermediary, with the intent to influence an official act or decision of a foreign government or political party. Typically, a case prosecuted under these provisions will involve an intent to influence governmental action.

Section 2C1.1 also applies to fraud involving the deprivation of the intangible right to honest services of government officials under 18 U.S.C. §§ 1341-1343 and conspiracy to defraud by interference with governmental functions under 18 U.S.C. § 371. Such fraud offenses typically involve an improper use of government influence that harms the operation of government in a manner similar to bribery offenses.

Offenses involving attempted bribery are frequently not completed because the offense is reported to authorities or an individual involved in the offense is acting in an undercover capacity. Failure to complete the offense does not lessen the defendant's culpability in attempting to use public position for personal gain. Therefore, solicitations and attempts are treated as equivalent to the underlying offense.

<u>Historical Note</u>: Effective November 1, 1987. Amended effective January 15, 1988 (<u>see</u> Appendix C, amendment 18); November 1, 1989 (<u>see</u> Appendix C, amendments 120-122); November 1, 1991 (<u>see</u> Appendix C, amendments 367 and 422); November 1, 1997 (<u>see</u> Appendix C, amendment 547); November 1, 2001 (<u>see</u> Appendix C, amendment 617); November 1, 2002 (<u>see</u> Appendix C, amendment 639); November 1, 2003 (<u>see</u> Appendix C, amendment 653); November 1, 2004 (<u>see</u> Appendix C, amendment 666); November 1, 2007 (<u>see</u> Appendix C, amendment 699); November 1, 2008 (<u>see</u> Appendix C, amendment 720); November 1, 2010 (<u>see</u> Appendix C, amendment 746).

§2C1.2. Offering, Giving, Soliciting, or Receiving a Gratuity

(a) Base Offense Level:

    (1) **11**, if the defendant was a public official; or

    (2) **9**, otherwise.

(b) Specific Offense Characteristics

    (1) If the offense involved more than one gratuity, increase by **2** levels.

    (2) If the value of the gratuity exceeded $5,000, increase by the number of levels from the table in §2B1.1 (Theft, Property Destruction, and Fraud) corresponding to that amount.

    (3) If the offense involved an elected public official or any public official in a high-level decision-making or sensitive position, increase by **4** levels. If the resulting offense level is less than level **15**, increase to level **15**.

(4) If the defendant was a public official who facilitated (A) entry into the United States for a person, a vehicle, or cargo; (B) the obtaining of a passport or a document relating to naturalization, citizenship, legal entry, or legal resident status; or (C) the obtaining of a government identification document, increase by **2** levels.

(c) Special Instruction for Fines - Organizations

(1) In lieu of the pecuniary loss under subsection (a)(3) of §8C2.4 (Base Fine), use the value of the unlawful payment.

Commentary

Statutory Provisions: 18 U.S.C. §§ 201(c)(1), 212-214, 217. For additional statutory provision(s), see Appendix A (Statutory Index).

Application Notes:

1. Definitions.—For purposes of this guideline:

"Government identification document" means a document made or issued by or under the authority of the United States Government, a State, or a political subdivision of a State, which, when completed with information concerning a particular individual, is of a type intended or commonly accepted for the purpose of identification of individuals.

"Public official" shall be construed broadly and includes the following:

(A) "Public official" as defined in 18 U.S.C. § 201(a)(1).

(B) A member of a state or local legislature. "State" means a State of the United States, and any commonwealth, territory, or possession of the United States.

(C) An officer or employee or person acting for or on behalf of a state or local government, or any department, agency, or branch of government thereof, in any official function, under or by authority of such department, agency, or branch of government, or a juror.

(D) Any person who has been selected to be a person described in subdivisions (A), (B), or (C), either before or after such person has qualified.

(E) An individual who, although not otherwise covered by subdivisions (A) through (D): (i) is in a position of public trust with official responsibility for carrying out a government program or policy; (ii) acts under color of law or official right; or (iii) participates so substantially in government operations as to possess de facto authority to make governmental decisions (e.g., which may include a leader of a state or local political party who acts in the manner described in this subdivision).

2. *Application of Subsection (b)(1).*—Related payments that, in essence, constitute a single gratuity (*e.g.*, separate payments for airfare and hotel for a single vacation trip) are to be treated as a single gratuity, even if charged in separate counts.

3. *Application of Subsection (b)(3).*—

(A) *Definition.*—"High-level decision-making or sensitive position" means a position characterized by a direct authority to make decisions for, or on behalf of, a government department, agency, or other government entity, or by a substantial influence over the decision-making process.

(B) *Examples.*—Examples of a public official in a high-level decision-making position include a prosecuting attorney, a judge, an agency administrator, a law enforcement officer, and any other public official with a similar level of authority. Examples of a public official who holds a sensitive position include a juror, a law enforcement officer, an election official, and any other similarly situated individual.

4. *Inapplicability of §3B1.3.*—Do not apply the adjustment in §3B1.3 (Abuse of Position of Trust or Use of Special Skill).

Background: This section applies to the offering, giving, soliciting, or receiving of a gratuity to a public official in respect to an official act. It also applies in cases involving (1) the offer to, or acceptance by, a bank examiner of a loan or gratuity; (2) the offer or receipt of anything of value for procuring a loan or discount of commercial bank paper from a Federal Reserve Bank; and (3) the acceptance of a fee or other consideration by a federal employee for adjusting or cancelling a farm debt.

Historical Note: Effective November 1, 1987. Amended effective November 1, 1989 (*see* Appendix C, amendment 121); November 1, 1991 (*see* Appendix C, amendment 422); November 1, 1995 (*see* Appendix C, amendment 534); November 1, 2001 (*see* Appendix C, amendment 617); November 1, 2004 (*see* Appendix C, amendment 666); November 1, 2010 (*see* Appendix C, amendment 746).

PART J - OFFENSES INVOLVING THE ADMINISTRATION OF JUSTICE

§2J1.2. Obstruction of Justice

(a) Base Offense Level: **14**

(b) Specific Offense Characteristics

(1) (Apply the greatest):

(A) If the (i) defendant was convicted under 18 U.S.C. § 1001; and (ii) statutory maximum term of eight years' imprisonment applies because the matter relates to sex offenses under 18 U.S.C. § 1591 or chapters 109A, 109B, 110, or 117 of title 18, United States Code, increase by **4** levels.

(B) If the offense involved causing or threatening to cause physical injury to a person, or property damage, in order to obstruct the administration of justice, increase by **8** levels.

(C) If the (i) defendant was convicted under 18 U.S.C. § 1001 or § 1505; and (ii) statutory maximum term of eight years' imprisonment applies because the matter relates to international terrorism or domestic terrorism, increase by **12** levels.

(2) If the offense resulted in substantial interference with the administration of justice, increase by **3** levels.

(3) If the offense (A) involved the destruction, alteration, or fabrication of a substantial number of records, documents, or tangible objects; (B) involved the selection of any essential or especially probative record, document, or tangible object, to destroy or alter; or (C) was otherwise extensive in scope, planning, or preparation, increase by **2** levels.

(c) Cross Reference

(1) If the offense involved obstructing the investigation or prosecution of a criminal offense, apply §2X3.1 (Accessory After the Fact) in respect to that criminal offense, if the resulting offense level is greater than that determined above.

Commentary

Statutory Provisions: 18 U.S.C. §§ 1001 (when the statutory maximum term of eight years' imprisonment applies because the matter relates to international terrorism or domestic terrorism, or to sex offenses under 18 U.S.C. § 1591 or chapters 109A, 109B, 110, or 117 of title 18, United States Code), 1503, 1505-1513, 1516, 1519. For additional statutory provision(s), see Appendix A (Statutory Index).

Application Notes:

1. Definitions.—For purposes of this guideline:

"Domestic terrorism" has the meaning given that term in 18 U.S.C. § 2331(5).

"International terrorism" has the meaning given that term in 18 U.S.C. § 2331(1).

"Records, documents, or tangible objects" includes (A) records, documents, or tangible objects that are stored on, or that are, magnetic, optical, digital, other electronic, or other storage mediums or devices; and (B) wire or electronic communications.

"Substantial interference with the administration of justice" includes a premature or improper termination of a felony investigation; an indictment, verdict, or any judicial determination based upon perjury, false testimony, or other false evidence; or the unnecessary expenditure of substantial governmental or court resources.

2. Chapter Three Adjustments.—

(A) Inapplicability of §3C1.1.—For offenses covered under this section, §3C1.1 (Obstructing or Impeding the Administration of Justice) does not apply, unless the defendant obstructed the investigation, prosecution, or sentencing of the obstruction of justice count.

(B) Interaction with Terrorism Adjustment.—If §3A1.4 (Terrorism) applies, do not apply subsection (b)(1)(C).

3. Convictions for the Underlying Offense.—In the event that the defendant is convicted of an offense sentenced under this section as well as for the underlying offense (i.e., the offense that is the object of the obstruction), see the Commentary to Chapter Three, Part C (Obstruction and Related Adjustments), and to §3D1.2(c) (Groups of Closely Related Counts).

4. Upward Departure Considerations.—If a weapon was used, or bodily injury or significant property damage resulted, an upward departure may be warranted. See Chapter Five, Part K (Departures). In a case involving an act of extreme violence (for example, retaliating against a government witness by throwing acid in the witness's face) or a particularly serious sex offense, an upward departure would be warranted.

5. Subsection (b)(1)(B).—The inclusion of "property damage" under subsection (b)(1)(B) is designed to address cases in which property damage is caused or threatened as a means of intimidation or retaliation (e.g., to intimidate a witness from, or retaliate against a witness for, testifying). Subsection (b)(1)(B) is not intended to apply, for example, where the offense consisted of destroying a ledger containing an incriminating entry.

Background: This section addresses offenses involving the obstruction of justice generally prosecuted under the above-referenced statutory provisions. Numerous offenses of varying seriousness may constitute obstruction of justice: using threats or force to intimidate or influence a juror or federal officer; obstructing a civil or administrative proceeding; stealing or altering court records; unlawfully intercepting grand jury deliberations; obstructing a criminal investigation; obstructing a state or local investigation of illegal gambling; using intimidation or force to influence testimony, alter evidence, evade legal process, or obstruct the communication of a judge or law enforcement officer; or causing a witness bodily injury or property damage in retaliation for providing testimony, information or evidence in a federal proceeding. The conduct that gives rise to the violation may, therefore, range from a mere threat to an act of extreme violence.

The specific offense characteristics reflect the more serious forms of obstruction. Because the conduct covered by this guideline is frequently part of an effort to avoid punishment for an offense that the defendant has committed or to assist another person to escape punishment for an offense, a cross reference to §2X3.1 (Accessory After the Fact) is provided. Use of this cross reference will provide an enhanced offense level when the obstruction is in respect to a particularly serious offense, whether such offense was committed by the defendant or another person.

<u>Historical Note</u>: *Effective November 1, 1987. Amended effective November 1, 1989 (<u>see</u> Appendix C, amendments 172-174); November 1, 1991 (<u>see</u> Appendix C, amendment 401); January 25, 2003 (<u>see</u> Appendix C, amendment 647); November 1, 2003 (<u>see</u> Appendix C, amendment 653); October 24, 2005 (<u>see</u> Appendix C, amendment 676); November 1, 2006 (<u>see</u> Appendix C, amendment 690); November 1, 2007 (<u>see</u> Appendix C, amendment 701); November 1, 2011 (<u>see</u> Appendix C, amendment 758); November 1, 2013 (<u>see</u> Appendix C, amendment 777).*

§2J1.3. Perjury or Subornation of Perjury; Bribery of Witness

(a) Base Offense Level: **14**

(b) Specific Offense Characteristics

   (1) If the offense involved causing or threatening to cause physical injury to a person, or property damage, in order to suborn perjury, increase by **8** levels.

   (2) If the perjury, subornation of perjury, or witness bribery resulted in substantial interference with the administration of justice, increase by **3** levels.

(c) Cross Reference

   (1) If the offense involved perjury, subornation of perjury, or witness bribery in respect to a criminal offense, apply §2X3.1 (Accessory After the Fact) in respect to that criminal offense, if the resulting offense level is greater than that determined above.

(d) Special Instruction

   (1) In the case of counts of perjury or subornation of perjury arising from testimony given, or to be given, in separate proceedings, do not group the counts together under §3D1.2 (Groups of Closely Related Counts).

Commentary

Statutory Provisions: 18 U.S.C. §§ 201(b)(3), (4), 1621-1623. For additional statutory provision(s), see Appendix A (Statutory Index).

Application Notes:

1. "Substantial interference with the administration of justice" includes a premature or improper termination of a felony investigation; an indictment, verdict, or any judicial determination based upon perjury, false testimony, or other false evidence; or the unnecessary expenditure of substantial governmental or court resources.

2. For offenses covered under this section, §3C1.1 (Obstructing or Impeding the Administration of Justice) does not apply, unless the defendant obstructed the investigation or trial of the perjury count.

3. In the event that the defendant is convicted under this section as well as for the underlying offense (i.e., the offense with respect to which he committed perjury, subornation of perjury, or witness bribery), see the Commentary to §3C1.1, and to §3D1.2(c) (Groups of Closely Related Counts).

4. If a weapon was used, or bodily injury or significant property damage resulted, an upward departure may be warranted. See Chapter Five, Part K (Departures).

5. "Separate proceedings," as used in subsection (d)(1), includes different proceedings in the same case or matter (e.g., a grand jury proceeding and a trial, or a trial and retrial), and proceedings in separate cases or matters (e.g., separate trials of codefendants), but does not include multiple grand jury proceedings in the same case.

Background: This section applies to perjury, subornation of perjury, and witness bribery, generally prosecuted under the referenced statutes. The guidelines provide a higher penalty for perjury than the pre-guidelines practice estimate of ten months imprisonment. The Commission believes that perjury should be treated similarly to obstruction of justice. Therefore, the same considerations for enhancing a sentence are applied in the specific offense characteristics, and an alternative reference to the guideline for accessory after the fact is made.

Historical Note: Effective November 1, 1987. Amended effective November 1, 1989 (see Appendix C, amendment 175); November 1, 1991 (see Appendix C, amendments 401 and 402); November 1, 1993 (see Appendix C, amendment 481); November 1, 2003 (see Appendix C, amendment 653); November 1, 2011 (see Appendix C, amendment 758); November 1, 2013 (see Appendix C, amendment 777).

PART S - MONEY LAUNDERING AND MONETARY TRANSACTION REPORTING

§2S1.1. Laundering of Monetary Instruments; Engaging in Monetary Transactions in Property Derived from Unlawful Activity

(a) Base Offense Level:

(1) The offense level for the underlying offense from which the laundered funds were derived, if (A) the defendant committed the underlying offense (or would be accountable for the underlying offense under subsection (a)(1)(A) of §1B1.3 (Relevant Conduct)); and (B) the offense level for that offense can be determined; or

(2) 8 plus the number of offense levels from the table in §2B1.1 (Theft, Property Destruction, and Fraud) corresponding to the value of the laundered funds, otherwise.

(b) Specific Offense Characteristics

(1) If (A) subsection (a)(2) applies; and (B) the defendant knew or believed that any of the laundered funds were the proceeds of, or were intended to promote (i) an offense involving the manufacture, importation, or distribution of a controlled substance or a listed chemical; (ii) a crime of violence; or (iii) an offense involving firearms, explosives, national security, or the sexual exploitation of a minor, increase by 6 levels.

(2) (Apply the Greatest):

(A) If the defendant was convicted under 18 U.S.C. § 1957, increase by 1 level.

(B) If the defendant was convicted under 18 U.S.C. § 1956, increase by 2 levels.

(C) If (i) subsection (a)(2) applies; and (ii) the defendant was in the business of laundering funds, increase by 4 levels.

(3) If (A) subsection (b)(2)(B) applies; and (B) the offense involved sophisticated laundering, increase by 2 levels.

Commentary

Statutory Provisions: 18 U.S.C. §§ 1956, 1957, 1960 (but only with respect to unlicensed money transmitting businesses as defined in 18 U.S.C. §

1960(b)(1)(C)). For additional statutory provision(s), see Appendix A (Statutory Index).

Application Notes:

1. *Definitions.—For purposes of this guideline:*

"Crime of violence" has the meaning given that term in subsection (a)(1) of §4B1.2 (Definitions of Terms Used in Section 4B1.1).

"Criminally derived funds" means any funds derived, or represented by a law enforcement officer, or by another person at the direction or approval of an authorized Federal official, to be derived from conduct constituting a criminal offense.

"Laundered funds" means the property, funds, or monetary instrument involved in the transaction, financial transaction, monetary transaction, transportation, transfer, or transmission in violation of 18 U.S.C. § 1956 or § 1957.

"Laundering funds" means making a transaction, financial transaction, monetary transaction, or transmission, or transporting or transferring property, funds, or a monetary instrument in violation of 18 U.S.C. § 1956 or § 1957.

"Sexual exploitation of a minor" means an offense involving (A) promoting prostitution by a minor; (B) sexually exploiting a minor by production of sexually explicit visual or printed material; (C) distribution of material involving the sexual exploitation of a minor, or possession of material involving the sexual exploitation of a minor with intent to distribute; or (D) aggravated sexual abuse, sexual abuse, or abusive sexual contact involving a minor. "Minor" means an individual under the age of 18 years.

2. *Application of Subsection (a)(1).—*

   (A) *Multiple Underlying Offenses.—In cases in which subsection (a)(1) applies and there is more than one underlying offense, the offense level for the underlying offense is to be determined under the procedures set forth in Application Note 3 of the Commentary to §1B1.5 (Interpretation of References to Other Offense Guidelines).*

   (B) *Defendants Accountable for Underlying Offense. In order for subsection (a)(1) to apply, the defendant must have committed the underlying offense or be accountable for the underlying offense under §1B1.3(a)(1)(A). The fact that the defendant was involved in laundering criminally derived funds after the commission of the underlying offense, without additional involvement in the underlying offense, does not establish that the defendant committed, aided, abetted, counseled, commanded, induced, procured, or willfully caused the underlying offense.*

(C) Application of Chapter Three Adjustments.—Notwithstanding §1B1.5(c), in cases in which subsection (a)(1) applies, application of any Chapter Three adjustment shall be determined based on the offense covered by this guideline (i.e., the laundering of criminally derived funds) and not on the underlying offense from which the laundered funds were derived.

3. *Application of Subsection (a)(2).—*

(A) In General.—Subsection (a)(2) applies to any case in which (i) the defendant did not commit the underlying offense; or (ii) the defendant committed the underlying offense (or would be accountable for the underlying offense under §1B1.3(a)(1)(A)), but the offense level for the underlying offense is impossible or impracticable to determine.

(B) Commingled Funds.—In a case in which a transaction, financial transaction, monetary transaction, transportation, transfer, or transmission results in the commingling of legitimately derived funds with criminally derived funds, the value of the laundered funds, for purposes of subsection (a)(2), is the amount of the criminally derived funds, not the total amount of the commingled funds, if the defendant provides sufficient information to determine the amount of criminally derived funds without unduly complicating or prolonging the sentencing process. If the amount of the criminally derived funds is difficult or impracticable to determine, the value of the laundered funds, for purposes of subsection (a)(2), is the total amount of the commingled funds.

(C) Non-Applicability of Enhancement.—Subsection (b)(2)(B) shall not apply if the defendant was convicted of a conspiracy under 18 U.S.C. § 1956(h) and the sole object of that conspiracy was to commit an offense set forth in 18 U.S.C. § 1957.

4. *Enhancement for Business of Laundering Funds.—*

(A) In General.—The court shall consider the totality of the circumstances to determine whether a defendant who did not commit the underlying offense was in the business of laundering funds, for purposes of subsection (b)(2)(C).

(B) Factors to Consider.—The following is a non-exhaustive list of factors that may indicate the defendant was in the business of laundering funds for purposes of subsection (b)(2)(C):

(i) The defendant regularly engaged in laundering funds.

(ii) The defendant engaged in laundering funds during an extended period of time.

(iii) The defendant engaged in laundering funds from multiple sources.

(iv) The defendant generated a substantial amount of revenue in return for laundering funds.

(v) At the time the defendant committed the instant offense, the defendant had one or more prior convictions for an offense under 18 U.S.C. § 1956 or § 1957, or under 31 U.S.C. § 5313, § 5314, § 5316, § 5324 or § 5326, or any similar offense under state law, or an attempt or conspiracy to commit any such federal or state offense. A conviction taken into account under subsection (b)(2)(C) is not excluded from consideration of whether that conviction receives criminal history points pursuant to Chapter Four, Part A (Criminal History).

(vi) During the course of an undercover government investigation, the defendant made statements that the defendant engaged in any of the conduct described in subdivisions (i) through (iv).

5. (A) Sophisticated Laundering under Subsection (b)(3).—For purposes of subsection (b)(3), "sophisticated laundering" means complex or intricate offense conduct pertaining to the execution or concealment of the 18 U.S.C. § 1956 offense.

Sophisticated laundering typically involves the use of—

(i) fictitious entities;

(ii) shell corporations;

(iii) two or more levels (i.e., layering) of transactions, transportation, transfers, or transmissions, involving criminally derived funds that were intended to appear legitimate; or

(iv) offshore financial accounts.

(B) Non-Applicability of Enhancement.—If subsection (b)(3) applies, and the conduct that forms the basis for an enhancement under the guideline applicable to the underlying offense is the only conduct that forms the basis for application of subsection (b)(3) of this guideline, do not apply subsection (b)(3) of this guideline.

6. Grouping of Multiple Counts.—In a case in which the defendant is convicted of a count of laundering funds and a count for the underlying offense from which the laundered funds were derived, the counts shall be grouped pursuant to subsection (c) of §3D1.2 (Groups of Closely-Related Counts).

Historical Note: Effective November 1, 1987. Amended effective November 1, 1989 (see Appendix C, amendments 212-214); November 1, 1991 (see Appendix C, amendments 378 and 422); November 1, 2001 (see Appendix C, amendment 634); November 1, 2003 (see Appendix C, amendment 655).

§2S1.3. Structuring Transactions to Evade Reporting Requirements; Failure to Report Cash or Monetary Transactions; Failure to File Currency and Monetary Instrument Report; Knowingly Filing False Reports; Bulk Cash Smuggling; Establishing or Maintaining Prohibited Accounts

(a) Base Offense Level:

(1) **8**, if the defendant was convicted under 31 U.S.C. § 5318 or § 5318A; or

(2) **6** plus the number of offense levels from the table in §2B1.1 (Theft, Property Destruction, and Fraud) corresponding to the value of the funds, if subsection (a)(1) does not apply.

(b) Specific Offense Characteristics

(1) If (A) the defendant knew or believed that the funds were proceeds of unlawful activity, or were intended to promote unlawful activity; or (B) the offense involved bulk cash smuggling, increase by **2** levels.

(2) If the defendant (A) was convicted of an offense under subchapter II of chapter 53 of title 31, United States Code; and (B) committed the offense as part of a pattern of unlawful activity involving more than $100,000 in a 12-month period, increase by **2** levels.

(3) If (A) subsection (a)(2) applies and subsections (b)(1) and (b)(2) do not apply; (B) the defendant did not act with reckless disregard of the source of the funds; (C) the funds were the proceeds of lawful activity; and (D) the funds were to be used for a lawful purpose, decrease the offense level to level **6**.

(c) Cross Reference

(1) If the offense was committed for the purposes of violating the Internal Revenue laws, apply the most appropriate guideline from Chapter Two, Part T (Offenses Involving Taxation) if the resulting offense level is greater than that determined above.

Commentary

Statutory Provisions: 18 U.S.C. § 1960 (but only with respect to unlicensed money transmitting businesses as defined in 18 U.S.C. § 1960(b)(1)(A) and (B)); 26 U.S.C. §§ 7203 (if a violation based upon 26 U.S.C. § 6050I), 7206 (if a violation based upon 26 U.S.C. § 6050I); 31 U.S.C. §§ 5313, 5314, 5316, 5318, 5318A(b), 5322, 5324, 5326, 5331, 5332. For additional statutory provision(s), *see* Appendix A (Statutory Index).

Application Notes:

1. *Definition of "Value of the Funds".*—For purposes of this guideline, "value of the funds" means the amount of the funds involved in the structuring or reporting conduct. The relevant statutes require monetary reporting without regard to whether the funds were lawfully or unlawfully obtained.

2. *Bulk Cash Smuggling.*—For purposes of subsection (b)(1)(B), "bulk cash smuggling" means (A) knowingly concealing, with the intent to evade a currency reporting requirement under 31 U.S.C. § 5316, more than $10,000 in currency or other monetary instruments; and (B) transporting or transferring (or attempting to transport or transfer) such currency or monetary instruments into or outside of the United States. "United States" has the meaning given that term in Application Note 1 of the Commentary to §2B5.1 (Offenses Involving Counterfeit Bearer Obligations of the United States).

3. *Enhancement for Pattern of Unlawful Activity.*—For purposes of subsection (b)(2), "pattern of unlawful activity" means at least two separate occasions of unlawful activity involving a total amount of more than $100,000 in a 12-month period, without regard to whether any such occasion occurred during the course of the offense or resulted in a conviction for the conduct that occurred on that occasion.

Background: Some of the offenses covered by this guideline relate to records and reports of certain transactions involving currency and monetary instruments. These reports include Currency Transaction Reports, Currency and Monetary Instrument Reports, Reports of Foreign Bank and Financial Accounts, and Reports of Cash Payments Over $10,000 Received in a Trade or Business.

This guideline also covers offenses under 31 U.S.C. §§ 5318 and 5318A, pertaining to records, reporting and identification requirements, prohibited accounts involving certain foreign jurisdictions, foreign institutions, and foreign banks, and other types of transactions and types of accounts.

Historical Note: Effective November 1, 1987. Amended effective November 1, 1989 (see Appendix C, amendments 216-218); November 1, 1991 (see Appendix C, amendments 379 and 422); November 1, 1993 (see Appendix C, amendment 490); November 1, 2001 (see Appendix C, amendments 617 and 634); November 1, 2002 (see Appendix C, amendment 637); November 1, 2003 (see Appendix C, amendment 655).

CHAPTER THREE–ADJUSTMENTS

PART B–ROLE IN THE OFFENSE

§3B1.3. Abuse of Position of Trust or Use of Special Skill

If the defendant abused a position of public or private trust, or used a special skill, in a manner that significantly facilitated the commission or concealment of the offense, increase by **2** levels. This adjustment may not be employed if an abuse of trust or skill is included in the base offense level or specific offense characteristic. If this adjustment is based upon an abuse of a position of trust, it may be employed in addition to an adjustment under §3B1.1 (Aggravating Role); if this adjustment is based solely on the use of a special skill, it may not be employed in addition to an adjustment under §3B1.1 (Aggravating Role).

Commentary

Application Notes:

1. *Definition of "Public or Private Trust".*—*"Public or private trust" refers to a position of public or private trust characterized by professional or managerial discretion (i.e., substantial discretionary judgment that is ordinarily given considerable deference). Persons holding such positions ordinarily are subject to significantly less supervision than employees whose responsibilities are primarily non-discretionary in nature. For this adjustment to apply, the position of public or private trust must have contributed in some significant way to facilitating the commission or concealment of the offense (e.g., by making the detection of the offense or the defendant's responsibility for the offense more difficult). This adjustment, for example, applies in the case of an embezzlement of a client's funds by an attorney serving as a guardian, a bank executive's fraudulent loan scheme, or the criminal sexual abuse of a patient by a physician under the guise of an examination. This adjustment does not apply in the case of an embezzlement or theft by an ordinary bank teller or hotel clerk because such positions are not characterized by the above-described factors.*

2. *Application of Adjustment in Certain Circumstances.*—*Notwithstanding Application Note 1, or any other provision of this guideline, an adjustment under this guideline shall apply to the following:*

(A) An employee of the United States Postal Service who engages in the theft or destruction of undelivered United States mail.

(B) A defendant who exceeds or abuses the authority of his or her position in order to obtain, transfer, or issue unlawfully, or use without authority, any means of identification. "Means of identification" has the meaning given that term in 18 U.S.C. § 1028(d)(7). The following are examples to which this subdivision would apply: (i) an employee of a state motor vehicle department who exceeds or abuses the authority of his or her position by knowingly issuing a driver's license based on false, incomplete, or misleading information; (ii) a hospital orderly who exceeds or abuses the authority of his

or her position by obtaining or misusing patient identification information from a patient chart; and (iii) a volunteer at a charitable organization who exceeds or abuses the authority of his or her position by obtaining or misusing identification information from a donor's file.

3. This adjustment also applies in a case in which the defendant provides sufficient indicia to the victim that the defendant legitimately holds a position of private or public trust when, in fact, the defendant does not. For example, the adjustment applies in the case of a defendant who (A) perpetrates a financial fraud by leading an investor to believe the defendant is a legitimate investment broker; or (B) perpetrates a fraud by representing falsely to a patient or employer that the defendant is a licensed physician. In making the misrepresentation, the defendant assumes a position of trust, relative to the victim, that provides the defendant with the same opportunity to commit a difficult-to-detect crime that the defendant would have had if the position were held legitimately.

4. "Special skill" refers to a skill not possessed by members of the general public and usually requiring substantial education, training or licensing. Examples would include pilots, lawyers, doctors, accountants, chemists, and demolition experts.

5. The following additional illustrations of an abuse of a position of trust pertain to theft or embezzlement from employee pension or welfare benefit plans or labor unions:

(A) If the offense involved theft or embezzlement from an employee pension or welfare benefit plan and the defendant was a fiduciary of the benefit plan, an adjustment under this section for abuse of a position of trust will apply. "Fiduciary of the benefit plan" is defined in 29 U.S.C. § 1002(21)(A) to mean a person who exercises any discretionary authority or control in respect to the management of such plan or exercises authority or control in respect to management or disposition of its assets, or who renders investment advice for a fee or other direct or indirect compensation with respect to any moneys or other property of such plan, or has any authority or responsibility to do so, or who has any discretionary authority or responsibility in the administration of such plan.

(B) If the offense involved theft or embezzlement from a labor union and the defendant was a union officer or occupied a position of trust in the union (as set forth in 29 U.S.C. § 501(a)), an adjustment under this section for an abuse of a position of trust will apply.

Background: This adjustment applies to persons who abuse their positions of trust or their special skills to facilitate significantly the commission or concealment of a crime. The adjustment also applies to persons who provide sufficient indicia to the victim that they legitimately hold a position of public or private trust when, in fact, they do not. Such persons generally are viewed as more culpable.

Historical Note: Effective November 1, 1987. Amended effective November 1, 1990 (see Appendix C, amendment 346); November 1, 1993 (see Appendix C, amendment 492); November 1, 1998 (see Appendix C, amendment 580); November 1, 2001 (see Appendix C, amendment 617); November 1, 2005 (see Appendix C, amendment 677); November 1, 2009 (see Appendix C, amendment 726).

PART C - OBSTRUCTION

§3C1.1. Obstructing or Impeding the Administration of Justice

If (1) the defendant willfully obstructed or impeded, or attempted to obstruct or impede, the administration of justice with respect to the investigation, prosecution, or sentencing of the instant offense of conviction, and (2) the obstructive conduct related to (A) the defendant's offense of conviction and any relevant conduct; or (B) a closely related offense, increase the offense level by **2** levels.

Commentary

Application Notes:

1. In General.—This adjustment applies if the defendant's obstructive conduct (A) occurred with respect to the investigation, prosecution, or sentencing of the defendant's instant offense of conviction, and (B) related to (i) the defendant's offense of conviction and any relevant conduct; or (ii) an otherwise closely related case, such as that of a co-defendant.

Obstructive conduct that occurred prior to the start of the investigation of the instant offense of conviction may be covered by this guideline if the conduct was purposefully calculated, and likely, to thwart the investigation or prosecution of the offense of conviction.

2. Limitations on Applicability of Adjustment.—This provision is not intended to punish a defendant for the exercise of a constitutional right. A defendant's denial of guilt (other than a denial of guilt under oath that constitutes perjury), refusal to admit guilt or provide information to a probation officer, or refusal to enter a plea of guilty is not a basis for application of this provision. In applying this provision in respect to alleged false testimony or statements by the defendant, the court should be cognizant that inaccurate testimony or statements sometimes may result from confusion, mistake, or faulty memory and, thus, not all inaccurate testimony or statements necessarily reflect a willful attempt to obstruct justice.

3. Covered Conduct Generally.—Obstructive conduct can vary widely in nature, degree of planning, and seriousness. Application Note 4 sets forth examples of the types of conduct to which this adjustment is intended to apply. Application Note 5 sets forth examples of less serious forms of conduct to which this enhancement is not intended to apply, but that ordinarily can appropriately be sanctioned by the determination of the particular sentence within the otherwise applicable guideline range. Although the conduct to which this adjustment applies is not subject to precise definition, comparison of the examples set forth in Application Notes 4 and 5 should assist the court in determining whether application of this adjustment is warranted in a particular case.

4. Examples of Covered Conduct.—The following is a non-exhaustive list of examples of the types of conduct to which this adjustment applies:

(A) threatening, intimidating, or otherwise unlawfully influencing a co-defendant, witness, or juror, directly or indirectly, or attempting to do so;

(B) committing, suborning, or attempting to suborn perjury, including during the course of a civil proceeding if such perjury pertains to conduct that forms the basis of the offense of conviction;

(C) producing or attempting to produce a false, altered, or counterfeit document or record during an official investigation or judicial proceeding;

(D) destroying or concealing or directing or procuring another person to destroy or conceal evidence that is material to an official investigation or judicial proceeding (e.g., shredding a document or destroying ledgers upon learning that an official investigation has commenced or is about to commence), or attempting to do so; however, if such conduct occurred contemporaneously with arrest (e.g., attempting to swallow or throw away a controlled substance), it shall not, standing alone, be sufficient to warrant an adjustment for obstruction unless it resulted in a material hindrance to the official investigation or prosecution of the instant offense or the sentencing of the offender;

(E) escaping or attempting to escape from custody before trial or sentencing; or willfully failing to appear, as ordered, for a judicial proceeding;

(F) providing materially false information to a judge or magistrate judge;

(G) providing a materially false statement to a law enforcement officer that significantly obstructed or impeded the official investigation or prosecution of the instant offense;

(H) providing materially false information to a probation officer in respect to a pre¬sentence or other investigation for the court;

(I) other conduct prohibited by obstruction of justice provisions under Title 18, United States Code (e.g., 18 U.S.C. §§ 1510, 1511);

(J) failing to comply with a restraining order or injunction issued pursuant to 21 U.S.C. § 853(e) or with an order to repatriate property issued pursuant to 21 U.S.C. § 853(p);

(K) threatening the victim of the offense in an attempt to prevent the victim from reporting the conduct constituting the offense of conviction.

This adjustment also applies to any other obstructive conduct in respect to the official investigation, prosecution, or sentencing of the instant offense where there is a separate count of conviction for such conduct.

5. Examples of Conduct Ordinarily Not Covered.—Some types of conduct ordinarily do not warrant application of this adjustment but may warrant a greater sentence within the otherwise applicable guideline range or affect the determination of whether other guideline adjustments apply (e.g., §3E1.1

(Acceptance of Responsibility)). However, if the defendant is convicted of a separate count for such conduct, this adjustment will apply and increase the offense level for the underlying offense (i.e., the offense with respect to which the obstructive conduct occurred). See Application Note 8, below.

The following is a non-exhaustive list of examples of the types of conduct to which this application note applies:

(A) providing a false name or identification document at arrest, except where such conduct actually resulted in a significant hindrance to the investigation or prosecution of the instant offense;

(B) making false statements, not under oath, to law enforcement officers, unless Application Note 4(G) above applies;

(C) providing incomplete or misleading information, not amounting to a material falsehood, in respect to a presentence investigation;

(D) avoiding or fleeing from arrest (see, however, §3C1.2 (Reckless Endangerment During Flight));

(E) lying to a probation or pretrial services officer about defendant's drug use while on pre-trial release, although such conduct may be a factor in determining whether to reduce the defendant's sentence under §3E1.1 (Acceptance of Responsibility).

6. "Material" Evidence Defined.—"Material" evidence, fact, statement, or information, as used in this section, means evidence, fact, statement, or information that, if believed, would tend to influence or affect the issue under determination.

7. Inapplicability of Adjustment in Certain Circumstances.—If the defendant is convicted of an offense covered by §2J1.1 (Contempt), §2J1.2 (Obstruction of Justice), §2J1.3 (Perjury or Subornation of Perjury; Bribery of Witness), §2J1.5 (Failure to Appear by Material Witness), §2J1.6 (Failure to Appear by Defendant), §2J1.9 (Payment to Witness), §2X3.1 (Accessory After the Fact), or §2X4.1 (Misprision of Felony), this adjustment is not to be applied to the offense level for that offense except if a significant further obstruction occurred during the investigation, prosecution, or sentencing of the obstruction offense itself (e.g., if the defendant threatened a witness during the course of the prosecution for the obstruction offense).

Similarly, if the defendant receives an enhancement under §2D1.1(b)(15)(D), do not apply this adjustment.

8. Grouping Under §3D1.2(c).—If the defendant is convicted both of an obstruction offense (e.g., 18 U.S.C. § 3146 (Penalty for failure to appear); 18 U.S.C. § 1621 (Perjury generally)) and an underlying offense (the offense with respect to which the obstructive conduct occurred), the count for the obstruction offense will be grouped with the count for the underlying offense under subsection (c) of §3D1.2 (Groups of Closely Related Counts). The offense level for that group of closely related counts will be the offense level for the underlying offense increased by the 2-level adjustment specified by this section, or the offense level for the obstruction offense, whichever is greater.

9. _Accountability for §1B1.3(a)(1)(A) Conduct._—_Under this section, the defendant is accountable for the defendant's own conduct and for conduct that the defendant aided or abetted, counseled, commanded, induced, procured, or willfully caused._

Historical Note: Effective November 1, 1987. Amended effective November 1, 1989 (see Appendix C, amendments 251 and 252); November 1, 1990 (see Appendix C, amendment 347); November 1, 1991 (see Appendix C, amendment 415); November 1, 1992 (see Appendix C, amendment 457); November 1, 1993 (see Appendix C, amendment 496); November 1, 1997 (see Appendix C, amendment 566); November 1, 1998 (see Appendix C, amendments 579, 581, and 582); November 1, 2002 (see Appendix C, amendment 637); November 1, 2004 (see Appendix C, amendment 674); November 1, 2006 (see Appendix C, amendment 693); November 1, 2010 (see Appendix C, amendments 746, 747, and 748); November 1, 2011 (see Appendix C, amendments 750 and 758); November 1, 2014 (see Appendix C, amendment 783).

PART E - ACCEPTANCE OF RESPONSIBILITY

§3E1.1. Acceptance of Responsibility

(a) If the defendant clearly demonstrates acceptance of responsibility for his offense, decrease the offense level by **2** levels.

(b) If the defendant qualifies for a decrease under subsection (a), the offense level determined prior to the operation of subsection (a) is level **16** or greater, and upon motion of the government stating that the defendant has assisted authorities in the investigation or prosecution of his own misconduct by timely notifying authorities of his intention to enter a plea of guilty, thereby permitting the government to avoid preparing for trial and permitting the government and the court to allocate their resources efficiently, decrease the offense level by **1** additional level.

Commentary

Application Notes:

1. In determining whether a defendant qualifies under subsection (a), appropriate considerations include, but are not limited to, the following:

(A) truthfully admitting the conduct comprising the offense(s) of conviction, and truthfully admitting or not falsely denying any additional relevant conduct for which the defendant is accountable under §1B1.3 (Relevant Conduct). Note that a defendant is not required to volunteer, or affirmatively admit, relevant conduct beyond the offense of conviction in order to obtain a reduction under subsection (a). A defendant may remain silent in respect to relevant conduct beyond the offense of conviction without affecting his ability to obtain a reduction under this subsection. However, a defendant who falsely *denies, or frivolously contests, relevant conduct that the court determines to be true has acted in a manner inconsistent with acceptance of responsibility;*

(B) voluntary termination or withdrawal from criminal conduct or associations;

(C) voluntary payment of restitution prior to adjudication of guilt;

(D) voluntary surrender to authorities promptly after commission of the offense;

(E) voluntary assistance to authorities in the recovery of the fruits and instrumentalities of the offense;

(F) voluntary resignation from the office or position held during the commission of the offense;

(G) post-offense rehabilitative efforts (e.g., counseling or drug treatment); and

(H) the timeliness of the defendant's conduct in manifesting the acceptance of responsibility.

2. This adjustment is not intended to apply to a defendant who puts the government to its burden of proof at trial by denying the essential factual elements of guilt, is convicted, and only then admits guilt and expresses remorse. Conviction by trial, however, does not automatically preclude a defendant from consideration for such a reduction. In rare situations a defendant may clearly demonstrate an acceptance of responsibility for his criminal conduct even though he exercises his constitutional right to a trial. This may occur, for example, where a defendant goes to trial to assert and preserve issues that do not relate to factual guilt (e.g., to make a constitutional challenge to a statute or a challenge to the applicability of a statute to his conduct). In each such instance, however, a determination that a defendant has accepted responsibility will be based primarily upon pre-trial statements and conduct.

3. Entry of a plea of guilty prior to the commencement of trial combined with truthfully admitting the conduct comprising the offense of conviction, and truthfully admitting or not falsely denying any additional relevant conduct for which he is accountable under §1B1.3 (Relevant Conduct) (see Application Note 1(A)), will constitute significant evidence of acceptance of responsibility for the purposes of subsection (a). However, this evidence may be outweighed by conduct of the defendant that is inconsistent with such acceptance of responsibility. A defendant who enters a guilty plea is not entitled to an adjustment under this section as a matter of right.

4. Conduct resulting in an enhancement under §3C1.1 (Obstructing or Impeding the Administra¬tion of Justice) ordinarily indicates that the defendant has not accepted responsibility for his criminal conduct. There may, however, be extraordinary cases in which adjustments under both §§3C1.1 and 3E1.1 may apply.

5. The sentencing judge is in a unique position to evaluate a defendant's acceptance of responsibility. For this reason, the determination of the sentencing judge is entitled to great deference on review.

6. Subsection (a) provides a 2-level decrease in offense level. Subsection (b) provides an additional 1-level decrease in offense level for a defendant at offense level 16 or greater prior to the operation of subsection (a) who both qualifies for a decrease under subsection (a) and who has assisted authorities in the investigation or prosecution of his own misconduct by taking the steps set forth in subsection (b). The timeliness of the defendant's acceptance of responsibility is a consideration under both subsections, and is context specific. In general, the conduct qualifying for a decrease in offense level under subsection (b) will occur particularly early in the case. For example, to qualify under subsection (b), the defendant must have notified authorities of his intention to enter a plea of guilty at a sufficiently early point in the process so that the government may avoid preparing for trial and the court may schedule its calendar efficiently.

Because the Government is in the best position to determine whether the defendant has assisted authorities in a manner that avoids preparing for trial, an adjustment under subsection (b) may only be granted upon a formal motion by the Government at the time of sentencing. See section 401(g)(2)(B) of Public Law 108–21. The government should not withhold such a motion based on interests not identified in §3E1.1, such as whether the defendant agrees to waive his or her right to appeal.

If the government files such a motion, and the court in deciding whether to grant the motion also determines that the defendant has assisted authorities in the investigation or prosecution of his own misconduct by timely notifying authorities of his intention to enter a plea of guilty, thereby permitting the government to avoid preparing for trial and permitting the government and the court to allocate their resources efficiently, the court should grant the motion.

Background: The reduction of offense level provided by this section recognizes legitimate societal interests. For several reasons, a defendant who clearly demonstrates acceptance of responsibility for his offense by taking, in a timely fashion, the actions listed above (or some equivalent action) is appropriately given a lower offense level than a defendant who has not demonstrated acceptance of responsibility.

Subsection (a) provides a 2-level decrease in offense level. Subsection (b) provides an additional 1-level decrease for a defendant at offense level 16 or greater prior to operation of subsection (a) who both qualifies for a decrease under subsection (a) and has assisted authorities in the investigation or prosecution of his own misconduct by taking the steps specified in subsection (b). Such a defendant has accepted responsibility in a way that ensures the certainty of his just punishment in a timely manner, thereby appropriately meriting an additional reduction. Subsection (b) does not apply, however, to a defendant whose offense level is level 15 or lower prior to application of subsection (a). At offense level 15 or lower, the reduction in the guideline range provided by a 2-level decrease in offense level under subsection (a) (which is a greater proportional reduction in the guideline range than at higher offense levels due to the structure of the Sentencing Table) is adequate for the court to take into account the factors set forth in subsection (b) within the applicable guideline range.

Section 401(g) of Public Law 108–21 directly amended subsection (b), Application Note 6 (including adding the first sentence of the second paragraph of that application note), and the Background Commentary, effective April 30, 2003.

Historical Note: Effective November 1, 1987. Amended effective January 15, 1988 (see Appendix C, amendment 46); November 1, 1989 (see Appendix C, amendment 258); November 1, 1990 (see Appendix C, amendment 351); November 1, 1992 (see Appendix C, amendment 459); April 30, 2003 (see Appendix C, amendment 649); November 1, 2010 (see Appendix C, amendments 746 and 747); November 1, 2013 (see Appendix C, amendment 775).

CHAPTER FIVE–DETERMINING THE SENTENCE

Introductory Commentary

For certain categories of offenses and offenders, the guidelines permit the court to impose either imprisonment or some other sanction or combination of sanctions. In determining the type of sentence to impose, the sentencing judge should consider the nature and seriousness of the conduct, the statutory purposes of sentencing, and the pertinent offender characteristics. A sentence is within the guidelines if it complies with each applicable section of this chapter. The court should impose a sentence sufficient, but not greater than necessary, to comply with the statutory purposes of sentencing. 18 U.S.C. § 3553(a).

Historical Note: Effective November 1, 1987.

PART A - SENTENCING TABLE

[see p. 425]

PART C - IMPRISONMENT

§5C1.1.   Imposition of a Term of Imprisonment

If (1) the defendant willfully obstructed or impeded, or attempted to obstruct or impede, the administration of justice with respect to the investigation, prosecution, or sentencing of the instant offense of conviction, and (2) the obstructive conduct related to (A) the defendant's offense of conviction and any relevant conduct; or (B) a closely related offense, increase the offense level by **2** levels.

Commentary

Application Notes:

1. In General.—This adjustment applies if the defendant's obstructive conduct (A) occurred with respect to the investigation, prosecution, or sentencing of the defendant's instant offense of conviction, and (B) related to (i) the defendant's offense of conviction and any relevant conduct; or (ii) an otherwise closely related case, such as that of a co-defendant.

Obstructive conduct that occurred prior to the start of the investigation of the instant offense of conviction may be covered by this guideline if the conduct was purposefully calculated, and likely, to thwart the investigation or prosecution of the offense of conviction.

2. Limitations on Applicability of Adjustment.—This provision is not intended to punish a defendant for the exercise of a constitutional right. A defendant's denial of guilt (other than a denial of guilt under oath that constitutes perjury), refusal to admit guilt or provide information to a probation officer, or refusal to enter a plea of guilty is not a basis for application of this provision. In applying this provision in respect to alleged false testimony or statements by the defendant, the court should be cognizant that inaccurate testimony or statements sometimes may result from confusion, mistake, or faulty memory and, thus, not all inaccurate testimony or statements necessarily reflect a willful attempt to obstruct justice.

3. Covered Conduct Generally.—Obstructive conduct can vary widely in nature, degree of planning, and seriousness. Application Note 4 sets forth examples of the types of conduct to which this adjustment is intended to apply. Application Note 5 sets forth examples of less serious forms of conduct to which this enhancement is not intended to apply, but that ordinarily can appropriately be sanctioned by the determination of the particular sentence within the otherwise applicable guideline range. Although the conduct to which this adjustment applies is not subject to precise definition, comparison of the examples set forth in Application Notes 4 and 5 should assist the court in determining whether application of this adjustment is warranted in a particular case.

4. Examples of Covered Conduct.—The following is a non-exhaustive list of examples of the types of conduct to which this adjustment applies:

(A) threatening, intimidating, or otherwise unlawfully influencing a co-defendant, witness, or juror, directly or indirectly, or attempting to do so;

(B) committing, suborning, or attempting to suborn perjury, including during the course of a civil proceeding if such perjury pertains to conduct that forms the basis of the offense of conviction;

(C) producing or attempting to produce a false, altered, or counterfeit document or record during an official investigation or judicial proceeding;

(D) destroying or concealing or directing or procuring another person to destroy or conceal evidence that is material to an official investigation or judicial proceeding (e.g., shredding a document or destroying ledgers upon learning that an official investigation has commenced or is about to commence), or attempting to do so; however, if such conduct occurred contemporaneously with arrest (e.g., attempting to swallow or throw away a controlled substance), it shall not, standing alone, be sufficient to warrant an adjustment for obstruction unless it resulted in a material hindrance to the official investigation or prosecution of the instant offense or the sentencing of the offender;

(E) escaping or attempting to escape from custody before trial or sentencing; or willfully failing to appear, as ordered, for a judicial proceeding;

(F) providing materially false information to a judge or magistrate judge;

(G) providing a materially false statement to a law enforcement officer that significantly obstructed or impeded the official investigation or prosecution of the instant offense;

(H) providing materially false information to a probation officer in respect to a pre¬sentence or other investigation for the court;

(I) other conduct prohibited by obstruction of justice provisions under Title 18, United States Code (e.g., 18 U.S.C. §§ 1510, 1511);

(J) failing to comply with a restraining order or injunction issued pursuant to 21 U.S.C. § 853(e) or with an order to repatriate property issued pursuant to 21 U.S.C. § 853(p);

(K) threatening the victim of the offense in an attempt to prevent the victim from reporting the conduct constituting the offense of conviction.

This adjustment also applies to any other obstructive conduct in respect to the official investigation, prosecution, or sentencing of the instant offense where there is a separate count of conviction for such conduct.

5. Examples of Conduct Ordinarily Not Covered.—Some types of conduct ordinarily do not warrant application of this adjustment but may warrant a greater sentence within the otherwise applicable guideline range or affect the determination of whether other guideline adjustments apply (e.g., §3E1.1 (Acceptance of Responsibility)). However, if the defendant is convicted of a separate count for such conduct, this adjustment will apply and increase the offense level for the underlying offense (i.e., the offense with respect to which the obstructive conduct occurred). See Application Note 8, below.

The following is a non-exhaustive list of examples of the types of conduct to which this application note applies:

(A) providing a false name or identification document at arrest, except where such conduct actually resulted in a significant hindrance to the investigation or prosecution of the instant offense;

(B) making false statements, not under oath, to law enforcement officers, unless Application Note 4(G) above applies;

(C) providing incomplete or misleading information, not amounting to a material falsehood, in respect to a presentence investigation;

(D) avoiding or fleeing from arrest (see, however, §3C1.2 (Reckless Endangerment During Flight));

(E) lying to a probation or pretrial services officer about defendant's drug use while on pre-trial release, although such conduct may be a factor in determining whether to reduce the defendant's sentence under §3E1.1 (Acceptance of Responsibility).

6. "Material" Evidence Defined.—"Material" evidence, fact, statement, or information, as used in this section, means evidence, fact, statement, or information that, if believed, would tend to influence or affect the issue under determination.

7. Inapplicability of Adjustment in Certain Circumstances.—If the defendant is convicted of an offense covered by §2J1.1 (Contempt), §2J1.2 (Obstruction of Justice), §2J1.3 (Perjury or Subornation of Perjury; Bribery of Witness), §2J1.5 (Failure to Appear by Material Witness), §2J1.6 (Failure to Appear by Defendant), §2J1.9 (Payment to Witness), §2X3.1 (Accessory After the Fact), or §2X4.1 (Misprision of Felony), this adjustment is not to be applied to the offense level for that offense except if a significant further obstruction occurred during the investigation, prosecution, or sentencing of the obstruction offense itself (e.g., if the defendant threatened a witness during the course of the prosecution for the obstruction offense).

Similarly, if the defendant receives an enhancement under §2D1.1(b)(15)(D), do not apply this adjustment.

8. Grouping Under §3D1.2(c).—If the defendant is convicted both of an obstruction offense (e.g., 18 U.S.C. § 3146 (Penalty for failure to appear); 18 U.S.C. § 1621 (Perjury generally)) and an underlying offense (the offense with respect to which the obstructive conduct occurred), the count for the obstruction offense will be grouped with the count for the underlying offense under subsection (c) of §3D1.2 (Groups of Closely Related Counts). The offense level for that group of closely related counts will be the offense level for the underlying offense increased by the 2-level adjustment specified by this section, or the offense level for the obstruction offense, whichever is greater.

9. *Accountability for §1B1.3(a)(1)(A) Conduct.*—Under this section, the defendant is accountable for the defendant's own conduct and for conduct that the defendant aided or abetted, counseled, commanded, induced, procured, or willfully caused.

Historical Note: Effective November 1, 1987. Amended effective November 1, 1989 (see Appendix C, amendments 251 and 252); November 1, 1990 (see Appendix C, amendment 347); November 1, 1991 (see Appendix C, amendment 415); November 1, 1992 (see Appendix C, amendment 457); November 1, 1993 (see Appendix C, amendment 496); November 1, 1997 (see Appendix C, amendment 566); November 1, 1998 (see Appendix C, amendments 579, 581, and 582); November 1, 2002 (see Appendix C, amendment 637); November 1, 2004 (see Appendix C, amendment 674); November 1, 2006 (see Appendix C, amendment 693); November 1, 2010 (see Appendix C, amendments 746, 747, and 748); November 1, 2011 (see Appendix C, amendments 750 and 758); November 1, 2014 (see Appendix C, amendment 783).

PART F - SENTENCING OPTIONS

§5F1.1.   Community Confinement

Community confinement may be imposed as a condition of probation or supervised release.

Commentary

Application Notes:

1.   "Community confinement" means residence in a community treatment center, halfway house, restitution center, mental health facility, alcohol or drug rehabilitation center, or other community facility; and participation in gainful employment, employment search efforts, community service, vocational training, treatment, educational programs, or similar facility-approved programs during non-residential hours.

2.   Community confinement generally should not be imposed for a period in excess of six months. A longer period may be imposed to accomplish the objectives of a specific rehabilitative program, such as drug rehabilitation. The sentencing judge may impose other discretionary conditions of probation or supervised release appropriate to effectuate community confinement.

Historical Note: Effective November 1, 1987. Amended effective November 1, 1989 (see Appendix C, amendment 302); November 1, 2002 (see Appendix C, amendment 646).

§5F1.2. Home Detention

Home detention may be imposed as a condition of probation or supervised release, but only as a substitute for imprisonment.

Commentary

Application Notes:

1.   *"Home detention" means a program of confinement and supervision that restricts the defendant to his place of residence continuously, except for authorized absences, enforced by appropriate means of surveillance by the probation office. When an order of home detention is imposed, the defendant is required to be in his place of residence at all times except for approved absences for gainful employment, community service, religious services, medical care, educational or training programs, and such other times as may be specifically authorized. Electronic monitoring is an appropriate means of surveillance and ordinarily should be used in connection with home detention. However, alternative means of surveillance may be used so long as they are as effective as electronic monitoring.*

2.   *The court may impose other conditions of probation or supervised release appropriate to effectuate home detention. If the court concludes that the amenities available in the residence of a defendant would cause home detention not to be sufficiently punitive, the court may limit the amenities available.*

3.   *The defendant's place of residence, for purposes of home detention, need not be the place where the defendant previously resided. It may be any place of residence, so long as the owner of the residence (and any other person(s) from whom consent is necessary) agrees to any conditions that may be imposed by the court, e.g., conditions that a monitoring system be installed, that there will be no "call forwarding" or "call waiting" services, or that there will be no cordless telephones or answering machines.*

Background: The Commission has concluded that the surveillance necessary for effective use of home detention ordinarily requires electronic monitoring. However, in some cases home detention may effectively be enforced without electronic monitoring, e.g., when the defendant is physically incapacitated, or where some other effective means of surveillance is available. Accordingly, the Commission has not required that electronic monitoring be a necessary condition for home detention. Nevertheless, before ordering home detention without electronic monitoring, the court should be confident that an alternative form of surveillance will be equally effective.

In the usual case, the Commission assumes that a condition requiring that the defendant seek and maintain gainful employment will be imposed when home detention is ordered.

Historical Note: Effective November 1, 1987. Amended effective November 1, 1989 (see Appendix C, amendments 271 and 302).

§5F1.3.   Community Service

Community service may be ordered as a condition of probation or supervised release.

Commentary

Application Note:

1.   *Community service generally should not be imposed in excess of 400 hours. Longer terms of community service impose heavy administrative burdens relating to the selection of suitable placements and the monitoring of attendance.*

Historical Note: Effective November 1, 1987. Amended effective November 1, 1989 (see Appendix C, amendments 283 and 302); November 1, 1991 (see Appendix C, amendment 419).

§5F1.4.   Order of Notice to Victims

The court may order the defendant to pay the cost of giving notice to victims pursuant to 18 U.S.C. § 3555. This cost may be set off against any fine imposed if the court determines that the imposition of both sanctions would be excessive.

Commentary

Background: In cases where a defendant has been convicted of an offense involving fraud or "other intentionally deceptive practices," the court may order the defendant to "give reasonable notice and explanation of the conviction, in such form as the court may approve" to the victims of the offense. 18 U.S.C. § 3555. The court may order the notice to be given by mail, by advertising in specific areas or through specific media, or by other appropriate means. In determining whether a notice is appropriate, the court must consider the generally applicable sentencing factors listed in 18 U.S.C. § 3553(a) and the cost involved in giving the notice as it relates to the loss caused by the crime. The court may not require the defendant to pay more than $20,000 to give notice.

If an order of notice to victims is under consideration, the court must notify the government and the defendant. 18 U.S.C. § 3553(d). Upon motion of either party, or on its own motion, the court must: (1) permit the parties to submit affidavits and memoranda relevant to the imposition of such an order; (2) provide counsel for both parties the opportunity to address orally, in open court, the appropriateness of such an order; and (3) if it issues such an order, state its reasons for doing so. The court may also order any additional procedures that will not unduly complicate or prolong the sentencing process.

Historical Note: Effective November 1, 1987. Amended effective November 1, 1989 (see Appendix C, amendments 284 and 302).

§5F1.5.   Occupational Restrictions

(a) The court may impose a condition of probation or supervised release prohibiting the defendant from engaging in a specified occupation, business, or profession, or limiting the terms on which the defendant may do so, only if it determines that:

    (1)   a reasonably direct relationship existed between the defendant's occupation, business, or profession and the conduct relevant to the offense of conviction; and

    (2)   imposition of such a restriction is reasonably necessary to protect the public because there is reason to believe that, absent such restriction, the defendant will continue to engage in unlawful conduct similar to that for which the defendant was convicted.

(b) If the court decides to impose a condition of probation or supervised release restricting a defendant's engagement in a specified occupation, business, or profession, the court shall impose the condition for the minimum time and to the minimum extent necessary to protect the public.

Commentary

Background: The Comprehensive Crime Control Act authorizes the imposition of occupational restrictions as a condition of probation, 18 U.S.C. § 3563(b)(5), or supervised release, 18 U.S.C. § 3583(d). Pursuant to § 3563(b)(5), a court may require a defendant to:

[R]efrain, in the case of an individual, from engaging in a specified occupation, business, or profession bearing a reasonably direct relationship to the conduct constituting the offense, or engage in such a specified occupation, business, or profession only to a stated degree or under stated circumstances.

Section 3583(d) incorporates this section by reference. The Senate Judiciary Committee Report on the Comprehensive Crime Control Act explains that the provision was "intended to be used to preclude the continuation or repetition of illegal activities while avoiding a bar from employment that exceeds that needed to achieve that result." S. Rep. No. 225, 98th Cong., 1st Sess. 96-97. The condition "should only be used as reasonably necessary to protect the public. It should not be used as a means of punishing the convicted person." Id. at 96. Section 5F1.5 accordingly limits the use of the condition and, if imposed, limits its scope, to the minimum reasonably necessary to protect the public.

The appellate review provisions permit a defendant to challenge the imposition of a probation condition under 18 U.S.C. § 3563(b)(5) if the sentence includes a more limiting condition of probation or supervised release than the maximum established in the guideline. See 18 U.S.C. § 3742(a)(3). The government may appeal if the sentence includes a less limiting condition of probation than the minimum established in the guideline. See 18 U.S.C. § 3742(b)(3).

Historical Note: Effective November 1, 1987. Amended effective November 1, 1989 (see Appendix C, amendments 285 and 302); November 1, 1991 (see Appendix C, amendment 428); November 1, 2002 (see Appendix C, amendment 646).

PART K - DEPARTURES

1. SUBSTANTIAL ASSISTANCE TO AUTHORITIES

§5K1.1. Substantial Assistance to Authorities (Policy Statement)

Upon motion of the government stating that the defendant has provided substantial assistance in the investigation or prosecution of another person who has committed an offense, the court may depart from the guidelines.

(a) The appropriate reduction shall be determined by the court for reasons stated that may include, but are not limited to, consideration of the following:

(1) the court's evaluation of the significance and usefulness of the defendant's assistance, taking into consideration the government's evaluation of the assistance rendered;

(2) the truthfulness, completeness, and reliability of any information or testimony provided by the defendant;

(3) the nature and extent of the defendant's assistance;

(4) any injury suffered, or any danger or risk of injury to the defendant or his family resulting from his assistance;

(5) the timeliness of the defendant's assistance.

Commentary

Application Notes:

1.   Under circumstances set forth in 18 U.S.C. § 3553(e) and 28 U.S.C. § 994(n), as amended, substantial assistance in the investigation or prosecution of another person who has committed an offense may justify a sentence below a statutorily required minimum sentence.

2.   The sentencing reduction for assistance to authorities shall be considered independently of any reduction for acceptance of responsibility. Substantial assistance is directed to the investigation and prosecution of criminal activities by persons other than the defendant, while acceptance of responsibility is directed to the defendant's affirmative recognition of responsibility for his own conduct.

3.   Substantial weight should be given to the government's evaluation of the extent of the defendant's assistance, particularly where the extent and value of the assistance are difficult to ascertain.

Background: A defendant's assistance to authorities in the investigation of criminal activities has been recognized in practice and by statute as a mitigating sentencing factor.   The nature, extent, and significance of assistance can involve a broad spectrum of conduct that must be evaluated by the court on an individual basis.   Latitude is, therefore, afforded the sentencing judge to reduce a sentence based upon variable relevant factors, including those listed above. The sentencing judge must, however, state the reasons for reducing a sentence under this section. 18 U.S.C. § 3553(c).   The court may elect to provide its reasons to the defendant *in camera* and in writing under seal for the safety of the defendant or to avoid disclosure of an ongoing investigation.

Historical Note: Effective November 1, 1987. Amended effective November 1, 1989 (see Appendix C, amendment 291).

§5K1.2.   Refusal to Assist (Policy Statement)

A defendant's refusal to assist authorities in the investigation of other persons may not be considered as an aggravating sentencing factor.

Historical Note: Effective November 1, 1987. Amended effective November 1, 1989 (see Appendix C, amendment 291).

§5K2.0. Grounds for Departure (Policy Statement)

(a)   UPWARD DEPARTURES IN GENERAL AND DOWNWARD DEPARTURES IN CRIMINAL CASES OTHER THAN CHILD CRIMES AND SEXUAL OFFENSES.—

(1) IN GENERAL.—The sentencing court may depart from the applicable guideline range if—

    (A) in the case of offenses other than child crimes and sexual offenses, the court finds, pursuant to 18 U.S.C. § 3553(b)(1), that there exists an aggravating or mitigating circumstance; or

    (B) in the case of child crimes and sexual offenses, the court finds, pursuant to 18 U.S.C. § 3553(b)(2)(A)(i), that there exists an aggravating circumstance,

of a kind, or to a degree, not adequately taken into consideration by the Sentencing Commission in formulating the guidelines that, in order to advance the objectives set forth in 18 U.S.C. § 3553(a)(2), should result in a sentence different from that described.

(2) DEPARTURES BASED ON CIRCUMSTANCES OF A KIND NOT ADEQUATELY TAKEN INTO CONSIDERATION.—

    (A) IDENTIFIED CIRCUMSTANCES.—This subpart (Chapter Five, Part K, Subpart 2 (Other Grounds for Departure)) identifies some of the circumstances that the Commission may have not adequately taken into consideration in determining the applicable guideline range (e.g., as a specific offense characteristic or other adjustment). If any such circumstance is present in the case and has not adequately been taken into consideration in determining the applicable guideline range, a departure consistent with 18 U.S.C. § 3553(b) and the provisions of this subpart may be warranted.

    (B) UNIDENTIFIED CIRCUMSTANCES.—A departure may be warranted in the exceptional case in which there is present a circumstance that the Commission has not identified in the guidelines but that nevertheless is relevant to determining the appropriate sentence.

(3) DEPARTURES BASED ON CIRCUMSTANCES PRESENT TO A DEGREE NOT ADEQUATELY TAKEN INTO CONSIDERATION.—A departure may be warranted in an exceptional case, even though the circumstance that forms the basis for the departure is taken into consideration in determining the guideline range, if the court determines that such circumstance is present in the offense to a degree substantially in excess of, or substantially below, that which ordinarily is involved in that kind of offense.

(4) DEPARTURES BASED ON NOT ORDINARILY RELEVANT OFFENDER CHARACTERISTICS AND OTHER CIRCUMSTANCES.—An offender characteristic or other circumstance identified in Chapter Five, Part H (Offender Characteristics) or elsewhere in the guidelines as not ordinarily relevant in determining whether a departure is warranted may be relevant to this determination only if such offender characteristic or other circumstance is present to an exceptional degree.

(b) DOWNWARD DEPARTURES IN CHILD CRIMES AND SEXUAL OFFENSES.—Under 18 U.S.C. § 3553(b)(2)(A)(ii), the sentencing court may impose a sentence below the range established by the applicable guidelines only if the court finds that there exists a mitigating circumstance of a kind, or to a degree, that—

(1) has been affirmatively and specifically identified as a permissible

ground of downward departure in the sentencing guidelines or policy statements issued under section 994(a) of title 28, United States Code, taking account of any amendments to such sentencing guidelines or policy statements by act of Congress;

(2) has not adequately been taken into consideration by the Sentencing

Commission in formulating the guidelines; and

(3) should result in a sentence different from that described.

The grounds enumerated in this Part K of Chapter Five are the sole grounds that have been affirmatively and specifically identified as a permissible ground of downward departure in these sentencing guidelines and policy statements. Thus, notwithstanding any other reference to authority to depart downward elsewhere in this Sentencing Manual, a ground of downward departure has not been affirmatively and specifically identified as a permissible ground of downward departure within the meaning of section 3553(b)(2) unless it is expressly enumerated in this Part K as a ground upon which a downward departure may be granted.

(c) LIMITATION ON DEPARTURES BASED ON MULTIPLE CIRCUMSTANCES.—The court may depart from the applicable guideline range based on a combination of two or more offender characteristics or other circumstances, none of which independently is sufficient to provide a basis for departure, only if—

(1) such offender characteristics or other circumstances, taken together,

make the case an exceptional one; and

(2) each such offender characteristic or other circumstance is—

(A) present to a substantial degree; and

(B) identified in the guidelines as a permissible ground for

departure, even if such offender characteristic or other circumstance is not ordinarily relevant to a determination of whether a departure is warranted.

(d) PROHIBITED DEPARTURES.—Notwithstanding subsections (a) and (b) of this policy statement, or any other provision in the guidelines, the court may not depart from the applicable guideline range based on any of the following circumstances:

(1) Any circumstance specifically prohibited as a ground for departure in

§§5H1.10 (Race, Sex, National Origin, Creed, Religion, and Socio-Economic Status), 5H1.12 (Lack of Guidance as a Youth and Similar Circumstances), the last sentence of 5H1.4 (Physical Condition,

Including Drug or Alcohol Dependence or Abuse; Gambling Addiction), and the last sentence of 5K2.12 (Coercion and Duress).

(2) The defendant's acceptance of responsibility for the offense, which may be taken into account only under §3E1.1 (Acceptance of Responsibility).

(3) The defendant's aggravating or mitigating role in the offense, which may be taken into account only under §3B1.1 (Aggravating Role) or §3B1.2 (Mitigating Role), respectively.

(4) The defendant's decision, in and of itself, to plead guilty to the offense or to enter a plea agreement with respect to the offense (i.e., a departure may not be based merely on the fact that the defendant decided to plead guilty or to enter into a plea agreement, but a departure may be based on justifiable, non-prohibited reasons as part of a sentence that is recommended, or agreed to, in the plea agreement and accepted by the court. See §6B1.2 (Standards for Acceptance of Plea Agreement).

(5) The defendant's fulfillment of restitution obligations only to the extent required by law including the guidelines (i.e., a departure may not be based on unexceptional efforts to remedy the harm caused by the offense).

(6) Any other circumstance specifically prohibited as a ground for departure in the guidelines.

(e) **REQUIREMENT OF SPECIFIC WRITTEN REASONS FOR DEPARTURE.**—If the court departs from the applicable guideline range, it shall state, pursuant to 18 U.S.C. § 3553(c), its specific reasons for departure in open court at the time of sentencing and, with limited exception in the case of statements received in camera, shall state those reasons with specificity in the statement of reasons form.

Commentary

Application Notes:

1. Definitions.—For purposes of this policy statement:

"Circumstance" includes, as appropriate, an offender characteristic or any other offense factor.

"Depart", "departure", "downward departure", and "upward departure" have the meaning given those terms in Application Note 1 of the Commentary to §1B1.1 (Application Instructions).

2. Scope of this Policy Statement.—

(A) Departures Covered by this Policy Statement.—This policy statement covers departures from the applicable guideline range based on offense characteristics or offender characteristics of a kind, or to a degree, not adequately taken into consideration in determining that range. See 18 U.S.C. § 3553(b).

Subsection (a) of this policy statement applies to upward departures in all cases covered by the guidelines and to downward departures in all such cases except for downward departures in child crimes and sexual offenses.

Subsection (b) of this policy statement applies only to downward departures in child crimes and sexual offenses.

(B) Departures Covered by Other Guidelines.—This policy statement does not cover the following departures, which are addressed elsewhere in the guidelines: (i) departures based on the defendant's criminal history (see Chapter Four (Criminal History and Criminal Livelihood), particularly §4A1.3 (Departures Based on Inadequacy of Criminal History Category)); (ii) departures based on the defendant's substantial assistance to the authorities (see §5K1.1 (Substantial Assistance to Authorities)); and (iii) departures based on early disposition programs (see §5K3.1 (Early Disposition Programs)).

3. Kinds and Expected Frequency of Departures under Subsection (a).—As set forth in subsection (a), there generally are two kinds of departures from the guidelines based on offense characteristics and/or offender characteristics: (A) departures based on circumstances of a kind not adequately taken into consideration in the guidelines; and (B) departures based on circumstances that are present to a degree not adequately taken into consideration in the guidelines.

(A) Departures Based on Circumstances of a Kind Not Adequately Taken into Account in Guidelines.—Subsection (a)(2) authorizes the court to depart if there exists an aggravating or a mitigating circumstance in a case under 18 U.S.C. § 3553(b)(1), or an aggravating circumstance in a case under 18 U.S.C. § 3553(b)(2)(A)(i), of a kind not adequately taken into consideration in the guidelines.

(i) Identified Circumstances.—This subpart (Chapter Five, Part K, Subpart 2) identifies several circumstances that the Commission may have not adequately taken into consideration in setting the offense level for certain cases. Offense guidelines in Chapter Two (Offense Conduct) and adjustments in Chapter Three (Adjustments) sometimes identify circumstances the Commission may have not adequately taken into consideration in setting the offense level for offenses covered by those guidelines. If the offense guideline in Chapter Two or an adjustment in Chapter Three does not adequately take that circumstance into consideration in setting the offense level for the offense, and only to the extent not adequately taken into consideration, a departure based on that circumstance may be warranted.

(ii) Unidentified Circumstances.—A case may involve circumstances, in addition to those identified by the guidelines, that have not adequately been taken into consideration by the Commission, and the presence of any such circumstance may warrant departure from the guidelines in that case. However, inasmuch as the Commission has continued to monitor and refine the guidelines since their inception to take into consideration relevant circumstances in sentencing, it is expected that departures based on such unidentified circumstances will occur rarely and only in exceptional cases.

(B) Departures Based on Circumstances Present to a Degree Not Adequately Taken into Consideration in Guidelines.—

(i) In General.—Subsection (a)(3) authorizes the court to depart if there exists an aggravating or a mitigating circumstance in a case under 18 U.S.C. § 3553(b)(1), or an aggravating circumstance in a case under 18 U.S.C. § 3553(b)(2)(A)(i), to a degree not adequately taken into consideration in the guidelines. However, inasmuch as the Commission has continued to monitor and refine the guidelines since their inception to determine the most appropriate weight to be accorded the mitigating and aggravating circumstances specified in the guidelines, it is expected that departures based on the weight accorded to any such circumstance will occur rarely and only in exceptional cases.

(ii) Examples.—As set forth in subsection (a)(3), if the applicable offense guideline and adjustments take into consideration a circumstance identified in this subpart, departure is warranted only if the circumstance is present to a degree substantially in excess of that which ordinarily is involved in the offense. Accordingly, a departure pursuant to §5K2.7 for the disruption of a governmental function would have to be substantial to warrant departure from the guidelines when the applicable offense guideline is bribery or obstruction of justice. When the guideline covering the mailing of injurious articles is applicable, however, and the offense caused disruption of a governmental function, departure from the applicable guideline range more readily would be appropriate. Similarly, physical injury would not warrant departure from the guidelines when the robbery offense guideline is applicable because the robbery guideline includes a specific adjustment based on the extent of any injury. However, because the robbery guideline does not deal with injury to more than one victim, departure may be warranted if several persons were injured.

(C) Departures Based on Circumstances Identified as Not Ordinarily Relevant.—Because certain circumstances are specified in the guidelines as not ordinarily relevant to sentencing (see, e.g., Chapter Five, Part H (Specific Offender Characteristics)), a departure based on any one of such circumstances should occur only in exceptional cases, and only if the circumstance is present in the case to an exceptional degree. If two or more of such circumstances each is present in the case to a substantial degree, however, and taken together make the case an exceptional one, the court may consider whether a departure would be warranted pursuant to subsection (c). Departures based on a combination of not ordinarily relevant circumstances that are present to a substantial degree should occur extremely rarely and only in exceptional cases.

In addition, as required by subsection (e), each circumstance forming the basis for a departure described in this subdivision shall be stated with specificity in the statement of reasons form.

4. Downward Departures in Child Crimes and Sexual Offenses.—

(A) Definition.—For purposes of this policy statement, the term "child crimes and sexual offenses" means offenses under any of the following: 18 U.S.C. §

1201 (involving a minor victim), 18 U.S.C. § 1591, or chapter 71, 109A, 110, or 117 of title 18, United States Code.

(B) Standard for Departure.—

(i) Requirement of Affirmative and Specific Identification of Departure Ground.— The standard for a downward departure in child crimes and sexual offenses differs from the standard for other departures under this policy statement in that it includes a requirement, set forth in 18 U.S.C. § 3553(b)(2)(A)(ii)(I) and subsection (b)(1) of this guideline, that any mitigating circumstance that forms the basis for such a downward departure be affirmatively and specifically identified as a ground for downward departure in this part (i.e., Chapter Five, Part K).

(ii) Application of Subsection (b)(2).—The commentary in Application Note 3 of this policy statement, except for the commentary in Application Note 3(A)(ii) relating to unidentified circumstances, shall apply to the court's determination of whether a case meets the requirement, set forth in subsection 18 U.S.C. § 3553(b)(2)(A)(ii)(II) and subsection (b)(2) of this policy statement, that the mitigating circumstance forming the basis for a downward departure in child crimes and sexual offenses be of kind, or to a degree, not adequately taken into consideration by the Commission.

5. Departures Based on Plea Agreements.—Subsection (d)(4) prohibits a downward departure based only on the defendant's decision, in and of itself, to plead guilty to the offense or to enter a plea agreement with respect to the offense. Even though a departure may not be based merely on the fact that the defendant agreed to plead guilty or enter a plea agreement, a departure may be based on justifiable, non-prohibited reasons for departure as part of a sentence that is recommended, or agreed to, in the plea agreement and accepted by the court. See §6B1.2 (Standards for Acceptance of Plea Agreements). In cases in which the court departs based on such reasons as set forth in the plea agreement, the court must state the reasons for departure with specificity in the statement of reasons form, as required by subsection (e).

Background: This policy statement sets forth the standards for departing from the applicable guideline range based on offense and offender characteristics of a kind, or to a degree, not adequately considered by the Commission. Circumstances the Commission has determined are not ordinarily relevant to determining whether a departure is warranted or are prohibited as bases for departure are addressed in Chapter Five, Part H (Offender Characteristics) and in this policy statement. Other departures, such as those based on the defendant's criminal history, the defendant's substantial assistance to authorities, and early disposition programs, are addressed elsewhere in the guidelines.

As acknowledged by Congress in the Sentencing Reform Act and by the Commission when the first set of guidelines was promulgated, "it is difficult to prescribe a single set of guidelines that encompasses the vast range of human conduct potentially relevant to a sentencing decision." (See Chapter One, Part A). Departures, therefore, perform an integral function in the sentencing guideline system. Departures permit courts to impose an appropriate sentence in the exceptional case in which mechanical application of the guidelines would fail to achieve the statutory purposes and goals of sentencing. Departures also help maintain "sufficient flexibility to permit individualized sentences when warranted by mitigating or aggravating factors not taken into account in the establishment of general sentencing practices." 28 U.S.C. § 991(b)(1)(B). By monitoring when courts depart from the guidelines and by analyzing their stated reasons for doing so, along with appellate cases reviewing these departures, the Commission can further refine the guidelines to specify more precisely when departures should and should not be permitted.

As reaffirmed in the Prosecutorial Remedies and Other Tools to end the Exploitation of Children Today Act of 2003 (the "PROTECT Act", Public Law 108–21), circumstances warranting departure should be rare. Departures were never intended to permit sentencing courts to substitute their policy judgments for those of Congress and the Sentencing Commission. Departure in such circumstances would produce unwarranted sentencing disparity, which the Sentencing Reform Act was designed to avoid.

In order for appellate courts to fulfill their statutory duties under 18 U.S.C. § 3742 and for the Commission to fulfill its ongoing responsibility to refine the guidelines in light of information it receives on departures, it is essential that sentencing courts state with specificity the reasons for departure, as required by the PROTECT Act.

This policy statement, including its commentary, was substantially revised, effective October 27, 2003, in response to directives contained in the PROTECT Act, particularly the directive in section 401(m) of that Act to–

"(1) review the grounds of downward departure that are authorized by the sentencing guidelines, policy statements, and official commentary of the Sentencing Commission; and

(2) promulgate, pursuant to section 994 of title 28, United States Code—

(A) appropriate amendments to the sentencing guidelines, policy statements, and official commentary to ensure that the incidence of downward departures is substantially reduced;

(B) a policy statement authorizing a departure pursuant to an early disposition program; and

(C) any other conforming amendments to the sentencing guidelines, policy statements, and official commentary of the Sentencing Commission necessitated by the Act, including a revision of ...section 5K2.0".

The substantial revision of this policy statement in response to the PROTECT Act was intended to refine the standards applicable to departures while giving due regard for concepts, such as the "heartland", that have evolved in departure jurisprudence over time.

Section 401(b)(1) of the PROTECT Act directly amended this policy statement to add subsection (b), effective April 30, 2003.

Historical Note: Effective November 1, 1987. Amended effective June 15, 1988 (see Appendix C, amendment 57); November 1, 1990 (see Appendix C, amendment 358); November 1, 1994 (see Appendix C, amendment 508); November 1, 1997 (see Appendix C, amendment 561); November 1, 1998 (see Appendix C, amendment 585); April 30, 2003 (see Appendix C, amendment 649); October 27, 2003 (see Appendix C, amendment 651); November 1, 2008 (see Appendix C, amendment 725); November 1, 2010 (see Appendix C, amendment 739); November 1, 2011 (see Appendix C, amendment 757); November 1, 2012 (see Appendix C, amendment 770).

CHAPTER EIGHT - SENTENCING OF ORGANIZATIONS

Introductory Commentary

The guidelines and policy statements in this chapter apply when the convicted defendant is an organization. Organizations can act only through agents and, under federal criminal law, generally are vicariously liable for offenses committed by their agents. At the same time, individual agents are responsible for their own criminal conduct. Federal prosecutions of organizations therefore frequently involve individual and organizational co-defendants. Convicted individual agents of organizations are sentenced in accordance with the guidelines and policy statements in the preceding chapters. This chapter is designed so that the sanctions imposed upon organizations and their agents, taken together, will provide just punishment, adequate deterrence, and incentives for organizations to maintain internal mechanisms for preventing, detecting, and reporting criminal conduct.

This chapter reflects the following general principles:

First, the court must, whenever practicable, order the organization to remedy any harm caused by the offense. The resources expended to remedy the harm should not be viewed as punishment, but rather as a means of making victims whole for the harm caused.

Second, if the organization operated primarily for a criminal purpose or primarily by criminal means, the fine should be set sufficiently high to divest the organization of all its assets.

Third, the fine range for any other organization should be based on the seriousness of the offense and the culpability of the organization. The seriousness of the offense generally will be reflected by the greatest of the pecuniary gain, the pecuniary loss, or the amount in a guideline offense level fine table. Culpability generally will be determined by six factors that the sentencing court must consider. The four factors that increase the ultimate punishment of an organization are: (i) the involvement in or tolerance of criminal activity; (ii) the prior history of the organization; (iii) the violation of an order; and (iv) the obstruction of justice. The two factors that mitigate the ultimate punishment of an organization are: (i) the existence of an effective compliance and ethics program; and (ii) self-reporting, cooperation, or acceptance of responsibility.

Fourth, probation is an appropriate sentence for an organizational defendant when needed to ensure that another sanction will be fully implemented, or to ensure that steps will be taken within the organization to reduce the likelihood of future criminal conduct.

These guidelines offer incentives to organizations to reduce and ultimately eliminate criminal conduct by providing a structural foundation from which an organization may self-police its own conduct through an effective compliance and ethics program. The prevention and detection of criminal conduct, as facilitated by an effective compliance and ethics program, will assist an organization in encouraging ethical conduct and in complying fully with all applicable laws.

Historical Note: Effective November 1, 1991 (see Appendix C, amendment 422). Amended effective November 1, 2004 (see Appendix C, amendment 673).

PART A - GENERAL APPLICATION PRINCIPLES

§8A1.1. Applicability of Chapter Eight

This chapter applies to the sentencing of all organizations for felony and Class A misdemeanor offenses.

Commentary

Application Notes:

1. *"Organization" means "a person other than an individual." 18 U.S.C. § 18. The term includes corporations, partnerships, associations, joint-stock companies, unions, trusts, pension funds, unincorporated organizations, governments and political subdivisions thereof, and non-profit organizations.*

2. *The fine guidelines in §§8C2.2 through 8C2.9 apply only to specified types of offenses. The other provisions of this chapter apply to the sentencing of all organizations for all felony and Class A misdemeanor offenses. For example, the restitution and probation provisions in Parts B and D of this chapter apply to the sentencing of an organization, even if the fine guidelines in §§8C2.2 through 8C2.9 do not apply.*

Historical Note: Effective November 1, 1991 (see Appendix C, amendment 422).

§8A1.2. Application Instructions - Organizations

(a) Determine from Part B, Subpart 1 (Remedying Harm from Criminal Conduct) the sentencing requirements and options relating to restitution, remedial orders, community service, and notice to victims.

(b) Determine from Part C (Fines) the sentencing requirements and options relating to fines:

(1) If the organization operated primarily for a criminal purpose or primarily by criminal means, apply §8C1.1 (Determining the Fine - Criminal Purpose Organizations).

(2) Otherwise, apply §8C2.1 (Applicability of Fine Guidelines) to identify the counts for which the provisions of §§8C2.2 through 8C2.9 apply. For such counts:

(A) Refer to §8C2.2 (Preliminary Determination of Inability to Pay Fine) to determine whether an abbreviated determination of the guideline fine range may be warranted.

(B) Apply §8C2.3 (Offense Level) to determine the offense level from Chapter Two (Offense Conduct) and Chapter Three, Part D (Multiple Counts).

(C) Apply §8C2.4 (Base Fine) to determine the base fine.

(D) Apply §8C2.5 (Culpability Score) to determine the culpability score. To determine whether the organization had an effective compliance and ethics program for purposes of §8C2.5(f), apply §8B2.1 (Effective Compliance and Ethics Program).

(E) Apply §8C2.6 (Minimum and Maximum Multipliers) to determine the minimum and maximum multipliers corresponding to the culpability score.

(F) Apply §8C2.7 (Guideline Fine Range - Organizations) to determine the minimum and maximum of the guideline fine range.

(G) Refer to §8C2.8 (Determining the Fine Within the Range) to determine the amount of the fine within the applicable guideline range.

(H) Apply §8C2.9 (Disgorgement) to determine whether an increase to the fine is required.

For any count or counts not covered under §8C2.1 (Applicability of Fine Guidelines), apply §8C2.10 (Determining the Fine for Other Counts).

(3) Apply the provisions relating to the implementation of the sentence of a fine in Part C, Subpart 3 (Implementing the Sentence of a Fine).

(4) For grounds for departure from the applicable guideline fine range, refer to Part C, Subpart 4 (Departures from the Guideline Fine Range).

(c) Determine from Part D (Organizational Probation) the sentencing requirements and options relating to probation.

(d) Determine from Part E (Special Assessments, Forfeitures, and Costs) the sentencing requirements relating to special assessments, forfeitures, and costs.

Commentary

Application Notes:

1. Determinations under this chapter are to be based upon the facts and information specified in the applicable guideline. Determinations that reference other chapters are to be made under the standards applicable to determinations under those chapters.

2. The definitions in the Commentary to §1B1.1 (Application Instructions) and the guidelines and commentary in §§1B1.2 through 1B1.8 apply to determinations under this chapter unless otherwise specified. The adjustments in Chapter Three, Parts A (Victim-Related Adjustments), B (Role in the Offense), C (Obstruction and Related Adjustments), and E (Acceptance of Responsibility) do not apply. The provisions of Chapter Six (Sentencing Procedures, Plea Agreements, and Crime Victims' Rights) apply to proceedings in which the defendant is an organization. Guidelines and policy statements not referenced in this chapter, directly or indirectly, do not apply when the defendant is an organization; e.g., the policy statements in Chapter Seven (Violations of Probation and Supervised Release) do not apply to organizations.

3. The following are definitions of terms used frequently in this chapter:

(A) "Offense" means the offense of conviction and all relevant conduct under §1B1.3 (Relevant Conduct) unless a different meaning is specified or is otherwise clear from the context. The term "instant" is used in connection with "offense," "federal offense," or "offense of conviction," as the case may be, to distinguish the violation for which the defendant is being sentenced from a prior or subsequent offense, or from an offense before another court (e.g., an offense before a state court involving the same underlying conduct).

(B) "High-level personnel of the organization" means individuals who have substantial control over the organization or who have a substantial role in the making of policy within the organization. The term includes: a director; an executive officer; an individual in charge of a major business or functional unit of the organization, such as sales, administration, or finance; and an individual with a substantial ownership interest. "High-level personnel of a unit of the organization" is defined in the Commentary to §8C2.5 (Culpability Score).

(C) "Substantial authority personnel" means individuals who within the scope of their authority exercise a substantial measure of discretion in acting on behalf of an organization. The term includes high-level personnel of the organization, individuals who exercise substantial supervisory authority (e.g., a plant manager, a sales manager), and any other individuals who, although not a part of an organization's management, nevertheless exercise substantial discretion when acting within the scope of their authority (e.g., an individual with authority in an organization to negotiate or set price levels or an individual authorized to negotiate or approve significant contracts). Whether an individual falls within this category must be determined on a case-by-case basis.

(D) "Agent" means any individual, including a director, an officer, an employee, or an independent contractor, authorized to act on behalf of the organization.

(E) An individual "condoned" an offense if the individual knew of the offense and did not take reasonable steps to prevent or terminate the offense.

(F) "Similar misconduct" means prior conduct that is similar in nature to the conduct underlying the instant offense, without regard to whether or not such conduct violated the same statutory provision. For example, prior Medicare fraud would be misconduct similar to an instant offense involving another type of fraud.

(G) "Prior criminal adjudication" means conviction by trial, plea of guilty (including an Alford plea), or plea of nolo contendere.

(H) "Pecuniary gain" is derived from 18 U.S.C. § 3571(d) and means the additional before-tax profit to the defendant resulting from the relevant conduct of the offense. Gain can result from either additional revenue or cost savings. For example, an offense involving odometer tampering can produce additional revenue. In such a case, the pecuniary gain is the additional revenue received because the automobiles appeared to have less mileage, i.e., the difference between the price received or expected for the automobiles with the apparent mileage and the fair market value of the automobiles with the actual mileage. An offense involving defense procurement fraud related to defective product testing can produce pecuniary gain resulting from cost savings. In such a case, the pecuniary gain is the amount saved because the product was not tested in the required manner.

(I) "Pecuniary loss" is derived from 18 U.S.C. § 3571(d) and is equivalent to the term "loss" as used in Chapter Two (Offense Conduct). See Commentary to §2B1.1 (Theft, Property Destruction, and Fraud), and definitions of "tax loss" in Chapter Two, Part T (Offenses Involving Taxation).

(J) An individual was "willfully ignorant of the offense" if the individual did not investigate the possible occurrence of unlawful conduct despite knowledge of circumstances that would lead a reasonable person to investigate whether unlawful conduct had occurred.

Historical Note: Effective November 1, 1991 (see Appendix C, amendment 422); November 1, 1997 (see Appendix C, amendment 546); November 1, 2001 (see Appendix C, amendment 617); November 1, 2004 (see Appendix C, amendment 673); November 1, 2010 (see Appendix C, amendment 747); November 1, 2011 (see Appendix C, amendment 758).

PART B - REMEDYING HARM FROM CRIMINAL CONDUCT, AND EFFECTIVE COMPLIANCE AND ETHICS PROGRAM

Historical Note: Effective November 1, 1991 (see Appendix C, amendment 422). Amended effective November 1, 2004 (see Appendix C, amendment 673).

1. REMEDYING HARM FROM CRIMINAL CONDUCT

Historical Note: Effective November 1, 2004 (see Appendix C, amendment 673).

Introductory Commentary

As a general principle, the court should require that the organization take all appropriate steps to provide compensation to victims and otherwise remedy the harm caused or threatened by the offense. A restitution order or an order of probation requiring restitution can be used to compensate identifiable victims of the offense. A remedial order or an order of probation requiring community service can be used to reduce or eliminate the harm threatened, or to repair the harm caused by the offense, when that harm or threatened harm would otherwise not be remedied. An order of notice to victims can be used to notify unidentified victims of the offense.

Historical Note: Effective November 1, 1991 (see Appendix C, amendment 422).

8B1.1. Restitution - Organizations

(a) In the case of an identifiable victim, the court shall --

(1) enter a restitution order for the full amount of the victim's loss, if such order is authorized under 18 U.S.C. § 2248, § 2259, § 2264, § 2327, § 3663, or § 3663A; or

(2) impose a term of probation or supervised release with a condition requiring restitution for the full amount of the victim's loss, if the offense is not an offense for which restitution is authorized under 18 U.S.C. § 3663(a)(1) but otherwise meets the criteria for an order of restitution under that section.

(b) Provided, that the provisions of subsection (a) do not apply --

(1) when full restitution has been made; or

(2) in the case of a restitution order under § 3663; a restitution order under 18 U.S.C. § 3663A that pertains to an offense against property described in 18 U.S.C. § 3663A(c)(1)(A)(ii); or a condition of restitution imposed pursuant to subsection (a)(2) above, to the extent the court finds, from facts on the record, that (A) the number of identifiable victims is so large as to make restitution impracticable; or (B) determining complex issues of fact related to the cause or amount of the victim's losses would complicate or prolong the sentencing process to a degree that the need to provide restitution to any victim is outweighed by the burden on the sentencing process.

(c) If a defendant is ordered to make restitution to an identifiable victim and to pay a fine, the court shall order that any money paid by the defendant shall first be applied to satisfy the order of restitution.

(d) A restitution order may direct the defendant to make a single, lump sum payment, partial payments at specified intervals, in-kind payments, or a combination of payments at specified intervals and in-kind payments. See 18 U.S.C. § 3664(f)(3)(A). An in-kind payment may be in the form of (1) return of property; (2) replacement of property; or (3) if the victim agrees, services rendered to the victim or to a person or organization other than the victim. See 18 U.S.C. § 3664(f)(4).

(e) A restitution order may direct the defendant to make nominal periodic payments if the court finds from facts on the record that the economic circumstances of the defendant do not allow the payment of any amount of a restitution order, and do not allow for the payment of the full amount of a restitution order in the foreseeable future under any reasonable schedule of payments.

(f) Special Instruction

(1) This guideline applies only to a defendant convicted of an offense committed on or after November 1, 1997. Notwithstanding the provisions of §1B1.11 (Use of Guidelines Manual in Effect on Date of Sentencing), use the former §8B1.1 (set forth in Appendix C, amendment 571) in lieu of this guideline in any other case.

Commentary

Background: Section 3553(a)(7) of Title 18, United States Code, requires the court, "in determining the particular sentence to be imposed," to consider "the need to provide restitution to any victims of the offense." Orders of restitution are authorized under 18 U.S.C. §§ 2248, 2259, 2264, 2327, 3663, and 3663A. For offenses for which an order of restitution is not authorized, restitution may be imposed as a condition of probation.

Historical Note: Effective November 1, 1991 (see Appendix C, amendment 422); November 1, 1997 (see Appendix C, amendment 571).

§8B1.2. Remedial Orders - Organizations (Policy Statement)

(a) To the extent not addressed under §8B1.1 (Restitution - Organizations), a remedial order imposed as a condition of probation may require the organization to remedy the harm caused by the offense and to eliminate or reduce the risk that the instant offense will cause future harm.

(b) If the magnitude of expected future harm can be reasonably estimated, the court may require the organization to create a trust fund sufficient to address that expected harm.

Commentary

Background: *The purposes of a remedial order are to remedy harm that has already occurred and to prevent future harm. A remedial order requiring corrective action by the organization may be necessary to prevent future injury from the instant offense, e.g., a product recall for a food and drug violation or a clean-up order for an environmental violation. In some cases in which a remedial order potentially may be appropriate, a governmental regulatory agency, e.g., the Environmental Protection Agency or the Food and Drug Administration, may have authority to order remedial measures. In such cases, a remedial order by the court may not be necessary. If a remedial order is entered, it should be coordinated with any administrative or civil actions taken by the appropriate governmental regulatory agency.*

Historical Note: Effective November 1, 1991 (see Appendix C, amendment 422).

§8B1.3. Community Service - Organizations (Policy Statement)

Community service may be ordered as a condition of probation where such community service is reasonably designed to repair the harm caused by the offense.

Commentary

Background: *An organization can perform community service only by employing its resources or paying its employees or others to do so. Consequently, an order that an organization perform community service is essentially an indirect monetary sanction, and therefore generally less desirable than a direct monetary sanction. However, where the convicted organization possesses knowledge, facilities, or skills that uniquely qualify it to repair damage caused by the offense, community service directed at repairing damage may provide an efficient means of remedying harm caused. In the past, some forms of community service imposed on organizations have not been related to the purposes of sentencing. Requiring a defendant to endow a chair at a university or to contribute to a local charity would not be consistent with this section unless such community service provided a means for preventive or corrective action directly related to the offense and therefore served one of the purposes of sentencing set forth in 18 U.S.C. § 3553(a).*

<u>Historical Note</u>: Effective November 1, 1991 (<u>see</u> Appendix C, amendment 422).

§8B1.4. Order of Notice to Victims - Organizations
Apply §5F1.4 (Order of Notice to Victims).

<u>Historical Note</u>: Effective November 1, 1991 (<u>see</u> Appendix C, amendment 422).

2. EFFECTIVE COMPLIANCE AND ETHICS PROGRAM

<u>Historical Note</u>: Effective November 1, 2004 (<u>see</u> Appendix C, amendment 673).

§8B2.1. <u>Effective Compliance and Ethics Program</u>

(a) To have an effective compliance and ethics program, for purposes of subsection (f) of §8C2.5 (Culpability Score) and subsection (b)(1) of §8D1.4 (Recommended Conditions of Probation - Organizations), an organization shall—

(1) exercise due diligence to prevent and detect criminal conduct; and

(2) otherwise promote an organizational culture that encourages ethical conduct and a commitment to compliance with the law.

Such compliance and ethics program shall be reasonably designed, implemented, and enforced so that the program is generally effective in preventing and detecting criminal conduct. The failure to prevent or detect the instant offense does not necessarily mean that the program is not generally effective in preventing and detecting criminal conduct.

(b) Due diligence and the promotion of an organizational culture that encourages ethical conduct and a commitment to compliance with the law within the meaning of subsection (a) minimally require the following:

(1) The organization shall establish standards and procedures to prevent and detect criminal conduct.

(2) (A) The organization's governing authority shall be knowledgeable about the content and operation of the compliance and ethics program and shall exercise reasonable oversight with respect to the implementation and effectiveness of the compliance and ethics program.

(B) High-level personnel of the organization shall ensure that the organization has an effective compliance and ethics program, as described in this guideline. Specific individual(s) within high-level personnel shall be assigned overall responsibility for the compliance and ethics program.

(C) Specific individual(s) within the organization shall be delegated

day-to-day operational responsibility for the compliance and ethics program. Individual(s) with operational responsibility shall report periodically to high-level personnel and, as appropriate, to the governing authority, or an appropriate subgroup of the governing authority, on the effective¬ness of the compliance and ethics program. To carry out such operational responsibility, such individual(s) shall be given adequate resources, appropriate authority, and direct access to the governing authority or an appropriate subgroup of the governing authority.

(3) The organization shall use reasonable efforts not to include within

the substantial authority personnel of the organization any individual whom the organization knew, or should have known through the exercise of due diligence, has engaged in illegal activities or other conduct inconsistent with an effective compliance and ethics program.

(4) (A) The organization shall take reasonable steps to communicate

periodically and in a practical manner its standards and procedures, and other aspects of the compliance and ethics program, to the individuals referred to in subparagraph (B) by conducting effective training programs and otherwise disseminating information appropriate to such individuals' respective roles and responsibilities.

(B) The individuals referred to in subparagraph (A) are the members

of the governing authority, high-level personnel, substantial authority personnel, the organization's employees, and, as appropriate, the organization's agents.

(5) The organization shall take reasonable steps—

(A) to ensure that the organization's compliance and ethics program is

followed, including monitoring and auditing to detect criminal conduct;

(B) to evaluate periodically the effectiveness of the organization's

compliance and ethics program; and

(C) to have and publicize a system, which may include mechanisms

that allow for anonymity or confidentiality, whereby the organization's employees and agents may report or seek guidance regarding potential or actual criminal conduct without fear of retaliation.

(6) The organization's compliance and ethics program shall be promoted

and enforced consistently throughout the organization through (A) appropriate incentives to perform in accordance with the compliance and ethics program; and (B) appropriate disciplinary measures for engaging in criminal conduct and for failing to take reasonable steps to prevent or detect criminal conduct.

(7) After criminal conduct has been detected, the organization shall take

reasonable steps to respond appropriately to the criminal conduct and to prevent further similar criminal conduct, including making any necessary modifications to the organization's compliance and ethics program.

(c) In implementing subsection (b), the organization shall periodically assess the risk of criminal conduct and shall take appropriate steps to design, implement, or modify each requirement set forth in subsection (b) to reduce the risk of criminal conduct identified through this process.

Commentary

Application Notes:

1. *Definitions.*—*For purposes of this guideline:*

"Compliance and ethics program" means a program designed to prevent and detect criminal conduct.

"Governing authority" means the (A) the Board of Directors; or (B) if the organization does not have a Board of Directors, the highest-level governing body of the organization.

"High-level personnel of the organization" and "substantial authority personnel" have the meaning given those terms in the Commentary to §8A1.2 (Application Instructions - Organizations).

"Standards and procedures" means standards of conduct and internal controls that are reasonably capable of reducing the likelihood of criminal conduct.

2. *Factors to Consider in Meeting Requirements of this Guideline.*—

(A) In General.—*Each of the requirements set forth in this guideline shall be met by an organization; however, in determining what specific actions are necessary to meet those requirements, factors that shall be considered include: (i) applicable industry practice or the standards called for by any applicable governmental regulation; (ii) the size of the organization; and (iii) similar misconduct.*

(B) Applicable Governmental Regulation and Industry Practice.—*An organization's failure to incorporate and follow applicable industry practice or the standards called for by any applicable governmental regulation weighs against a finding of an effective compliance and ethics program.*

(C) The Size of the Organization.—

(i) In General.—*The formality and scope of actions that an organization shall take to meet the requirements of this guideline, including the necessary features of the organization's standards and procedures, depend on the size of the organization.*

(ii) Large Organizations.—*A large organization generally shall devote more formal operations and greater resources in meeting the requirements of this guideline than shall a small organization. As appropriate, a large organization should encourage small organizations (especially those that have, or seek to have, a business relationship with the large organization) to implement effective compliance and ethics programs.*

(iii) Small Organizations.—In meeting the requirements of this guideline, small organizations shall demonstrate the same degree of commitment to ethical conduct and compliance with the law as large organizations. However, a small organiza¬tion may meet the requirements of this guideline with less formality and fewer resources than would be expected of large organizations. In appropriate circumstances, reliance on existing resources and simple systems can demonstrate a degree of commitment that, for a large organization, would only be demonstrated through more formally planned and implemented systems.

Examples of the informality and use of fewer resources with which a small organization may meet the requirements of this guideline include the following: (I) the governing authority's discharge of its responsibility for oversight of the compliance and ethics program by directly managing the organization's compliance and ethics efforts; (II) training employees through informal staff meetings, and monitoring through regular "walk-arounds" or continuous observation while managing the organization; (III) using available personnel, rather than employing separate staff, to carry out the compliance and ethics program; and (IV) modeling its own compliance and ethics program on existing, well-regarded compliance and ethics programs and best practices of other similar organizations.

(D) Recurrence of Similar Misconduct.—Recurrence of similar misconduct creates doubt regarding whether the organization took reasonable steps to meet the requirements of this guideline. For purposes of this subparagraph, "similar misconduct" has the meaning given that term in the Commentary to §8A1.2 (Application Instructions - Organizations).

3. Application of Subsection (b)(2).—High-level personnel and substantial authority personnel of the organization shall be knowledgeable about the content and operation of the compliance and ethics program, shall perform their assigned duties consistent with the exercise of due diligence, and shall promote an organizational culture that encourages ethical conduct and a commitment to compliance with the law.

If the specific individual(s) assigned overall responsibility for the compliance and ethics program does not have day-to-day operational responsibility for the program, then the individual(s) with day-to-day operational responsibility for the program typically should, no less than annually, give the governing authority or an appropriate subgroup thereof information on the implementation and effectiveness of the compliance and ethics program.

4. Application of Subsection (b)(3).—

(A) Consistency with Other Law.—Nothing in subsection (b)(3) is intended to require conduct inconsistent with any Federal, State, or local law, including any law governing employment or hiring practices.

(B) Implementation.—In implementing subsection (b)(3), the organization shall hire and promote individuals so as to ensure that all individuals within the high-level personnel and substantial authority personnel of the organization will perform their assigned duties in a manner consistent with the exercise of due diligence and the promotion of an organizational culture

that encourages ethical conduct and a commitment to compliance with the law under subsection (a). With respect to the hiring or promotion of such individuals, an organization shall consider the relatedness of the individual's illegal activities and other misconduct (i.e., other conduct inconsistent with an effective compliance and ethics program) to the specific responsibilities the individual is anticipated to be assigned and other factors such as: (i) the recency of the individual's illegal activities and other misconduct; and (ii) whether the individual has engaged in other such illegal activities and other such misconduct.

5. *Application of Subsection (b)(6).*—*Adequate discipline of individuals responsible for an offense is a necessary component of enforcement; however, the form of discipline that will be appropriate will be case specific.*

6. *Application of Subsection (b)(7).*—*Subsection (b)(7) has two aspects.*

First, the organization should respond appropriately to the criminal conduct. The organization should take reasonable steps, as warranted under the circumstances, to remedy the harm resulting from the criminal conduct. These steps may include, where appropriate, providing restitution to identifiable victims, as well as other forms of remediation. Other reasonable steps to respond appropriately to the criminal conduct may include self-reporting and cooperation with authorities.

Second, the organization should act appropriately to prevent further similar criminal conduct, including assessing the compliance and ethics program and making modifications necessary to ensure the program is effective. The steps taken should be consistent with subsections (b)(5) and (c) and may include the use of an outside professional advisor to ensure adequate assessment and implementation of any modifications.

7. *Application of Subsection (c).*—*To meet the requirements of subsection (c), an organization shall:*

(A) Assess periodically the risk that criminal conduct will occur, including assessing the following:

(i) The nature and seriousness of such criminal conduct.

(ii) The likelihood that certain criminal conduct may occur because of the nature of the organization's business. If, because of the nature of an organization's business, there is a substantial risk that certain types of criminal conduct may occur, the organization shall take reasonable steps to prevent and detect that type of criminal conduct. For example, an organization that, due to the nature of its business, employs sales personnel who have flexibility to set prices shall establish standards and procedures designed to prevent and detect price-fixing. An organization that, due to the nature of its business, employs sales personnel who have flexibility to represent the material characteristics of a product shall establish standards and procedures designed to prevent and detect fraud.

(iii) The prior history of the organization. The prior history of an organization may indicate types of criminal conduct that it shall take actions to prevent and detect.

(B) Prioritize periodically, as appropriate, the actions taken pursuant to any requirement set forth in subsection (b), in order to focus on preventing and detecting the criminal conduct identified under subparagraph (A) of this note as most serious, and most likely, to occur.

(C) Modify, as appropriate, the actions taken pursuant to any requirement set forth in subsection (b) to reduce the risk of criminal conduct identified under subparagraph (A) of this note as most serious, and most likely, to occur.

Background: This section sets forth the requirements for an effective compliance and ethics program. This section responds to section 805(a)(5) of the Sarbanes-Oxley Act of 2002, Public Law 107–204, which directed the Commission to review and amend, as appropriate, the guidelines and related policy statements to ensure that the guidelines that apply to organizations in this chapter "are sufficient to deter and punish organizational criminal misconduct."

The requirements set forth in this guideline are intended to achieve reasonable prevention and detection of criminal conduct for which the organization would be vicariously liable. The prior diligence of an organization in seeking to prevent and detect criminal conduct has a direct bearing on the appropriate penalties and probation terms for the organization if it is convicted and sentenced for a criminal offense.

Historical Note: Effective November 1, 2004 (see Appendix C, amendment 673). Amended effective November 1, 2010 (see Appendix C, amendment 744); November 1, 2011 (see Appendix C, amendment 758); November 1, 2013 (see Appendix C, amendment 778).

PART C - FINES

1.   DETERMINING   THE   FINE   -   CRIMINAL PURPOSE ORGANIZATIONS

§8C1.1. Determining the Fine - Criminal Purpose Organizations

If, upon consideration of the nature and circumstances of the offense and the history and characteristics of the organization, the court determines that the organization operated primarily for a criminal purpose or primarily by criminal means, the fine shall be set at an amount (subject to the statutory maximum) sufficient to divest the organization of all its net assets. When this section applies, Subpart 2 (Determining the Fine - Other Organizations) and §8C3.4 (Fines Paid by Owners of Closely Held Organizations) do not apply.

Commentary

Application Note:

1. "Net assets," as used in this section, means the assets remaining after payment of all legitimate claims against assets by known innocent bona fide creditors.

Background: This guideline addresses the case in which the court, based upon an examination of the nature and circumstances of the offense and the history and characteristics of the organization, determines that the organization was operated primarily for a criminal purpose (*e.g.,* a front for a scheme that was designed to commit fraud; an organization established to participate in the illegal manufacture, importation, or distribution of a controlled substance) or operated primarily by criminal means (*e.g.,* a hazardous waste disposal business that had no legitimate means of disposing of hazardous waste). In such a case, the fine shall be set at an amount sufficient to remove all of the organization's net assets. If the extent of the assets of the organization is unknown, the maximum fine authorized by statute should be imposed, absent innocent bona fide creditors.

Historical Note: Effective November 1, 1991 (see Appendix C, amendment 422).

* * * * *

2. DETERMINING THE FINE - OTHER ORGANIZATIONS

§8C2.1. Applicability of Fine Guidelines

The provisions of §§8C2.2 through 8C2.9 apply to each count for which the applicable guideline offense level is determined under:

(a) §§2B1.1, 2B1.4, 2B2.3, 2B4.1, 2B5.3, 2B6.1;
§§2C1.1, 2C1.2, 2C1.6;
§§2D1.7, 2D3.1, 2D3.2;
§§2E3.1, 2E4.1, 2E5.1, 2E5.3;
§2G3.1;
§§2K1.1, 2K2.1;
§2L1.1;
§2N3.1;
§2R1.1;
§§2S1.1, 2S1.3;
§§2T1.1, 2T1.4, 2T1.6, 2T1.7, 2T1.8, 2T1.9, 2T2.1, 2T2.2, 2T3.1; or

(b) §§2E1.1, 2X1.1, 2X2.1, 2X3.1, 2X4.1, with respect to cases in which the offense level for the underlying offense is determined under one of the guideline sections listed in subsection (a) above.

Commentary

Application Notes:

1. If the Chapter Two offense guideline for a count is listed in subsection (a) or (b) above, and the applicable guideline results in the determination of the offense level by use of one of the listed guidelines, apply the provisions of §§8C2.2 through 8C2.9 to that count. For example, §§8C2.2 through 8C2.9 apply to an offense under §2K2.1 (an offense guideline listed in subsection (a)), unless the cross reference in that guideline requires the offense level to be determined under an offense guideline section not listed in subsection (a).

2. If the Chapter Two offense guideline for a count is not listed in subsection (a) or (b) above, but the applicable guideline results in the determination of the offense level by use of a listed guideline, apply the provisions of §§8C2.2 through 8C2.9 to that count. For example, where the conduct set forth in a count of conviction ordinarily referenced to §2N2.1 (an offense guideline not listed in subsection (a)) establishes §2B1.1 (Theft, Property Destruction, and Fraud) as the applicable offense guideline (an offense guideline listed in subsection (a)), §§8C2.2 through 8C2.9 would apply because the actual offense level is determined under §2B1.1 (Theft, Property Destruction, and Fraud).

Background: The fine guidelines of this subpart apply only to offenses covered by the guideline sections set forth in subsection (a) above. For example, the provisions of §§8C2.2 through 8C2.9 do not apply to counts for which the applicable guideline offense level is determined under Chapter Two, Part Q (Offenses Involving the Environment). For such cases, §8C2.10 (Determining the Fine for Other Counts) is applicable.

Historical Note: Effective November 1, 1991 (see Appendix C, amendment 422). Amended effective November 1, 1992 (see Appendix C, amendment 453); November 1, 1993 (see Appendix C, amendment 496); November 1, 2001 (see Appendix C, amendments 617, 619, and 634); November 1, 2005 (see Appendix C, amendment 679).

§8C2.2. Preliminary Determination of Inability to Pay Fine

(a) Where it is readily ascertainable that the organization cannot and is not likely to become able (even on an installment schedule) to pay restitution required under §8B1.1 (Restitution - Organizations), a determination of the guideline fine range is unnecessary because, pursuant to §8C3.3(a), no fine would be imposed.

(b) Where it is readily ascertainable through a preliminary determination of the minimum of the guideline fine range (see §§8C2.3 through 8C2.7) that the organization cannot and is not likely to become able (even on an installment schedule) to pay such minimum guideline fine, a further determination of the guideline fine range is unnecessary. Instead, the court may use the preliminary determination and impose the fine that would result from the application of §8C3.3 (Reduction of Fine Based on Inability to Pay).

Commentary

Application Notes:

1. In a case of a determination under subsection (a), a statement that "the guideline fine range was not determined because it is readily ascertainable that the defendant cannot and is not likely to become able to pay restitution" is recommended.

2. In a case of a determination under subsection (b), a statement that "no precise determination of the guideline fine range is required because it is readily ascertainable that the defendant cannot and is not likely to become able to pay the minimum of the guideline fine range" is recommended.

Background: Many organizational defendants lack the ability to pay restitution. In addition, many organizational defendants who may be able to pay restitution lack the ability to pay the minimum fine called for by §8C2.7(a). In such cases, a complete determination of the guideline fine range may be a needless exercise. This section provides for an abbreviated determination of the guideline fine range that can be applied where it is readily ascertainable that the fine within the guideline fine range determined under §8C2.7 (Guideline Fine Range - Organizations) would be reduced under §8C3.3 (Reduction of Fine Based on Inability to Pay).

Historical Note: Effective November 1, 1991 (see Appendix C, amendment 422).

§8C2.3. Offense Level

(a) For each count covered by §8C2.1 (Applicability of Fine Guidelines), use the applicable Chapter Two guideline to determine the base offense level and apply, in the order listed, any appropriate adjustments contained in that guideline.

(b) Where there is more than one such count, apply Chapter Three, Part D (Multiple Counts) to determine the combined offense level.

Commentary

Application Notes:

1. In determining the offense level under this section, "defendant," as used in Chapter Two, includes any agent of the organization for whose conduct the organization is criminally responsible.

2. In determining the offense level under this section, apply the provisions of §§1B1.2 through 1B1.8. Do not apply the adjustments in Chapter Three, Parts A (Victim-Related Adjustments), B (Role in the Offense), C (Obstruction), and E (Acceptance of Responsibility).

Historical Note: Effective November 1, 1991 (see Appendix C, amendment 422).

§8C2.4. Base Fine

(a) The base fine is the greatest of:

(1) the amount from the table in subsection (d) below corresponding to the offense level determined under §8C2.3 (Offense Level); or

(2) the pecuniary gain to the organization from the offense; or

(3) the pecuniary loss from the offense caused by the organization, to the extent the loss was caused intentionally, knowingly, or recklessly.

(b) *Provided*, that if the applicable offense guideline in Chapter Two includes a special instruction for organizational fines, that special instruction shall be applied, as appropriate.

(c) *Provided, further*, that to the extent the calculation of either pecuniary gain or pecuniary loss would unduly complicate or prolong the sentencing process, that amount, i.e., gain or loss as appropriate, shall not be used for the determination of the base fine.

(d) <u>Offense Level Fine Table</u>

<u>Offense Level</u>	<u>Amount</u>
6 or less	$5,000
7	$7,500
8	$10,000
9	$15,000
10	$20,000
11	$30,000
12	$40,000
13	$60,000
14	$85,000
15	$125,000
16	$175,000
17	$250,000
18	$350,000
19	$500,000
20	$650,000
21	$910,000
22	$1,200,000
23	$1,600,000
24	$2,100,000
25	$2,800,000
26	$3,700,000
27	$4,800,000
28	$6,300,000
29	$8,100,000
30	$10,500,000
31	$13,500,000
32	$17,500,000
33	$22,000,000
34	$28,500,000
35	$36,000,000
36	$45,500,000
37	$57,500,000
38 or more	$72,500,000.

Commentary

Application Notes:

1. *"Pecuniary gain," "pecuniary loss," and "offense" are defined in the Commentary to §8A1.2 (Application Instructions - Organizations). Note that subsections (a)(2) and (a)(3) contain certain limitations as to the use of pecuniary gain and pecuniary loss in determining the base fine. Under subsection (a)(2), the pecuniary gain used to determine the base fine is the pecuniary gain to the organization from the offense. Under subsection (a)(3), the pecuniary loss used to determine the base fine is the pecuniary loss from the offense caused by the organization, to the extent that such loss was caused intentionally, knowingly, or recklessly.*

2. *Under 18 U.S.C. § 3571(d), the court is not required to calculate pecuniary loss or pecuniary gain to the extent that determination of loss or gain would unduly complicate or prolong the sentencing process. Nevertheless, the court may need to approximate loss in order to calculate offense levels under Chapter Two. See Commentary to §2B1.1 (Theft, Property Destruction, and Fraud). If loss is approximated for purposes of determining the applicable offense level, the court should use that approximation as the starting point for calculating pecuniary loss under this section.*

3. *In a case of an attempted offense or a conspiracy to commit an offense, pecuniary loss and pecuniary gain are to be determined in accordance with the principles stated in §2X1.1 (Attempt, Solicitation, or Conspiracy).*

4. *In a case involving multiple participants (i.e., multiple organizations, or the organization and individual(s) unassociated with the organization), the applicable offense level is to be determined without regard to apportionment of the gain from or loss caused by the offense. See §1B1.3 (Relevant Conduct). However, if the base fine is determined under subsections (a)(2) or (a)(3), the court may, as appropriate, apportion gain or loss considering the defendant's relative culpability and other pertinent factors. Note also that under §2R1.1(d)(1), the volume of commerce, which is used in determining a proxy for loss under §8C2.4(a)(3), is limited to the volume of commerce attributable to the defendant.*

5. *Special instructions regarding the determination of the base fine are contained in §§2B4.1 (Bribery in Procurement of Bank Loan and Other Commercial Bribery); 2C1.1 (Offering, Giving, Soliciting, or Receiving a Bribe; Extortion Under Color of Official Right; Fraud Involving the Deprivation of the Intangible Right to Honest Services of Public Officials; Conspiracy to Defraud by Interference with Governmental Functions); 2C1.2 (Offering, Giving, Soliciting, or Receiving a Gratuity); 2E5.1 (Offering, Accepting, or Soliciting a Bribe or Gratuity Affecting the Operation of an Employee Welfare or Pension Benefit Plan; Prohibited Payments or Lending of Money by Employer or Agent to Employees, Representatives, or Labor*

Organizations); and 2R1.1 (Bid-Rigging, Price-Fixing or Market-Allocation Agreements Among Competitors).

Background: Under this section, the base fine is determined in one of three ways: (1) by the amount, based on the offense level, from the table in subsection (d); (2) by the pecuniary gain to the organization from the offense; and (3) by the pecuniary loss caused by the organization, to the extent that such loss was caused intentionally, knowingly, or recklessly. In certain cases, special instructions for determining the loss or offense level amount apply. As a general rule, the base fine measures the seriousness of the offense. The determinants of the base fine are selected so that, in conjunction with the multipliers derived from the culpability score in §8C2.5 (Culpability Score), they will result in guideline fine ranges appropriate to deter organizational criminal conduct and to provide incentives for organizations to maintain internal mechanisms for preventing, detecting, and reporting criminal conduct. In order to deter organizations from seeking to obtain financial reward through criminal conduct, this section provides that, when greatest, pecuniary gain to the organization is used to determine the base fine. In order to ensure that organizations will seek to prevent losses intentionally, knowingly, or recklessly caused by their agents, this section provides that, when greatest, pecuniary loss is used to determine the base fine in such circumstances. Chapter Two provides special instructions for fines that include specific rules for determining the base fine in connection with certain types of offenses in which the calculation of loss or gain is difficult, e.g., price-fixing. For these offenses, the special instructions tailor the base fine to circumstances that occur in connection with such offenses and that generally relate to the magnitude of loss or gain resulting from such offenses.

Historical Note: Effective November 1, 1991 (see Appendix C, amendment 422). Amended effective November 1, 1993 (see Appendix C, amendment 496); November 1, 1995 (see Appendix C, amendment 534); November 1, 2001 (see Appendix C, amendment 634); November 1, 2004 (see Appendix C, amendments 666 and 673).

§8C2.5. Culpability Score

(a) Start with **5** points and apply subsections (b) through (g) below.

(b) Involvement in or Tolerance of Criminal Activity

If more than one applies, use the greatest:

    (1) If --

        (A) the organization had 5,000 or more employees and

(i) an individual within high-level personnel of the organization participated in, condoned, or was willfully ignorant of the offense; or

(ii) tolerance of the offense by substantial authority personnel was pervasive throughout the organization; or

(B) the unit of the organization within which the offense was committed had 5,000 or more employees and

(i) an individual within high-level personnel of the unit participated in, condoned, or was willfully ignorant of the offense; or

(ii) tolerance of the offense by substantial authority personnel was pervasive throughout such unit,

add **5** points; or

(2) If --

(A) the organization had 1,000 or more employees and

(i) an individual within high-level personnel of the organization participated in, condoned, or was willfully ignorant of the offense; or

(ii) tolerance of the offense by substantial authority personnel was pervasive throughout the organization; or

(B) the unit of the organization within which the offense was committed had 1,000 or more employees and

(i) an individual within high-level personnel of the unit participated in, condoned, or was willfully ignorant of the offense; or

(ii) tolerance of the offense by substantial authority personnel was pervasive throughout such unit,

add **4** points; or

(3) If --

(A) the organization had 200 or more employees and

(i) an individual within high-level personnel of the organization participated in, condoned, or was willfully ignorant of the offense; or

(ii) tolerance of the offense by substantial authority personnel was pervasive throughout the organization; or

(B) the unit of the organization within which the offense was committed had 200 or more employees and

(i) an individual within high-level personnel of the unit participated in, condoned, or was willfully ignorant of the offense; or

(ii) tolerance of the offense by substantial authority personnel was pervasive throughout such unit,

add **3** points; or

(4) If the organization had 50 or more employees and an individual within substantial authority personnel participated in, condoned, or was willfully ignorant of the offense, add **2** points; or

(5) If the organization had 10 or more employees and an individual within substantial authority personnel participated in, condoned, or was willfully ignorant of the offense, add **1** point.

(c) <u>Prior History</u>

If more than one applies, use the greater:

(1) If the organization (or separately managed line of business) committed any part of the instant offense less than 10 years after (A) a criminal adjudication based on similar misconduct; or (B) civil or administrative adjudication(s) based on two or more separate instances of similar misconduct, add **1** point; or

(2) If the organization (or separately managed line of business) committed any part of the instant offense less than 5 years after (A) a criminal adjudication based on similar misconduct; or (B) civil or administrative adjudication(s) based on two or more separate instances of similar misconduct, add **2** points.

(d) <u>Violation of an Order</u>

If more than one applies, use the greater:

(1) (A) If the commission of the instant offense violated a judicial order or injunction, other than a violation of a condition of probation; or (B) if the organization (or separately managed line of business) violated a condition of probation by engaging in similar misconduct, <u>i.e.</u>, misconduct similar to that for which it was placed on probation, add **2** points; or

(2) If the commission of the instant offense violated a condition of probation, add **1** point.

(e) <u>Obstruction of Justice</u>

If the organization willfully obstructed or impeded, attempted to obstruct or impede, or aided, abetted, or encouraged obstruction of justice during the investigation, prosecution, or sentencing of the instant offense, or, with knowledge thereof, failed to take reasonable steps to prevent such obstruction or impedance or attempted obstruction or impedance, add **3** points.

(f) <u>Effective Compliance and Ethics Program</u>

(1) If the offense occurred even though the organization had in place at the time of the offense an effective compliance and ethics program, as provided in §8B2.1 (Effective Compliance and Ethics Program), subtract **3** points.

(2) Subsection (f)(1) shall not apply if, after becoming aware of an offense, the organization unreasonably delayed reporting the offense to appropriate governmental authorities.

(3) (A) Except as provided in subparagraphs (B) and (C), subsection (f)(1) shall not apply if an individual within high-level personnel of the organization, a person within high-level personnel of the unit of the organization within which the offense was committed where the unit had 200 or more employees, or an individual described in §8B2.1(b)(2)(B) or (C), participated in, condoned, or was willfully ignorant of the offense.

(B) There is a rebuttable presumption, for purposes of subsection (f)(1), that the organization did not have an effective compliance and ethics program if an individual—

(i) within high-level personnel of a small organization; or

(ii) within substantial authority personnel, but not within high-level personnel, of any organization,

participated in, condoned, or was willfully ignorant of, the offense.

(C) Subparagraphs (A) and (B) shall not apply if—

(i) the individual or individuals with operational responsibility for the compliance and ethics program (see §8B2.1(b)(2)(C)) have direct reporting obligations to the governing authority or an appropriate subgroup thereof (e.g., an audit committee of the board of directors);

(ii) the compliance and ethics program detected the offense before discovery outside the organization or before such discovery was reasonably likely;

(iii) the organization promptly reported the offense to appropriate governmental authorities; and

(iv) no individual with operational responsibility for the compliance and ethics program participated in, condoned, or was willfully ignorant of the offense.

(g) <u>Self-Reporting, Cooperation, and Acceptance of Responsibility</u>

If more than one applies, use the greatest:

(1) If the organization (A) prior to an imminent threat of disclosure or government investigation; and (B) within a reasonably prompt time after becoming aware of the offense, reported the offense to appropriate governmental authorities, fully cooperated in the investigation, and clearly demonstrated recognition and affirmative acceptance of responsibility for its criminal conduct, subtract **5** points; or

(2) If the organization fully cooperated in the investigation and clearly demonstrated recognition and affirmative acceptance of responsibility for its criminal conduct, subtract **2** points; or

(3) If the organization clearly demonstrated recognition and affirmative acceptance of responsibility for its criminal conduct, subtract **1** point.

Commentary

Application Notes:

1. *Definitions.*—*For purposes of this guideline, "condoned", "prior criminal adjudication", "similar misconduct", "substantial authority personnel", and "willfully ignorant of the offense" have the meaning given those terms in Application Note 3 of the Commentary to §8A1.2 (Application Instructions - Organizations).*

"Small Organization", for purposes of subsection (f)(3), means an organization that, at the time of the instant offense, had fewer than 200 employees.

2. *For purposes of subsection (b), "unit of the organization" means any reasonably distinct operational component of the organization. For example, a large organization may have several large units such as divisions or subsidiaries, as well as many smaller units such as specialized manufacturing, marketing, or accounting operations within these larger units. For purposes of this definition, all of these types of units are encompassed within the term "unit of the organization."*

3. *"High-level personnel of the organization" is defined in the Commentary to §8A1.2 (Application Instructions - Organizations). With respect to a unit with 200 or more employees, "high-level personnel of a unit of the organization" means agents within the unit who set the policy for or control that unit. For example, if the managing agent of a unit with 200 employees participated in an offense, three points would be added under subsection (b)(3); if that organization had 1,000 employees and the managing agent of the unit with 200 employees were also within high-level personnel of the organization in its entirety, four points (rather than three) would be added under subsection (b)(2).*

4. *Pervasiveness under subsection (b) will be case specific and depend on the number, and degree of responsibility, of individuals within substantial authority personnel who participated in, condoned, or were willfully ignorant of the offense. Fewer individuals need to be involved for a finding of pervasiveness if those individuals exercised a relatively high degree of authority. Pervasiveness can occur either within an organization as a whole or within a unit of an organization. For example, if an offense were committed in an organization with 1,000 employees but the tolerance of the offense was pervasive only within a unit of the organization with 200 employees (and no high-level personnel of the organization participated in, condoned, or was willfully ignorant of the offense), three points would be added under subsection (b)(3). If, in the same organization, tolerance of the offense was pervasive throughout the organization as a whole, or an individual within high-level personnel of the organization participated in the offense, four points (rather than three) would be added under subsection (b)(2).*

5. A "separately managed line of business," as used in subsections (c) and (d), is a subpart of a for-profit organization that has its own management, has a high degree of autonomy from higher managerial authority, and maintains its own separate books of account. Corporate subsidiaries and divisions frequently are separately managed lines of business. Under subsection (c), in determining the prior history of an organization with separately managed lines of business, only the prior conduct or criminal record of the separately managed line of business involved in the instant offense is to be used. Under subsection (d), in the context of an organization with separately managed lines of business, in making the determination whether a violation of a condition of probation involved engaging in similar misconduct, only the prior misconduct of the separately managed line of business involved in the instant offense is to be considered.

6. Under subsection (c), in determining the prior history of an organization or separately managed line of business, the conduct of the underlying economic entity shall be considered without regard to its legal structure or ownership. For example, if two companies merged and became separate divisions and separately managed lines of business within the merged company, each division would retain the prior history of its predecessor company. If a company reorganized and became a new legal entity, the new company would retain the prior history of the predecessor company. In contrast, if one company purchased the physical assets but not the ongoing business of another company, the prior history of the company selling the physical assets would not be transferred to the company purchasing the assets. However, if an organization is acquired by another organization in response to solicitations by appropriate federal government officials, the prior history of the acquired organization shall not be attributed to the acquiring organization.

7. Under subsections (c)(1)(B) and (c)(2)(B), the civil or administrative adjudication(s) must have occurred within the specified period (ten or five years) of the instant offense.

8. Adjust the culpability score for the factors listed in subsection (e) whether or not the offense guideline incorporates that factor, or that factor is inherent in the offense.

9. Subsection (e) applies where the obstruction is committed on behalf of the organization; it does not apply where an individual or individuals have attempted to conceal their misconduct from the organization. The Commentary to §3C1.1 (Obstructing or Impeding the Administration of Justice) provides guidance regarding the types of conduct that constitute obstruction.

10. Subsection (f)(2) contemplates that the organization will be allowed a reasonable period of time to conduct an internal investigation. In addition, no reporting is required by subsection (f)(2) or (f)(3)(C)(iii) if the organization

reasonably concluded, based on the information then available, that no offense had been committed.

11. For purposes of subsection (f)(3)(C)(i), an individual has "direct reporting obligations" to the governing authority or an appropriate subgroup thereof if the individual has express authority to communicate personally to the governing authority or appropriate subgroup thereof (A) promptly on any matter involving criminal conduct or potential criminal conduct, and (B) no less than annually on the implementation and effectiveness of the compliance and ethics program.

12. "Appropriate governmental authorities," as used in subsections (f) and (g)(1), means the federal or state law enforcement, regulatory, or program officials having jurisdiction over such matter. To qualify for a reduction under subsection (g)(1), the report to appropriate governmental authorities must be made under the direction of the organization.

13. To qualify for a reduction under subsection (g)(1) or (g)(2), cooperation must be both timely and thorough. To be timely, the cooperation must begin essentially at the same time as the organization is officially notified of a criminal investigation. To be thorough, the cooperation should include the disclosure of all pertinent information known by the organization. A prime test of whether the organization has disclosed all pertinent information is whether the information is sufficient for law enforcement personnel to identify the nature and extent of the offense and the individual(s) responsible for the criminal conduct. However, the cooperation to be measured is the cooperation of the organization itself, not the cooperation of individuals within the organization. If, because of the lack of cooperation of particular individual(s), neither the organization nor law enforcement personnel are able to identify the culpable individual(s) within the organization despite the organization's efforts to cooperate fully, the organization may still be given credit for full cooperation.

14. Entry of a plea of guilty prior to the commencement of trial combined with truthful admission of involvement in the offense and related conduct ordinarily will constitute significant evidence of affirmative acceptance of responsibility under subsection (g), unless outweighed by conduct of the organization that is inconsistent with such acceptance of responsibility. This adjustment is not intended to apply to an organization that puts the government to its burden of proof at trial by denying the essential factual elements of guilt, is convicted, and only then admits guilt and expresses remorse. Conviction by trial, however, does not automatically preclude an organization from consideration for such a reduction. In rare situations, an organization may clearly demonstrate an acceptance of responsibility for its criminal conduct even though it exercises its constitutional right to a trial. This may occur, for example, where an organization goes to trial to assert and preserve issues that do not relate to factual guilt (e.g., to make a constitutional challenge to a statute or a challenge to the applicability of a statute to its conduct). In each such instance, however, a determination that an organization has accepted responsibility will be based primarily upon pretrial statements and conduct.

15. In making a determination with respect to subsection (g), the court may determine that the chief executive officer or highest ranking employee of an organization should appear at sentencing in order to signify that the organization has clearly demonstrated recognition and affirmative acceptance of responsibility.

Background: The increased culpability scores under subsection (b) are based on three interrelated principles. First, an organization is more culpable when individuals who manage the organization or who have substantial discretion in acting for the organization participate in, condone, or are willfully ignorant of criminal conduct. Second, as organizations become larger and their managements become more professional, participation in, condonation of, or willful ignorance of criminal conduct by such management is increasingly a breach of trust or abuse of position. Third, as organizations increase in size, the risk of criminal conduct beyond that reflected in the instant offense also increases whenever management's tolerance of that offense is pervasive. Because of the continuum of sizes of organizations and professionalization of management, subsection (b) gradually increases the culpability score based upon the size of the organization and the level and extent of the substantial authority personnel involvement.

Historical Note: Effective November 1, 1991 (see Appendix C, amendment 422). Amended effective November 1, 2004 (see Appendix C, amendment 673); November 1, 2006 (see Appendix C, amendment 695); November 1, 2010 (see Appendix C, amendment 744).

§8C2.6. Minimum and Maximum Multipliers

Using the culpability score from §8C2.5 (Culpability Score) and applying any applicable special instruction for fines in Chapter Two, determine the applicable minimum and maximum fine multipliers from the table below.

Culpability Score	Minimum Multiplier	Maximum Multiplier
10 or more	2.00	4.00
9	1.80	3.60
8	1.60	3.20
7	1.40	2.80
6	1.20	2.40
5	1.00	2.00
4	0.80	1.60
3	0.60	1.20
2	0.40	0.80
1	0.20	0.40
0 or less	0.05	0.20.

Commentary

Application Note:

1. A special instruction for fines in §2R1.1 (Bid-Rigging, Price-Fixing or Market-Allocation Agreements Among Competitors) sets a floor for minimum and maximum multipliers in cases covered by that guideline.

Historical Note: Effective November 1, 1991 (see Appendix C, amendment 422).

§8C2.7. Guideline Fine Range - Organizations

(a) The minimum of the guideline fine range is determined by multiplying the base fine determined under §8C2.4 (Base Fine) by the applicable minimum multiplier determined under §8C2.6 (Minimum and Maximum Multipliers).

(b) The maximum of the guideline fine range is determined by multiplying the base fine determined under §8C2.4 (Base Fine) by the applicable maximum multiplier determined under §8C2.6 (Minimum and Maximum Multipliers).

Historical Note: Effective November 1, 1991 (see Appendix C, amendment 422).

§8C2.8. Determining the Fine Within the Range (Policy Statement)

(a) In determining the amount of the fine within the applicable guideline range, the court should consider:

(1) the need for the sentence to reflect the seriousness of the offense, promote respect for the law, provide just punishment, afford adequate deterrence, and protect the public from further crimes of the organization;

(2) the organization's role in the offense;

(3) any collateral consequences of conviction, including civil obligations arising from the organization's conduct;

(4) any nonpecuniary loss caused or threatened by the offense;

(5) whether the offense involved a vulnerable victim;

(6) any prior criminal record of an individual within high-level personnel of the organization or high-level personnel of a unit of the organization who participated in, condoned, or was willfully ignorant of the criminal conduct;

(7) any prior civil or criminal misconduct by the organization other than that counted under §8C2.5(c);

(8) any culpability score under §8C2.5 (Culpability Score) higher than 10 or lower than 0;

(9) partial but incomplete satisfaction of the conditions for one or more of the mitigating or aggravating factors set forth in §8C2.5 (Culpability Score);

(10) any factor listed in 18 U.S.C. § 3572(a); and

(11) whether the organization failed to have, at the time of the instant offense, an effective compliance and ethics program within the meaning of §8B2.1 (Effective Compliance and Ethics Program).

(b) In addition, the court may consider the relative importance of any factor used to determine the range, including the pecuniary loss caused by the offense, the pecuniary gain from the offense, any specific offense characteristic used to determine the offense level, and any aggravating or mitigating factor used to determine the culpability score.

Commentary

Application Notes:

1. Subsection (a)(2) provides that the court, in setting the fine within the guideline fine range, should consider the organization's role in the offense. This consideration is particularly appropriate if the guideline fine range does not take the organization's role in the offense into account. For example, the guideline fine range in an antitrust case does not take into consideration whether the organization was an organizer or leader of the conspiracy. A higher fine within the guideline fine range ordinarily will be appropriate for an organization that takes a leading role in such an offense.

2. Subsection (a)(3) provides that the court, in setting the fine within the guideline fine range, should consider any collateral consequences of conviction, including civil obligations arising from the organization's conduct. As a general rule, collateral consequences that merely make victims whole provide no basis for reducing the fine within the guideline range. If criminal and civil sanctions are unlikely to make victims whole, this may provide a basis for a higher fine within the guideline fine range. If punitive collateral sanctions have been or will be imposed on the organization, this may provide a basis for a lower fine within the guideline fine range.

3. Subsection (a)(4) provides that the court, in setting the fine within the guideline fine range, should consider any nonpecuniary loss caused or threatened by the offense. To the extent that nonpecuniary loss caused or threatened (e.g., loss of or threat to human life; psychological injury; threat to national security) by the offense is not adequately considered in setting the guideline fine range, this factor provides a basis for a higher fine within the range. This factor is more likely to be applicable where the guideline fine range is determined by pecuniary loss or gain, rather than by offense level, because the Chapter Two offense levels frequently take actual or threatened nonpecuniary loss into account.

4. Subsection (a)(6) provides that the court, in setting the fine within the guideline fine range, should consider any prior criminal record of an individual within high-level personnel of the organization or within high-level personnel of a unit of the organization. Since an individual within high-level personnel either exercises substantial control over the organization or a unit of the organization or has a substantial role in the making of policy within the organization or a unit of the organization, any prior criminal misconduct of such an individual may be relevant to the determination of the appropriate fine for the organization.

5. Subsection (a)(7) provides that the court, in setting the fine within the guideline fine range, should consider any prior civil or criminal misconduct by the organization other than that counted under §8C2.5(c). The civil and criminal misconduct counted under §8C2.5(c) increases the guideline fine range. Civil or criminal misconduct other than that counted under §8C2.5(c) may provide a basis for a higher fine within the range. In a case involving a pattern of illegality, an upward departure may be warranted.

6. Subsection (a)(8) provides that the court, in setting the fine within the guideline fine range, should consider any culpability score higher than ten or lower than zero. As the culpability score increases above ten, this may provide a basis for a higher fine within the range. Similarly, as the culpability score decreases below zero, this may provide a basis for a lower fine within the range.

7. Under subsection (b), the court, in determining the fine within the range, may consider any factor that it considered in determining the range. This allows for courts to differentiate between cases that have the same offense level *but differ in seriousness (e.g., two fraud cases at offense level 12, one resulting in a loss of $21,000, the other $40,000). Similarly, this allows for courts to differentiate between two cases that have the same aggravating factors, but in which those factors vary in their intensity (e.g., two cases with upward adjustments to the culpability score under §8C2.5(c)(2) (prior criminal adjudications within 5 years of the commencement of the instant offense, one involving a single conviction, the other involving two or more convictions).*

Background: Subsection (a) includes factors that the court is required to consider under 18 U.S.C. §§ 3553(a) and 3572(a) as well as additional factors that the Commission has determined may be relevant in a particular case. A number of factors required for consideration under 18 U.S.C. § 3572(a) (e.g., pecuniary loss, the size of the organization) are used under the fine guidelines in this subpart to determine the fine range, and therefore are not specifically set out again in subsection (a) of this guideline. In unusual cases, factors listed in this section may provide a basis for departure.

Historical Note: Effective November 1, 1991 (see Appendix C, amendment 422). Amended effective November 1, 2004 (see Appendix C, amendment 673).

§8C2.9. Disgorgement

The court shall add to the fine determined under §8C2.8 (Determining the Fine Within the Range) any gain to the organization from the offense that has not and will not be paid as restitution or by way of other remedial measures.

Commentary

Application Note:

1. This section is designed to ensure that the amount of any gain that has not and will not be taken from the organization for remedial purposes will be added to the fine. This section typically will apply in cases in which the organization has received gain from an offense but restitution or remedial efforts will not be required because the offense did not result in harm to identifiable victims, e.g., money laundering, obscenity, and regulatory reporting offenses. Money spent or to be spent to remedy the adverse effects of the offense, e.g., the cost to retrofit defective products, should be considered as disgorged gain. If the cost of remedial efforts made or to be made by the organization equals or exceeds the gain from the offense, this section will not apply.

Historical Note: Effective November 1, 1991 (see Appendix C, amendment 422).

§8C2.10. Determining the Fine for Other Counts

For any count or counts not covered under §8C2.1 (Applicability of Fine Guidelines), the court should determine an appropriate fine by applying the provisions of 18 U.S.C. §§ 3553 and 3572. The court should determine the appropriate fine amount, if any, to be imposed in addition to any fine determined under §8C2.8 (Determining the Fine Within the Range) and §8C2.9 (Disgorgement).

Commentary

Background: The Commission has not promulgated guidelines governing the setting of fines for counts not covered by §8C2.1 (Applicability of Fine Guidelines). For such counts, the court should determine the appropriate fine based on the general statutory provisions governing sentencing. In cases that have a count or counts not covered by the guidelines in addition to a count or counts covered by the guidelines, the court shall apply the fine guidelines for the count(s) covered by the guidelines, and add any additional amount to the fine, as appropriate, for the count(s) not covered by the guidelines.

Historical Note: Effective November 1, 1991 (see Appendix C, amendment 422).

* * * * *

3. IMPLEMENTING THE SENTENCE OF A FINE

§8C3.1. Imposing a Fine

(a) Except to the extent restricted by the maximum fine authorized by statute or any minimum fine required by statute, the fine or fine range shall be that determined under §8C1.1 (Determining the Fine - Criminal Purpose Organizations); §8C2.7 (Guideline Fine Range - Organizations) and §8C2.9 (Disgorgement); or §8C2.10 (Determining the Fine for Other Counts), as appropriate.

(b) Where the minimum guideline fine is greater than the maximum fine authorized by statute, the maximum fine authorized by statute shall be the guideline fine.

(c) Where the maximum guideline fine is less than a minimum fine required by statute, the minimum fine required by statute shall be the guideline fine.

Commentary

Background: This section sets forth the interaction of the fines or fine ranges determined under this chapter with the maximum fine authorized by statute and any minimum fine required by statute for the count or counts of conviction. The general statutory provisions governing a sentence of a fine are set forth in 18 U.S.C. § 3571.

When the organization is convicted of multiple counts, the maximum fine authorized by statute may increase. For example, in the case of an organization convicted of three felony counts related to a $200,000 fraud, the maximum fine authorized by statute will be $500,000 on each count, for an aggregate maximum authorized fine of $1,500,000.

Historical Note: Effective November 1, 1991 (see Appendix C, amendment 422).

§8C3.2. Payment of the Fine - Organizations

(a) If the defendant operated primarily for a criminal purpose or primarily by criminal means, immediate payment of the fine shall be required.

(b) In any other case, immediate payment of the fine shall be required unless the court finds that the organization is financially unable to make immediate payment or that such payment would pose an undue burden on the organization. If the court permits other than immediate payment, it shall require full payment at the earliest possible date, either by requiring payment on a date certain or by establishing an installment schedule.

Commentary

Application Note:

1. When the court permits other than immediate payment, the period provided for payment shall in no event exceed five years. 18 U.S.C. § 3572(d).

Historical Note: Effective November 1, 1991 (see Appendix C, amendment 422).

§8C3.3. Reduction of Fine Based on Inability to Pay

(a) The court shall reduce the fine below that otherwise required by §8C1.1 (Determining the Fine - Criminal Purpose Organizations), or §8C2.7 (Guideline Fine Range - Organizations) and §8C2.9 (Disgorgement), to the extent that imposition of such fine would impair its ability to make restitution to victims.

(b) The court may impose a fine below that otherwise required by §8C2.7 (Guideline Fine Range - Organizations) and §8C2.9 (Disgorgement) if the court finds that the organization is not able and, even with the use of a reasonable installment schedule, is not likely to become able to pay the minimum fine required by §8C2.7 (Guideline Fine Range - Organizations) and §8C2.9 (Disgorgement).

Provided, that the reduction under this subsection shall not be more than necessary to avoid substantially jeopardizing the continued viability of the organization.

Commentary

Application Note:

1. For purposes of this section, an organization is not able to pay the minimum fine if, even with an installment schedule under §8C3.2 (Payment of the Fine - Organizations), the payment of that fine would substantially jeopardize the continued existence of the organization.

Background: Subsection (a) carries out the requirement in 18 U.S.C. § 3572(b) that the court impose a fine or other monetary penalty only to the extent that such fine or penalty will not impair the ability of the organization to make restitution for the offense; however, this section does not authorize a criminal purpose organization to remain in business in order to pay restitution.

Historical Note: Effective November 1, 1991 (see Appendix C, amendment 422).

§8C3.4. Fines Paid by Owners of Closely Held Organizations

The court may offset the fine imposed upon a closely held organization when one or more individuals, each of whom owns at least a 5 percent interest in the organization, has been fined in a federal criminal proceeding for the same offense conduct for which the organization is being sentenced. The amount of such offset shall not exceed the amount resulting from multiplying the total fines imposed on those individuals by those individuals' total percentage interest in the organization.

Commentary

Application Notes:

1. For purposes of this section, an organization is closely held, regardless of its size, when relatively few individuals own it. In order for an organization to be closely held, ownership and management need not completely overlap.

2. This section does not apply to a fine imposed upon an individual that arises out of offense conduct different from that for which the organization is being sentenced.

Background: For practical purposes, most closely held organizations are the alter egos of their owner-managers. In the case of criminal conduct by a closely held corporation, the organization and the culpable individual(s) both may be convicted. As a general rule in such cases, appropriate punishment may be achieved by offsetting the fine imposed upon the organization by an amount that reflects the percentage ownership interest of the sentenced *individuals and the magnitude of the fines imposed upon those individuals. For example, an organization is owned by five individuals, each of whom has a twenty percent interest; three of the individuals are convicted; and the combined fines imposed on those three equals $100,000. In this example, the fine imposed upon the organization may be offset by up to 60 percent of their combined fine amounts, i.e., by $60,000.*

Historical Note: Effective November 1, 1991 (see Appendix C, amendment 422).

* * * * *

§8C4.1. Substantial Assistance to Authorities - Organizations (Policy Statement)

(a) Upon motion of the government stating that the defendant has provided substantial assistance in the investigation or prosecution of another organization that has committed an offense, or in the investigation or prosecution of an individual not directly affiliated with the defendant who has committed an offense, the court may depart from the guidelines.

(b) The appropriate reduction shall be determined by the court for reasons stated on the record that may include, but are not limited to, consideration of the following:

> (1) the court's evaluation of the significance and usefulness of the organization's assistance, taking into consideration the government's evaluation of the assistance rendered;
>
> (2) the nature and extent of the organization's assistance; and
>
> (3) the timeliness of the organization's assistance.

Commentary

Application Note:

1. Departure under this section is intended for cases in which substantial assistance is provided in the investigation or prosecution of crimes committed by individuals not directly affiliated with the organization or by other organizations. It is not intended for assistance in the investigation or prosecution of the agents of the organization responsible for the offense for which the organization is being sentenced.

Historical Note: Effective November 1, 1991 (see Appendix C, amendment 422).

§8C4.2. Risk of Death or Bodily Injury (Policy Statement)

If the offense resulted in death or bodily injury, or involved a foreseeable risk of death or bodily injury, an upward departure may be warranted. The extent of any such departure should depend, among other factors, on the nature of the harm and the extent to which the harm was intended or knowingly risked, and the extent to which such harm or risk is taken into account within the applicable guideline fine range.

Historical Note: Effective November 1, 1991 (see Appendix C, amendment 422).

§8C4.3. Threat to National Security (Policy Statement)

If the offense constituted a threat to national security, an upward departure may be warranted.

Historical Note: Effective November 1, 1991 (see Appendix C, amendment 422).

§8C4.4. Threat to the Environment (Policy Statement)

If the offense presented a threat to the environment, an upward departure may be warranted.

Historical Note: Effective November 1, 1991 (see Appendix C, amendment 422).

§8C4.5. Threat to a Market (Policy Statement)

If the offense presented a risk to the integrity or continued existence of a market, an upward departure may be warranted. This section is applicable to both private markets (e.g., a financial market, a commodities market, or a market for consumer goods) and public markets (e.g., government contracting).

Historical Note: Effective November 1, 1991 (see Appendix C, amendment 422).

§8C4.6. Official Corruption (Policy Statement)

If the organization, in connection with the offense, bribed or unlawfully gave a gratuity to a public official, or attempted or conspired to bribe or unlawfully give a gratuity to a public official, an upward departure may be warranted.

Historical Note: Effective November 1, 1991 (see Appendix C, amendment 422).

§8C4.7. Public Entity (Policy Statement)

If the organization is a public entity, a downward departure may be warranted.

Historical Note: Effective November 1, 1991 (see Appendix C, amendment 422).

§8C4.8. Members or Beneficiaries of the Organization as Victims (Policy Statement)

If the members or beneficiaries, other than shareholders, of the organization are direct victims of the offense, a downward departure may be warranted. If the members or beneficiaries of an organization are direct victims of the offense, imposing a fine upon the organization may increase the burden upon the victims of the offense without achieving a deterrent effect. In such cases, a fine may not be appropriate. For example, departure may be appropriate if a labor union is convicted of embezzlement of pension funds.

Historical Note: Effective November 1, 1991 (see Appendix C, amendment 422).

§8C4.9. Remedial Costs that Greatly Exceed Gain (Policy Statement)

If the organization has paid or has agreed to pay remedial costs arising from the offense that greatly exceed the gain that the organization received from the offense, a downward departure may be warranted. In such a case, a substantial fine may not be necessary in order to achieve adequate punishment and deterrence. In deciding whether departure is appropriate, the court should consider the level and extent of substantial authority personnel involvement in the offense and the degree to which the loss exceeds the gain. If an individual within high-level personnel was involved in the offense, a departure would not be appropriate under this section. The lower the level and the more limited the extent of substantial authority personnel involvement in the offense, and the greater the degree to which remedial costs exceeded or will exceed gain, the less will be the need for a substantial fine to achieve adequate punishment and deterrence.

Historical Note: Effective November 1, 1991 (see Appendix C, amendment 422).

§8C4.10. Mandatory Programs to Prevent and Detect Violations of Law (Policy Statement)

If the organization's culpability score is reduced under §8C2.5(f) (Effective Compliance and Ethics Program) and the organization had implemented its program in response to a court order or administrative order specifically directed at the organization, an upward departure may be warranted to offset, in part or in whole, such reduction.

Similarly, if, at the time of the instant offense, the organization was required by law to have an effective compliance and ethics program, but the organization did not have such a program, an upward departure may be warranted.

Historical Note: Effective November 1, 1991 (see Appendix C, amendment 422). Amended effective November 1, 2004 (see Appendix C, amendment 673).

§8C4.11. Exceptional Organizational Culpability (Policy Statement)

If the organization's culpability score is greater than 10, an upward departure may be appropriate.

If no individual within substantial authority personnel participated in, condoned, or was willfully ignorant of the offense; the organization at the time of the offense had an effective program to prevent and detect violations of law; and the base fine is determined under §8C2.4(a)(1), §8C2.4(a)(3), or a special instruction for fines in Chapter Two (Offense Conduct), a downward departure may be warranted. In a case meeting these criteria, the court may find that the organization had exceptionally low culpability and therefore a fine based on loss, offense level, or a special Chapter Two instruction results in a guideline fine range higher than necessary to achieve the purposes of sentencing. Nevertheless, such fine should not be lower than if determined under §8C2.4(a)(2).

Historical Note: Effective November 1, 1991 (see Appendix C, amendment 422).

Worksheet A (Offense Level)

Defendant _____   District/Office _____

Docket Number (Year-Sequence-Defendant No.)   ___ ___-___ ___ ___ ___-___ ___

Count Number(s) _____   U.S. Code Title & Section _____ : _____

_____ : _____

Guidelines Manual Edition Used: 20___ *(NOTE: worksheets keyed to the Manual effective November 1, 2010)*

Instructions:

For each count of conviction (or stipulated offense), complete a separate Worksheet A. Exception: Use only a single Worksheet A where the offense level for a group of closely related counts is based primarily on aggregate value or quantity (see §3D1.2(d)) or where a count of conspiracy, solicitation, or attempt is grouped with a substantive count that was the sole object of the conspiracy, solicitation, or attempt (see §3D1.2(a) and (b)).

1. **Offense Level** (See Chapter Two)

Enter the applicable base offense level and any specific offense characteristics from Chapter Two and explain the bases for these determinations. Enter the sum in the box provided.

Guideline	Description	Level
_____	_____	_____
_____	_____	_____
_____	_____	_____
_____	_____	_____
_____	_____	_____
_____	_____	_____

Sum   ☐

2. **Victim-Related Adjustments** (See Chapter Three, Part A)

Enter the applicable section and adjustment. If more than one section is applicable, list each section and enter the combined adjustment. If no adjustment is applicable enter "0."   §_____   ☐

3. **Role in the Offense Adjustments** (See Chapter Three, Part B)

Enter the applicable section and adjustment. If more than one section is applicable, list each section and enter the combined adjustment. If the adjustment reduces the offense level, enter a minus (-) sign in front of the adjustment. If no adjustment is applicable, enter "0."   §_____   ☐

4. **Obstruction Adjustments** (See Chapter Three, Part C)

Enter the applicable section and adjustment. If more than one section is applicable, list each section and enter the combined adjustment. If no adjustment is applicable, enter "0."   §_____   ☐

5. **Adjusted Offense Level**

Enter the sum of Items 1-4. If this worksheet does not cover all counts of conviction or stipulated offenses, complete Worksheet B. Otherwise, enter this result on Worksheet D, Item 1.   ☐

☐   *Check if the defendant is convicted of a single count. In such case, Worksheet B need not be completed.*

☐   *If the defendant has no criminal history, enter criminal history "I" here and on Item 4, Worksheet D. In such case, Worksheet C need not be completed.*

U.S. Sentencing Commission
November 22, 2010
H:\oesp\TRAINING\Worksheets\Worksheets-November2010.wpd

Worksheet B
(Multiple Counts or Stipulation to Additional Offenses)

Defendant _____   Docket Number _____

Instructions

Step 1: Determine if any of the counts group. (Note: All, some, or none of the counts may group. Some of the counts may have already been grouped in the application under Worksheet A, specifically, (1) counts grouped under §3D1.2(d), or (2) a count charging conspiracy, solicitation, or attempt that is grouped with the substantive count of conviction (see §3D1.2(a)). Explain the reasons for grouping:

_____

_____

Step 2: Using the box(es) provided below, for each group of closely related counts, enter the highest adjusted offense level from the various "A" Worksheets (Item 5) that comprise the group (see §3D1.3). (Note: A "group" may consist of a single count that has not grouped with any other count. In those instances, the offense level for the group will be the adjusted offense level for the single count.)

Step 3: Enter the number of units to be assigned to each group (see §3D1.4) as follows:

- One unit (1) for the group of closely related counts with the highest offense level
- An additional unit (1) for each group that is equally serious or 1 to 4 levels less serious
- An additional half unit (1/2) for each group that is 5 to 8 levels less serious
- No increase in units for groups that are 9 or more levels less serious

1. **Adjusted Offense Level for the First Group of Closely Related Counts**
   Count number(s):_____   [ ] _____ (unit)

2. **Adjusted Offense Level for the Second Group of Closely Related Counts**
   Count number(s):_____   [ ] _____ (unit)

3. **Adjusted Offense Level for the Third Group of Closely Related Counts**
   Count number(s):_____   [ ] _____ (unit)

4. **Adjusted Offense Level for the Fourth Group of Closely Related Counts**
   Count number(s):_____   [ ] _____ (unit)

5. **Adjusted Offense Level for the Fifth Group of Closely Related Counts**
   Count number(s):_____   [ ] _____ (unit)

6. **Total Units**   _____ (total units)

7. **Increase in Offense Level Based on Total Units (See §3D1.4)**   [ ]

1 unit:	no increase	2 1/2 - 3 units:	add 3 levels
1 1/2 units:	add 1 level	3 1/2 - 5 units:	add 4 levels
2 units:	add 2 levels	More than 5 units:	add 5 levels

8. **Highest of the Adjusted Offense Levels from Items 1-5 Above**   [ ]

9. **Combined Adjusted Offense Level (See §3D1.4)**   [ ]
   Enter the sum of Items 7 and 8 here and on Worksheet D, Item 1.

Worksheet C (Criminal History)

Defendant _____ Docket Number _____

Enter the Date Defendant Commenced Participation in Instant Offense (Earliest Date of Relevant Conduct)_____

1. 3 Points for each prior ADULT sentence of imprisonment EXCEEDING ONE YEAR AND ONE MONTH imposed within 15 YEARS of the defendant's commencement of the instant offense OR resulting in incarceration during any part of that 15-YEAR period. (See §§4A1.1(a) and 4A1.2.)

2. 2 Points for each prior sentence of imprisonment of AT LEAST 60 DAYS resulting from an offense committed ON OR AFTER the defendant's 18th birthday not counted under §4A1.1(a) imposed within 10 YEARS of the instant offense; and

   2 Points for each prior sentence of imprisonment of AT LEAST 60 DAYS resulting from an offense committed BEFORE the defendant's 18th birthday not counted under §4A1.1(a) from which the defendant was released from confinement within 5 YEARS of the instant offense. (See §§4A1.1(b) and 4A1.2.)

3. 1 Point for each prior sentence resulting from an offense committed ON OR AFTER the defendant's 18th birthday not counted under §4A1.1(a) or §4A1.1(b) imposed within 10 YEARS of the instant offense; and

   1 Point for each prior sentence resulting from an offense committed BEFORE the defendant's 18th birthday not counted under §4A1.1(a) or §4A1.1(b) imposed within 5 YEARS of the instant offense. (See §§4A1.1(c) and 4A1.2.)

   NOTE: A maximum sum of 4 Points may be given for the prior sentences in Item 3.

Date of Imposition	Offense	Sentence	Release Date[**]	Guideline Section	Criminal History Pts.

[*] Indicate with an asterisk those offenses where defendant was sentenced as a juvenile.

[**] A release date is required in only two instances:

   a. When a sentence covered under §4A1.1(a) was imposed more than 15 years prior to the commencement of the instant offense but release from incarceration occurred within such 15-year period;

   b. When a sentence counted under §4A1.1(b) was imposed for an offense committed prior to age 18 and more than 5 years prior to the commencement of the instant offense, but release from incarceration occurred within such 5-year period; and

4. Sum of Criminal History Points for prior sentences under §§4A1.1(a), 4A1.1(b), and 4A1.1(c) (Items 1,2,3).

U.S. Sentencing Commission
November 22, 2010
H:\oesp\TRAINING\Worksheets\Worksheets-November2010.wpd

Worksheet D (Guideline Worksheet)

Defendant _____   District _____

Docket Number _____

1. **Adjusted Offense Level** (From Worksheet A or B)
    If Worksheet B is required, enter the result from Worksheet B, Item 9.
    Otherwise, enter the result from Worksheet A, Item 5.

2. **Acceptance of Responsibility** (See Chapter Three, Part E)
    Enter the applicable reduction of 2 or 3 levels. If no adjustment is
    applicable, enter "0".

3. **Offense Level Total** (Item 1 less Item 2)

4. **Criminal History Category** (From Worksheet C)
    Enter the result from Worksheet C, Item 8.

5. **Terrorism/Career Offender/Criminal Livelihood/Armed
    Career Criminal/Repeat and Dangerous Sex Offender**
    (see Chapter Three, Part A, and Chapter Four, Part B)

    a. Offense Level Total

        If the provision for Career Offender (§4B1.1), Criminal
        Livelihood (§4B1.3), Armed Career Criminal (§4B1.4), or
        Repeat and Dangerous Sex Offender (§4B1.5) results in an
        offense level total higher than Item 3, enter the offense level
        total. Otherwise, enter "N/A."

    b. Criminal History Category

        If the provision for Terrorism (§3A1.4), Career Offender
        (§4B1.1), Armed Career Criminal (§4B1.4), or Repeat and
        Dangerous Sex Offender (§4B1.5) results in a criminal history
        category higher than Item 4, enter the applicable criminal history
        category. Otherwise, enter "N/A."

6. **Guideline Range from Sentencing Table**   Months
    Enter the applicable guideline range from Chapter Five, Part A.

7. **Restricted Guideline Range** (See Chapter Five, Part G)
    If the statutorily authorized maximum sentence or the statutorily   Months
    required minimum sentence restricts the guideline range (Item 6) (see
    §§5G1.1 and 5G1.2), enter either the restricted guideline range or any
    statutory maximum or minimum penalty that would modify the
    guideline range. Otherwise, enter "N/A."

    ☐ Check this box if §5C1.2 (Limitation on Applicability of Statutory Minimum Penalties in Certain Cases) is applicable.

8. **Undischarged Term of Imprisonment** (See §5G1.3)

    ☐ If the defendant is subject to an undischarged term of imprisonment, check this box and list the
        undischarged term(s) below.

    _____

    _____

U.S. Sentencing Commission
November 22, 2010
H:\oesp\TRAINING\Worksheets\Worksheets-November2010.wpd

Worksheet D

Page 2

Defendant _____   Docket Number _____

9. **Sentencing Options** (Check the applicable box that corresponds to the Guideline Range entered in Item 6 or Item 7, if applicable.)
(See Chapter Five, Sentencing Table)

☐   Zone A   If checked, the following options are available (see §5B1.1):

-    Fine (See §5E1.2(a))

-    "Straight" Probation

-    Imprisonment

☐   Zone B   If checked, the minimum term may be satisfied by:

-    Imprisonment

-    Imprisonment of at least one month plus supervised release with a condition that substitutes community confinement or home detention for imprisonment (see §5C1.1(c)(2))

-    Probation with a condition that substitutes intermittent confinement, community confinement, or home detention for imprisonment (see §5B1.1(a)(2) and §5C1.1(c)(3))

☐   Zone C   If checked, the minimum term may be satisfied by:

-    Imprisonment

-    Imprisonment of at least one-half of the minimum term plus supervised release with a condition that substitutes community confinement or home detention for imprisonment (see §5C1.1(d)(2))

☐   Zone D   If checked, the minimum term shall be satisfied by a sentence of imprisonment (see §5C1.1(f))

10. **Length of Term of Probation** (See §5B1.2)

If probation is imposed, the guideline for the length of such term of probation is: (Check applicable box)

☐   At least one year, but not more than five years if the offense level total is 6 or more

☐   No more than three years if the offense level total is 5 or less

11. **Conditions of Probation** (See §5B1.3)

List any mandatory conditions ((a)(1)-(10)), standard conditions ((c)(1)-(14)), and any other special conditions that may be applicable:

_____

_____

_____

_____

_____

_____

_____

Worksheet D

Page 3

Defendant _____   Docket Number _____

12. **Supervised Release** (See §§5D1.1 and 5D1.2)

   a. A term of supervised release is: (Check applicable box)

     ☐ Required because a term of imprisonment of more than one year is to be imposed or if required by statute

     ☐ Authorized but not required because a term of imprisonment of one year or less is to be imposed

   b. Length of Term (Guideline Range of Supervised Release): (Check applicable box)

     ☐ Class A or B Felony: Three to Five Year Term

     ☐ Class C or D Felony: Two to Three Year Term

     ☐ Class E Felony or Class A Misdemeanor: One Year Term

   c. Restricted Guideline Range of Supervision Release

     ☐ If a statutorily required term of supervised release impacts the guideline range, check this box and enter the required term. _____

13. **Conditions of Supervised Release** (See §5D1.3)
List any mandatory conditions ((a)(1)-(8)), standard conditions ((c)(1)-(15)), and any other special conditions that may be applicable: _____
_____

14. **Restitution** (See §5E1.1)

   a. If restitution is applicable, enter the amount. Otherwise enter "N/A" and the reason:_____
_____

   b. Enter whether restitution is statutorily mandatory or discretionary: _____
_____

   c. Enter whether restitution is by an order of restitution or solely as a condition of supervision. Enter the authorizing statute:
_____

15. **Fines** (Guideline Range of Fines for Individual Defendants) (See §5E1.2)

		Minimum	Maximum
a.	Special fine provisions ☐ Check box if any of the counts of conviction is for a statute with a special fine provision. (This does not include the general fine provisions of 18 USC § 3571(b)(2), (d))		
	Enter the sum of statutory maximum fines for all such counts		$_____
b.	Fine Table (§5E1.2(c)(3)) Enter the minimum and maximum fines	$_____	$_____
c.	Guideline Range of Fines (determined by the minimum of the fine table (Item 15(b)) and the greater maximum above (Item 15(a) or 15(b)))	$_____	$_____
d.	Ability to Pay		

     ☐ Check this box if the defendant does not have an ability to pay.

U.S. Sentencing Commission
November 22, 2010
H:\ossp\TRAINING\Worksheets\Worksheets-November2010.wpd

Worksheet D   Page 4

Defendant _____   Docket Number _____

16. **Special Assessments** (See §5E1.3)

Enter the total amount of special assessments required for all counts of conviction:

- $25 for each misdemeanor count of conviction

- Not less than $100 for each felony count of conviction

$ _____

17. **Additional Factors**

List any additional applicable guidelines, policy statements, and statutory provisions. Also list any applicable aggravating and mitigating factors that may warrant a sentence at a particular point either within or outside the applicable guideline range. Attach additional sheets as necessary.

_____

_____

_____

_____

_____

_____

_____

_____

_____

_____

_____

_____

_____

_____

_____

_____

_____

_____

_____

_____

_____

_____

_____

_____

Completed by _____   Date _____

U.S. Sentencing Commission
November 22, 2010
H:\oesp\TRAINING\Worksheets\Worksheets-November2010.wpd

SENTENCING TABLE
(in months of imprisonment)

	Offense Level	**Criminal History Category (Criminal History Points)**					
		I (0 or 1)	II (2 or 3)	III (4, 5, 6)	IV (7, 8, 9)	V (10, 11, 12)	VI (13 or more)
Zone A	1	0-6	0-6	0-6	0-6	0-6	0-6
	2	0-6	0-6	0-6	0-6	0-6	1-7
	3	0-6	0-6	0-6	0-6	2-8	3-9
	4	0-6	0-6	0-6	2-8	4-10	6-12
	5	0-6	0-6	1-7	4-10	6-12	9-15
	6	0-6	1-7	2-8	6-12	9-15	12-18
Zone B	7	0-6	2-8	4-10	8-14	12-18	15-21
	8	0-6	4-10	6-12	10-16	15-21	18-24
	9	4-10	6-12	8-14	12-18	18-24	21-27
Zone C	10	6-12	8-14	10-16	15-21	21-27	24-30
	11	8-14	10-16	12-18	18-24	24-30	27-33
	12	10-16	12-18	15-21	21-27	27-33	30-37
Zone D	13	12-18	15-21	18-24	24-30	30-37	33-41
	14	15-21	18-24	21-27	27-33	33-41	37-46
	15	18-24	21-27	24-30	30-37	37-46	41-51
	16	21-27	24-30	27-33	33-41	41-51	46-57
	17	24-30	27-33	30-37	37-46	46-57	51-63
	18	27-33	30-37	33-41	41-51	51-63	57-71
	19	30-37	33-41	37-46	46-57	57-71	63-78
	20	33-41	37-46	41-51	51-63	63-78	70-87
	21	37-46	41-51	46-57	57-71	70-87	77-96
	22	41-51	46-57	51-63	63-78	77-96	84-105
	23	46-57	51-63	57-71	70-87	84-105	92-115
	24	51-63	57-71	63-78	77-96	92-115	100-125
	25	57-71	63-78	70-87	84-105	100-125	110-137
	26	63-78	70-87	78-97	92-115	110-137	120-150
	27	70-87	78-97	87-108	100-125	120-150	130-162
	28	78-97	87-108	97-121	110-137	130-162	140-175
	29	87-108	97-121	108-135	121-151	140-175	151-188
	30	97-121	108-135	121-151	135-168	151-188	168-210
	31	108-135	121-151	135-168	151-188	168-210	188-235
	32	121-151	135-168	151-188	168-210	188-235	210-262
	33	135-168	151-188	168-210	188-235	210-262	235-293
	34	151-188	168-210	188-235	210-262	235-293	262-327
	35	168-210	188-235	210-262	235-293	262-327	292-365
	36	188-235	210-262	235-293	262-327	292-365	324-405
	37	210-262	235-293	262-327	292-365	324-405	360-life
	38	235-293	262-327	292-365	324-405	360-life	360-life
	39	262-327	292-365	324-405	360-life	360-life	360-life
	40	292-365	324-405	360-life	360-life	360-life	360-life
	41	324-405	360-life	360-life	360-life	360-life	360-life
	42	360-life	360-life	360-life	360-life	360-life	360-life
	43	life	life	life	life	life	life

November 1, 2012